STRUCTURAL CHANGE IN A
DEVELOPING ECONOMY

COLOMBIA'S PROBLEMS AND PROSPECTS

RICHARD R. NELSON

T. PAUL SCHULTZ

ROBERT L. SLIGHTON

PRINCETON UNIVERSITY PRESS, PRINCETON, N.J. 1971

Preface

This book is the last product of a multifaceted study of the Colombian economy undertaken at The Rand Corporation between 1966 and 1969 under the sponsorship of the Agency for International Development with supplementary funds provided by the Corporation. In the course of this study a large number of papers on various aspects of the structure of the Colombian economy were submitted to AID and published as separate Rand memoranda. An additional set of papers on political and bureaucratic constraints on policymaking in Colombia, a subject that lay outside our research mandate from AID, was completed with Rand sponsorship. The purpose of this volume is to bring together and integrate that subset of these two groups of papers on the Colombian economy and polity that we felt to be of general interest to students of the development process.

In several respects the Rand Colombia study was an experiment. It was experimental in that we attempted to understand the development process of a country both in breadth and depth through organization of a research group that held together for a substantial period of time. The three authors of this study were involved more or less full time for more than two years. In addition, significant participation was provided by Richard Maullin and Constantine Menges of Rand's Social Science Department, and by Leland Johnson, Paul Johnson, Merrill Bateman, and Edwin Mansfield, who were members of, or consultants to, the Economics Department at Rand. This approach enabled us to marshal or develop expertise and resources to study in detail and at length a number of different but linked facets of the development process, something that could not have been done either by one person working alone or by a group brought together for just a short time. The considerable duration of the project and continuity of the group gave us a chance to explore the links between the different facets and to evolve and elaborate our initial concepts regarding interactions that suggested the particular studies in the first place. We hope this approach has borne fruit in this volume, which is intended as a unified view of important processes and their interaction, rather than a collection of separate essays. The nature of this view will be discussed in the Introduction.

Although the detailed empirical analysis concentrated on Colombia, we viewed the basic objective not as trying to explain Colombia but as attempting to gain a better understanding of development processes generally. The objective might appear at first to call for a study of a large cross-country sample. Given time and resource constraints, however, we felt such a study to be inadvisable. Rather, we gambled that it would be more fruitful to work with an unbalanced sample, to study one country in considerable depth, with casual attention to other countries, largely to check whether the analysis seemed applicable to them as well. One reason for taking this approach was to increase the likelihood of achieving coherence of the parts. We judged that the focus on a single country would provide a common data base and arena of discourse among the study participants that would be far more difficult to arrive at with a set of cross-country studies. Second, we felt that there were many aspects of the development process that could be investigated only by generating a detailed knowledge of fine structure and nuance that would not have been feasible had we attempted to study a large sample of countries.

The authors are indebted to more individuals than can conveniently be identified within the confines of this Preface. However, they would particularly like to thank William Rhoads of USAID, Bogota; Lester Taylor, Richard Porter, and Karsten Laursen of the Harvard Development Advisory Service; Antonio Urdinola of the Departamento Administrativo de Planeacion of the Colombian government; Miguel Urrutia Montoya of the Junta Monetaria; Lauchlin Currie; and Richard Maullin and Leland Johnson of The Rand Corporation, for many useful suggestions.

Contents

List of Tables

List of Figures

STRUCTURAL CHANGE IN A DEVELOPING ECONOMY

CHAPTER I

Introduction

To some readers this book is mostly about Colombia. To us, the authors, it is about the development process generally. We do not pretend to have created a new "theory of development." However, the approach is quite different from traditional treatments. We have taken three important themes of the development process, examined and modeled these in some detail, and tried to show how these themes relate to each other. These themes are: the relationship between economic development and rapid growth of population and internal migration; development as a process of structural change in a technologically dualistic economy; and policymaking as a behavioral response by the government to the shifting policy preferences of the governed.

Why did we choose to organize this study around these three themes? First of all, it seemed to us that we could not hope to understand the development process unless population growth and rural-urban migration were built endogenously into the analysis and brought center stage. To be sure, the surge of population growth being experienced in Colombia and almost all other less developed countries is in part exogenous to their own internal developments—the result of widespread application of new public health techniques to control endemic disease. Nonetheless, part of the fall in the death rate must have been related to the sharp improvement in consumption levels coincident with the post-World War II spurt of economic growth. More important, the consequences of decreases in the death rate on the rate of growth of population depend on what happens to the birth rate, in particular, the extent and speed with which it declines, and this is in part a function of changes in economic structure. The pattern of migration is similarly endogenous to the development process, for migration is the reflection of a disequilibrium in the labor market that derives from uneven regional expansion of population, or economic opportunities, or both.

The literature on the determinants of population growth and

migration is quite sketchy. The material presented in Chapters II
and III aims to carry both theoretical and empirical analysis a
considerable distance forward. These chapters develop several
models and test them against data in a number of different
countries, not just Colombia.

It seemed natural that these chapters should come first. The
analysis of population growth and migration provides an extremely
useful way to cut into the network of simultaneous dynamic relationships that are involved in the growth process. Population
growth at once is a principal determinant of one of the major
factors of production—labor—and at the same time strongly influences the magnitude and composition of the evolution of other
factors, in particular, the growth of physical and human capital.
More generally, the facts of rapid population growth and rural-
urban migration are the pivotal ones behind the most dramatic
change that has occurred over the last twenty years in Colombia:
the transition from a predominantly rural, agricultural, and largely
self-contained economy and polity to one that is increasingly urban,
industrial, and dependent upon international trade or borrowing for
the resources needed to enable the economy to operate and expand.

Thus the analysis of population growth and migration leads us
naturally into our second major theme: development as a process
of structural transformation. In Chapter IV we begin the elabora-
tion of this theme. In attempting to develop an endogenous analysis
of population dynamics, a major research problem was the limited
amount of prior work. The literature on structural changes in a
developing economy is, of course, vast and diverse. Here our problem was that prior empirical studies within the most broadly employed framework, that of neoclassical growth theory, indicated
the need for some major rethinking and theoretical restructuring.
A detailed look beneath industry aggregates led us in the direction
of trying to model industrial development as a structural transformation process—a process by which modern technology is in
part grafted onto and in part replaces an older craft technology—rather than as a simple neoclassical process of factor aug-
mentation. Chapter IV constructs a model of such a "dual" industrial structure and describes and "explains" in detail certain
of the characteristics of Colombia within that analytic frame.

In Chapter V the demographic and structural transformation

themes are woven together. The focus is on urban unemployment and the dual income distribution. More specifically, the chapter is concerned with the relationships among the following variables: the rate of migration, overt unemployment, relative employment in the craft and modern sectors, and the distribution of income. The migration model of Chapter III leads us to expect that overt urban unemployment tends to be self-limiting to an extent. A rise in unemployment dampens migration; a fall in unemployment speeds it up. The structural transformation model with its emphasis on duality suggests that employment in the craft sector also serves as a buffer for overt unemployment, declining as employment grows rapidly in the modern sector, increasing when the modern sector slows down. This hypothesis is strongly confirmed. These phenomena, together with the fact that there is a significant and growing wage differential between the modern and craft sectors, carry interesting and important implications for changes in income distribution over the development process. These are examined in some detail.

The study of unemployment and income distribution of Chapter V pertains to developments over the past decade, a period that has seen a marked slowdown of growth of employment and also of output in the modern sector of Colombian industry. Chapter VI examines the reasons for this and, in so doing, sets the stage for the third major component of our analysis: a behavioral treatment of policymaking. The analysis in this chapter divides into two parts. The first is an attempt to explain the composition of the modern sector of the Colombian economy, a composition that implies dependence upon imports for operation and expansion. The problem here is to sketch the outlines of a theory of dynamic comparative advantage. But the central analytic core of the chapter is a reconsideration of the "two-gap" model of the constraints on the growth of the modern sector in terms of a model that encompasses prices—in particular, the effective exchange rate—as variables. The slowdown of the rate of growth of the modern sector since 1961 and consequent rise in employment and resurgence of the craft sector is shown to be the lagged consequence of a tightening import constraint which, in turn, is the result of the fall in coffee prices of the mid-1950s and the inadequacy of the Colombian policy response to this shift in the foreign exchange supply curve. A policy of gradual devaluation of the "real" exchange rate would almost certainly have reduced the magnitude of Colombia's difficulties, but no such policy was adopted.

Chapter VII attempts to understand why. It considers the structure and legacies of Colombian politics at the time of the coffee crisis, and how these constrained and molded the kinds of policies that could be considered in the 1960s. In this chapter we try to break from two traditions: that of treating policymaking exogenously, and that of explicitly or implicitly assuming that policy is, or can be, determined by "optimality" considerations. This chapter, probably more than any other, is specific to the Colombian scene. We are obviously unable to present any general model of policymaking, but we hope we have made a small contribution by showing that, in some cases at least, policies are largely predictable, that they are the outputs of decisionmaking systems where incentives and constraints are known and fairly stable.

The main conclusion of Chapter VII is that Colombian foreign exchange policy—a somewhat extreme version of the "disequilibrium system" of an overvalued currency, quantitative controls, and administrative pricing that is employed in some form or another by most of the less developed world—is not simply the creature of a technical bureaucracy that holds an ideology of growth demanding such a policy. Our argument is that the disequilibrium system is the policy that maximizes the electoral support of the government, given the electorate's perceptions of the effects of foreign exchange policy. It is politically "legitimate," and we suggest that many of the reasons why it is are deeply rooted in the behavioral characteristics of democratic government and hence are applicable to a wide range of less developed countries.

Chapter VIII considers policy changes we think would significantly enhance Colombia's growth performance. The principal components of an active population policy are discussed, both birth control policies and policies that would act on the family size goal. We explore various aspects of educational policy, attempting to identify areas where returns seem to be high. We also consider higher technical education where, in recent years, the "returns" signal has been ambiguous. An attempt is made to link, in terms of both justification and policy reinforcement, policies to higher education and to building an indigenous Colombian technical and scientific capability. Yet the key requirement would appear to be major reform of foreign exchange policy, rather than a relaxation of skill bottlenecks. We simply do not see how a country of Colombia's size and resource endowments can hope to achieve rapid economic growth unless stronger incentives are provided for export, the high and variable walls of protectionism are reduced, and market mechanisms are used to ration foreign exchange to a far greater extent than at present.

The positive arguments for these policy changes are neither particularly new nor subtle. The more interesting question is whether they are politically feasible. To approach this question we must first ask, "If these policies are so desirable, why have they not been adopted?" The message of Chapter VII is that the Colombian policymaking system gives—and, to maintain itself, must give—higher priority to income distribution goals than to the goal of rapid economic growth. We conclude by briefly considering the likelihood of modifying this scale of priorities through political innovation.

CHAPTER II

Population Growth: Investigation of a Hypothesis

INTRODUCTION

The population explosion is integral to the economic development problems and processes of most of today's less developed countries. Colombia is no exception. Indeed, in recent years she has experienced one of the world's most rapid population growth rates, more than three percent a year in the 1960s. Because of the population explosion, almost all features of the Colombian economic, political, and social scene have changed, are changing, and will change dramatically.

In later chapters we trace through some of the consequences of these changes. Suffice it to say here that because of the population explosion there are more children to be educated, more mouths to be fed, more hands to be employed. Rapid population growth has fueled massive rural-urban migration. Growth of labor demand in the urban modern sector has proceeded more slowly than has the growth of the migration-fed urban work force, and the urban poor, unemployed or employed at very low wages, are increasingly prominent. Rapid population growth caused by high fertility has manifestly complicated Colombia's problems. Old policies and institutions must be modified.

Under reasonable assumptions it can be shown that this rapid growth of population has retarded the rate of growth of average income in Colombia. Although we have a rough understanding of the mechanism relating changes in population growth to the pace of development and will explore certain facets of this relationship in later chapters, the converse mechanism—that relating changes in the economic and social environment to changes in the rate of population growth—has scarcely been explored.[1] This

[1] For a thoughtful discussion of the relationship between changes in population growth and the pace of economic development, together with a critique of certain widely accepted formulations of this mechanism, see Gunnar Myrdal, *Asian Drama*, Pantheon Books, New York, 1968, Vol. III, Appendix 7, pp. 2063–2075.

chapter addresses this second aspect of the population problem: the determinants of population growth.

The proximate cause of Colombia's accelerated rate of population growth was the abrupt decline in death rates following World War II from about twenty-five to fifteen per thousand. But to say this is not to understand the phenomenon, nor to be able to predict its future course, nor to be able to develop public policies that can better cope with it. The most salient issues that require answers are why has the birth rate not fallen more rapidly, what are likely future trends in the birth rate, and what variables (particularly ones that policy might influence) will affect these trends?

Historical experience with regimes in which the death rate has fallen sharply indicates that, almost invariably, the birth rate moves to offset changes in the death rate, sooner or later, and in varying degree. Developed countries experienced a fall in birth rates in concurrence with a series of other fundamental social and economic changes. Urbanization and the extension of universal education, among other changes, have been attributed a role in the reduction of birth rates in developed countries.

A closer look at today's less developed countries reveals that often birth rates are substantially lower among urban than among rural women. Since the population explosion is contributing to a rapid shift of population from the countryside to the cities, this redistribution of population may help to dampen the rate of population growth by instigating a decline in the average birth rate. This sanguine interpretation of the effect of rural-urban migration on the birth rate has been discounted by some observers, but is nevertheless generally accepted. This phenomenon is important enough to probe deeper to learn why rural and urban birth rates differ, and whether rural-urban migration will disturb these traditional differences. Perhaps by exploring this question one can sharpen one's understanding of the general determinants of birth rates and also discover how public policy can influence birth rates. To develop such a model of reproductive behavior is the aim of this chapter.

Can differences in birth rates be interpreted partly as reflecting differences in the number of births parents want, and if so, what aspects of the parents' environment are ultimately responsible for their different wants? Our model rests on the assumption that people tend to adjust their behavior when their environment affords them new opportunities and imposes on them new limitations. This tendency toward "rational" behavioral adjustment may be neither prompt nor complete, but it provides a working hypothesis regarding family planning behavior that is helpful in investigating the local environment for the possible determinants of local birth rates.

The second section of this chapter elaborates the conceptual framework of the family planning hypothesis and explores its empirical implications. In the third section certain facets of the model are evaluated empirically against the unfortunately limited Colombian data. Then, with the aid of two additional case studies, Puerto Rico and Taiwan, for which the limitations of data are less severe than for Colombia, further implications of the model are tested.

The Family Planning Hypothesis and the Economic Causes of Population Growth

The family planning model is built around two basic factors that are assumed to exert a systematic effect on the actual frequency of births in following periods: (1) a family size goal or a number of surviving children that parents want, this being determined by a host of environmental factors modifying the relative attractiveness of few versus many children; (2) the incidence of death, mainly among offspring, which necessitates a compensating adjustment in birth rates to achieve any particular family size goal.[2]

THE FAMILY SIZE GOAL

Parents value children for themselves; but, in less developed countries particularly, children also contribute from an early age to family resources. Balanced against the benefits of having children, there also are costs: opportunity costs of time parents spend with their children, and pecuniary costs of goods and services required to feed, clothe, shelter, and educate a child. Parents' resources, in terms of time and wealth, constrain the activities undertaken, including the number of children they can rear.

It is useful as an introduction to more formal and quantitative

___

[2] The model is elaborated more fully in T. Paul Schultz, *A Family Planning Hypothesis*, RM-5405-RC/AID, The Rand Corporation, Santa Monica, Dec. 1967, and in "An Economic Model of Family Planning and Fertility," *Journal of Political Economy*, Vol. 77, No. 2, March–April 1969.

analysis to discuss briefly several characteristics of a community that seem likely to affect the subjective or pecuniary net cost of having children and thus affect the number of surviving children parents desire. The following seem central: (1) opportunity income of women and men, (2) the allocation of children's time between school and work, (3) birth control, and (4) institutions.

Opportunity income of women and men. To devote her time to her children, a mother forgoes the opportunity to earn additional income or undertake other activities. This opportunity cost of children is an important part of the total costs of rearing children, and a part that appears to grow as a society advances economically. When women can easily find good jobs outside the home, they tend both to participate frequently in the labor force and to appreciate the opportunity costs associated with enlarging their family or lengthening their years of child rearing. One expects, therefore, in an environment where women can earn more income (per unit time), to find higher female participation rates, lower birth rates, and shorter intervals between births, other things being equal.[3]

Typically, the main source of family income is that of the male head of household. A change in his income may have a variety of effects on parents' desires for children. An unanticipated but permanent change in family income would appear to change, in the same direction, the number of children parents can expect to rear at their current standard of living.[4] However, in the long run, a permanent shift in income is usually translated into a new standard of living for parents and children alike. Although parents have some latitude in the standard of living they provide for their children, the standards deemed socially acceptable rise with

[3] Each of these simple associations among women's earnings, activity, and fertility can be verified with U.S. data, and international comparisons also appear to be generally consistent with these direct implications of the opportunity income hypothesis. For example, see G. G. Cain and A. Weininger, "Economic Determinants of Fertility," April 1967 (mimeo); G. G. Cain, *Married Women in the Labor Force: An Economic Analysis,* University of Chicago Press, Chicago, 1966; United Nations, *Population Bulletin,* No. 7, 1963; Pascal K. Whelpton, "Trends and Differentials in Spacing Births," *Demography,* Vol. 1, 1964.

[4] Because children represent a long-term irreversible commitment, parents are not likely to respond to a change in income by adjusting the final number of children they want unless they view the change as permanent. The timing of births, on the other hand, might be altered in response to transitory changes in income.

parents' income and status. Exactly how these countervailing effects of an unexpected permanent change in income and a subsequent change in child costs balance out cannot be predicted *a priori*.[5]

Child labor and education. Children may also be gainfully employed. Until children can earn more than they consume, they rely economically on the family. The extent to which potential child earnings are captured by the parent depends on the alternative opportunities for children to attend school or to assist their parents, as well as the social attitudes toward child labor practices within and outside the home. At a later age when children can earn more than they consume, a host of cultural and economic factors are likely to determine what fraction of this "net income" is claimed by parents. Regardless of the underlying determinants of child labor practices in the community, the prevalence of unpaid family workers should be associated with larger benefits or lower net costs for rearing children.

School for children, therefore, even when provided free by the state, imposes opportunity costs on parents. Even if children do not work outside the home, they provide help in the home by tending younger children and performing routine household chores. This help is restricted when they attend school. School attendance also adds as a rule to direct household outlays for better clothes, school materials, transportation, and support away from home. The parents' decision to send their children to school thus increases child costs and may be a strong determinant underlying the family size goal. Having fewer children and providing these with additional opportunities for schooling may be an important watershed in the transition from so-called traditional values, where reproductive behavior was consistent with a regime of high childhood mortality and low social mobility, to so-called modern values, where reproductive behavior adjusts to conditions of low mortality and higher mobility in accord with the individual's talents, training, and formal education.

The schooling of parents may also affect their family size goal. The education of parents is closely associated with their opportunity income, and thus with the opportunity cost of the parents' time spent attending to the needs of their children. And since chil-

[5] This issue is discussed at greater length in Schultz, "An Economic Model of Family Planning and Fertility."

dren tend to be a relatively time intensive involvement, parents' education may underlie their relative evaluation of whether to have a large family or to allocate more of their time and resources to other activities. Schooling may give parents easier (cheaper) access to birth control information, contributing to their earlier and more reliable adoption of family limitation. Behavioral patterns of better educated parents may be more flexible and capable of coping with environmental change, such as an unanticipated decline in death rates as has occurred in Colombia. Finally, the willingness of parents to invest in their child's education may hinge on how much schooling they had. It is possible, therefore, that the schooling of each generation paves the way for the increased educational opportunities enjoyed by the next, increasing the costs of rearing children.

Birth control. The costs of birth control consist of the efforts of acquiring and evaluating information about alternative contraceptive methods and then the outlays and inconvenience associated with using a method. Traditional methods of birth control are less reliable and less convenient than modern ones.[6] Where the range of alternatives is limited to traditional methods, large costs must be incurred to achieve a high degree of reliability, as in the extreme cases of ,continence, dissolution of marital unions, and induced abortion. It should be stressed, however, that the personal costs associated with the adoption and use of contraception are poorly understood and very difficult as yet to appraise empirically.

Institutions and other factors. Income and wealth transfers between generations and from active workers to the inactive aged and infirm depend in part on the structure of the family. The extended family tends to shelter both the old and young. Parents have socially approved claims on their offspring's future earnings if their own means of support are exhausted, just as young parents turn to the extended family for support of their children when their current earnings are deemed insufficient. The scope and necessity of these family production and redistribution relationships ap-

---

[6] Although pregnancy rates differ among populations practicing similar methods of contraception, largely because of differences in motivation and understanding, the greater reliability of modern compared with traditional methods of contraception is on the order of ten to one. Costs and convenience also appear to favor modern over traditional methods of contraception.

pear to be a function of the average level of wealth in the society and the specific activities undertaken by the state.[7] These family institutional factors are judged to be important by some observers in determining family size goals, but empirical evidence is scant, and Colombian data are not rich enough to specify this facet of the family setting.

Many other factors undoubtedly play a role in determining the relative attractiveness to parents of having few or many surviving children. Some may be jointly determined with fertility, such as the marital status of the population and female activity, and thus these must be interpreted with utmost caution. Other variables, representing features of the population that are commonly assumed to correlate with fertility, are also considered, such as rural-urban residence, migrant status of the community, male wage or income levels, and the agricultural composition of the labor force. For the scope of this study the above abbreviated list of more important factors provides a useful starting point for evaluating the predictive power of the family planning hypothesis for Colombia. It is assumed, of course, that the environmental variables that are omitted from the analysis are uncorrelated with those included. Having settled on a desirable number of surviving children, parents may then decide, prospectively and retrospectively, how many births are needed to achieve that family size goal.

THE INCIDENCE OF DEATH

In exercising some control over births to achieve a certain surviving size of family, parents must take into account the incidence of death among their offspring. Neglecting for the moment the uncertainty of outcome that stems from the unpredictability of births and deaths within a particular family, the family planning hypothesis implies that parents try to compensate for the *average* incidence of death by seeking the number of births that will give

---

[7] The government may, for example, proscribe child labor, enforce school attendance, institute support programs for the aged and unproductive persons, and provide compulsory insurance programs of disability, medical care, and retirement. Public policies further impinge directly on the costs and benefits of children versus other private resource uses by government tax and expenditure policies, which extend, on one hand, personal deductions and dependency allowances on taxes and, on the other hand, provide for public health, education, and welfare services.

them the desired number of surviving children. Two behavioral mechanisms may be involved in this compensating adjustment of birth rates to death rates: a long-run expectation mechanism that may work primarily via changes in accepted patterns of marriage, birth timing, and spacing; and a short-run replacement mechanism that may emerge most strongly among older women several decades after the onset of the decline in child death rates.

First, the established regime of childhood mortality may influence parents in planning their lifetime reproductive behavior to compensate for what they *expect* to be the incidence of death among their offspring. If the death rate for children is high, this adjustment may take the form of earlier marriage and earlier initiation of child bearing and more frequent remarriage. Moreover, the level of death rates is closely associated with the amount of uncertainty attaching to the family formation process. Where increased uncertainty has the effect of inducing parents to seek more births, both the direct effect of the expected level of death rates and the indirect effect of death rates operating through uncertainty will tend to influence objective birth rates in the same direction. In this case birth rates might be observed to overcompensate for the changes in death rates, leaving surviving family size smaller under a regime of low, compared with a regime of high, death rates.

Second, since mortality in childhood is concentrated in the first years of life, parents may make an extra effort to have an additional child when they lose one of their children. This presumes that some still fertile women already have the number of living children they want and, without their child's death, would seek to avoid further births. A decade or two after child death rates decline, when large numbers of parents reach their surviving family size goal before menopause, fluctuations in child death rates are likely to exert a pronounced effect on the birth rate among this group of older women.[8]

Although these two behavioral mechanisms are distinct, it is empirically difficult to distinguish between them with the available aggregate demographic data because the usual expectation model and the replacement model imply similar adjustment equations for

[8] This implication of the model is confirmed in analysis of Taiwan data reported later in this chapter.

the purposes of empirical estimation. Regardless of the relative importance of these two mechanisms, the implications are clear that, for a community, current birth rates are likely to be influenced by recent past and future expected death rates.

In summary, parents' decision to seek a particular number of births is interpreted as a function of (1) the character of their environment that affects their revealed preferences for surviving children, and (2) past or expected child death rates that necessitate compensating adjustment in birth rates. This family planning hypothesis is next translated into a model that yields implications for reproductive behavior that are subject to empirical verification.

TOWARD EMPIRICAL EVALUATION OF THE MODEL FOR COLOMBIA

This section presents a formal model based on the preceding qualitative discussion and some results of testing the model against Colombian data. The problem is to specify a relation between the number of births parents want and environmental variables that are not themselves determined simultaneously with, or subsequently by, the objective number of births. In this exploration of the implications of the family planning hypothesis, it is assumed that the factors determining birth rates are themselves predetermined.[9]

THE HYPOTHESIS, IMPLICATIONS, AND EVIDENCE

Our family planning hypothesis postulates a multivariate relationship between equilibrium birth rates and certain features of parents' environment.[10] Here we shall assume the relationship is approximately linear and additive.

---

[9] A later study of other developing countries will attempt to specify and estimate the more prominent simultaneous relationships, among them family decisions relating to the frequency or number of births wanted. Neglecting interactions among family behavioral decisions biases our estimates of the effects of environmental conditions on the frequency of births; but it is hoped this simultaneous equation bias is not large, and the findings of this partial analysis represent a tentative step toward understanding the complex of household decisions pertaining to labor force participation, migration, and fertility.

[10] Since in the case of Colombia one is unable to consider more than one cross-section of regional observations without reliable information on death rates, these dynamic aspects of the model are not further developed here. The assumptions and the entire econometric model implicit in this discussion are set forth in Schultz, *A Family Planning Hypothesis.*

Unfortunately, the model cannot be tested directly for Colombia because separate data for births and deaths are not available at the regional level. The major source of reliable regional data is the Census of Population.[11] The age composition of the population, as recorded in the Census at the municipality level, does not permit estimation of birth and child death rates independently of each other,[12] but it does provide a basis, albeit approximate because of migration flows, for estimating a measure of "surviving fertility."[13] If, as appears to be the general case, and as our model

[11] Three studies have attempted to examine fertility, mortality, and, in some cases, migration rates by Department. A United Nations study directed by Grauman sought to project demographic trends based on data for 1938–1951 and to analyze some of the implications of these trends. Cuervo in a CELADE paper studied the differences in fertility across Departments and demonstrated that the 1951 Census age compositions imply radically different fertility patterns from registered rates (which are grossly deficient in several Departments). Berry used Grauman's fertility and mortality estimates by Department, and he suggests how these vital rates may be linked to various social and demographic characteristics. None of these studies utilized the 1964 Census materials or examined data at the municipality level. Alvaro Lopez is preparing a study of Colombian population growth based on the 1964 Census results, but it was not available as of this writing. See *Some Aspects of Population Growth in Colombia,* prepared by the Secretariat of the Economic Commission for Latin America, Economic and Social Council, United Nations, E/CN.12/618, Nov. 10, 1962; Lilia Ines Cuervo Gomez, *Fecundidad Diferencial de Colombia por Secciones Politico-Administrativas,* Centro Latinoamericano de Demografia, Santiago, E/CN.CELADE/C.21 B.61.1/5. Rev. 1, 1964; R. Albert Berry, *Breve Estudio de los Determinantes del Crecimiento de la Poblacion en Colombia,* Centro de Estudios Sobre Desarrollo Economico (CEDE), Universidad de los Andes, Bogota, March 1965.

[12] Even if the assumptions required for quasi-stable population theory estimates of vital rates were granted, there is no general way to contend with interregional migration, which radically affects the age compositions of regional populations. At the national level it may be assumed that net migration flows into or out of Colombia in this period were negligible, and thus it is feasible to estimate Colombian national average birth and death rates. But regional estimates of vital rates must rely on less reliable evidence of the net balance between birth and child death rates, as reflected in child-woman and child-population ratios of the traditional sort. See T. Paul Schultz, *Population Growth and Internal Migration in Colombia,* RM-5765-AID/RC, The Rand Corporation, Santa Monica, July 1969, Appendix B.

[13] Four linear estimates of the crude birth rate (uncompensated for the incidence of child death) are computed and averaged, based on the ratio of children (age 0–4 and 5–9) to women of childbearing age (15–49) and on the ratio of children (age 0–4 and 5–9) to total population. The linear

implies, the levels of birth rates and child death rates are positively correlated across regions in Colombia, this synthetic measure of surviving fertility derived from child-woman and child-population ratios will vary less across regions than will actual birth rates.[14] In sum, as our dependent variable, we are forced to use, not the birth rate, but a proxy for the birth rate minus the child death rate. From these data, of course, we are unable to estimate the effect of the child death rate on the birth rate.

There are similar problems in obtaining indexes of the "independent" variables. No comprehensive Colombian data exist on a regional basis for wage rates for women. We assume here that women's participation in the labor force is predetermined by their income opportunities and is a satisfactory proxy for women's opportunity wage. The effect of the educational process is measured in two ways as suggested by our analysis above: school attendance among children, and educational attainment of adults.[15] No measure of age-specific labor force participation is available for Colombia by municipality, and thus the effect of unpaid family employment of children, or indeed any measure of the work experience of children, is omitted in this analysis.

Departing from the central components of the model, we find several other variables worth considering, though their relations

---

estimates are borrowed from a cross-sectional analysis of some fifty countries by Bogue and Palmore. The average of the four 1964 estimates is designated our estimate of surviving fertility for each municipality for the decade before the 1964 Census. For regression coefficients, see Donald J. Bogue and James A. Palmore, "Some Empirical and Analytic Relations Among Demographic Fertility Measures with Regression Models for Fertility Estimation," *Demography*, Vol. 1, 1964, Table 8, p. 325.

[14] The counterbalancing effects of interregional birth and child death rates and their impact on child-woman ratios are discussed by Warren C. Robinson, "Urbanization and Fertility: The Non-Western Experience," *Milbank Memorial Fund Quarterly*, Vol. 41, No. 3, July 1963, pp. 291–308. Puerto Rican data also reveal this interregional pattern. The family planning hypothesis, of course, implies that this pattern is behaviorally determined. See Schultz, "An Economic Model of Family Planning and Fertility."

[15] Multicollinearity is not as much a problem as might be expected in considering both child and adult schooling simultaneously in a regression model. For the Colombia sample the simple correlation coefficient between adult and child schooling variables is only .47 in the 1964 Census; for Puerto Rico from 1951 to 1957 it is .42; and for Taiwan it is .39 in 1965.

to preferred size of surviving family are more problematic.[16] Under the reasonable assumption that a rapid rise in real wages relaxes parents' resource constraint on having a larger number of children, it is plausible that the level and rate of growth (1952–1965) of local agricultural real wages may be associated with somewhat larger families, other things being equal.

Internal migration may also account for some of the inter-regional variation in surviving fertility. Women in rural areas have more children, on the average, than women living in urban areas. Since the bulk of internal migration in Colombia consists of persons moving from rural to urban residence, the migrant may bring with him more than the urban average number of young children, or continue to want and have a larger number of children than is typical among urban-born residents.[17] In this case regions in which a large proportion of the local population were in-migrants would tend to record higher levels of surviving fertility than regions, other-wise similar, in which in-migrants represented a smaller proportion of the population. To test this line of reasoning, the proportion of men in the municipality who were born outside the municipality is included in the regression model as an in-migration variable. In the next chapter migration and its determinants are the center of analysis.[18]

Turning again to the rural or urban nature of a locality, we have implicitly argued above that characterizing an environment

[16] It was also possible to test the hypothesis that the available stock of housing per capita reflected the relative cost of housing and, consequently, a constraint on desired family size. A moderate, but not statistically sig-nificant, positive association was found between the average number of rooms per capita in the 1951 Housing Census and surviving fertility in 1964 across the sample of Colombian municipalities.

[17] Zarate has sought to show that urban immigrants to Monterrey, Mexico, only gradually reduce their fertility toward the level sustained by native-born residents of the city. However, he neglects to make allowances for the differences that undoubtedly distinguish the family environment for the urban in-migrant parents and city-born parents, differences that may go far toward accounting for the different reproductive behavior he correlates with the two groups. Alvan O. Zarate, "Differential Fertility in Monterrey, Mexico," *Milbank Memorial Fund Quarterly*, Vol. 45, No. 2, Part 1, April 1967; and "Some Factors Associated with Urban-Rural Fertility Differentials in Mexico," *Population Studies*, Vol. 21, No. 3, Nov. 1967.

[18] There are strong reasons for treating both migration and population growth simultaneously, but, as noted later, this proved impossible given data limitations for Colombia.

as urban or rural conceals the more fundamental differences among environments that are only crudely described by this arbitrary dichotomy. For example, a change of residence from rural to urban areas frequently involves a number of changes in family organization and environment that on balance appear to add to the costs of rearing children. The result may thus be lower birth rates among urban than among rural populations. Many of these changes are directly incorporated into our model.[19] For much the same reason, agricultural activity is often thought to be more conducive to higher birth rates than nonagricultural activity. Both the proportion of the population in rural residence and the proportion of the labor force employed in agriculture are considered as possible explanatory variables in our regression analysis of surviving fertility in Colombia.

Finally, the proportion of adult women married or living in free unions is often considered as an intermediate cause for variation in surviving fertility. It must be emphasized, however, that the marriage rate represents an institutional variable which is not likely to be independent of desired or surviving fertility, for the timing of marriage patterns is heavily influenced by the environmental constraints and opportunities that simultaneously determine the number of children parents indeed want.[20] Therefore, the inclusion of the marriage rate in the regression model may bias the estimation of the direct effects of environmental variables on surviving fertility.

The data examined are derived from a 15 percent random sample of 131 Colombian municipalities for which unpublished

[19] A number of factors could add, on balance, to the real costs of rearing children in the urban compared with the rural environment: (1) direct costs of food and housing are likely to be greater for a large family; (2) opportunities to use the productive talents of children to add to family resources tend to be more limited; (3) the need to invest in children's schooling and skills is better understood in the urban environment, hence the associated costs are more often accepted; (4) opportunities for women to work outside of the home are greater, and consequently their potential contribution to family income that is forgone while children are young is larger.

[20] The postponement of marriage is the primary determinant of variation in the proportion of the adult female population married, and this form of institutional adjustment is commonly associated with the more fundamental changes in the environment already included in the analysis. To the extent that marriage is a response to the environmental constraints, its inclusion biases downward the other estimates for the environmental constraints.

1964 Census tabulations and published 1951 Census data are matched. Information from the two censuses yields estimates of local patterns of population growth and internal migration.[21]

EMPIRICAL FINDINGS FOR COLOMBIA

The association between regional surviving fertility, from the decade before 1964, as defined earlier, and characteristics of the local population and environment is estimated in Table 1 by ordinary least squares. The principal variables of the model—child and adult schooling rates and female activity rates—account for

[21] The design and shortcomings of this sample and associated census data are discussed in Schultz, *Population Growth and Internal Migration in Colombia*, Appendix B.

TABLE 1

REGRESSIONS ON ESTIMATED MUNICIPAL SURVIVING FERTILITY, COLOMBIA, 1964[a]

(in parentheses beneath regression coefficients are their t statistics, or the ratios of the coefficients to their standard errors)

Regression Number	Constant Term	Proportion with Some Primary Schooling Age 5–9	Age 15–59	Female Activity Rate	Proportion of Women Married	Proportion of Men Not Born in Locality	Annual Growth of Real Wages	R²
1	52.09	−.098 (−2.27)[b]	−.080 (−2.34)[b]	−.108 (−2.92)[c]	.037 (1.98)[b]	.028 (1.53)	.142 (1.34)	.266
2	52.31	−.086 (−2.02)[b]	−.084 (−2.46)[b]	−.112 (−3.03)[c]	.035 (1.87)	.028 (1.52)	NI	.256
3	52.32	−.095 (−2.24)[b]	−.067 (−2.07)[b]	−.116 (−3.12)[c]	.035 (1.85)	NI	NI	.242
4	54.46	−.109 (−2.59)[c]	−.059 (−1.81)	−.120 (−3.20)[c]	NI	NI	NI	.221

NOTES:

NI means "variable not included in regression."

[a] Independent variables expressed in percentages, with growth of real wages measured in agriculture on an average annual basis from 1952 to 1965. Surviving fertility is expressed in terms of a crude birth rate per thousand population that is approximately associated with the proportion of children in the regional population to women and adults of childbearing age (see footnotes 12 and 13).

[b] Coefficient significantly different from zero at the 5 percent level of confidence.

[c] Coefficient significantly different from zero at the 1 percent level of confidence.

SOURCE:

T. Paul Schultz, *Population Growth and Internal Migration in Columbia*, RM-5765-RC/AID, The Rand Corporation, Santa Monica, July 1969, Table 3, p. 23. Sample size is 131.

about 22 percent of the interregional variation in surviving fertility in Colombia. The predictive power of the relationship is less important, for our purposes, than the significance and size of the regression coefficients. Child school attendance and female activity rates are significantly associated with interregional differences in surviving fertility, but adult education falls marginally below the 5 percent confidence level, its coefficient being only 1.8 times its standard error. The marriage rate, in-migration rate, and growth of real wage variables all have the expected sign in relation to surviving fertility, but none adds significantly to overall relationships or is attributed a regression coefficient that is significantly different from zero.

Although there is a tendency for rural and agricultural regions to record higher fertility rates, it appears that these differences are largely accounted for by the education and female activity variables and make no significant additional contribution to explaining interregional variation in surviving fertility in the Colombian sample.

If the relationship estimated in Regression 4 of Table 1 were valid, a number of probable changes in Colombia would contribute to a reduction in the rate of population growth. A doubling of the child school attendance rate for the age group 5 to 9 from the level of 22 percent in 1964 would be associated with a 5 percent reduction in surviving fertility, and as the proportion of adults with some schooling increased from, say, 62 to 74 percent, this would be associated with an additional 1 percent reduction in surviving fertility. These findings are broadly consistent with those considered later for Puerto Rico and Taiwan. The school system appears to exert an influence on fertility more through the direct route associated with having children in school than through its delayed impact on the educational attainment of parents.[22] The participation of women in the labor force is likely to continue to increase in Colombia, and a doubling of the current low level of activity among women would be associated with a 4 percent decline in surviving fertility. Major changes such as these are likely to occur in the next decade or two, and according to the estimates presented here, these changes alone would be associated with a 10 percent reduction in surviving fertility and population growth.

[22] Schultz, *A Family Planning Hypothesis.*

EVIDENCE FROM OTHER COUNTRIES

It is not possible to estimate the child death rate in Colombia on a regional level.[23] Therefore, to examine the magnitude and speed of response of changes in birth rates as related to changes in child death rates, it is necessary to look to the experience of other countries. Moreover, to judge the effectiveness of birth control programs in hastening the reduction in birth rates, analysis must focus on one of the few developing countries where a major family planning program has been launched. In Colombia such a nationwide program is only now taking shape. Thus, as a way of probing these questions and further implications of the family planning model, experience in Puerto Rico and Taiwan are examined in the remainder of this chapter.

THE CASE OF PUERTO RICO

Puerto Rican data are generally better than Colombian. In particular, we have reliable observations on crude birth and death rates by municipality, so we can directly test more of the implications of the model. Table 2 contrasts the level of birth and death rates in Colombia, Puerto Rico, and Taiwan.

The model is reformulated and estimated from a time series of cross-sectional observations on 75 Puerto Rican municipalities for the period 1950 to 1957. First, the ratio of the variance of regional-specific to time-and-regional-independent disturbances is estimated. A transformation of the pooled data based in the estimated variance ratio then yields improved estimates of the

[23] Mortality among children in Colombia has undoubtedly decreased with the control of some infectious and microbial diseases, but childhood deaths are still much more common than in developed countries. Infant mortality is about four times greater in Colombia than in advanced countries, and death among preschool children (ages 1 to 7) may be thirty times higher. Protein-calorie malnutrition is thought to be responsible for the high death rate in Latin America, contributing to the susceptibility of children to the pneumonia-diarrhea complex of diseases. Essentially nonmicrobial, these diseases are not readily controlled by modern medical technology without a prior improvement in the child's diet and home environment. McDermott, "Modern Medicine and the Demographic/Disease Pattern of Overly Traditional Societies: A Technologic Misfit," paper presented at the Institute on International Medical Education of the Association of American Medical Colleges, Washington, D.C., March 28, 1966.

TABLE 2

CRUDE AND AGE-SPECIFIC BIRTH AND DEATH RATES IN
SELECTED COUNTRIES

Country and Year	Crude Birth Rate	Age-Specific Birth Rate							Crude Death Rate	Infant Mortality Rate
		15–19	20–24	25–29	30–35	39–40	40–44	45–49		
Taiwan										
1921–1925	41.2	n.a.	n.a.	n.a.	n.a.	n.a.	n.a.	n.a.	23.7	165[a]
1936–1940	43.6	n.a.	n.a.	n.a.	n.a.	n.a.	n.a.	n.a.	19.7	140[a]
1950	43.3	62	247	298	269	192	112	30	11.5	44.7[a]
1955	45.3	51	274	342	296	219	103	25	8.6	44.8
1960	39.5	49	254	334	256	170	79	13	6.9	35.0
1965	32.7	36	261	326	195	100	42	6	5.5	24.1
1966[b]	31.3	39	269	320	184	88	37	5	5.4	21.7
Puerto Rico										
1939–1941[c]	39.2	78	248	262	215	140	43	9	18.4	137
1950	39.0	99	280	260	200	143	53	12	9.9	68
1954	35.2	98	255	219	160	131	48	11	7.5	58
1958	33.2	104	291	203	133	104	42	10	6.9	53
1964	30.6	n.a.	257	193	116	88	34	7	7.2	52
Colombia (estimated)										
1951–1964	47	95	299	339	302	239	168	30	14	115
United States										
1964	21	73	220	179	104	50	14	1	9.4	25

NOTES:

n.a. means "not available."

[a] 1920–1940, George W. Barclay, *Colonial Development and Population in Taiwan*, Princeton University Press, Princeton, 1954; and from United Nations sources. 1950 entry is for 1952 1954, Tables 36, 39.

[b] Adjusted for shift in pattern of enumeration in December 1966 associated with Special Census.

[c] Underregistration is probably substantial at this time in Puerto Rico.

SOURCES:

Taiwan——*Demographic Reference Taiwan 1966*, Vol. VI, and adjusted 1966 crude birth rate bimonthly newsletter of the Taiwan Population Studies Center, Jan.–Feb. 1968.

Puerto Rico——United Nations *Demographic Yearbook* and U.S. vital statistics.

Colombia——Estimates from T. Paul Schultz, *Population Growth and Internal Migration in Colombia*, RM-5765-RC/AID, The Rand Corporation, Santa Monica, July 1969, Appendix A, Table A-3.

United States——Arthur Campbell, Alice Clague, Frank Godley, *Natality Statistics Analysis United States 1964*, National Center for Health Statistics, Series 21, No. 11, Feb. 1967, Table 3 p. 8.

parameters of the model analogous to generalized least squares.[24] These final Puerto Rican estimates of the basic family planning model are reported in Regression 1 of Table 3. The association between birth rates and prior death rates conforms to expectations. The estimates are statistically strong for two years and of diminishing positive value for three years when analyzed together against current birth rates. Both education variables are inversely associated with birth rates, as for Colombia, measuring in this case school attendance rates among children 7 to 13 and median years of adult schooling. The proxy for women's opportunity income, their participation rates in the labor force, is also negatively associated with birth rates, whereas the anticipated positive association with birth rates is observed when family members work for their parents without pay, reducing the cost of rearing children.

Regressions 2 and 3 of Table 3 show the additional associations between birth rates and two variables often related to fertility. Although in Puerto Rico, as in Colombia, rural and agricultural regions exhibit somewhat higher than average birth rates, the variables of the basic family planning model account fully for the differences in birth rates associated with these cruder distinctions among family environments.

Further details on the regional populations and their environment are obtained for Puerto Rico for testing additional implications of the model that could not be investigated for Colombia and are reported elsewhere.[25] The recent variability of death rates was used as a proxy for uncertainty stemming from these fluctuations in death rates, but without finding a statistically significant association with regional birth rates.[26] As with the Colombian

---

[24] For full discussion and derivation of estimation procedure for dynamic relations of a time series of cross-sections, see Schultz, *A Family Planning Hypothesis*, Appendix D.

[25] Schultz, *A Family Planning Hypothesis*, Table 8, p. 41.

[26] Since death rates fell abruptly in this period, 1943 to 1956, and declines were due largely to irreversible improvements in health and economic conditions, it is plausible that the greater the deviations in death rates from their trend value, the greater parents' difficulty in anticipating future death rates and interpreting trends accurately. Uncertainty in death rates is therefore estimated as the variance from a linear time trend. How well this proxy represents the parents' expectations of the uncertainty they face in forming their family is moot. As noted in the text, no significant association was found between this measure of uncertainty and birth rates after including the other control variables.

TABLE 3

TWO-STAGE REGRESSIONS ON CRUDE BIRTH RATES IN MUNICIPALITIES OF PUERTO RICO, 1950–1957

(in parentheses beneath regression coefficients are their t statistics,
or the ratios of the coefficients to their standard errors)

Regression Number	Constant Term	Education		Women Participation (percent)	Unpaid Family Workers (percent)	Crude Death Rates		Urbanization (percent)	Proportion Active in Agriculture (percent)	R^2
		Children Age 7–13 in School (percent)	Adults Age 25 and over (years)			Lagged 1 year	Lagged 2 years			
1	26.88	−.083 (2.24)[b]	−1.451 (4.90)[b]	−.179 (5.97)[b]	.766 (8.06)[b]	.835 (4.89)[b]	.304 (1.88)			.449
2	28.47	−.099 (2.54)[b]	−1.627 (5.02)[b]	−.185 (6.17)[b]	.759 (7.98)[b]	.817 (4.75)[b]	.263 (1.58)	.016 (1.31)		.451
3	26.20	−.078 (1.99)[a]	−1.382 (3.93)[b]	−.177 (5.92)[b]	.755 (7.63)[b]	.831 (4.83)[b]	.303 (1.86)		.007 (.39)	.449

NOTES:
[a] Coefficient significantly different from zero at the 5 percent level of confidence.
[b] Coefficient significantly different from zero at the .1 percent level of confidence.

SOURCE:
T. Paul Schultz, *A Family Planning Hypothesis and Some Empirical Evidence from Puerto Rico*, RM-5405-RC/AID, The Rand Corporation, Santa Monica, Dec. 1967, Table 9. Sample size is 525.

analysis, it is interesting to test for Puerto Rico whether differences in age, sex, and marital status of the population account for some part of the variation in crude birth rates not accounted for by the basic model. To test this hypothesis, two variables were constructed to measure the effect of these compositional characteristics on birth rates.[27] Adding either or both of these variables to the basic model does not add to its explanatory power, nor do these variables show a statistically significant association with birth rates or substantially alter the previous estimates of the model.[28]

One quantitative implication of these findings for Puerto Rico deserves emphasis. The estimated association between death and subsequent birth rates shown in Table 3 implies that a change in regional death rates is associated with a fully compensating change in birth rates within a few years; that is, the sum of the regression coefficients for the death rate exceeds one. A reduction in death rates in this period was not associated with a significant increase in the rate of population growth. If the association reflects causality, as the model postulates, reducing death rates, say, from fifteen to ten per thousand, by improving health and economic conditions of the population did not exacerbate the population growth problem in Puerto Rico. On the contrary, it directly facilitated the fertility transition to a birth rate five to six per thousand lower, actually reducing the rate of population growth within a

[27] As a proxy for the share of the population subject to the risk of child bearing, the proportion of adults married was used. Age-specific marital status data were not available by region for the purposes of deriving a measure of the fertile population subject to the risk of child bearing. The women in each age group were attributed the appropriate national age-specific birth rate, and the estimated number of births for each municipality was then divided by the population to derive an estimate of the municipal crude birth rate. This procedure assumes that age-specific birth rates do not vary appreciably across Puerto Rico, so that age-sex compositional differences will account for (some of) the observed interregional variation in crude birth rates.

[28] These demographic variables may not vary sufficiently across regions for us to identify their effect on birth rates, or their effect may have already been accounted for by underlying economic variables that themselves influence marriage rates and, through their effect on migration, change the age structure. But, regardless of the reasons, this simple test finds no support for the hypothesis that these compositional features of the municipal populations are helpful in understanding existing differences in municipal birth rates.

couple of years. This evidence may foreshadow future trends in Colombia.

In summary, four environmental variables lagged one year and death rates lagged one and two years constitute the core of the Puerto Rican test of the family planning model. In contrast with the Colombian test of the model, directly measured birth and death rates and unpaid family workers have been added. Additional environmental and demographic variables again do not account for a significant portion of the remaining unexplained interregional variation in birth rates in Puerto Rico. The salient features of the family's environment—mortality or health, education, and economic activity of women and children—account for almost half of the variation in Puerto Rican birth rates among 75 municipalities over seven years.

THE CASE OF TAIWAN

For Taiwan three new dimensions of the model can be examined. First, data on birth rates of women of various ages permit us to examine whether women appear to respond differently at different ages to constraints and opportunities on the family formation process. It was earlier conjectured that the effect of family planning would be more noticeable among older women, particularly as they might try to replace lost children quickly. Second, age-specific death rates allow us to refine our measure of child death rates and recast our model logarithmically to incorporate this information in another statistical form.[29] Third, in Taiwan it is possible to evaluate by means of our model the effectiveness of public policy aimed at hastening the spread and use of modern contraception to reduce birth rates.

Additional biological and behavioral information available for Taiwan enables us to sharpen the implications of the family planning model for age-specific reproductive behavior. Most family planning is avoiding unwanted births after having the number of surviving children wanted. Spacing of births is a subtle and uncommon refinement, for two reasons.[30] First, as fertility declines, birth

[29] See discussion later in note 41.

[30] For example, in Taiwan among women accepting an IUD (Intrauterine Device) in 1966, about 15 percent reported their objective was spacing as opposed to stopping further births. Among women over the age of 29, the proportion spacing births was only 5 percent. *Demographic Refer-*

intervals do not increase; rather, child bearing becomes increasingly concentrated in fewer years, usually while the mother is still in her twenties. It therefore appears that women prefer to have their children close together in their early years of marriage once reliable means of contraception are available, assuming the family environment is relatively stable and predictable.[31] Second, spacing of births relies on foresight, which is difficult to fathom in a rapidly changing environment such as is common in developing countries, whereas avoiding further births when enough children are already living necessitates no forethought and involves obvious reinforcement mechanisms.

As fertility declines secularly, it is common for the relative decline in birth rates for older women to exceed the decline for younger women, as is evidenced for Taiwan in Table 4. The proportion married in Taiwan has fallen of late for women age 15 to 19, but has not changed appreciably since 1959 for older women, though for older cohorts the secular trend has been toward an increasing proportion married. The postponement or early consummation of marriage, as is argued earlier, is one form of family planning and may, like others, adapt to environmental opportunities and constraints, such as a change in child mortality or an increase in returns to, and opportunities for, extended education. Consequently, our model is designed to predict age-specific birth rates and not age-specific birth rates of married women. To the extent to which the model accounts for regional differences in birth rates for women 15 to 19, two instruments of family planning are likely to be in operation: birth control within marriage, and postponement of marriage itself. More generally, however, the model has greatest relevance to the age-specific reproductive behavior of women over age 30, among whom birth control

---

ence—*Taiwan, Republic of China, 1967,* Vol. V, Taiwan Population Studies Center, Taiwan Provincial Department of Health, July 1967, Table 8.

[31] This pattern prevails in virtually all developed countries. One exception is the Netherlands, where fertility is still relatively high and the participation of women in the labor force is very low, particularly among married women. In the Netherlands one finds the unusual pattern of prolonged childbearing years and thus a more uniform relative downward shift in age-specific fertility rates at all ages than in most other advanced industrial countries. The growing concentration of childbearing in the younger years appears to be also emerging in many of the less developed countries that are experiencing a substantial decline in fertility.

TABLE 4
PERCENTAGE DECLINE IN TAIWAN BIRTH RATES, 1955–1966

Age of Women	Percentage Decline in Birth Rate
15–19	24
20–24	2
25–29	6
30–34	38
35–39	60
40–44	64
45–49	80
Total fertility rate[a]	28
Crude birth rate	31

NOTE:
   [a] Sum of age-specific fertility rates times five, the number of years in each cohort.
SOURCE:
   See Table 2.

is likely to become increasingly common as demographic transition progresses.

For Taiwan the analytical treatment of child mortality can be refined further than was possible for Puerto Rico, where only the crude death rate was available. The model implies that the death of a child to a still fertile mother is likely to induce her to have a somewhat higher subsequent birth rate than she would otherwise have had. Although the death of a child may motivate its mother to seek an additional offspring, this effect on her reproductive behavior may be difficult to distinguish in the short run if she is young and if her age cohort is likely to be having additional children regardless of the incidence of child mortality. If, on the other hand, the mother is older, say in her late thirties, when a sizable proportion of her cohort intends to avoid further births, her behavioral response to the child's death may distinguish her from others in her cohort in a relatively short time.[32]

---

[32] This implication of the family planning model allows us to discriminate between two possible causes for the association between child death rates and subsequent birth rates in a region. Some students of the subject have suggested that the statistical association may be due to a biological lag in the human reproductive process. The reasoning runs that, when a breast-feeding infant dies, the consequent cessation of lactation reduces the period

Although it is not possible from published data to trace the frequency of child death to mothers of a specific age, it is possible in each region to determine the age-specific death rate for children in several years. Since age-specific mortality is relatively low beyond age 14, the child death rate is defined in our analysis from birth through age 14.[33]

One final issue is germane to our inquiry: how long is the lag between the death of a child and its subsequent observable effect on births likely to be? Research on the average length of birth intervals for women not practicing contraception suggests that on the average two or three years will elapse.[34] For women between ages 20 and 29, when fecundity appears to be highest, a lag of two years seems most likely, at least for the United States, and perhaps three years for women 15 to 19 and over 29 years of age. To this biological lag a decisionmaking lag may be added, but there is no empirical evidence to guide one in estimating the probable length of this behavioral lag. Since we are restricted in Taiwan to a few years of consolidated and published data on death, experimentation with various lengths of lags is limited to 1966, where it is found that the three-year lag is statistically strongest for the age-standardized birth rate, although the two-year lag (not reported here) is marginally more powerful in accounting for the interregional variation in birth rates for women between ages 20

---

of postpartum sterility (amenorrhea) and thus increases the probability that the mother will conceive again. In some cultures intercourse during lactation is taboo, and various other customary and institutional arrangements work to increase birth intervals if the child survives, but are rescinded if the child dies. Were this the cause of the statistical association noted in Puerto Rico, the association should be significant for women of all ages and perhaps diminish with advancing age and declining fecundity. The family planning model that attributes this association to a behavioral decision would lead us to expect that the statistical association would be stronger among women over 30 and weaker among women in their twenties, when reproductive behavior is less immediately sensitive to child mortality.

[33] Age-specific death rates are summed for the region from birth through age 14. The infant survival rate was also investigated, but the statistical association was stronger when the child death variable was defined over the entire first 14 years of life. Beyond that age not only are death rates low, but an increasing fraction of the child deaths are likely to occur to parents who were beyond reproductive age and could not, therefore, change their reproductive behavior.

[34] Robert G. Potter, "Birth Intervals: Structure and Change," *Population Studies,* Vol. 17, No. 155, 1963, pp. 155–156.

and 29. This result is consistent with the other direct evidence on birth intervals mentioned above. The results reported here are for a fixed three-year lag for both 1964 and 1966.[35]

The Taiwan system of household registrations provides a rich and reliable source of certain types of demographic and economic data that have been compiled and published in the last few years for 361 administrative units of Taiwan—precincts, townships, and hsiangs.[36] From these data it is possible to estimate school attendance for children and educational attainment for adults, as in Colombia, and also to derive the occupational attachment for men.[37] Birth rates are analyzed for two years, 1964 and 1966.

[35] Using the two-year lag for the age-specific birth rates between 20 and 29 did not change appreciably the other regression coefficients, and since the two-year lagged death rates were not available for 1964, comparability was preserved by using the three-year lag for all regressions reported in Tables 5 through 7.

[36] These unique data for a less developed country are published by the Taiwan Department of Civil Affairs and reflect years of consultative effort on the part of the University of Michigan Population Studies Center under the direction of Ronald Freedman and the Taiwan Population Studies Center in Taichung under the direction of L. P. Chow. The Taiwan family planning program has become in recent years the prototype of a successful, large-scale, well-run program in a developing country. This reputation is probably closely related to the fact that a substantial fraction of the program's resources has been used both to improve the design of the program with the aid of carefully evaluated pilot programs (the Taichung experiment is discussed in Ronald Freedman and John Y. Takeshita, *Family Planning in Taiwan: An Experiment in Social Change,* Princeton University Press, Princeton, 1969) and to collect the basic demographic and program statistics that permit reliable evaluation of the program's success at each stage. For a brief survey of this much-studied program, see R. G. Potter, R. Freedman, and L. P. Chow, "Taiwan's Family Planning Program," *Science,* Vol. 160, May 24, 1968, pp. 848–853.

[37] Education and occupation data are available for only a year or two. Women's participation in the labor force was also examined (from unpublished tabulations of the household registry kindly provided by Paul Liu) but was not found to be significantly associated with birth rates. Liu finds from an evaluation check on the accuracy of the registry system that it performs well in measuring births, education, and male occupation, but is exceptionally inaccurate when it comes to current work status of women in the community. Paul K. C. Liu (tr. W. L. Parish), "The Use of Household Registration Records in Measuring the Fertility Level of Taiwan," *Economics Papers,* Selected English Series No. 2, The Institute of Economics, Academia Sinica, Taipei, Taiwan, p. 4. Ronald Freedman has pointed out that the adult education measure published from the household registration material provides information only on the average educational attainment of all persons 12 years or older who are no longer in school. It would

In the latter year the large-scale unofficial family planning program launched in 1964 may have begun to influence birth rates. It is initially assumed that the program's effect is uniform throughout the island, or at least uncorrelated with our exogenous variables, and later an adjustment for the effect of the program on birth rates is proposed. To explore these finer implications of the family planning hypothesis, a reformulation of the statistical model seems appropriate.

In mathematical notation, the relationship we want to characterize is

(1) $$B = f(D)s(X, Y, Z, \ldots)p(M)$$

where B represents the birth rate, $f(D)$ is a function of the child death rate, $s(X, Y, Z, \ldots)$ is a function of environmental factors $X, Y, Z, \ldots$ that determine the number of surviving children parents want, and $p(M)$ a function that relates family planning program inputs to the number of averted (unwanted) births.[38] The first function, that of the child death rate, can be given explicit form if it is assumed that parents adjust systematically for death rates to obtain a particular surviving family size. In this case the death variable enters multiplicatively into the model as $1/S$, where the survival rate $S = 1 - D$.[39]

(2) $$B = \left(\frac{1}{S}\right)^{\alpha} s(X, Y, Z, \ldots)p(M).$$

---

be distinctly preferable to have age-specific educational data, since only the potential parent population's education is germane to the hypothesis we seek to test. With 1966 Census materials, soon to be available, it should be possible to derive such a measure of age-specific educational attainment.

[38] The resources used in the family planning program should be recorded at the regional level of observation, valuing each input comparably at its opportunity value elsewhere in the national economy. For the purposes of program evaluation, aspects or activities of the program that operate through different instruments and can be reasonably combined in different proportions should be treated separately in the program cost accounts. This is particularly useful for human resources where doctors are aided by less skilled paramedical technicians and field workers, whose talents are less scarce than those of the doctor and may be substituted within certain limits for those of the doctor. Alternative propaganda efforts and promotional expenditure schemes may also be segregated and analyzed to help determine what mix of publicity, direct inducements, and human resources yields a desired effect on the birth rate at least cost.

[39] The death factor is defined as the reciprocal of the child "survival" rate (that is, one minus the sum of child death rates). For example, if

If parents compensated precisely for the change in child death rates to obtain a constant number of children surviving to a particular age, regardless of the expected incidence of child death, then $\alpha = 1$ in Equation (2). If $\alpha > 1$, birth rates would diminish as death rates declined by more than enough to hold constant the surviving number of children, and in this case surviving family size would fall. This might occur if parents not only adjusted to the decline in the expected incidence of death but also reacted plausibly to both the associated reduction in the uncertainty surrounding the child-rearing process and to the associated increase in the rate of return to investment in the child's schooling and vocational skills. Were $\alpha < 1$ and other factors did not change, the number of children reaching maturity would increase as child death rates declined.

Our estimating equation is in this case based on the assumption that all of the variables interact multiplicatively to determine birth rates or, in other words, that the elasticity of each independent variable with respect to birth rates is constant. The birth rate equation is thus explicitly shown in Equation (3) and conveniently estimated in logarithmic-linear form.[40]

$$(3) \qquad B = \left(\frac{1}{S}\right)^{\alpha} K X^{\beta_1} Y^{\beta_2} Z^{\beta_3} M^{\beta_4} u$$

where α and β_i ($i = 1, \ldots, 4$) are parameters of the model, K is an estimated scale factor, and u a properly behaved log normal disturbance term.[41]

---

80 percent of the children "survived" to age 15, then the child death factor would be about 1.25. Parents to have four surviving children would seek about five births ($4 \times 1.25 = 5$). It seems probable, however, that uncertainty enters this decisionmaking process. When, say, two decades ago, only 50 percent of the children survived to age 15 in the region, parents might still have only wanted four surviving children, but, to hedge against the greater uncertainty implicit in such a heavy regime of childhood mortality, they might have sought, not eight births ($4 \times [1/.5] = 8$), but perhaps nine or ten. In this case the reduction in child death rates would reduce the size of surviving (to age 15) family.

[40] Logarithmic regressions are performed on the logarithms (to the base 10) of the variables.

[41] The log-linear form of Eq. 3 implies that resources employed to disseminate information about birth control are subject to diminishing returns. But, because no resources were used in the family planning program in some regions, that is, $M_i = 0$ for some ith region, and the logarithm of

Estimates of this formulation of the family planning model between birth rates in 1964 and 1966 and appropriately lagged environmental variables are shown in Tables 5 and 6. This formulation of the model accounts for 23 percent of the interregional relative variation in the age-standardized birth rate in 1964 and 57 percent in 1966.[42] For the age-specific birth rates from age 30 to 44, the model accounts for 20 to 37 percent of the variation, but for the age 20–29 cohorts only 6 to 22 percent of the variance can be understood in terms of these environmental variables. These overall findings are consistent with our expectation that the model

---

zero is undefined, a small constant, δ, is added to this variable in all regions to represent latent knowledge of birth control present in the absence of the program. Alternative values of this constant may make a difference in the implied rate of diminishing returns to the family planning program input. In estimating the model, the constant is selected in order to maximize the fit or strengthen the association between the input variable and the birth rate and thereby maximize the predictive power of the entire model. This procedure modifies the constant elasticity property of the log-linear formulation, but the effect on the elasticity estimate appears to be minor, except for very small values of M. For a more complete discussion of the sensitivity of estimates to various specifications of the model, see T. Paul Schultz, "The Effectiveness of Family Planning in Taiwan," P-4069, The Rand Corporation, Santa Monica, April 1969, a paper presented at the Population Association of America Meetings, Atlantic City, New Jersey.

[42] The age-standardized and normalized birth rate defined for the ith region as

$$B_i / \sum_{j=1}^{7} B_j W_{ij}$$

where B_i is the number of births in the ith region, B_j is the national age-specific birth rate per thousand women in the jth age cohort, and W_{ij} is the number of thousand women in the jth age cohort in the ith region. For instance, if the age-specific birth rates in a region were identical to the national average age-specific rates, then the age-standardized birth rate would be unity. A possible source of error in our dependent variable is the adjustment procedure applied to correct regionally registered birth rates for the unusual effects of the 1966 Census, which concentrated birth registrations at the end of 1966. The adjustment procedure, we are informed by Ronald Freedman, was later found to be unsatisfactory, and an improved procedure is being developed. The results reported here are not greatly affected by the shift from adjusted to unadjusted series. Tables 6 and 7 are based on the adjusted figures as published in the *1966 Taiwan Demographic Factbook*, Department of Civil Affairs, Taiwan Provincial Government, Republic of China, Oct. 1967, Table 17.

TABLE 5
REGRESSIONS ON REGISTERED FERTILITY IN ADMINISTRATIVE REGIONS OF TAIWAN, 1964[a]
(in parentheses beneath regression coefficients are their t statistics, or the ratios of the coefficients to their standard errors)

Regression Number	Dependent Variable	Constant Term	Percent of Children Age 12–19 in School 1961	Percent of Adults with Primary School Certificate 1961[c]	Percent of Male Labor Force in Agriculture 1965	Reciprocal of Child Survival Probability 1961[d]	R^2
1	Birth rate normalized for age and sex composition[b]	.112	−.100 (−4.2)[f]	−.005 (−.12)	.017 (1.75)	1.218 (5.74)[f]	.225
	Age-specific birth rate per 1000 women of age:						
2	15–19	1.246	−.094 (−1.08)	.273 (1.76)	−.086 (−2.37)[e]	4.050 (5.16)[f]	.107
3	20–24	2.418	−.056 (−1.85)	.025 (.47)	.008 (.60)	.953 (3.47)[f]	.074
4	25–29	2.689	−.047 (−2.05)[e]	−.070 (−1.70)	.023 (2.36)[e]	−.186 (−.89)	.055
5	30–34	2.545	−.144 (−4.82)[f]	−.027 (−.51)	.017 (1.39)	1.238 (4.50)[f]	.202
6	35–39	2.441	−.224 (−5.01)[f]	−.109 (−1.37)	.052 (2.80)[e]	2.801 (6.96)[f]	.310
7	40–44	1.931	−.256 (−4.29)[f]	−.028 (−.27)	.077 (3.10)[e]	3.351 (6.22)[f]	.271

NOTES:

[a] All variables expressed as logarithms (to base 10). Sample size is 361.

[b] Actual crude birth rate divided by normalized crude birth rate derived by attributing the national age-specific birth rates to the seven age cohorts of women in each region. Deviations from one (or zero in the log form) therefore represent deviations in local crude birth rate from that expected nationally from the region's age/sex population composition.

[c] Adults considered to be all persons over the age of 12 and out of school.

[d] This variable is defined as the reciprocal of one minus the summed death rates for children from birth to age 15 in the region. Thus if d_i is the frequency of death per person age i in a region, the death variable for that region is defined as

$$1/(1-\sum_{i=1}^{15} d_i).$$

[e] Coefficient significantly different from zero at 1 percent level of confidence.

[f] Coefficient significantly different from zero at .1 percent level of confidence.

pertains primarily to the cohorts of older age, when birth control is practiced more widely.[43]

As before, the child death factor and child school attendance rates are the most powerful explanatory variables in the model. The association in both years between birth rates and the child death factor lagged three years is positive and statistically significant at the .1 percent confidence level, except in 1964 for women between ages 25 and 29. As indicated earlier, the reproductive behavior of this group is not likely to be influenced strongly by the contemporary regime of mortality. The coefficient for the child death factor in the age-standardized birth rate equation, α, exceeds unity in both years (1.2 [$\pm$.2] in 1964 and 1.9 [$\pm$.2] in 1966). This implies that a lower regional child death rate is associated significantly with a reduction in the number of children parents in that region are likely to have surviving to the age of 15. This evidence that parents overcompensate in their reproductive behavior for changes in child death rates suggests that they may also be responding to the decline in uncertainty attaching to the family formation process or to other concurrent developments that are strongly associated, and perhaps caused by, the reduction in child death rates.

Educational opportunities are also associated with lower birth rates. But, as before, for Colombia the association is more consistent and statistically significant for child school attendance rates than for adult education rates. The relationship between child schooling and the birth rate is stronger among women over 30, but by 1966 even among the younger women this association is statistically significant at the 5 percent level or better. Adult education, according to these findings, plays no noticeable role in 1964 but emerges as statistically significant in 1966 among women 20 to 29. This may be an indication that better educated women are beginning to space their births or practice birth control even during their twenties.

As noted in our consideration of Colombia, the proportion of the active population in agriculture is frequently linked to differences in birth rates, for it is plausibly reasoned that, to a great

---

[43] All regressions are significant at the 1 percent level according to the F ratio test of the overall interrelation. In Tables 6 and 7 all satisfy this test at the .1 percent level.

TABLE 6

Regressions on Adjusted Registered Fertility in Administrative Regions of Taiwan, 1966[a]

(in parentheses beneath regression coefficients are their t statistics, or the ratios of the coefficients to their standard errors)

Regression Number	Dependent Variable	Constant Term	Percent of Children Age 12–19 in School 1965	Percent of Adults with Primary School Certificate 1965[e]	Percent of Male Labor Force in Agriculture 1965	Reciprocal of Child Survival Probability 1963[d]	R^2
1	Birth rate normalized for age and sex composition[b]	.371	−.185 (−10.3)[f]	−.075 (−2.18)[e]	.013 (2.06)[e]	1.928 (12.46)[f]	.566
	Age-specific birth rate per 1000 women of age:						
2	15–19	1.756	−.198 (−2.31)[e]	.035 (.22)	−.054 (−1.73)	5.709 (7.71)[f]	.211
3	20–24	2.765	−.111 (−4.07)[f]	−.131 (−2.52)[e]	.021 (2.14)[e]	1.130 (4.81)[f]	.185
4	25–29	2.725	−.109 (−6.08)[f]	−.048 (−1.41)	.029 (4.46)[f]	.246 (1.58)	.216
5	30–34	2.695	−.211 (−6.61)[f]	−.087 (−1.44)	.009 (.76)	2.169 (7.89)[f]	.338
6	35–39	2.722	−.406 (−7.61)[f]	−.140 (−1.37)	.027 (1.36)	3.579 (7.74)[f]	.372
7	40–44	2.349	−.455 (−5.82)[f]	−.181 (−1.21)	.087 (3.05)[e]	4.458 (6.58)[f]	.312

NOTES:

[a] Birth rates in 1966 were adjusted for overregistration in the last quarter of the year due to the year end Census of Population. Unadjusted data yield very similar findings. For methodology and convincing rationale for adjustment procedures, see *Taiwan Demographic Factbook 1967*. All variables expressed as logarithms (to base 10). Sample size is 361.

[b] Actual births divided by normalized births derived by attributing the national age-specific birth rates to the seven age cohorts of women in each region. Deviations from one (or zero in the log form) therefore represent deviations in local crude birth rate from that expected nationally from the region's age/sex population composition.

[e] Adults considered to be all persons over the age of 12 and out of school.

[d] This variable is defined as the reciprocal of one minus the summed death rates for children from birth to age 15 in the region. Thus if d_i is the frequency of death per person of age i in a region, the death variable is defined as

$$1/(1 - \sum_{i=1}^{15} d_i).$$

[e] Coefficient significantly different from zero at 1 percent level of confidence.

[f] Coefficient significantly different from zero at .1 percent level of confidence.

extent, small-scale agriculture permits parents to utilize the productive contribution of children's time. Examining this relationship in Taiwan, we find it weak. In 1964 it does not satisfy the traditional test for significance at the 5 percent level, and in 1966 it hardly passes this test, revealing slightly higher age-standardized birth rates in areas of heavy agricultural dependence.[44] More interesting than the overall effect is the age-specific association. In areas where agricultural activity predominates, there is a tendency for birth rates to be lower for the 15–19 age cohort and higher for later ages. With the scarcity of land in Taiwan, it is not implausible that there would be a systematic tendency for marriage and child bearing to be delayed until land ownership or operation were within reach of the younger generation.[45]

Although it is not now possible to consider in adequate detail the influence of the Taiwan family planning program, this program may be operating to bias our estimates of environmental effects on regional births. A simple treatment of this factor is therefore better than none.[46] Other facets of this program are dealt with later in this study. One may interpret the family planning program

[44] It should be noted that the quantitative magnitude of this relationship between agricultural activity and higher birth rates is small indeed. The association suggests that, if the proportion of active men in agriculture in a region increased 100 percent, the age-standardized birth rates would increase 1.3 to 1.7 percent.

[45] A similar tendency was evident in England during the enclosures and industrial revolution, for the age at marriage fell more slowly in the rural setting than in the urban, where land and support on the land for a wife and children were generally not within the reach of young men. See P. G. Ohlin, "The Positive and the Preventive Check: A Study of the Rate of Growth of the Pre-Industrial Population," unpublished Ph.D. dissertation, Harvard University, 1955.

[46] The restricted measure of the impact of the family planning program in Taiwan that is considered here is defined in Note e to Table 7. Numerous studies have over the last several years sought to evaluate the effect of the program on behavior of the population. Most studies have analyzed the program measures of output: the number of persons "serviced" or the number of IUD and pill acceptors. Island-wide surveys have also documented the changing patterns of contraceptive use. Consequently, our method is in no sense unique in implying that the program has had a distinguishable impact on birth rates in Taiwan, but it does use indirect procedures of statistical inference that have not been widely applied. A more thorough investigation of the impact of the family planning program on birth rates is presented in Schultz, "The Effectiveness of Family Planning in Taiwan."

TABLE 7

Regressions on Adjusted Registered Fertility in Administrative Regions of Taiwan, Including a Measure of Inputs into the Family Planning Program, 1966[a]

(in parentheses beneath regression coefficients are their t statistics, or the ratio of the coefficients to their standard errors)

Regression Number	Dependent Variable	Constant Term	Percent of Children Age 12–19 in School 1965	Percent of Adults with Primary School Certificate[c] 1965	Percent of Male Labor Force in Agriculture 1965	Reciprocal of Child Survival Probability[d] 1963	Man Months of Effort Family Planning[e] 1964	R^2
1	Birth rate normalized for age and sex composition[b]	.306 (5.28)	−.156 (−8.85)[f]	−.0604 (−1.85)	.0126 (1.97)[g]	1.63 (10.48)[f]	−.0333 (−6.13)[f]	.607
	Age-specific birth rate per 1000 women of age:							
2	15–19	1.59 (5.56)	−.121 (−1.39)	.0748 (.47)	−.0613 (−1.94)	4.92 (6.40)[f]	−.0914 (−3.40)[f]	.238
3	20–24	2.73 (29.9)	−.0947 (−3.38)[h]	−.125 (−2.41)[h]	.0212 (2.09)[g]	.968 (3.93)[f]	−.0180 (−2.09)[h]	.193
4	25–29	2.71 (44.6)	−.103 (−5.55)[h]	−.0452 (−1.31)[h]	.0289 (4.41)[f]	.182 (1.11)	−.0071 (−1.23)	.220
5	30–34	2.63 (24.8)	−.180 (−5.56)[f]	−.0727 (−1.21)	.0076 (.65)	1.86 (6.51)[f]	−0.353 (−3.55)[f]	.360
6	35–39	2.56 (14.7)	−.334 (−6.26)[f]	−.106 (−1.07)	.0250 (1.29)	2.83 (6.04)[f]	−.0824 (−5.03)[f]	.414
7	40–44	2.06 (8.19)	−.331 (−4.29)[f]	−.117 (−.82)	.0813 (2.91)[h]	3.16 (4.66)[f]	−.145 (−6.10)[f]	.377
8	45–49	.686 (1.28)	.172 (1.05)	−.359 (−1.18)	.0359 (.60)	5.56 (3.86)[f]	−.0903 (1.79)[g]	.068

NOTES:

a All variables expressed as logarithms (to base 10). Sample size is 361.

b Actual births divided by normalized births derived by attributing the national age-specific birth rates to the seven age cohorts of women in each region. Deviations from one (or zero in the log form) therefore represent deviations in local crude birth rate from that expected nationally from the region's age/sex population composition.

c Adults considered to be all persons over the age of 12 and out of school.

d This variable is defined as the reciprocal of one minus the summed death rates for children in the region from birth to age 15. Thus if d_i is the frequency of death per person age i in a region, the death variable for that region is defined as

$$1/(1 - \sum_{i=1}^{15} d_i).$$

e This represents the number of man months of village-health-education nurses, prepregnancy-health workers, and doctors, allocated to each region in a particular year per 1000 women between the ages of 15 and 49 in that region. Since the equation is fitted in logarithmic form, and many regions received no manpower inputs in this initial year of the program, .1 man months per 1000 women in childbearing ages is arbitrarily added to the input for all regions, there being no logarithm for zero. The program input measured thus for the entire country increased from 1.47 in 1964 to 3.26 in 1965 and to 3.63 man months per 1000 women in 1966. The 1964 inputs should have an effect on birth rates in later years as well as 1966, and thus the effect estimated in this regression is *not* a long-run estimate of the effect of the program inputs in this initial year.

f Coefficient significantly different from zero at .1 percent level of confidence.

g Coefficient significantly different from zero at 5 percent level of confidence.

h Coefficient significantly different from zero at 1 percent level of confidence.

as an input that reduces the cost of contraception to persons in the region and thus makes it more convenient to place reliable limits on their family size. Inclusion in Table 7 of the man months of medical and nonmedical manpower employed in the region's family planning program in 1964 per 1000 women of childbearing age shows that the program's inputs in that year appear to have had a small, but very significant, impact on birth rates only two years later, particularly among young (15–19) and older (30+) women. The inclusion of the family planning program manpower input improves the explanatory power of the regression (about 4 percent overall) and slightly reduces the size and significance of the other estimates. Nevertheless, the only variable for which the change in estimates deserves comment is the adult education variable, which is no longer statistically significant at the 5 percent level after the inclusion of the family planning program variable. The significance of this result will become clearer when the policy implications of family planning programs are considered in a later chapter.

SUMMARY AND CONCLUSIONS

Quantitative analysis of interregional variation in birth rates in Colombia and two other less developed countries suggests the organizing and explanatory power of the family planning hypothesis as a framework for guiding study of the determinants of population growth.

Certain features of the parents' environment could be measured in each country, while other features could not; and their omission or indirect treatment by means of proxies introduce serious problems for our interpretation of these statistical findings. Nevertheless, the empirical evidence, though richer and perhaps more reliable for Puerto Rico and Taiwan than for Colombia, is for all three countries generally consistent with our model. General support is given to our working hypothesis that variations in reproductive behavior are the outcome of parents' behavioral responses to the opportunities and constraints of their environment. Several links between the environment and reproductive behavior emerge as quantitatively and statistically very significant. Later in this book their implications for the design of public policy will be explored in greater detail, but a word of summary here may be worthwhile.

In Colombia our proxy for the net balance between birth and child death rates, surviving fertility, should closely parallel the size of surviving family. The model postulates that, to the extent that the number of surviving children parents have is influenced by differences in parents' desires, the proxy for surviving fertility should be associated across regions with characteristics of those regions that make more or fewer children attractive to parents. Schooling for children is one such feature of the local environment that indicates that parents bear additional costs in the rearing of children, which may contribute to their acceptance of a reduced family size goal. Education for the adult parent population also increases the opportunity value of parents' time and may alter their revealed preferences toward more goods and fewer children. Finally, where women participate in the labor force with greater frequency, a higher value is attached to a woman's time and, consequently, child rearing becomes more costly.[47] Each of these features of the municipal environment and population in Colombia is associated with lower surviving fertility as implied by the model. No significant association remains, after these variables are considered, between the level of surviving fertility and rural-urban residence, growth of wages, or extent of prior local in-migration. What do these findings suggest for policy?

Increased income or urbanization may not necessarily reduce population growth by itself, though these changes may bring about a salutary reduction in both birth and child death rates without necessarily directly affecting population growth or migration rates. Rather, the family environment must change to make more parents seek fewer surviving children. Furthermore, parents must be advised on the most humane and safe means to achieve their diminished family size goal. This may necessitate an active program hastening the diffusion of birth control innovations of the kind that has been mounted in Taiwan. The selective expansion of health, education, and welfare programs may do much to encourage parents to seek fewer children.

The association between surviving fertility and parents' environ-

---

[47] Not all forms of economic activity undertaken by women necessarily raise the cost of child rearing, for some types of activity may be undertaken in the home or in the company of one's children and thus not represent a conflicting claim on the mother's family-rearing responsibilities.

ment, though statistically weak in the fragmentary and indirect data examined for Colombia, is revealed with greater clarity and richness when better data from Puerto Rico and Taiwan are studied.

Although much more research is needed for adequate specification of a model of human reproductive behavior in terms that are appropriately simple but useful, as well as for estimation of its parameters for a variety of populations, the analysis offered in this chapter points to important areas of interaction between a parent's environment and reproductive behavior. To control or cope with population growth, these interactions must be understood. In addition to family planning programs that subsidize the spread of innovative modern means of birth control, slowing population growth in less developed countries such as Colombia may depend in large measure on the priority given to promoting change in certain features of the family's environment. Among these the extension of basic education and the improvement of child health may prove crucial.

CHAPTER III

Internal Migration: A Quantitative Study of Rural-Urban Migration in Colombia

INTRODUCTION

The most prominent manifestation of Colombia's population explosion has been massive rural-urban migration. In the past twenty-five years the percentage of Colombia's population living in urban communities has increased from 30 to 52 percent. Like the birth rate, the migration rate has widespread economic and social consequences, and although the determinants of migration are thought to be explicable in terms of people's wants, remarkably few studies have sought to analyze internal migration to find out what exactly motivates the migrant. It is obvious that the design of policy measures to cope with the problems associated with migration and urbanization in Colombia requires a broad understanding of why migration takes place.

There is some evidence that the excess of births over deaths is of about the same magnitude in rural and urban areas of much of Latin America.[1] But although the natural rates of increase of the rural and urban populations may be similar, the growth of each population and the distribution of the population within each category have been altered drastically by internal migration. As shown in Table 8, between 1951 and 1964 the rural population grew at about 1 percent per year, while the urban population in-

---

[1] This approximate parity between regional birth and death rates conceals two significant underlying differences. Both birth and death rates appear to be higher among rural than among urban residents. In addition, differences in crude birth rates do not adequately reflect fertility differences in the two populations, for rural-urban migration has reduced the proportion of women of childbearing age in the rural compared with the urban population. In Colombia, without reliable vital statistics or other direct evidence of regional fertility, the most one can observe is that as of 1964 the ratio of young children (less than 5 years of age) to women in childbearing age (15–49) is about 40 percent higher in rural than in urban areas. For estimates of vital rates for rural and urban regions of Venezuela, Mexico, and Chile, see E. Arriaga, "Components of City Growth in Selected Latin American Countries," *Milbank Memorial Fund Quarterly*, Vol. 46, No. 2, April 1968, Part 2, Table 6, p. 246.

TABLE 8
Growth of Population and Labor Force in Colombia

	1938 Census (thousands)	1938–1951 Annual Rate of Growth (percent)	1951 Census (thousands)	1951–1964 Annual Rate of Growth (percent)	1964 Census (thousands)	1964–1974 Annual Estimated Rate of Growth (percent)	1974 Estimate of Labor Force (thousands)
Adjusted population totals							
Men	4,395	(2.1)	5,759	(3.2)	8,657	a	
Women	4,465	(2.1)	5,829	(3.3)	8,910	a	
Both sexes	8,850	(2.1)	11,589	(3.3)	17,567	a	
Urban (cabeceras)	2,610	(4.2)	4,482	(5.6)	9,094	b	b
Rural (other regions)	6,240	(.9)	7,106	(1.2)	8,361	b	b
Labor force totals							
Men	c		3,150	(2.1)	4,102	(3.4)	5,715d
Women	c		724	(2.8)	1,032	(3.3)	1,424d
Both sexes	c		3,874	(2.2)	5,134	(3.4)	7,139d

Notes:
a Dependent on future level of birth rates.
b Dependent on future developments of Colombian rural and urban sectors.
c Incomparable data on labor force from 1938 Census.
d It is assumed that age- and sex-specific activity rates will be the same in 1974 as in 1964, and that survival rates comparable to the mortality level 14 of the West life tables would prevail in the decade 1964–1974. For detailed discussion of these labor force projections, see source below.

Source:
T. Paul Schultz, Population Growth and Internal Migration in Colombia, RM-5765-RC/AID, The Rand Corporation, Santa Monica, July 1969, Appendix A, Table A-3.

TABLE 9

POPULATION GROWTH IN THE MAJOR CITIES OF COLOMBIA
BETWEEN CENSUSES 1938–1964

City by Size in 1964	Census Population Total (thousands)			Annual Average Rate of Growth (percent)	
	1938	1951	1964	1938–1951	1951–1964
Bogota D.E.	356	715	1,697	5.4	6.8
Medellin	168	358	773	6.1	6.0
Cali	102	284	638	8.3	6.3
Barranquilla	152	280	498	4.8	4.5
Cartagena	85	129	242	3.3	4.9
Bucairamanga	51	112	230	6.3	5.6
Manrzales	86	126	222	3.0	4.4
Pereia	60	115	188	5.2	3.8
Cucuta	57	95	175	4.0	5.4
Ibague	61	99	164	3.6	3.9
Palmira	41	81	141	4.7	4.3
Armenia	51	78	137	3.4	5.4
Monteria	64	77	126	2.7	3.8
Cienega	47	57	113	1.4	5.4
Pasto	50	81	113	3.9	2.5
Santa Marta	33	47	104	2.8	6.2
Total population	8,850	11,589	17,567	2.1	3.3

SOURCE:
Bolletin Mensual de Estadistica, DANE, Bogota, No. 176, Nov. 1964, p. 7.

creased 5 percent annually. The major cities of Colombia increased even more rapidly, as may be seen from Table 9, with Bogota growing between the last two censuses at the rate of 6.8 percent per year. The total labor force grew at 2.2 percent per year between 1951 and 1964, the rural and urban labor forces growing at .4 percent and 4.4 percent per year respectively. To take an extreme case of the impact of internal migration, Table 10 shows that the majority of the residents of rapidly growing Bogota in 1964 were in-migrants to that city; among the economically active ages (15–59) three-fourths were born outside of the city, and almost half had migrated into the city within the past eleven years.

The rest of this chapter attempts to probe the fine structure and the causes of internal migration. Migration is first considered in the context of overall Colombian development and urbanization. Then migration rates are estimated for various groups in the population to clarify who migrates and to where. A model of inter-

TABLE 10

PERCENT OF PERMANENT POPULATION IN BOGOTA
METROPOLITAN AREA IN 1964 WHO MIGRATED TO CITY,
BY SEX, AGE, AND DURATION OF RESIDENCE IN BOGOTA

Sex and Age	Total Migrants	Duration of Residence in Bogota (years)		
		0–5	6–11	12 or more
Male				
0–14	23	18	5	1
15–59	73	30	15	28
60 or more	81	18	10	54
All ages	51	24	11	17
Female				
0–14	26	20	5	1
15–59	75	30	16	29
60 or more	84	20	11	53
All ages	56	25	12	19
Both sexes all ages	54	25	11	18

SOURCE:
  Derived from unpublished 1964 Census tabulations.

regional migration is finally set forth and estimated for a sample
of Colombian municipalities, from which we can infer the responsiveness of migration to some economic, demographic, and
political developments in the rural and urban sectors of the society.

INTERNAL MIGRATION RATES

A net migration rate is defined as the ratio of a net migration
flow to local average population size. If the observation period
is short, deaths, births, and migration are small relative to the
base population, and the measurement of a migration rate presents
no particular problems. However, when the time interval is longer,
as in Colombia, thirteen years having elapsed between censuses,
and the registration of births and deaths is incomplete, a number
of assumptions are required to estimate regional net migration
rates. These assumptions and the estimation procedure they entail
are discussed and evaluated elsewhere.[2]

  [2] Basically, the national regime of mortality was estimated from various
demographic sources. The age- and sex-specific death rates are then applied

Sex- and region-specific net migration rates for 1951–1964 are estimated for each five-year age cohort in 1951 between ages 0 and 44 (which had attained the ages of 13–57 by 1964).[3] The estimated net migration rates examined here do not necessarily add up to zero for all regions, for they apply to populations of different sizes, and the sample of municipalities, for various reasons, is not always representative of the entire Colombian population.[4] In particular, Bogota, Cali, and Medellin are not included in the randomly selected sample of municipalities. Since the findings pertain to the municipal average tendency for net migration to occur, however, we do not think this omission radically affects our results.[5]

The annual average migration rate estimates are summarized in Table 11 for various components of the sampled population.

---

for thirteen years to the age- and sex-specific population enumerated in each region in 1951. The difference between this "no-migration estimate" and the number of persons enumerated in that region in the 1964 Census is defined as net in- or out-migration. The continuously compounded migration rate is then calculated that would have yielded the estimated amount of in- or out-migration. For a more detailed treatment of this procedure, see T. Paul Schultz, *Population Growth and Internal Migration in Colombia*, RM-5765-RC/AID, The Rand Corporation, Santa Monica, July 1969, Appendix B.

[3] Without information on the exact number of births between the censuses, it is not possible to estimate the migration among individuals less than 13 years old in 1964 who were not born at the time of the 1951 Census. It was judged that age misreporting became a serious enough problem after the age of 50 not to warrant the computation of migration rates beyond the age cohort 40–44 in 1951 that had attained the ages of 53–57 by 1964. The youngest and oldest age-cohort migration rates are, probably, the least reliable.

[4] The randomized probability sample was based on all Colombian municipalities for which there were coterminous 1951 and 1964 Census data. The sample consisted of 131 municipalities, or about 15 percent of the municipalities of Colombia, and they contained about 12 percent of the Colombian population. The probability of the selection of a municipality was proportional to the average population size of a municipality in its Department.

[5] A number of students of migration have argued the case for analyzing gross migration flows, for net flows obscure the skill-specific cross-flows of gross migration that are possibly responding to different forces. Although the argument is sound, its import in the Colombian case is much less than in developed countries such as United States. This subject is dealt with later in the chapter in the discussion of the homogeneous nature of migration.

TABLE 11

ANNUAL AVERAGE MIGRATION RATES FOR A REPRESENTATIVE SAMPLE OF COLOMBIAN MUNICIPALITIES BY REGION, AGE, AND SEX, 1951–1964

(in percent of average age cohort between 1951 and 1964)

Region and Sex (Sample Size)	Initial Age Cohort in 1951									
	0–4	5–9	10–14	15–19	20–24	25–29	30–34	35–39	40–44	0–44
Cities:										
1. Cabeceras – greater than 10,000 in 1964 (17)										
Male	2.62	2.21	1.38	2.22	1.68	2.30	1.89	1.96	1.64	2.12
Female	3.55	3.34	2.33	1.45	1.24	1.53	1.89	.93	1.37	2.38
Both sexes	3.11	2.83	1.90	1.80	1.45	1.89	1.89	1.41	1.50	2.26
Towns:										
2. Cabeceras – less than 10,000 in 1964 (114)										
Male	.33	−2.26	−3.04	.27	.41	.48	.36	.39	.24	−.49
Female	1.24	−.08	−1.92	−1.30	−.65	−.20	.19	−.73	−.26	−.26
Both sexes	.81	−1.05	−2.42	−.58	−.17	.11	.27	−.21	−.02	−.36
Countryside:										
3. Rural areas outside of all Cabeceras (131)										
Male	−2.50	−4.17	−4.62	−3.30	−3.57	−2.12	−1.97	−2.35	−2.02	−3.23
Female	−3.17	−4.19	−3.42	−3.07	−2.96	−2.74	−2.06	−3.56	−3.01	−3.34
Both sexes	−2.82	−4.18	−4.02	−3.19	−3.27	−2.41	−2.01	−2.89	−2.45	−3.2

NOTE:

A negative migration rate means a net out-migration from the region, and conversely for a positive migration rate. A sample of 131 municipalities (about 15 percent) of Colombia was drawn randomly from those for which 1951 and 1964 census data were available on a comparable basis. Cohort survival probabilities were estimates for the country as a whole and were assumed to pertain to each municipal population in order to compute compounded average annual migration rates for each age and sex cohort. The table shows the specific migration rates from the sample and need not equal zero for the entire sample because of different population bases. For more detailed discussion of these estimates, their weaknesses, and their analysis, see T. Paul Schultz, *Population Growth and Internal Migration in Colombia*, RM-5765-RC/AID, The Rand Corporation, Santa Monica, July 1969.

Since it is not generally possible to discern at what age migration takes place during this period, nor indeed whether the rate of migration increased or decreased in the interim, it is convenient for our purposes to refer to this cohort by age, 0 to 44, in 1951 at the beginning of the observation period, even though this gives the appearance that many migrants are very young. Migration rates are presented for the entire municipality as well as for its urban component, the municipal administrative center or Cabecera, and for the rural regions outside the Cabecera. Since many of the municipalities have only a small Cabecera, those greater than 10,000 in 1964 are singled out for special consideration as "cities." From the total of 131 municipalities sampled, 17 qualify by this criterion as containing a large Cabecera and accordingly are called cities. This two-way division of the urban sample underlies the findings shown in Table 11.

REGIONAL DISTRIBUTION OF MIGRATION

The cities with populations in excess of 10,000 in 1964 gained greatly from migration, although even in this sample there are several exceptions.[6] Taking the group as a whole, we find that men migrated, on balance, into the cities at an annual rate of 2.1 percent and women at 2.4 percent. For the smaller towns (Cabeceras of less than 10,000), the net out-migration of men occurred at an annual rate of .5 percent and women at a slower .3 percent. The sex compositions among net migrants out of the rural regions were more nearly balanced, with men leaving at a net rate of 3.2 percent per year and the women at 3.3 percent per year. Viewing the sample as a whole, we see that the localities lost each year, on the average, 1.7 percent of the men between the active ages of 0 and 44 and 1.4 percent of the women. This decline reflects the net flow to the larger cities, which are under-represented in our sample. The limitations of the census data and the consequent method of constructing the sample are later seen to affect the character and magnitude of this net outflow of persons from the sampled municipalities.[7]

[6] See Schultz, *Population Growth and Internal Migration in Colombia*, Table 5.

[7] These are weighted average municipal migration rates for the three distinguished regions: cities, towns, and rural areas. But averages across regions need not approximate the aggregate migration rates for all sampled regions. A 2 percent inflow into large city-dominated municipalities might

SEX SELECTIVITY

Rural out-migration is not markedly sex selective, but urban in-migration appears to be somewhat selective of women. Where, then, do the remaining men go? Two regions are underrepresented in the Colombian sample: the larger cities, which received the same probability of selection in our sample as the less populous rural municipalities, and the frontier territories for which census data are not compiled in 1951 and 1964 on a comparable basis and therefore are excluded from the sample frame. Evidence from Bogota and other large cities suggests that, on balance, more women than men migrate into these metropolitan centers as into "cities," and thus this flow does not explain the slight preponderance of men migrating out of the sampled regions.[8] The frontier territories, however, contain more men than women and have been growing rapidly. These regions contained 3.4 percent of the Colombian population in 1951 and 4.2 percent in 1964. This growth is more rapid than can be explained without resort to large in-migration. The sex ratio for the regions included and excluded

TABLE 12
NUMBER OF MEN FOR EACH HUNDRED WOMEN BY REGION IN COLOMBIA, 1964

Region	Total Municipality	Cabeceras (Urban)	Other Areas (Rural)
Established Departments from which municipal sample drawn	96.8	88.2	107.4
of which Bogota D.E. (Metropolitan Area)	87.5	87.3	95.1
Frontier regions not represented in municipal sample	105.5	94.2	111.1
All of Colombia	97.1	88.4	107.6

SOURCE:
   Bolletin Mensual de Estadistica, DANE, Bogota, No. 194, May 1967, p. 12.

appear to counterbalance a 2 percent outflow from small town municipalities. The number of persons entering the cities would nevertheless exceed the number leaving the rural regions because of different-sized population bases.

   [8] Marco F. Reyes Carmona, *Estudio Socio-Economico del Fenomeno de la Immigration a Bogota*, Economia Colombiana, Bogota, Jan. 1965, pp. 5–11.

in the national sample are shown in Table 12, and they suggest the countervailing sex imbalances in the cities and frontier territories of Colombia that undoubtedly reflect the effects of past migration.[9] Thus, in summary, net migration from established rural regions of Colombia to the frontier agricultural regions is strongly male selective, whereas migration from the countryside to the cities is slightly female selective. Migration in other periods and places has sometimes followed parallel patterns of sex selectivity when open frontiers and urbanization provide alternative goals for the migrant.[10]

[9] The sex imbalance increases to 125 men to 100 women when one considers only the frontier Amazon regions, namely, Meta, Aranca, Caqueta, Amazonas, Guinia, Putamavo, Vaupes, and Cichada.

[10] Among urban immigrants in Latin America, women tend to be more numerous than men. Since Ravenstein observed this phenomenon during the industrial revolution in England and called it a "law of migration," it has been frequently rediscovered among various rural-urban migration groups. E. J. Ravenstein, "The Laws of Migration," *Journal of the [Royal] Statistical Society,* Vol. 48, No. 2, June 1885. Employment and social opportunities in the city compared with the countryside appear to be relatively more attractive to women than they are to men, *if they have enjoyed equal opportunities for education.* Men's skills are specific to agriculture, whereas women's are more readily adapted to the demands of the urban labor market, particularly in Latin America where the city demand for domestic help is strong. Exceptions to the female selectivity of migration have their own instructive explanations. Where the impetus to urbanization is very strong, as in Caracas and Sao Paulo, the expansion of male employment opportunities may be sufficient to secure a migrant ratio between the sexes of nearly one. Longer-distance migration is more frequently dominated by men, and thus the international migration to these two cities was predictably male selective. T. Paul Schultz, "Demographic Conditions of Economic Development in Latin America," P-3885, The Rand Corporation, Santa Monica, July 1968. In the United States from 1940 to 1944, when employment and military demands fueled the exodus from the land, the out-migration from rural areas was greater for men than women. C. Taueber, "Recent Trends in Rural-Urban Migration in the United States," *Milbank Memorial Fund Quarterly,* Vol. 25, No. 2, April 1947. In Africa and Asia the rural-urban migrant is more often male than female, but for Ghana, at least, it has been shown that this pattern is due to the greater educational attainment of men than women, and the sex selectivity of rural-urban migration disappears in the recent period as educational opportunities between the sexes have equalized. J. C. Caldwell, "Determinants of Rural-Urban Migration in Ghana," *Population Studies,* Vol. 22, No. 3, Nov. 1968. See also E. S. Lee *et al., Population Redistribution and Economic Growth, United States 1870–1950,* Vol. 1, *Methodological Considerations and Reference Tables,* American Philosophical Society, Philadelphia, 1957.

AGE SELECTIVITY

Migration draws forth young, able-bodied, and unencumbered workers. The highest age-specific migration rates occur for men who were between ages 10 and 14 in 1951. Until ages 30–34 migration rates for men decrease, and thereafter stabilize or perhaps increase slightly. Among women, fluctuations in age-specific migration rates are less than among men; they reach their peak at a younger age, between 5 and 9, decline gradually until ages 30–34, and then rise again. For women to migrate earlier is not implausible, for once they are married or with children, the costs associated with their migration must increase. With the relatively high level of mortality in Colombia, a substantial proportion of women are widowed by age 40, and this may contribute to the increase of out-migration of women from rural areas after they reach age 40. On the other hand, this may be a spurious result stemming from the tendency of older women to overstate their age.

Between urban and rural regions of the municipalities the age-sex patterns of migration are similar to those estimated for the entire municipality. In the towns in the sample the outflow of men is concentrated entirely in the age cohorts 5–9 and 10–14, and thereafter men on balance migrate in. We suspect that a good portion of this outflow is to the largest cities, in particular Bogota, Medellin, and Cali. Women leave the towns later than they do the rural regions; town out-migration rates reach a maximum for those age 10 to 14. This could be due to earlier marriage in the rural areas (which probably deters migration) and greater opportunity for women to attend schools and find employment in urban areas than in rural ones. In the rural areas older women tend to migrate out of the community more often than older men; at these ages women may be widowed and generally less tied to agriculture than men of comparable ages.[11]

On balance, the small towns lose many of their young men and

[11] Housekeeper skills are more in demand in the urban environment than in the rural one and may require less youthful flexibility for women to learn at middle age than for a man to acquire a new trade. See also Bruce Herrick, *Urban Migration and Economic Development*, MIT Press, Cambridge, 1965; and Joan M. Nelson, "Migrants, Urban Poverty, and Instability in New Nations: Critique of a Myth," Center for International Affairs, Harvard University (draft, n.d.).

some women at all ages, but they attract a net inflow of older men who are probably displaced from traditional agricultural and rural craft occupations. The cities draw men and women in large numbers, women mostly at young ages and men somewhat more often at older ages. One may infer from various evidence that some of the young men leaving established rural regions are making their way to the frontier territories, while the majority, of course, migrate to the cities. Women of all ages, on the other hand, are gravitating predominantly to the big cities where their services are most in demand.

From the data considered here it is not possible to distinguish migrants by their origin and destination, or even estimate gross migration rates. One cannot, therefore, infer to what extent migration follows a "stepwise" course in Colombia, with rural residents moving to small towns and town-dwellers migrating on to cities. Scattered evidence, however, confirms the "stepwise" process, particularly in more developed, urbanized countries such as Chile.[12] In a survey of immigrants of Bogota the proportion from Cabeceras (municipal administrative centers regarded as urban) was 87 percent. On the other hand, many Cabeceras are very small towns. Another sample from a barrio of Bogota found 59 percent of the household heads who had migrated to the city were from areas with a population of less than 2,000.[13] To assess the prevalence of "stepwise" and "return" migration will require more detailed data and more thorough analyses than are now available.

This review of the general flows of migration in Colombia prepares us in the next section to develop an explicit framework for interpreting migration rates primarily as a response to disequilibrium in the local labor markets. Since the migration rates estimated for the rural population are greater and more uniform across age and sex cohorts than those estimated for towns and cities, it is this rural exodus that dominates the migration rates estimated for

---

[12] Herrick, *Urban Migration and Economic Development.*
[13] Miguel M. Urrutia and Luis Castellanos Ch., *Estudios Economico Social de la Poblacion de Bogota,* Corporacion Automa Regional, Bogota, 1962; Marco F. Reyes Carmona, *Estudio Socio-Economico del Fenomeno de la Immigracion a Bogota,* Centro de Estudios Sobre Desarrollo Economico, Universidad de los Andes, Economia Colombiana, Bogota, 1965; William L. Flinn, "Rural to Urban Migration: A Colombian Case," research paper, Land Tenure Center, University of Wisconsin, Madison, July 1966.

the entire municipality. Identification of the economic, social, and political forces that account for these high rates of out-migration from the rural Colombian population is the objective of the next section.

A MODEL OF INTERREGIONAL MIGRATION

Our basic hypothesis is that migration, like population growth, is largely the result of purposeful behavior. In general, people migrate because they have reason to believe that, by migrating, they can improve their condition and that of their family.

In this view, the massive interregional shifts of population that are associated with the development process are a dynamic adjustment to large imbalances between regional supply and demand for labor.[14] A high rate of migration thus reflects substantial interregional inequalities in either the rate of expansion of economic activity or population growth or both.[15]

There are, of course, many other factors that affect the decision to migrate: the cost of migration; the relative quality of the non-economic environment; relative educational opportunities; and, in Colombia, interregional differences in the level of violence. Then, too, migration is the movement of individuals rather than "repre-

[14] This is the general view of migration set forth by Simon Kuznets, "Introduction: Population Redistribution, Migration and Economic Growth," in H. T. Eldridge and D. S. Thomas (eds.), *Population, Redistribution and Economic Growth, United States 1870–1950,* Vol. III: *Demographic Analyses and Interrelations,* American Philosophical Society, Philadelphia, 1964.

[15] If interregional migration is to be analyzed as a stochastic process for which the parameters can be estimated by ordinary regression analysis, there are powerful reasons to define the dependent variable, migration, as a population rate or average propensity, rather than as an absolute number (of migrants). This procedure, first of all, provides a clear link between the aggregate estimated model and the underlying rationale of individual behavior. But, in addition, this specification of the dependent variable as a rate, rather than as an absolute number, corrects for serious sources of bias and inefficiency in the estimating procedure that are introduced by the unequal size of regional populations and their frequent association with other social and economic determinants of the migration process itself. When absolute gross flows of migrants are analyzed, as in Sahota's analysis of migration in Brazil, the behavioral or statistical interpretation of the econometric findings is in no sense obvious. G. S. Sahota, "An Economic Analysis of Internal Migration in Brazil," *Journal of Political Economy,* Vol. 76, No. 2, March/April 1968, pp. 218–245.

sentative men." The young are still relatively unencumbered and
can look forward to many rewarding years in a new location; the
better educated are equipped to evaluate the opportunities and
uncertainties associated with migration; and women often have
more to gain from leaving traditional rural society—all these
people can be expected to differ in their susceptibility to migration.
A model that takes into account regional differences in the composition of the population with respect to age, sex, and educational
attainment should thus possess greater predictive power than one
that does not.

Given this basic hypothesis as to the nature of migration, the
critical problem in constructing an explanatory model is finding
some way to measure the balance between the supply and demand
for labor. To a considerable extent this balance is reflected in the
level and structure of wages within each community. The decision
to migrate can be expected to be conditioned by the differences
between local wage rates and those in other areas.

Information on wages in rural areas is limited to the rate paid
male agricultural day laborers. Data for urban areas include both
the rates paid to agricultural workers in the vicinity and the rates
paid in modern manufacturing. The migrant, however, is likely to
be excluded initially by his lack of urban skills and connections
from employment in the latter sector.[16] For this reason interregional differences in the balance between labor supply and demand are specified as the difference between the local wage paid
to agricultural labor and an implicit "urban" wage that is assumed
to be perceived equally by all potential migrants.[17]

---

[16] For a more complete discussion of this phenomenon, see R. L. Slighton,
*Relative Wages, Skill Shortages, and Changes in Income Distribution in
Colombia*, RM-5651-RC/AID, The Rand Corporation, Santa Monica, Oct.
1968. The same dichotomy may be seen in Colombian agriculture. Many
government policies have probably contributed to the deterioration in rural
relative wages and the increasing dualism within the agricultural sector
itself. Two forthcoming studies of Colombian agriculture pursue these points
in greater detail: L. Jay Atkinson, "Agricultural Production and Technology
in Colombia," U.S. Department of Agriculture, Economic Research Service,
Jan. 1969, draft; R. Albert Berry, "Agricultural Development of Colombia,"
Yale University, 1968, draft. In particular, Atkinson probes the problem
of involving the traditional peasant farmer in the modernizing process,
rather than of following the current policy of permitting the dualism within
agriculture to widen further.

[17] In the estimation equation for the model, only the local wage to agricul-

Labor markets are far from perfect, however, and the interregional pattern of unemployment—and hence the probability of
a migrant's obtaining a job—need not be consonant with the interregional structure of wages.[18] Unfortunately, reliable data on local
rates of unemployment are not available for Colombia and almost
by definition are incomparable between rural and urban sectors of
a low-income country. A surrogate measure of unemployment at
the current wage is needed, and is here assumed to be a linear
function of the rate of growth of the potential labor force—population growth without interregional migration as measured at the
beginning of the migration period. The greater the population
growth in a given community, the lower the probability of obtaining local employment and hence the greater the tendency for out-
migration.

The role of Colombia's mountainous terrain in constraining the
course of internal migration within regional "watersheds" could not
be confirmed with available data,[19] and evidence reported later in
this chapter supports the conclusion that the pecuniary costs and
time requirements of transportation are relatively unimportant in
understanding migration compared with the trauma of uprooting

---

tural day labor is introduced, and the constant term is assumed to represent
in part the attraction of the commonly perceived "urban" opportunity wage.
For example, in an area where the local wage in agriculture is relatively
high, the differential between local wages and wages in other (unspecified)
areas would be positive, and hence the pressure to emigrate is relatively
small.

[18] The marginal productivity of labor, hence a measure of the equilibrium
long-run competitive wage, is likely to be an increasing function of the
supplies of complementary factors of production per worker: land and
capital. In addition, factor proportions or the labor intensity of agricultural
production in Colombia appear to differ depending on the land tenure
arrangements. Thus it was decided to explore how these variables might
be associated with net migration rates in conjunction with the directly
observed current daily wage. Measures of inputs (land and capital) in
agriculture could not be satisfactorily measured, but the proxies from the
1960 Agricultural Census that were examined bore no particular relationship
to net migration. Nor did the proportion of the arable land farmed by
tenant farmers capture the anticipated effect of *minifundia* versus *latifundia*
on the derived demand for labor in Colombian agriculture.

[19] Exploratory investigation did not find any association between the level
of wages in the modern manufacturing sector of the nearest large (six
largest) city. But this is consistent with the dualism of the urban labor
market discussed earlier and elaborated in Chapter V.

from a local community, regardless of initial location and final destination.[20]

Although we are forced to treat the geographical distribution of employment opportunities in this simplified fashion, it is still possible to test a simplified form of the hypothesis that migration rates are responsive to locational factors. In particular, we can examine the conjecture that the distance of migration reflects the costs of the migration process. Because the urban center is the main focus of migration, the distance between the municipal center and the state (Department) capital is examined as a factor influencing the rate of migration. The terrain of Colombia is so varied and so often impenetrable in the highlands that the measure of geographic distance was translated into hours required to travel the distance. Since it is doubtful that travel costs are linearly related to time, we have proposed the logarithm of time as the final proxy for the "cost" of migration from the municipality to the Department capital or another more accessible major city.[21]

A further factor of potential importance to the explanation of migration rates in Colombia is the incidence of violence. It is commonly alleged that a part of the rural-urban migration in Colombia has been simply the result of the search for physical security from the violence that raged in many areas of rural Colombia during the 1950s and continues in abated form to this day.[22] To test this

[20] Although land transportation across the mountain divides in Colombia remains difficult except in a few places, the network of government-subsidized bus lines reaches into virtually every inhabited valley and most highland communities.

[21] For the estimates of time to travel from municipality to capital, see *Circunscripciones Electorales y Division Politico-Administrativo De Colombia, 1964,* Registraducia Nacional del Estado Civil, Bogota, 1964. Logarithms to the base 10 of travel time in hours are used in the study as the distance variable, and where in two cases the municipality was the Department capital, the time was assumed to be .01 hours, there being no logarithm of zero.

[22] Organized rural violence in Colombia, *la Violencia,* along regional, class, and political lines claimed the lives of an estimated 200,000 persons during the 1950s. It is alleged that this destructive and pervasive reign of violence in the countryside contributed to the rapid rural-urban migration. In the department of Tolima, for example, it is claimed that 42 percent of the residents were forced to leave their homes to escape the widespread violence. Whatever are the social, political, or economic roots of this malaise, it must be considered in any comprehensive explanation of postwar regional migration rates. The classic study of this phenomenon is the data source

conjecture, we examine the relationship between population flows and the frequency of politically motivated homicide from 1958 to 1963. Although the geographic pattern of violence in this period may not be the same as for earlier years, these data are the best publicly available proxy for the local incidence of violence for the entire 1951–1964 period.[23]

The final set of factors influencing migration that we shall consider here are characteristics of individual migrants. The migration rates presented in the previous section indicate that rural-urban migration is selective with respect to age and sex as well as region, and a model that treats migration as a homogeneous interregional flow is thus of limited value. We use two general methods for coping with the differences in responsiveness of different groups of potential migrants. One is to examine subpopulations that are homogeneous with respect to the particular characteristics. Accordingly, thirty-six groups are distinguished by age, sex, and rural-urban residence and analyzed separately as well as combined into various population aggregates. It is not possible, however, to control for educational attainment by computing education-specific migration rates, for the necessary information on the educational attainment of municipal populations was not published for the 1951 Census. Hence an alternative approach is necessary. The influence of educational attainment on migration is estimated by constructing an aggregate measure of educational attainment in the community and introducing this variable as a determinant of the community migration rate.[24]

---

used here: Guzman, Fals, and Umana, *La Violencia en Colombia*, Monografias Sociological, Vol. 1, No. 12, National University, Bogota, 1962, and Vol. 2, Ediciones Tercer Mundo, Bogota, 1964. For discussions in English, see Robert C. Williamson, "Toward a Theory of Political Violence: The Case of Rural Colombia," *Western Political Quarterly*, Vol. 18, No. 1, March 1965, pp. 35–44, and R. S. Weinert, "Violence in Pre-Modern Societies: Rural Colombia," *American Political Science Review*, Vol. 60, No. 2, June 1966, pp. 340–347.

[23] Guzman, Fals, and Umana, *La Violencia en Colombia*, Vol. 2, Table III, Appendix, Chap. II, pp. 301–325.

[24] Another and more satisfactory method for treating the heterogeneous nature of labor with its various skill attributes is proposed in a recent paper by Welch. He estimates the linear weights for aggregating different levels of schooling as a production input. Finis Welch, "Linear Synthesis of Skill Distribution," *Journal of Human Resources*, Vol. 4, No. 3, Summer 1969.

Education may influence the rate of migration in at least two countervailing directions, however. On one hand, children who are educated are more likely to migrate once they are economically independent of their parents. Migration tends to be selective of the better educated, probably because the educated can evaluate their opportunities outside the local labor market and because they tend to be more adaptable to the demands placed on the migrant. In addition, evidence from Bogota suggests that the returns to completion of primary, secondary, and vocational schooling are substantial and that the migrant appears to receive no less for his services than a native-born resident of Bogota of the same age, sex, and education.[25] Since it appears that schooling is valued less highly in rural than in urban activities,[26] the returns to rural-urban migration are therefore likely to be higher for individuals of relatively high educational attainment.[27]

On the other hand, a municipality that educates a large proportion of its child population provides a free service which may be valued highly by local residents, particularly parents of school-age

---

[25] T. Paul Schultz, *Returns to Education in Bogota, Colombia,* RM-5645-RC/AID, The Rand Corporation, Santa Monica, Sept. 1968, p. 21.

[26] See income data for 1965–1966 in Schultz, *Population Growth and Internal Migration in Colombia,* Appendix Tables B-6 and B-7.

[27] This raises the rate-of-return formulation of the migration process as an investment activity undertaken when discounted benefits sufficiently outweigh the associated costs. As a formal predictive model, this human capital framework for analyzing migration places great demands on the data base, requiring information on future earning profiles for individuals in a variety of locations and direct and opportunity costs associated with moving from one location to another. Largely for this reason, we suspect, the basic hypothesis underlying this approach, that migration occurs in response to the rate of return, has not been very rigorously tested. Were information available on alternative labor market opportunities and migration costs, one could solve for a pecuniary rate of return to migration between all alternative environments and add to our model this predictive variable. This single variable would, nevertheless, neglect the effects of uncertainty, imperfect capital markets, the cost of information, and nonpecuniary costs and benefits associated with migration. Since even the pecuniary rate of return cannot be calculated from available data, we have turned to proxies for the intermediate variables that determine the pecuniary rate of return: wages, unemployment, and the costs of migration. See L. Sjaastad, "The Costs and Returns of Human Migration," in *Investment in Human Beings,* supplement to the *Journal of Political Economy,* Vol. 70, No. 5, Part 2, Oct. 1962.

children. This public service or nonwage benefit adds to the attractiveness of the locality to a potential migrant.

Given the *a priori* complexity of the relationship between the propensity to migrate and local educational opportunities, we think it useful to employ at least two separate indexes of a community's inputs into education and their allocation: the proportion of children age 5–9 attending school, and the proportion of children age 10–14 so enrolled. Because of the relatively high premium paid to primary school graduates and those with some secondary training, our initial hypothesis is that the tendency to migrate should be related more closely to the latter variable than to the former.

Although the above adjustments should be sufficient to deal with most of the problems associated with treating net migration as a homogeneous flow, the elusive problem of the quality dimension of migration remains. We think this problem is not serious in the case of Colombia. It seems probable, as argued by Sjaastad, that interregional migration in an industrially developed and mobile economy, such as the United States, should be characterized as heterogeneous, for different concurrent interregional gross migration flows contain very different human capital components and respond to various special market inducements.[28] The more nearly unidirectional flow of migrants in Colombia, from established agricultural regions and small towns to the cities, does not in all probability conceal deep cross-currents of skill-specific gross migration. Indeed, the skills of the migrant from the rural sector are probably not so different from the skills of the migrant returning to the rural sector as to be fruitfully disaggregated. Consequently, in developing countries such as Colombia where heavy net migration follows the traditional course from countryside to city and specialized talents are relatively unimportant, it is probably acceptable to treat labor in a migration model as homogeneous within age and sex cohorts.

In summary, the model of interregional migration that is tested here, within the limitations of available Colombian data, interprets local rates of migration as an approximately linear function of six independent variables: local wage rates in agriculture; the estimated local rate of population increase in the absence of migration;

---

[28] For a review of the economic logic, see L. Sjaastad, "The Costs and Returns of Human Migration."

distance to the nearest large town; the level of political violence; and two measures of schooling. That is,

$$(4) \quad M_i/P_i = a_0 + a_1W_i + a_2P_i + a_3D_i + a_4(V_i/P_i) \\ + a_5E_{1_i} + a_6E_{2_i} + u_i,$$

where

M_i/P_i is the net migration rate for the local ith region's population, greater than zero if there is net in-migration, and less than zero if there is net out-migration,

W_i is the local agricultural daily wage including food,

P_i is the estimated growth rate of the local potential labor supply,

D_i is the logarithm of the time required to travel from the locality to the nearest major city or state capital,

V_i/P_i is the frequency of political violence in the locality,

E_{1_i} is the school enrollment rate for children between 5 and 9 years,

E_{2_i} is the school enrollment rate for children between 10 and 14 years,

u_i is a normally distributed stochastic disturbance term, and the a's are model parameters to be estimated.

A problem of estimating Equation 4 arises from the probable simultaneous determination of several of the "exogenous" variables.[29] The frequency of violence and the growth of the potential labor force, both of which foster out-migration, may not be predetermined, but rather may be influenced simultaneously by the economic attributes of the local environment and its population. Although the current rate of entry into the labor force that influences current migration is largely determined ten to twenty years

---

[29] The object is to specify a plausible behavioral relation between migration and the environmental variables that are not themselves determined simultaneously with, or subsequently by, the migration decision. It should be clear that a more realistic conception of migration would place it in the context of other household decisions (education, participation, marriage, fertility) and the regional allocation of other resources over time. It is hoped, however, that the simultaneous interactions that lead to estimation bias are relatively small here, and that this partial analysis of the underlying system of dynamic relations represents a step toward more satisfactory quantitative analysis of migration in developing countries. A summary of the definitions of the variables used in the regression analysis is given in the notes to Table 13.

earlier by the parents' environment (Chapter II), this prior environment is not strictly independent of the current environment, which is also observed to be associated with migration. Yet without a deeper knowledge of the underlying causes of rural violence and information on the earlier regional environment, simultaneous estimation of these three relationships is not feasible.[30]

REGRESSION FINDINGS

This section presents and discusses the least squares regression findings of our investigation of interregional migration in Colombia for a sample of 131 municipalities. The migration model is first estimated for net migration rates based on the entire municipal population less than 44 years of age in 1951, and then reestimated for age- and sex- and region-specific migration flows.

AGGREGATE MIGRATION

The two local-labor-condition variables acted as expected (see Tables 13 and 14). High local wages reduce out-migration. Population pressure or our proxy for the natural rate of increase of the population accelerates out-migration. Also as expected, the prevalence of violence adds further to the outflow. The regression coefficients for these variables exceed twice their standard errors and thus seem to reflect statistically significant associations in the directions implied by the model.

The coefficients on education provide a puzzle. Incidence of education of the 10–14 age bracket is, as expected, strongly associated with out-migration and provides a much greater stimulus to migration than education for the 5–9 bracket. The surprising result is that the coefficient on 5–9 education has an unexpected sign. That is, the effect of greater education at this level seems to be associated with less out-migration (or greater in-migration). This is hard to understand. As we shall see shortly, greater disaggregation does not completely clear up the puzzle.[31]

---

[30] Schultz, *Population Growth and Internal Migration in Colombia*, Appendix C, briefly explores the evidence on the causes of the rural violence and shows what environmental factors are associated with this phenomenon.

[31] Because the wage variable may correspond roughly to the amount of resources available in the community for educational purposes, the two additional age-specific school enrollment variables may indicate how these resources are allocated. Are they spent to give a majority of the children

TABLE 13

REGRESSIONS ON AVERAGE ANNUAL MIGRATION RATE FOR ALL PERSONS AGE 7 TO 51 IN 1958 IN COLOMBIA, 1951–1964

(in parentheses beneath regression coefficients are their t statistics, or the ratios of the coefficients to their standard errors)

Regression Number	Constant Term	Wage[a] 1956	Percent with Some Primary Schooling[b]		Population Pressure[c] (surviving fertility in 1940–1951)	Frequency of Violence[d] (1958–1963)	Distance to City[e] (log time)	R^2
			Age 5–9	Age 10–14				
1	5.06	.761 (2.94)	.110 (3.18)	−.101 (−5.04)	−.103 (−2.21)	−.034 (−4.77)	NI	.314
2	8.13	.658 (2.62)	.090 (2.64)	−.113 (5.87)	−.127 (−2.83)	−.034 (−4.82)	−1.26 (−3.54)	.366

NOTES:

NI means "variable not included in regression."

[a] 1956 quarterly average of agricultural wages paid to men including food.

[b] 1964 Census percentage of age group with some primary schooling.

[c] 1951 Census estimate of surviving fertility from decade before census approximating the potential rate of growth of the local supply of labor. See Chapter II for detailed derivation of this surviving fertility estimate.

[d] 1958–1964 reported frequency of violence per 10,000 persons in 1964 Census.

[e] Logarithm (base 10) of the time required to travel from municipality's Cabecera to its Department capital or closer city, expressed in hours.

TABLE 14
MEANS, STANDARD DEVIATIONS, AND CORRELATION COEFFICIENTS OF VARIABLES USED IN OVERALL REGRESSION ANALYSIS

	Municipality Migration Rate Age 7–51 in 1958	Wage 1956	Primary Schooling		Population Pressure	Frequency of Violence	Distance to City
			Age 5–9	Age 10–14			
Mean	−2.25	2.37	22.2	69.8	40.9	8.76	.484
Standard Deviation	2.26	.70	8.2	13.8	3.7	24.9	.519
Simple Correlation Coefficient							
Wage	.000	—					
Schooling							
5–9	.011	−.033	—				
10–14	−.241	.068	.796	—			
Population	−.195	.110	−.260	−.180	—		
Violence	−.337	.408	−.103	−.022	.102	—	
Distance	−.191	−.098	−.500	−.438	.036	.027	—

NOTE:
See Notes to Table 13 for variable definitions.

Among the small town migrants the effect of greater distance to the nearest city appears to be to spur migration, not damp it (Regression 4, Table 15). Here rationalization is somewhat easier. For people with some exposure to modern urban life, geographical isolation from the major metropolitan centers may create a special incentive to migrate, and this added incentive may be stronger than the disincentive to migration implied by the greater cost of migrating a longer distance.

DISAGGREGATED MIGRATION

As a first step toward disaggregation, we consider separately the migration behavior by sex of the urban (Cabecera) and rural portions of the municipality. These results are given in Table 15. The estimates confirm that the migration model, as specified and as limited by data, is better able to capture the inducements for rural-urban migration than interurban migration. Further disaggregation of migration by age as well as sex and region leads to the model estimates reported in Tables 16 (the total sample), 17 (the rural sample), and 18 (the urban sample). At this finer level of analysis a number of additional patterns emerge about the responsiveness of particular groups to the forces that propel the migration process.

The association between daily wages in agriculture and migration is strongest for the young, among whom migration is most common. No effect of rural wages on male migration rates is evident after age 26. Since wages for women are reported for only a few municipalities, the wage variable pertains only to men's wages. The women's migration rate is thus understandably less sensitive than men's to this measure of wages. However, in the overall sample the effect of local wages is powerful. The estimates

---

a brief one- or two-year exposure to primary schooling, as is a common strategy in rural areas of Colombia? Or are they spent to give a complete five-year primary education to a select fraction of the school-age population? If, as we surmise, it is the more extensive exposure to the education process that pays returns (particularly in the urban labor market) and fosters out-migration from rural areas, the younger enrollment variable could be partially associated with lower out-migration, and the older enrollment variable could be associated with higher out-migration, when wages are included in the regression model.

TABLE 15

REGRESSIONS ON AVERAGE ANNUAL MIGRATION RATES FOR PERSONS AGE 7 TO 51 IN 1958
IN COLOMBIA, 1951–1964, BY REGION AND SEX

(in parentheses beneath regression coefficients are their t statistics,
or the ratios of the coefficients to their standard errors)

Regression Number and Dependent Variable	Constant Term	Wage 1956	With Some Primary Schooling		Population Pressure	Frequency of Violence	Distance to City	R^2
			Age 5–9	Age 10–14				
1. Both sexes Total municipality	8.13	.658 (2.62)	.090 (2.64)	−.113 (5.87)	−.127 (−2.83)	−.034 (−4.82)	−1.260 (−3.54)	.366
2. Men Total municipality	7.71	.781 (2.90)	.089 (2.42)	−.118 (−5.74)	−.117 (−2.43)	−.033 (−4.39)	−1.300 (−3.40)	.345
3. Women Total municipality	8.35	.544 (2.25)	.091 (2.77)	−.107 (−5.78)	−.133 (−3.08)	−.035 (−5.13)	−1.234 (−3.60)	.406
4. Both sexes Cabeceras (urban)	3.77	.235 (.66)	.037 (.76)	−.027 (−1.01)	−.070 (−1.11)	−.011 (−1.11)	−1.327 (−2.64)	.102
5. Men Cabeceras (urban)	3.38	.310 (.78)	.055 (1.01)	−.044 (−1.43)	−.057 (−.79)	−.006 (−.58)	−1.514 (−2.67)	.095
6. Women Cabeceras (urban)	3.71	.243 (.71)	.030 (.64)	−.021 (−.80)	−.073 (−1.19)	−.014 (−1.50)	−1.296 (−2.68)	.113
7. Both sexes Other regions (rural)	6.77	.560 (1.88)	.077 (1.91)	−.115 (−5.05)	−.108 (−2.04)	−.040 (−4.80)	−.205 (−.49)	.331
8. Men Other regions (rural)	6.41	.710 (2.28)	.077 (1.82)	−.119 (−5.02)	−.100 (−1.79)	−.038 (−4.45)	−.351 (−.80)	.311
9. Women Other regions (rural)	6.82	.419 (1.43)	.074 (1.84)	−.107 (−4.79)	−.115 (−2.18)	−.042 (−5.12)	−.008 (−.02)	.342

NOTE:
See Notes to Table 13 for variable definitions.

TABLE 16

REGRESSIONS ON AGE- AND SEX-SPECIFIC AVERAGE ANNUAL MIGRATION RATES FOR TOTAL REPRESENTATIVE SAMPLE OF MUNICIPALITIES IN COLOMBIA, 1951–1964[a]

(after regression coefficients are their t statistics, or the ratios of the coefficients to their standard errors)

Sex and Age in 1958	Wage 1956 Coef.	t	Primary Schooling Age 5–9 Coef.	t	Age 10–14 Coef.	t	Population Pressure Coef.	t	Frequency of Violence Coef.	t	Distance to City Coef.	t	R^2
Men 7–11	.665	2.50	.125	3.43	−.127	−6.23	−.130	−2.72	−.033	−4.48	−1.124	−2.98	.384
12–16	1.207	3.79	.090	2.07	−.147	−6.04	−.201	−3.53	−.021	−2.42	−1.721	−3.81	.376
17–21	1.224	3.50	.062	1.31	−.144	−5.40	−.257	−4.12	−.016	−1.67	−1.766	−3.57	.354
22–26	.968	3.13	.075	1.78	−.123	−5.21	−.187	−3.37	−.030	−3.47	−1.294	−2.95	.333
27–31	.358	1.14	.092	2.15	−.080	−3.36	−.015	−.27	−.042	−4.82	−.714	−1.62	.248
32–36	.356	1.34	.074	2.05	−.061	−3.02	−.008	−.18	−.046	−6.22	−.702	−1.86	.317
37–41	.185	.71	.083	2.33	−.071	−3.55	.016	.34	−.041	−5.71	−.512	−1.86	.303
42–46	.224	.88	.079	2.26	−.061	−3.14	.002	.04	−.041	−5.72	−.728	−2.00	.304
47–51	−.110	−.41	.085	2.31	−.059	−2.88	.021	.43	−.032	−4.26	−.644	−1.69	.242
Women 7–11	.699	2.77	.110	3.19	−.118	−6.12	−.145	−3.22	−.037	−5.25	−1.311	−3.67	.426
12–16	1.103	3.86	.087	2.23	−.136	−6.26	−.240	−4.70	−.037	−4.62	−1.818	−4.49	.459
17–21	.704	2.43	.091	2.31	−.140	−6.33	−.219	−4.23	−.029	−3.62	−1.552	−3.78	.409
22–26	.278	1.03	.080	2.16	−.095	−4.60	−.107	−2.22	−.031	−4.09	−1.132	−2.95	.305
27–31	.157	.65	.081	2.45	−.062	−3.34	−.057	−1.32	−.031	−4.59	−.589	−1.71	.265
32–36	.297	1.22	.074	2.21	−.068	−3.63	−.044	−1.01	−.035	−5.12	−.655	−1.89	.282
37–41	.065	.28	.097	3.10	−.081	−4.61	−.031	−.75	−.034	−5.29	−.807	−2.48	.350
42–46	.353	1.52	.074	2.34	−.072	−4.08	−.044	−1.06	−.037	−5.78	−.960	−2.92	.344
47–51	.167	.67	.099	2.93	−.069	−3.68	−.013	−.30	−.032	−4.60	−1.016	−2.90	.302

NOTES:
See Notes to Table 13 for variable definitions.
[a] Sample size is 131.

TABLE 17
REGRESSIONS ON AGE- AND SEX-SPECIFIC AVERAGE ANNUAL MIGRATION RATES FOR RURAL PORTIONS OF COLOMBIA, 1951–1964[a]

(after regression coefficients are their t statistics, or the ratios of the coefficients to their standard errors)

Sex and Age in 1958	Wage 1956		Primary Schooling Age 5–9		Primary Schooling Age 10–14		Population Pressure		Frequency of Violence		Distance to City		R_2
	Coef.	t	Coef.	t	Coef.	t	Coef.	t	Coef.	t	Coef.	t	
Men													
7–11	.581	1.45	.124	2.27	−.144	−4.70	−.107	−1.49	−.039	−3.47	−.473	−.83	.246
12–16	1.245	3.57	.041	.87	−.132	−4.98	−.200	−3.21	−.025	−2.59	−.568	−1.15	.325
17–21	1.333	3.51	.030	.57	−.138	−4.77	−.273	−4.02	−.021	−1.97	−.779	−1.45	.331
22–26	.905	2.59	.078	1.64	−.135	−5.05	−.182	−2.90	−.035	−3.60	−.445	−.90	.308
27–31	.169	.45	.114	2.25	−.097	−3.42	.032	.48	−.048	−4.67	−.115	−.22	.240
32–36	.114	.36	.089	2.03	−.072	−2.93	.022	.39	−.051	−5.72	.099	.22	.286
37–41	.065	.21	.105	2.51	−.080	−3.42	.039	.72	−.047	−5.51	.365	.84	.297
42–46	.119	.39	.085	2.02	−.058	−2.48	.010	.18	−.044	−5.08	.192	.44	.238
47–51	−.225	−.66	.071	1.53	−.048	−1.86	.043	.71	−.036	−3.81	.170	.35	.175
Women													
7–11	.495	1.73	.077	1.98	−.116	−5.33	−.094	−1.84	−.042	−5.32	.131	.32	.375
12–16	1.019	3.14	.042	.94	−.130	−5.25	−.215	−3.71	−.042	−4.67	−.286	−.62	.394
17–21	.677	2.04	.068	1.51	−.134	−5.28	−.209	−3.51	−.035	−3.77	−.432	−.92	.344
22–26	.227	.75	.108	2.60	−.114	−4.89	−.067	−1.22	−.039	−4.64	−.173	−.40	.307
27–31	−.018	−.06	.119	2.73	−.084	−3.44	−.029	−.51	−.038	−4.33	.217	.48	.246
32–36	−.080	.25	.075	1.72	−.072	−2.97	−.041	−.72	−.041	−4.61	.300	.66	.239
37–41	−.014	−.04	.084	1.95	−.075	−3.13	−.028	−.49	−.046	−5.22	.424	.95	.286
42–46	.204	.64	.054	1.25	−.061	−2.52	−.042	−.74	−.044	−4.98	.167	.37	.235
47–51	.062	.19	.097	2.16	−.067	−2.66	.018	.31	−.042	−4.58	.215	.46	.219

NOTES:
See Notes to Table 13 for variable definitions.
[a] Rural portions defined as those areas of municipalities other than the Cabeceras or municipal administrative center. Sample size is 131.

TABLE 18

REGRESSIONS ON AGE- AND SEX-SPECIFIC AVERAGE ANNUAL MIGRATION RATES FOR THE CABECERAS OR URBAN PORTIONS OF COLOMBIA, 1951–1964[a]

(after regression coefficients are their t statistics, or the ratios of the coefficients to their standard errors)

Sex and Age in 1958	Wage 1956		Primary Schooling Age 5-9		Primary Schooling Age 10-14		Population Pressure		Frequency of Violence		Distance to City		R_2
	Coef.	t	Coef.	t	Coef.	t	Coef.	t	Coef.	t	Coef.	t	
Men													
7–11	.376	.92	.045	.81	−.026	−.83	−.113	−1.55	−.017	−1.47	−1.080	−1.86	.092
12–16	.622	1.37	.074	1.19	−.066	−1.89	−.091	−1.20	−.008	−.64	−2.237	−3.48	.150
17–21	.045	.08	.053	.72	−.061	−1.48	−.102	−1.06	.003	.26	−2.149	−2.81	.087
22–26	−7.358	−1.69	−.166	−.27	.288	.87	−.540	−.70	.056	.46	−1.802	−.29	.039
27–31	.033	.07	.052	.76	.001	.05	−.085	−.95	−.000	−.03	−.105	−.15	.031
32–36	.430	.97	−.012	−.21	.028	.83	−.063	−.80	−.017	−1.38	−.450	−.72	.049
37–41	−.050	−.11	.008	.13	.006	.17	.016	.19	−.015	−1.24	−.273	−.43	.022
42–46	−.016	−.03	.003	.05	.001	.03	.049	.61	−.019	−1.51	−.577	−.91	.034
47–51	.129	.30	.155	2.62	−.060	−1.81	−.020	−.26	−.012	−1.00	.138	.22	.076
Women													
7–11	.394	.95	.018	.31	.020	.63	−.111	−1.50	−.020	−1.75	−1.172	−1.99	.138
12–16	.457	1.02	.040	.65	−.024	−.71	−.140	−1.75	−.020	−1.64	−1.783	−2.82	.141
17–21	.121	.29	.055	.98	−.072	−2.31	−.162	−2.21	−.016	−1.39	−1.904	−3.28	.162
22–26	−.323	−.74	.001	.01	−.013	−.37	−.071	−.90	−.007	−.57	−1.413	−2.28	.064
27–31	.379	1.10	.023	.49	.006	.23	.006	.10	−.008	−.87	−.672	−1.37	.061
32–36	.317	.82	.008	.15	−.016	−.55	−.017	−.24	−.016	−1.54	−.441	−.81	.028
37–41	−.220	−.68	.016	.37	−.014	−.55	−.036	−.63	−.003	−.34	−.892	−1.95	.051
42–46	.435	1.22	.047	.98	−.028	−1.04	−.020	−.31	−.019	−1.92	−.674	−1.33	.068
47–51	−.397	−1.13	.004	.08	.007	.27	.009	.14	−.006	−.61	−1.120	−2.25	.080

NOTES:
See Notes to Table 13 for variable definitions.
[a] Sample size is 131.

imply that, if rural wages were doubled (and city wages held constant), migration might be reduced by about 70 percent.

The relation between population pressure and out-migration is most noticeable for the young (up to about age 26). Perhaps because each generation is a poor substitute for another, the youngest generation experiences the strongest competitive employment pressure from the growth of their own age group, a pressure that depresses local returns to their labor and forces them to migrate from the country to the city or frontier territory.[32] According to the estimated relationship taken at regression means, a 20 percent reduction in surviving fertility is associated with a 40 percent reduction in the out-migration of men and a 50 percent reduction in the out-migration of women.[33] A modest reduction in birth rates is thus associated with a substantial decline in internal migration.

The distance-to-city variable helps to account for differences in migration rates among the Cabeceras *only*. Young men and women living in remote towns are *more* likely to migrate from their community than are those living close to the big city.[34] This relationship is statistically strong for men until age 21, persists for women until age 26, and reappears again for women between ages 47 and 51.[35] Distance to the city does not appear to affect the propensity of the rural population to migrate.

[32] Caldwell has substantiated by an analysis of individual survey data that in Ghana a person is more likely to migrate from his rural residence to the city if he is born into a large family. Indeed, the total number of siblings of the same sex is an even stronger predictor of the propensity to migrate. This micro-individual evidence is, of course, consistent with our hypothesis that communities that experience more rapid population growth and sustain larger increases in family size are also likely to experience higher out-migration rates among their youth. J. C. Caldwell, "Determinants of Rural-Urban Migration in Ghana," p. 371.

[33] Regressions 2 and 3 to Table 15.

[34] To translate the implications of the coefficients estimated in Regression 1 of Table 15 into quantitative terms, the average municipality in the sample was about three hours travel time from the capital of its state (*Departamento*). If the municipality were six hours from the capital, the associated out-migration rate would be some 16 percent greater than for the municipality which was the average three hours from its capital. If the municipality were only one hour away from the capital, the out-migration rate would be 26 percent less than for the average, other things being equal.

[35] This empirical result may be spurious, for since remote areas are likely to sustain higher death rates than less remote urban-oriented areas, out-migration rates would be overestimated for these remote areas by our procedure for estimating migration, namely, assuming a uniform regime of age-

Violence is rurally contained, so far as it is associated with rural out-migration in Colombia. In only one age-sex group, men between ages 17 and 21 (the violence makers), is out-migration from rural areas *not* statistically associated with the frequency of violence (Table 17). Among Cabecera populations there appears to be no relation between the region's violence rate and its migration rate for any age or sex component of the population. Nonetheless, one death by violence is associated with a net out-migration of approximately forty persons from the immediate *rural* area. Middle-aged men are slightly more sensitive to this inducement to migrate than are younger men, and women in both the very young and older age cohorts depart from the violence-torn regions at the highest rates.[36] According to these estimates, if the average municipal incidence of violent deaths had been nil, rather than the figure recorded of 8.7 per 10,000, the associated overall migration rate out of the sampled regions would have been 13 percent lower, or reduced from 2.25 to 1.95 percent per year.[37]

The puzzling education results are not resolved by disaggregation. School enrollment for the 10–14 age bracket is associated with out-migration for all age groups and both sexes. The effect is smallest for the older people in the sample, suggesting that the older group may have already been denuded through migration and thus is no longer particularly susceptible to migration. Education of the 5–9 group continues to deter out- or foster in-migration. The pattern of coefficients across age brackets is plausible. The coefficient is largest for those of the age cohort that are in school. But the positive sign for other age groups (except possibly the group of parents with children in school) is hard to understand.

---

and sex-specific mortality for all regions of Colombia. However, since this relationship between remoteness and out-migration does not emerge strongly in the rural areas where the regime of mortality is probably most severe, we reserve judgment.

[36] It should be noted that this estimate of the migration effect of violence is likely to be an overestimate, for the definition of migration includes any decline in regional population in excess of normal mortality. Some of the violent deaths are undoubtedly being attributed to out-migration and thus inflating the true effect of violence on the migration of the surviving population.

[37] Elasticity response computed at variable means from Regression 1, Table 15. For only the rural subsector the reduction in average migration implied by Regression 7, Table 15, would have been 10 percent, from 3.06 to 2.71 per year, in the absence of any violence.

..t prospects does the future hold? The key probably lies in the effect of the "population explosion." Population pressure, as estimated here, increased 20 percent from 1951 to 1964, and our analysis in Chapter II suggests that population growth is unlikely to slow greatly over the coming decade. This means that the average population pressure in the next years will increase and exceed the average of the 1951–1964 period. The consequence is likely to be a faster rate of rural-urban migration, unless offset by a significant increase in rural wages and employment opportunities relative to urban.

SUMMARY AND CONCLUSIONS

One-third of the rural Colombian population under the age of 40 in 1951 that lived outside of the Cabeceras had left these areas by 1964. This large outflow of migrants approximately equaled the excess of births over deaths in these rural areas, and consequently the rural population grew very slowly between these census years. Only among the youngest and oldest age groups did the rural population increase. Small towns, on balance, also lost people to migration. The growth of towns larger than 10,000 was spurred by in-migration of more than 2 percent per year. About half of the population growth of these larger towns and cities appears to have been due to in-migration between 1951 and 1964. Because the migrant tended to be young and economically active, the in-migration contributed relatively more to the growth of the urban labor force than their numbers would imply, and held the rural labor force virtually constant. In Bogota, to cite an extreme, 45 percent of the 1964 residents in the economically active ages had migrated to the city in the prior eleven years.

This wave of rural-urban migration appears to have been heightened by the increase in the rate of population growth that followed improved sanitation, nutrition, and health practices after the 1940s. The further reduction in infant and child mortality since 1950 should add to these pressures of population growth in the 1960s and further increase the already high rate of migration from the rural labor market into the cities in search of better employment. Reducing the incidence of rural violence will contribute to reducing rural-urban migration rates, but this factor is not quantitatively as important as the underlying "population explosion."

There is also evidence that schooling, though a local attraction to parents, later facilitates out-migration of students, equipping them to better evaluate and respond to employment opportunities in the city, where returns to education appear to be higher than in the countryside.

Migration in Colombia appears to follow predictable lines, reducing disequilibrium between regional labor markets. Our evidence confirms that interregional migration responds strongly to market forces drawing rural labor to the cities from regions where the returns to labor are relatively low and the supply of labor is growing relatively rapidly. Although incomes of much of the urban labor force have stagnated during the last decade (as we shall see in Chapter V), they are nevertheless still substantially in excess of those earned by comparably educated persons in the countryside.[38] Internal migration of the magnitude recently experienced by Colombia is therefore the consequence of fundamental forces that will not be turned aside lightly.

In terms of the economic objectives of raising labor productivity and increasing national income, migration per se is nothing to be alarmed about. Indeed, given population growth, migration is likely to have a beneficial effect for the migrant. For the community as a whole, migration performs an important function in the development process, facilitating structural change and keeping the difference between rural and urban incomes within bounds. Given the apparent rationality of the migration process, it seems likely that, if migration were to become strongly dysfunctional and urban unemployment rates were to rise very sharply, the process would be more or less self-correcting. If this is true, the benefits of migration may well outweigh the social costs incurred in providing housing and public services at a higher cost in the urban than in the rural areas.[39]

[38] See Schultz, *Population Growth and Internal Migration in Colombia*, Appendix B, Part III, for evidence on the stagnation of urban wages in the traditional sectors. See also Slighton, *Relative Wages, Skill Shortages, and Changes in Income Distribution in Colombia*.

[39] There is no solid evidence of the social externalities associated with the migration process to weigh against the private benefits. But, as Joan Nelson concludes in her review of the literature on migrants, the private benefits are unambiguous: "Research is virtually unanimous on the point that most migrants consider themselves better off, and probably are in fact better off than they were before they moved. In view of conditions

Aside from the economic costs and benefits of internal migration, many of which are admittedly difficult to appraise, there are
possible political repercussions of rapid urbanization in the less
developed world, sustained by heavy rural-urban migration. The
concentration of poor and unemployed in the cities may pose political problems that are easier to manage, if not resolve, when the
poor are dispersed about the countryside. As yet the potentially
explosive political tinder seems to be damp. Indeed, it would appear that internal migration contributes to the conservative character of the cities and, for better or for worse, strengthens the
status quo.[40]

---

in the city this is a shocking testimonial to even worse conditions in the
countryside." "Migrants, Urban Poverty, and Instability in New Nations:
Critique of a Myth," p. 22. From the "economist's point of view," gathering
quantitative materials on the externalities of migration and urbanization
in the developing world is a priority objective on the research agenda.
This point is elaborated by Bruce Herrick, "Urbanization and Urban Migration in Latin America: An Economist's View," in Francine Rabinowitz
and Felicity Trueblood (eds.), *The Latin American Urban Annual* (forthcoming), Sage Publishing Co.
   [40] The evidence we have seen from sociological surveys of migrant barrios
of Latin American cities suggests that the urban immigrant tends to be
politically conservative, to accept middle-class values, and to work harder
and experience less unemployment than his native-city-born counterpart.
The first generation urban immigrant improves his lot and shows few radical
tendencies, but the story may be somewhat different for the second generation urban immigrant who does not have the perspective on rural poverty
from which to judge his current state of affairs. See, for example, the
survey by Richard M. Morse, "Recent Research on Latin American Urbanization," *Latin American Research Review,* Vol. 1, No. 1, Fall 1965.
A thoughtful and thorough analysis of the evidence on migrant status,
progress, and political activities in the less developed countries leads Joan
Nelson to conclude that "Scattered evidence on current behavior, historical
material and survey data concur, then, in the finding that rural-to-urban
migrants are not politically disruptive" but, in fact, are a conservative force
in the political arena. "Migrants, Urban Poverty, and Instability in New
Nations: Critique of a Myth," p. 16.

CHAPTER IV

Manufacturing Development: Factor Endowments and Dualism

The preceding chapter observed and analyzed the flow of people from the countryside to the cities, pulled there by expectations of an improvement in the standard of living for themselves and their children. In this chapter we begin an analysis of a key sector in the cities—manufacturing. The pace at which employment opportunities, at satisfactory income levels, expand in urban communities will be in large part determined by how, and how fast, the manufacturing sector develops.

UNDERDEVELOPMENT IN THE MANUFACTURING SECTOR: SYMPTOMS, PROBLEMS, AND PROXIMATE CAUSES

Many of Colombia's present economic problems are caused by, or are related to, certain characteristics of her manufacturing sector that constrain the ability of the sector to absorb the rapidly growing urban labor force. Compared with the manufacturing sector in more developed countries, employment in manufacturing comprises a far smaller fraction of total employment, productivity is much lower, and there are certain important differences in composition. To a considerable extent these characteristics are merely symptoms of Colombia's stage of development. In some respects, however, the Colombian situation is atypical. This section compares Colombia with other countries of roughly the same, and higher, levels of development and discusses why certain characteristics of the manufacturing sector peculiar to Colombia are causing problems.

SMALL SHARE OF EMPLOYMENT

In 1964 manufacturing employment in Colombia amounted to 280,000 persons, or about 6 percent of the work force, according to the data published by the Colombian central statistical bureau.[1]

---

[1] Data presented in this section are from three sources. Those for Colombia are from DANE (the central statistical bureau) and for the

United Nations statistics, which are based on census data, give about 16 percent.[2] The discrepancy is largely accounted for by the inclusion of self-employed "craftsmen" in the latter total. But, however delineated, relative employment in manufacturing in Colombia is far smaller than in more developed countries. This is typical of less developed countries. Figure 1 shows percent of the labor force in manufacturing versus GNP per capita for a large number of different countries. The positive relationship is striking.[3]

The manufacturing sector, while small, generates income far above that produced by most of the rest of the economy. This is the reason for the migration to the cities discussed in the preceding chapter. Focusing on the narrower definition of manufacturing employment, the 6 percent of the work force engaged in manufacturing produces 17 percent of the total value added.[4] Value added per worker is about five times that in agriculture, and average wage rates probably three times as great. In contrast, in the United States value added per worker in manufacturing is roughly double that in agriculture. As Figure 2 shows, the relative difference between productivity in manufacturing and in the rest of the economy tends to be far greater in less developed than in more developed economies. Value added per worker in manufacturing rises with per capita income, but much less than in pro-

---

United States from the Department of Commerce *1954, 1958, and 1963 Census of Manufactures, General Summary* when these two countries are compared alone. In the larger samples used to derive the (least squares) regression lines, the data source was the United Nations, *Growth of World Industry: National Tables, 1938–1958,* Vol. I, New York, 1963. In the U.S.–Colombia comparisons, Colombian data were deflated with the principal import exchange rate. In the regression sample, census results from each of the twenty-nine countries were switched to 1962 currency via the implicit GNP deflator from the United Nations, *Yearbook of National Account Statistics,* New York, 1964, then converted to dollars using the 1962 exchange rate (the free market rate) wherever possible. There are significant differences between the DANE data and those from the U.S. source both in the size of establishments covered and, to some extent, in the subsector inclusions. In particular, the U.S. data include many small, low-productivity firms excluded by DANE.

[2] In Chapter V the data discrepancies will be discussed in some detail.

[3] Although the regression line has been fitted as a linear function, the well-known evidence of curvature is obvious from the graph.

[4] Productivity and incomes in the manufacturing sector excluded by the narrow definition will be examined later. Suffice it to say here that productivity there is much lower.

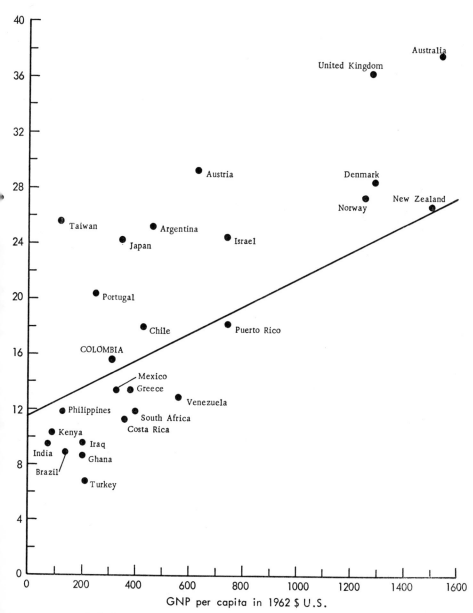

1. Labor Force in Manufacturing versus GNP per Capita

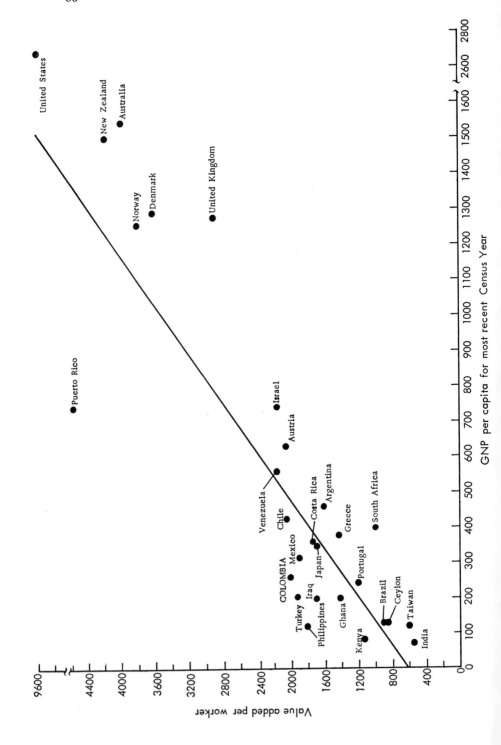

portion.[5] Although manufacturing productivity is low in less developed countries, the relative productivity gap from advanced countries is even greater in agriculture.[6]

That value added per worker in manufacturing is significantly higher than in the rest of the economy means that an expansion of the percentage of employment in manufacturing (without a decline in productivity) in itself will raise per capita income. This fact plays a major role in Lewis and Ranis-Fei development models.[7] But, as we have seen, this difference also exerts a drawing power, pulling people from the country to the cities. Given the relatively small size of the manufacturing sector, it must grow at a very rapid relative rate to keep up with the number of people seeking jobs, even if the flow of people from the country to the city is but a small fraction of the rural population.

LOW PRODUCTIVITY AND INCOMES COMPARED WITH THOSE IN MORE DEVELOPED ECONOMIES

Although productivity and wages in Colombian manufacturing are high relative to those in Colombian agriculture, they are low compared with those of more highly developed economies. Even for the narrow definition of manufacturing, value added per worker in Colombian industry is only about one-quarter that in the United States. In 1964 the figures were about $3,000 and $11,800. As shown in Figure 2, countries that lie in between the United States and Colombia in per capita income also tend to lie in between in productivity in manufacturing.[8]

[5] Differences in percent of the population engaged in economic activity is not a significant causal factor. See S. Kuznets, *Modern Economic Growth,* Yale University Press, New Haven, 1966.

[6] *Ibid.;* and A. Maizels, *Industrial Growth and World Trade,* Cambridge University Press, Cambridge, 1963.

[7] W. A. Lewis, *The Theory of Economic Growth,* George Allen & Unwin, London, 1955; and G. Ranis and J. Fei, "A Theory of Economic Development," *American Economic Review,* Vol. 51, No. 4, Sept. 1961, pp. 533–565.

[8] The data suggest that, although Colombia has low productivity relative to the highest-income countries, it compares favorably with other countries of comparable GNP per capita. See, for example, B. S. Minhas, *An International Comparison of Factor Costs and Factor Use,* North Holland Publishing Company, Amsterdam, 1963; and K. J. Arrow, H. B. Chenery, B. S. Minhas, and R. M. Solow, "Capital-Labor Substitution and Economic Efficiency," *Review of Economics and Statistics,* Vol. 43, No. 3, Aug.

Low productivity in Colombia has been reflected more than proportionately in the form of lower real wages, which average one-seventh that of the United States and constitute 27 percent of value added versus 48 percent in the United States. Although fringe benefits, such as social security, unemployment compensation, and so forth, are a larger fraction of wages in Colombia than in the United States, official Colombian figures for total labor cost suggest a labor share of well under 50 percent. Figure 3 shows, as many writers have noted, that low labor share in manufacturing is a phenomenon typical of less developed countries.[9]

In contrast to wage rates that average roughly one-seventh those of the United States, the average rate of return on capital probably is somewhat higher. Previous estimates of the capital-labor ratio for the two countries,[10] together with the estimates of labor's share presented above, imply a minimum estimate of the average gross rate of return of 25 percent in Colombia, compared with somewhere around 20 percent in the United States.[11] Our own calculations suggest an even higher rate of return in Colombia.[12]

1961. In part, however, this may be a statistical illusion. The figures for value added per worker reflect undervaluation or overvaluation of domestic currency relative to the dollar and different degrees of effective protection from foreign competition provided to industry and agriculture, as well as real productivity differences.

[9] See Arrow *et al.*, "Capital-Labor Substitution and Economic Efficiency." This was also reported in S. Kuznets, *Modern Economic Growth.*

[10] Capital data for the United States are from S. Kuznets, *Capital in the American Economy,* National Bureau of Economic Research, Princeton, 1961; the data have been adjusted for recent growth of capital. The $7,000 figure for Colombia is from the ECLA estimate of a capital–value added ratio of roughly two, reported in United Nations, *Analysis and Projections of Economic Development, Part III: The Economic Development of Colombia,* ECLA, Geneva, 1957. A similar estimate is found in J. Delaplaine, "The Structure of Economic Growth in Colombia and Argentina," unpublished manuscript.

[11] The very high rate of return on capital in Colombia may be unusual. For cross-country comparisons, see E. Mitchell, *An Econometric Study of International and Interindustrial Differences in Labor Productivity,* RM-5125-PR, The Rand Corporation, Santa Monica, Dec. 1966, and B. S. Minhas, *An International Comparison of Factor Costs and Factor Use.*

[12] Our own calculations suggest that the profit rate before taxes in modern manufacturing was at least 30 percent in 1964 and probably was closer to 40 percent. By "profit rate" we mean the ratio of value added less total labor costs and depreciation to the sum of fixed capital (valued in terms of replacement cost), inventories, and that part of working capital

The low productivity of Colombian industry imposes a floor under prices, given prevailing real wage rates and expected rates of return on capital. Perhaps its most important consequence has been to limit the ability of the sector to set prices low enough to develop an export market without reducing real wage rates or accepting lower profit rates. Indeed, in many cases low productivity has meant that protection from foreign competition is required if profit rates and wages for those employed by the sector are to be maintained.

DIFFERENCES IN PATTERN AND COMPOSITION

Low productivity and wages relative to that in richer countries are phenomena that hold across the board, industry by industry, as shown in Table 19. There is some tendency for the same industries to stand relatively high or low with respect to value added per worker and the wage rate in Colombia as in the United States. Lary and Kuznets have observed this similarity of pattern of value added per worker to hold across a variety of countries; Mitchell has shown it for value added and wage rates.[13] As a first approxi-

---

not financed by accounts payable. If there is no long-term fixed debt, this will be the rate of return on equity. We have used DANE data for value added, labor cost, and investment in plant, equipment, and inventories. The estimates for the fixed capital stock were obtained by cumulating DANE figures for gross investment on a revised version of the Economic Commission for Latin America (ECLA) estimate of the value of the fixed capital stock in manufacturing in 1953. The revision in this case consisted of reducing the ECLA estimate by 33 percent. All data had first been expressed in terms of 1964 investment goods prices. Depreciation was assumed to be 5 percent of the annual stock. Even so, the marginal capital-output ratio implied by these assumptions is only 0.8. Given these assumptions, the average before-tax profit rate in 1964 was slightly more than 30 percent. Without revision of the ECLA estimate and with the assumption of an 8 percent depreciation rate, the marginal capital-output ratio over the period 1953–1954 implied by the DANE data for manufacturing is actually negative. The implication is rather strong that the official data understate investment (and profits). This is also the consensus of the accounting profession in Colombia. If it is assumed that actual investment is 33 percent higher than reported (and profits are higher by that absolute amount), the average profit rate in modern manufacturing in 1964 was about 40 percent.

[13] H. Lary, *Exports of Manufactures by the Less Developed Countries*, National Industrial Conference Board, June 1966; S. Kuznets, *Modern Economic Growth;* and E. Mitchell, *An Econometric Study of International and Interindustrial Differences in Labor Productivity.*

84

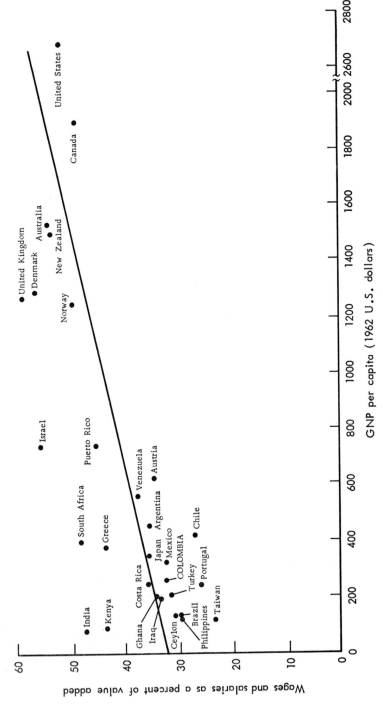

3. Wage and Salary Share versus GNP per Capita

TABLE 19
Value Added Per Worker and Wage Rate Per Worker[a]

Industry	United States, 1963[b] Value Added Per Worker	Wage Rate Per Worker	Colombia, 1964[b] Value Added Per Worker	Wage Rate Per Worker	Ratio of Colombian to U.S. VA/W
Industry average	$11,833	$5,746	$ 2,966	$ 793	.25
Food[c]	13,283	5,257	3,157	685⎱	.47[d]
Beverages	n.a.	n.a.	7,537	1,138⎰	
Tobacco	21,733	4,274	11,293	1,070	.52
Textiles	7,093	3,921	2,581	861	.36
Clothing and footwear	6,144	3,457	1,173	468	.19
Wood and wood products	7,140	4,153	1,313	551	.18
Furniture	8,148	4,586	1,234	546	.15
Paper and paper products	12,577	5,966	4,219	1,029	.34
Printing	11,472	6,039	2,042	796	.18
Chemicals	23,848	6,740	4,447	1,007	.19
Petroleum	24,193	7,387	12,153	2,084	.50
Rubber products	11,215	5,697	3,326	1,053	.30
Leather products	6,347	3,749	2,067	653	.33
Nonmetallic minerals	12,275	5,598	1,937	733	.16
Basic metals	13,547	6,865	5,605	816	.41
Metal products	10,896	5,903	1,976	720	.18
Machinery, excl. elec.	11,862	6,558	2,172	671	.18
Electrical machinery	11,252	6,141	2,844	831	.25
Transportation equip.	14,218	7,406	1,445	792	.10

Notes:
  n.a. means "not available."
  [a] 1963 exchange rate: 12 pesos = 1 dollar.
  [b] Comparable figures were not available for the same year.
  [c] Includes beverages in the U.S. figures.
  [d] Food and beverages were combined for Colombia using labor force weights, which were .712 for food and .288 for beverages. The ratio with U.S. value added per worker is based on VA per worker of $4,418 in Colombia.
Sources:
  United States——U.S. Department of Commerce, *1963 Census of Manufactures*, (USA), *General Summary*, Washington, D.C., 1966.
  Colombia——DANE.

mation, it does appear meaningful to think of a general level of manufacturing productivity and wages in a country, with inter-industry patterns being roughly in proportion across countries. Yet there still remains considerable variance in that tendency. The ratio of value added per worker (or wages) in Colombia to that in the United States is relatively high in tobacco, textiles, and petroleum (between one-third and one-half that in the United

States).[14] The ratio is relatively low (less than one-fifth that in the United States) in lumber, apparel, nonmetallic minerals, basic metals, and in the metal processing industries.

Part of the explanation for these varying ratios is the grossness of the two-digit industry category; metal processing, for example, includes both pots and pans and aircraft. Nevertheless, many of the differences between Colombia and the United States in the pattern of output per worker by industry are typical of all such comparisons between developed and less developed nations. We can verify this partially by examining Figure 4. For example, the difference between value added per worker between high and low income countries tends to be less for textiles and food products than for basic metals and metal processing. We can also check the effect of possible differences in composition of output by industry by examining finer data.[15]

There also were important differences between Colombia and the United States in the composition of manufacturing output and employment (Table 20). In 1964 in Colombia the food, beverages, and tobacco complex accounted for 22 percent of employment and 36 percent of value added; the textiles, clothing, leather, and footwear complex accounted for an additional 28 percent of employment and 19 percent of value added. In the United States these industries accounted for only 11 and 14 percent of employment and 12 and 8 percent of value added. (The relatively large Colombian industries tended to be ones in which productivity was relatively high compared with the United States.) In the United States the basic metals and metal processing industries, which include machinery and transportation equipment as well as other metal products, accounted for 42 percent of employment and 45 percent of value added. In Colombia these industries accounted for only about 18 percent of employment and 14 percent of value added. These differences in composition between manufacturing sectors in developed and less developed countries are well known.[16]

[14] See Tables 4 and 5.

[15] Finer detail here means at the three-digit level. The results obtained by the authors were roughly comparable to those in the tables in the appendix of K. J. Arrow et al., "Capital-Labor Substitution and Economic Efficiency."

[16] See, for example, S. Kuznets, *Modern Economic Growth;* H. Chenery, "Patterns of Industrial Growth," *American Economic Review,* Vol. 50,

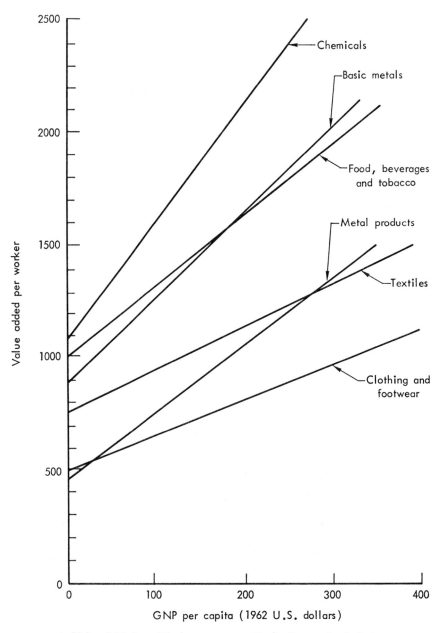

4. Value Added per Worker versus per Capita Income by Industry

TABLE 20
DISTRIBUTION OF VALUE ADDED AND LABOR FORCE
(in percent)

Industry	United States, 1963[a]		Colombia, 1964[a]	
	Value Added	Labor Force	Value Added	Labor Force
Food[b]	11.4	10.1	15.6	14.6
Beverages	—	—	14.9	5.9
Tobacco	.9	.5	5.1	1.3
Textiles	3.2	5.3	13.5	15.5
Clothing and footwear	4.1	7.9	4.4	11.1
Wood and wood products	2.1	3.5	.9	2.1
Furniture	1.6	2.3	.7	1.7
Paper and paper products	3.8	3.6	2.7	1.9
Printing	5.5	5.6	2.9	4.2
Chemicals	9.2	4.5	10.5	7.0
Petroleum	1.7	.9	2.9	.7
Rubber products	2.4	2.6	2.7	2.4
Leather products	1.1	2.0	1.1	1.6
Nonmetallic minerals	3.7	3.5	5.9	9.0
Basic metals	7.9	6.9	2.4	1.3
Metal products	6.1	6.7	4.5	6.7
Machinery, excl. elec.	9.0	9.0	1.3	1.7
Electrical machinery	8.9	9.3	3.1	3.2
Transportation equipment	11.9	9.9	2.5	5.2

NOTES:
    [a] Comparable figures were not available for the same year.
    [b] Includes beverages in the U.S. figures.
SOURCES:
    United States——U.S. Department of Commerce, *1963 Census of Manufacturers,* *(USA)*, *General Summary*, Washington, D.C., 1966.
    Colombia——DANE.

Figure 5 presents illustrative regression lines of the percentage of total manufacturing value added in several industries versus per capita income.[17] Colombia's composition is reasonably well predicted by the regressions, but the share of value added accounted for by textiles and food processing is somewhat high, and the share of metal processing somewhat low.

No. 4, Sept. 1960, pp. 624–654; W. G. Hoffman, *The Growth of Industrial Economies*, Oxford University Press, New York, 1958; and A. Maizels, *Industrial Growth and World Trade*.

    [17] Only a few industries are presented because a quite complete analysis is available in H. Chenery, "Patterns of Industrial Growth."

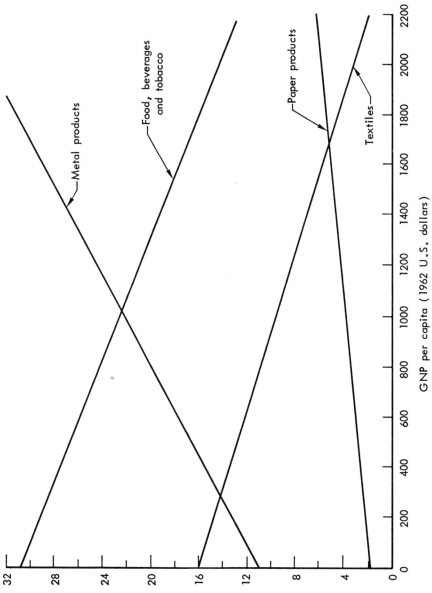

5. Percent of Manufacturing Value Added in Industry versus GNP per Capita

The discussion above was concerned with composition at the two-digit level. For more narrowly defined products, there are many that Colombia does not produce at all, among them many kinds of machinery, certain kinds of intermediate goods such as specialty chemicals, and various electrical components. These differences in pattern and in composition mean that Colombian industry is dependent upon imports for operation (intermediate goods) and expansion (capital goods). For many products needed to permit the manufacturing sector to operate, domestic production is sharply limited. A large share of Colombia's new capital equipment is imported in final form, and most of the rest is assembled by Colombian firms out of imported components. Where Colombia does produce intermediate and capital goods, productivity and quality tend to be low and prices relatively high.

INTERACTIONS OF THE CHARACTERISTICS

The combination of low productive capacity and low productivity in the capital and intermediate goods industries can be pernicious. The requirement for industrial growth sufficiently rapid to avoid rising urban unemployment in the face of migration, together with the manufacturing sector's difficulty in generating exports in sufficient amount to satisfy import requirements, potentially pose an awkward economic and political problem. There need not be such a problem. If access to imports can be attained through primary sector exports, the manufacturing sector can grow rapidly. But in this area the Colombian experience has been exceedingly unfortunate. Later we shall discuss in detail the history of Colombia's access to foreign exchange. Suffice it to say here that, largely because of a rise in coffee prices, Colombia's real export earnings rose significantly over the 1945–1955 period and then fell precipitously as coffee prices fell. Between 1955 and 1960 total exports, in dollar terms, declined by about 30 percent. Since that time exports have grown, but they have not yet struggled back to mid-1950 levels. After a sharp fall in imports, major foreign exchange assistance from the World Bank, International Monetary Fund, and the Agency for International Development permitted Colombian imports to pick up again after 1960, though they never reached the levels of the mid-1950s. Since then the import con-

straint has tightened again.[18] The last few years have seen the unfortunate dynamic consequences of this foreign exchange shortage,
namely, a slowing down of the rate of growth of manufacturing
output and employment, rising urban unemployment, and a
sequence of balance-of-payments crises.

In order to design sensible policies to deal with these characteristics and the problems they cause, it is necessary to understand
the factors that lie behind them. In the remainder of this chapter
we shall develop an explanation for low productivity. In Chapter
VI we shall examine the import dependency phenomenon and explore the constraints on the evolution of the Colombian manufacturing sector.

NEOCLASSICAL THEORY—ITS POWER AND ITS DEFICIENCY[19]

Over the past decade a considerable literature has developed
that attempts to explain the cross-country differences in labor productivity discussed in the preceding section. The descriptive and
qualitative literature has suggested a great number of variables
as being potentially significant in explaining these differences and
it has used (implicitly) a wide variety of models. However, in the
more quantitative literature using a formal model, the theoretical
analysis almost invariably starts from two assumptions. The first is
that within an industry all firms, both in a country and in different
countries, are in some basic sense employing the same neoclassical
production function. Differences in output per worker therefore
ought to be explainable by differences in the suppply of complementary factors per worker. The second assumption is that factors
are homogeneous and perfectly mobile within an industry in a
country and that factor prices are determined on competitive markets. Prices or returns of different factors are thus the same for
all firms in the country and are equal to marginal productivity.
Together these two assumptions imply that in each country the
industry is the representative firm writ large. Intercountry produc-

---

[18] For data, see John Sheahan, "Imports, Investment, and Growth:
Colombian Experience Since 1950," Center for Development Economics,
Williams College, Sept. 1966.

[19] This and the following section closely follow R. Nelson, "A Diffusion
Model of International Productivity Differences," *American Economic Review*, Vol. 58, No. 5, Part 1, Dec. 1968, pp. 1219–1248.

tivity differences thus reflect differences in factor proportions used by the representative firms.[20]

The point of view that we wish to stress later in this chapter breaks significantly from these assumptions. We have been led to adopt a quite different point of view, in large part because of growing awareness that the early attempts to employ the model empirically suggested some basic problems with the neoclassical framework. It will be useful therefore to set the stage by describing these problems.

The best point of departure is an attempt by Arrow, Chenery, Minhas, and Solow to relate cross-country differences in value added per worker to differences in the capital-labor ratio.[21] Capital and labor were defined so that their returns added up to value added. Thus other factors implicitly were assumed to influence average quality or effectiveness of one or both of these two basic inputs. For our purposes the pertinent questions to which their research pertains can be posed as follows. Given the observed level of value added per worker and of capital per worker in an industry in a less developed country, what would value added per worker be in that country if the capital-labor ratio were equal to that in a developed country, assuming both were on the same production function? How much of the observed difference in value added per worker can be explained in the sense above by the difference in the capital-labor ratio?

The answers, of course, depend on the "shape" of the production function. The basic assumptions constrain the shape. Output per worker, Q/L, must be an increasing and concave function of the capital-labor ratio, K/L, given other factors that will be denoted by Y. Thus

(1) $$\frac{Q}{L} = F\left(\frac{K}{L}, Y\right).$$

[20] In a way, this is too strict. Several of the papers admit the possibility of total factor productivity differences across nations. But this is brought in as an empirical fact of life, not as something intrinsic to the basic model. For a survey of much of the relevant literature, see M. Nerlove, "Recent Empirical Studies of the CES and Related Production Functions," in M. Brown (ed.), *The Theory and Empirical Analysis of Production,* National Bureau of Economic Research, New York, 1967.

[21] See K. J. Arrow *et al.,* "Capital-Labor Substitution and Economic Efficiency."

Or, for a constant Y,

(1a) $$\frac{Q}{L} = f\left\{\frac{K}{L}\right\}, \qquad f' > 0, \qquad f'' < 0.$$

Notice that $f(\cdot)$ may differ across countries if Y differs.

Observation of output and capital per worker identifies a point on the function. Further observation of the rate of return on capital, or of capital's share of value added, serves to identify the slope and the elasticity of the function at that point. Since the model implies that the rate of return on capital is equal to capital's marginal productivity,

(2) $$f'(K/L)_0 = r_0,$$

and

$$(S_K)_0 = [f'(K/L)_0](K/L)_0/f(K/L)_0$$

where r and S_K refer to the rate of return on capital and capital's share of value added respectively, and the subscript "0" indicates the present level of a variable.

This information suffices for estimation by linear extrapolation (see Figure 6) of the effect on output per worker of small changes in the capital-labor ratio. For large changes something must be known about the degree of concavity of the function—the rate of diminishing returns. This can be measured by the elasticity of substitution between capital and labor which determines how the elasticity of the function changes as the capital-labor ratio changes.

(3) $$\frac{d \log S_K}{d \log \left(\frac{K}{L}\right)} = (1 - S_K)\left(\frac{E - 1}{E}\right)$$

where E is the elasticity of substitution.[22] In general, E will not

---

22

(1) $$S_K = \frac{f_k K}{Q} = \left\{\frac{f_k}{f_L}\right\}\left\{\frac{K}{L}\right\} \qquad S_L = \left\{\frac{f_k}{f_L}\right\}\left\{\frac{K}{L}\right\}\{1 - S_k\}.$$

(2) $$\frac{dS_k}{d\frac{K}{L}} = -\left[\frac{f_k}{f_L}\frac{K}{L}\right]\frac{dS_k}{d\frac{K}{L}} + \frac{f_k}{f_L}\{1 - S_k\} + \{1 - S_k\}\frac{K}{L}\frac{d\left\{\frac{f_k}{f_1}\right\}}{d\frac{K}{L}}.$$

be a constant but will itself change with K/L. However, in the Arrow *et al.* specification, the production function is assumed to have a constant elasticity of substitution. Thus, if one knows a point on the curve, its slope at that point, and the elasticity of substitution, one can specify the entire (partial) production function. One can then directly answer the two questions posed above.

Let us apply this model to Colombia and ask: How much larger would value added per worker have been in the Colombian manufacturing industry if Colombia had had a capital stock per worker roughly comparable to that in the United States (but no other changes affecting productivity were made)? To recall the relevant numbers, as of 1964 value added per worker in Colombia was about \$3,000 (compared with \$12,000 in the United States).[23] The capital-labor ratio was about \$6,000 (compared with \$24,000 in the United States). This is a point on the production function.

Noting that

$$E = -\left(\frac{d\frac{K}{L}}{d\frac{f_k}{f_L}}\right)\left(\frac{\frac{f_k}{f_L}}{\frac{K}{L}}\right),$$

that

$$\frac{f_k K}{f_L L} = \frac{S_k}{1 - S_k}, \quad \text{and} \quad 1 + \frac{S_k}{1 - S_k} = \frac{1}{1 - S_k},$$

then by regrouping,

$$(3) \qquad \frac{dS_k}{d\left\{\frac{K}{L}\right\}}\left\{\frac{1}{1 - S_k}\right\} = \frac{f_k}{f_L}\{1 - S_k\}\left[1 - \frac{1}{E}\right].$$

Since, from Eq. 1,

$$\frac{f_k}{f_L}\{1 - S_k\} = \frac{L}{K}S_k,$$

then

$$(4) \qquad \frac{dS_k}{d\frac{K}{L}} = S_k\{1 - S_k\}\left\{\frac{E - 1}{E}\right\}\frac{L}{K}.$$

Eq. 3 in the text follows immediately.

[23] R. Nelson, *A Study of Industrialization in Colombia: Part I, Analysis*, RM-5412-AID, The Rand Corporation, Santa Monica, Aug. 1967.

The elasticity of the function at that point can be estimated by capital share—about .7. Let us take an estimate of the elasticity of substitution from Arrow *et al.* at about .6. (Later we shall discuss how they arrived at that figure.) Assuming a constant elasticity of substitution between capital and labor Equation 1a can be written:[24]

$$
(4) \qquad \frac{\dfrac{Q}{L}}{\left(\dfrac{Q}{L}\right)_0} = \left[S_K^0 \left[\frac{\left\{\dfrac{K}{L}\right\}}{\left\{\dfrac{K}{L}\right\}_0} \right]^{\frac{E-1}{E}} + S_L^0 \right]^{\frac{E}{E-1}}
$$

Calculations show that, if this function holds, output per worker would be slightly more than twice as great—approximately $6,900—if the capital-labor ratio was the same as that in the United States but other variables influencing relative productivities

[24] Output per worker can be written

$$
(1) \qquad \frac{Q}{L} = A \left[\delta \left\{\frac{K}{L}\right\}^{\frac{E-1}{E}} + 1 - \delta \right]^{\frac{E}{E-1}}.
$$

The ratios of the factor shares can be shown to be

$$
(2) \qquad \frac{S_k}{S_L} = \frac{\delta}{1-\delta} \left[\frac{K}{L}\right]^{\frac{E-1}{E}}.
$$

Rewriting Eq. 1,

$$
(3) \qquad \frac{Q}{L} = A \left[\delta \left\{\frac{K}{L}\right\}_0^{\frac{E-1}{E}} \left[\frac{\left\{\dfrac{K}{L}\right\}}{\left\{\dfrac{K}{L}\right\}_0} \right]^{\frac{E-1}{E}} + 1 - \delta \right]^{\frac{E}{E-1}}.
$$

Substituting from Eq. 2 and rearranging,

$$
(4) \qquad \frac{Q}{L} = \frac{A\{1-\delta\}}{S_L^0} \left[S_k^0 \left[\frac{\left\{\dfrac{K}{L}\right\}}{\left\{\dfrac{K}{L}\right\}_0} \right]^{\frac{E-1}{E}} + S_L^0 \right]^{\frac{E}{E-1}}.
$$

Recognizing that $\left\{\dfrac{Q}{L}\right\}_0$ must equal $\dfrac{A\{1-\delta\}}{S_L^0}$,

$$
(5) \qquad \frac{Q}{L} = \left\{\frac{Q}{L}\right\}_0 \left[S_k^0 \left[\frac{\left\{\dfrac{K}{L}\right\}}{\left\{\dfrac{K}{L}\right\}_0} \right]^{\frac{E-1}{E}} + S_L^0 \right]^{\frac{E}{E-1}}.
$$

were not changed from levels existing in Colombia. Or, differences in the capital-labor ratio alone explain only about one-third of the observed productivity difference. The rate of return on capital, which at Colombia's existing capital-labor ratio is somewhat greater than in the United States, would be significantly lower at a higher capital-labor ratio, if nothing else changed. All this is shown in Figure 6.

What was just done is *not* exactly what Arrow *et al.* did, although the calculations are directly implied by their model and their estimate of the (constant) elasticity of substitution. Arrow *et al.* were interested in explaining productivity differences among a number of countries, and for many of them reliable capital stock data did not exist. However, if one assumes, for the moment, that capital-labor ratio differences are the only distinguishing differences

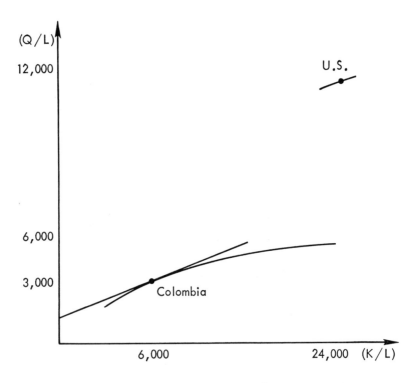

The elasticity of the function at K/L = 6,000 is 0.7, and the elasticity of substitution is 0.6

6. CES Calculations for a Colombian–U.S. Comparison

between rich and poor countries, given the general neoclassical production function and the assumption that labor is paid its marginal product, one can obtain a monotonic increasing relationship between the wage rate and the capital-labor ratio:

$$(5) \qquad w = g\left\{\frac{K}{L}\right\}.$$

This relationship provides an indirect measure of the capital-labor ratio and permits (1a) to be written as follows:

$$(6) \qquad \frac{Q}{L} = f[g^{-1}(w)] = h(w).$$

If one knows $f(\cdot)$ one can specify both $g(\cdot)$ and $h(\cdot)$. The reverse is, in general, not true. However, the form of $f(\cdot)$ implies a form for $h(\cdot)$, and from estimates of some of the parameters of $h(\cdot)$ one can infer some (but not all) of the parameters of $f(\cdot)$. In particular, one can infer the elasticity of substitution. It is in this manner that Arrow *et al.* obtained their estimate of the elasticity of substitution.

Notice that in reality what is happening is that the elasticity of substitution is being estimated so as to fit the observed differences in labor share (or capital share) between high and low wage countries. Dividing both sides of (6) by w and inverting yields

$$(7) \qquad \frac{Lw}{Q} = \frac{w}{h(w)}$$

or

$$S_L = j(w).$$

As shown earlier, it is an empirical fact that the share of labor is higher in high wage than in low wage countries, and this will be reflected in the estimated parameters of (6). Since w is assumed to be related only to K/L, it follows from (5), (6), and (7) that the wage share increases as the capital-labor ratio increases. This means that, as the model is specified, the statistical results will be interpreted as implying an elasticity of substitution between capital and labor of less than unity. (Note Equation 3.)

But there clearly is something misspecified about the model. For where capital data are available it is possible to go back and estimate what output per worker would be at a different capital-labor ratio. From the assumptions of the model, the result should be that lifting the capital-labor ratios in poor countries to a level comparable to that in the United States should yield an output per worker estimate equal to that in the United States. As we have seen, it does not. Arrow *et al.* did not show this negative result the way we did. Instead, they used a factor price frontier argument that we shall discuss and use later. But first let us try to see in what basic way the model might be misspecified.

Let us maintain for the moment the key assumptions of the model—the common linear homogeneous production function and competitive factor pricing—but drop the special assumption used in Equation 1a that differences in capital-labor ratios are the only differences between countries. Instead, let us admit, as before, that there may be other factors, Y as well as K/L, that vary across countries and affect both Q/L and the marginal productivity of labor (assumed to equal the wage rate). Then

(1) $$\frac{Q}{L} = F\left(\frac{K}{L}, Y\right)$$

and

(8) $$w = G\left(\frac{K}{L}, Y\right)$$

If, speaking intuitively, $F(\cdot)$ and $G(\cdot)$ have the same isoquants, we can write

(9) $$\frac{Q}{L} = H(w)$$

exactly as before.[25]

If this is what is going on, we can explain why Arrow *et al.* can get such a good fit for the equation estimating the elasticity of substitution in spite of the fact that differences in capital-labor ratios alone can explain only a small portion of intercountry productivity differences. For Equations 9 and 6 are indistinguishable. The equation they actually fitted is consistent with a wide variety of factors, not just higher capital-labor ratios, that distinguish rich countries from poor. Although something that might be called an elasticity of substitution can be derived, there is no reason why the number so estimated need have anything at all to do with

---

[25] More precisely, the set of inverse sets for $G(\cdot)$ is identical to that for $F(\cdot)$.

an elasticity of substitution (holding other factors constant) between K and L.[26]

One implication of the above is that there is no reason why the Arrow *et al.* estimate of the "elasticity of substitution" should be used in Equation 4. However, if the "share equals elasticity" assumption is maintained, there is little explanatory leverage in the elasticity of substitution. If the elasticity of substitution is higher than .6, then diminishing returns will set in less rapidly and a higher capital-labor ratio will contribute more to higher output.

TABLE 21
OUTPUT PER WORKER AS A FUNCTION OF CAPITAL PER WORKER AND THE ELASTICITY OF SUBSTITUTION

$\dfrac{(K/L)}{(K/L)_0}$	$(Q/L)/(Q/L)_0$				
	E				
	.4	.6	.8	1.0	1.5
2	1.49	1.57	1.60	1.63	1.65
4	1.88	2.28	2.50	2.64	2.81
6	2.03	2.73	3.21	3.51	3.88

NOTE:
Calculations based on Eq. 4 of the text assuming $(S_K) = .7$.

But, as shown in Table 21, even with a high elasticity of substitution, it still is not possible to explain more than half of the observed differences in value added per worker in this way. If a linear homogeneous production function common to all nations and competitive factor pricing are assumed, then differences between rich and poor countries must transcend differences in the capital-labor ratio.

[26] For example, consider two countries with exactly the same capital-labor ratio, but one with a higher output per worker because of, say, higher educational attainments. Assume that the rate of return on capital is the same in both countries with the wage rate and, hence, wage share higher in the high-income country. From the CES calculations described above, the statistician would obtain an estimate of the elasticity of substitution between capital and labor (less than one), despite the fact that there is no difference in the capital-labor ratios in the two cases.

We noted earlier that Arrow *et al.* also deduced this conclusion. Their argument was based on the following fact. A neoclassical production function with two factors of production, say, capital and labor, implies a factor price frontier, if we assume competitive factor pricing. Thus the general model

$$\frac{Q}{L} = f\left\{\frac{K}{L}\right\}; \qquad f' > 0 \qquad f'' < 0$$

where

$$w = \frac{\partial Q}{\partial L}, \qquad r = \frac{\partial Q}{\partial K}$$

implies a factor price frontier that can be characterized as

$$(10) \qquad S(w, r) = 0, \qquad \frac{\partial w}{\partial r} < 0.$$

Both factor prices are uniquely related to K/L, one positively and one negatively. If the wage rate is higher in one country than another (because of more capital per worker), the rate of return on capital must be lower. Recall that the slope of $f(K/L)$ declined with K/L in Figure 6.

However, several studies have shown that the rate of return on capital in high wage countries is nowhere near as low, in comparison with the rate of return on capital in low wage countries, as is implied by the factor price frontier.[27] It is this fact that led Arrow *et al.* to recognize that something else, as well as differences in capital-labor ratios, must distinguish high from low wage countries.

One might have expected this result. After all, there are international capital markets. The question then becomes, why does the rate of return on capital in less developed countries fall to roughly world levels at such a low capital-labor ratio? What are the key differences between less and more developed countries that repress both output per worker and the return to capital in the former?

An obvious next step is to put into the model other factors that seem positively related to value added per worker. Mitchell (along with many others) has suggested a measure of skill or edu-

---

[27] E. Mitchell, *An Econometric Study of International and Interindustrial Differences in Labor Productivity.*

cation endowments.[28] His particular formulation is in terms of an index of skill mix of the labor force, which he designates by the ratio of skilled labor, L_1, to total labor, L.

$$(11) \qquad \frac{Q}{L} = F\left(\frac{K}{L}, \frac{L_1}{L}, Y^*\right).$$

It is clear that the ratio of skilled to total labor is far smaller in Colombia than in the United States. To cite just a few numbers, the percentage of the manufacturing work force in Bogota with at least some college level training was only about 3 percent in 1965. In the United States over 20 percent of the urban work force has had some college education. Further, almost 70 percent of the workers employed in manufacturing activity in Bogota had had no secondary education at all, compared with less than 20 percent in the U.S. urban work force.[29]

We shall not attempt here to calculate how much difference this might make to productivity. The Mitchell specification of the way education enters the production function is only one of many. We shall propose a significantly different specification in a later chapter. But it is highly unlikely that any neoclassical specification would permit education to close the gap in explanatory power of the neoclassical model.

To understand this, consider again the factor price frontier. The Mitchell model implies a factor price frontier as follows:

$$(12) \qquad S(w_1, w_2, r) = 0 \qquad \left[\frac{\partial w_i}{\partial r}\right]_{w_j} < 0 \qquad \left[\frac{\partial w_i}{\partial w_j}\right]_r < 0$$

where w_1 and w_2 are the wages of skilled and unskilled labor. If one assumes $r = \bar{r}$ (rates of return on capital do not differ much across countries), then if unskilled workers are paid more in high income countries, skilled workers must be paid less, not just relatively but absolutely. The result on the factor price frontier for a two-factor model is easily generalized to a three- or indeed an n-factor model. If one factor is paid less in one situation (country) than in another, there must be at least one other factor that is

---

[28] *Ibid.*

[29] We shall examine the educational distribution of the Colombian labor force in some detail in a later chapter.

paid more.[30] What limited data we have seen suggest that, if we exclude managerial personnel (who will be discussed later), this is not the case. Engineers, scientists, doctors, lawyers, skilled mechanics—all tend to be paid less, not more, in less developed countries than in more developed ones. Certainly this is so in Colombia. In part there may be quality differences. But the so-called brain drain shows that many of these people can go from a country where they are "scarce" to one in which they are "plentiful" and earn more money.

If one drops the assumption of constancy across countries in rates of return on capital and admits higher rates of return in low wage countries, the conclusion is less clear. However, there is still strong reason to suspect that a full explanation of international productivity differences transcends capital and skill endowments per worker.[31] As other factors are progressively brought

---

[30] Assume a linear homogeneous production function $A = f\{X_1 \ldots X_n\}$. Assume price, marginal cost, and average cost are all equal to one, and further assume cost minimization so that $w_i = f_i$ for all i. Assume the isoquants are strictly convex, and at least some of each factor is needed to produce any output. The linear homogeneity assumption guarantees that one can calculate the nature of possible variations in factor price compatible with these assumptions by considering only one isoquant. Using vector notation, consider two such compatible factor price vectors, W_0 and W_1, and their associated minimum cost factor inputs, X_0 and X_1. We know

$$(1) \qquad \operatorname*{Min}_X W_0 X = W_0 X_0 = 1 < W_0 X_1,$$

and

$$(2) \qquad \operatorname*{Min}_X W_1 X = W_1 X_1 = 1 < W_1 X_0.$$

Thus

$$(3) \qquad W_0 X_0 < W_1 X_0 \quad \text{or} \quad W_0 \ngtr W_1$$

and

$$(4) \qquad W_1 X_1 < W_0 X_1 \quad \text{or} \quad W_1 \ngtr W_0.$$

That is, neither factor price vector, compatible with the assumptions, can be strictly greater than the other. If one observes two such systems of factor prices, if one of the components of one is greater than the same component in the other, some other component must be less.

[31] Denison's study of U.S.–European productivity differences identifies a large number of factors, but also a significant "total factor productivity" difference. Anne Krueger's unpublished study of U.S.–Indian productivity differences, while concluding that capital and education are a lot of the story, also has an unexplained residual. See E. Denison (assisted by J. P. Poullier), *Why Economic Growth Rates Differ*, Brookings Institution, Washington, D.C., 1967; and A. Krueger, "Factor Endowments and Per Capita Income Differences Among Countries," unpublished manuscript.

into the analysis, the unexplained residual will be further reduced. And clearly there are some important measurement errors that need to be treated. But there are no reasons why the two basic assumptions of the model—a common linear homogeneous production function and perfect competitive factor markets—should be held sacrosanct.

THE CASE FOR ABANDONING THE BASIC ASSUMPTIONS: MANUFACTURING AS A DIFFUSION PROCESS

The assumptions of a common production function and perfect and competitive factor markets have proved both convenient and fruitful for modeling many economic phenomena. Yet they appear to obscure our understanding of international differences in productivity, particularly differences between advanced and underdeveloped economies.

It has been clear for some time that growth and structural transformation of the manufacturing sector in advanced economies is, in considerable part, the result of technological advance and not simply the result of increases in the various factors of production. Because of the accounting identity between the value of output and the returns to inputs, it always is possible to "explain" output changes by input changes (suitably measured). Many of these input changes themselves, however, must be attributed to technological advances. Technological advance itself can be attributed in some part to inputs invested for the purpose of advancing technology. Hence, in some sense perhaps, changes in output can be attributed to changes in inputs (although the relationship almost certainly will not be linear homogeneous). Even so, no one would deny that in advanced countries, in a quite fundamental sense, production functions have changed and are changing over time. Although this is a statement about growth over time within a country, it also has important implications regarding differences, at any moment of time, across countries.

Recent research by Keesing, Vernon, Hufbauer,[32] and others

[32] See G. C. Hufbauer, *Synthetic Materials and the Theory of International Trade,* Duckworth, London, 1966; R. Vernon, "International Investment and International Trade in Product Cycles," *Quarterly Journal of Economics,* Vol. 80, No. 2, May 1966, pp. 190–207; and D. Keesing, "The Impact of Research and Development in U.S. Trade," *Journal of Political Economy,* Vol. 75, No. 1, Feb. 1967, pp. 38–48, for an introduction to a rapidly growing literature.

suggests strongly that trade patterns in manufactured products reflect more than differences in resource endowments. A considerable portion of U.S. manufacturing exports is in new products that other countries have not yet begun to produce in quantity. Vernon and Hufbauer go on to show that, with a lag, the other major manufacturing nations pick up and employ U.S. technology (and gradually cut the United States out of export markets). With a greater lag, eventually less developed countries begin to adopt and employ this technology (if it has not already become obsolete).

The technological-lead, product-cycle theory suggests a quite different analysis of international differences in productivity than is implied by the model discussed in the preceding section. The engine of manufacturing development is technological advance in the developed countries, particularly the United States. The United States is the leading country in creating new products, in part because of its "endowment" of managers, scientists, engineers, and its innovative and flexible people. It is clear that the United States has a real technological "lead." More generally, the position of any country in the diffusion hierarchy may well be a function of factor endowments, particularly supply of sophisticated managers, technicians, and easily trainable labor. But there is no reason to believe that these factors enter in the way implied by conventional neoclassical analysis. Viewing the economic development process as a diffusion process naturally leads one to abandon the two basic assumptions of the neoclassical model, that all firms in all countries are on the same production function and that markets are in full equilibrium.

Within the country where the inventing is going on, the firms doing it have at least a potential head start over the others. Other firms may themselves have been close to making the invention and be able to follow quite quickly. Other firms may lag considerably. Within the adopting countries, firms may differ greatly in their ability to adopt quickly. Some may be subsidiaries of the innovating firms in the countries doing the inventing. Among the domestically owned firms there may be great variation in technical and managerial capability to adopt new technology. Various studies of diffusion show that, in general, it takes a considerable time for a new technique to spread to most of the firms in an industry. Thus at any given time one would expect to find considerable variation among firms with respect to the vintage of their technology, certainly between countries, but even within a country.[33]

Variation among firms with respect to vintage of technology is certainly compatible with perfect factor markets. The Solow embodiment model and various versions of the putty clay model,[34] for example, involve both differences among firms in the vintage of their technology and perfect factor markets. But such models require perfect knowledge and foresight on the part of firm managers and perfect knowledge and mobility on the part of factors. Although the studies of diffusion are consistent with the assumption that entrepreneurial decisions move the systems in the direction of equilibrium, they do not indicate that the adjustment rate is so rapid that, for all practical purposes, all firms always have the same rate of return on capital. Clearly they do not. Similarly, the various studies of labor mobility, while indicating that labor moves from poorer to better paying jobs, far from indicate a perfect labor market.[35] Our earlier treatment of migration has stressed lagged and imperfect labor mobility.

It would appear, therefore, that data on value added per worker in a particular industry represent the weighted average of a distribution that may have considerable range and variance.

(13)
$$\frac{Q}{L} = \sum_{\left(\frac{Q}{L}\right)_{min}}^{\left(\frac{Q}{L}\right)_{max}} \left(\frac{Q}{L}\right)_i \frac{L_i}{L} .$$

In comparing less with more developed countries, it is clear that $(Q/L)_{max}$ is likely to be smaller in the former both because of differences in factor prices and because some firms in the more developed countries are simply ahead technologically. And

---

[33] For a survey of the diffusion literature, see R. Nelson, M. J. Peck, and E. Kalachek, *Technology, Economic Growth, and Public Policy,* Brookings Institution, Washington, D.C., 1967, Chap. 5.

[34] See W. E. G. Salter, *Productivity and Technical Change,* Cambridge University Press, Cambridge, 1960; and R. M. Solow, "Investment and Technical Progress," in Arrow, Karlin, and Suppes (eds.), *Mathematical Methods in the Social Sciences,* Stanford University Press, Stanford, 1960.

[35] Nelson, Peck, and Kalachek, *Technology, Economic Growth, and Public Policy,* Chaps. 5 and 7.

$(Q/L)_{min}$ is likely to be smaller in the less developed country, for factor price reasons if for no other.

It also is likely (although far from certain) that the range of productivity will be greater in the less developed country, for two basic reasons. First, the responsiveness of investment to a new, even highly profitable, technological opportunity, although positive, is likely to be less strong. Managerial talent is more limited, and it is likely that differences in management capabilities show up more sharply in ability to appraise and exploit new opportunities than in any other way. There are also apt to be a large number of specific input bottlenecks, such as particular skills and machinery that must be purchased from abroad. Second, imperfect domestic factor markets, another well-known characteristic of less developed countries, further tend to slow the adoption process by increasing the cost of expanding firms. Slow adoption not only reduces the density of the upper tail of the distribution in Equation 13, it also reduces pressure on lagging firms.[36]

It seems worthwhile to illustrate how some of these relationships work by the following highly stylized and simplified model. Many of the simplifying assumptions used in this model will be abandoned later. But for the present assume that at time t_0 full competitive equilibrium exists on product and factor markets, all firms have the same (linear homogeneous) production functions and (within any country) face the same factor prices, have the same costs, and are making a normal profit. Any initial differences in output per worker across countries will then be a function of relative factor endowments which, in turn, will be reflected in relative and absolute factor prices. To simplify matters, assume that capital and labor are the only factors (one can interpret capital as broadly as one wishes). Thus at time t_0

$$(14) \qquad \left(\frac{Q}{L}\right) = f\left(\frac{K}{L}\right) = g(w, r)$$

where $g(\cdot)$ is homogeneous of degree zero and w and r are the costs of labor and capital respectively.

Assume that at time t_0 a new technology is invented that is

---

[36] In Sidney Winter's terms, slow adoption makes survival space less constraining. See S. Winter, "Economic National Selection and the Theory of the Firm," *Yale Economic Essays,* Spring 1964.

α times more productive for every factor mix.[37] At time $t_0 + \theta$ the new technology is first brought into use at a small level. The lag between invention and introduction, θ, may differ across countries. After time $t_0 + \theta$ productivity will be

$$(15) \qquad \left(\frac{Q}{L}\right) = g(w_1, r_1)\frac{L_1}{L} + \alpha g(w_2, r_2)\frac{L_2}{L}.$$

In the formulation above, subscript 1 refers to the old technology and subscript 2 to the new technology.[38] For heuristic reasons, and to link the model of this section with the empirical analysis of the next section, we shall call the new subsector "modern" and the old subsector "craft." The use of the subscript for factor prices indicates that factor prices may differ for firms using the two technologies, although initially they are assumed equal.[39]

Unit costs for the two technologies will be:

$$(16) \qquad\qquad C_1 = h_1(w_1, r_1),$$

and

$$C_2 = h_2(w_2, r_2) = \frac{h_1(w_2, r_2)}{\alpha}$$

[37] The assumption that the superiority of new technology is neutral (with respect to the relative marginal products of labor and capital) is very bothersome. Later we shall present some evidence that the new technology is capital-using relative to the old, but this proves more complex mathematically in the context of the present. Even more important, we should like to introduce a "learning" phenomenon, with the necessity of time elapsing or experience accumulating before the productivity advantages of the new technology are fully realized, and we shall do this later. But, again, for this preliminary model the costs of added complexity seem too high.

[38] The intramanufacturing dualism model obviously has a kinship with the Ranis-Fei agricultural-manufacturing dualism model. G. Ranis and J. Fei, "A Theory of Economic Development." In "The Pareto Distribution and the Cobb-Douglas Production Function in Activity Analysis," *Review of Economic Studies*, Vol. 23(1), No. 60, 1955–1956, pp. 27–31, H. Houthakker has an interesting model of distribution of firms in which, as in the present one, looking at the aggregate obscures what is really going on.

[39] Eq. 15 appears to introduce a logical inconsistency into the model, for the $g(\cdot)$ expression assumes perfect and competitive factor markets, and Eq. 18 explicitly denies it. As with the oversimplifications of this preliminary model, this can be remedied, but with an undesirable increase in complexity. Instead, the apparent inconsistency will be resolved by assuming that, although the factor market is not perfect between the two classes of firms, it is perfect within each class.

where $h_i(\cdot)$ is a linear homogeneous function of factor prices.[40] It is assumed that price is initially equal to C_1 and hence exceeds cost achievable with modern technology.

Instead of assuming full equilibrium throughout the diffusion process, assume rather that the system moves toward equilibrium. Let the rate of expansion (or contraction) of output from a particular technology be proportional to unit profits (or losses).

$$(17) \qquad \left(\frac{\dot{Q}}{Q}\right)_i = \lambda[P - h_i(w_i, r_i)], \qquad \lambda > 0,$$
$$Q_1 + Q_2 = Q$$

where P is the product price. Assume that profitable (and expanding) firms have to pay more for their factors than firms breaking even or losing money (and hence declining). Without specifying at the moment the relative (dynamic) elasticities of supply of the two factors, let the cost equations be

$$(18) \qquad h_i(w_i, r_i) = h_i(\bar{w}, \bar{r}) + b[P - h_i(\bar{w}, \bar{r})],$$
$$0 \le b < 1,$$

where $\bar{w}$ and $\bar{r}$ are the factor prices firms just breaking even have to pay and b is, in a sense, a "sharing" factor determining the split of rents between profits and factor payments. There may or may not be a trend in $\bar{w}$, $\bar{r}$. Like θ, λ and b may differ across countries.

Finally, let the demand equation be

$$(1a) \qquad\qquad P = P(Q), \qquad P' \le 0.$$

As we shall see, either a positive trend in factor prices or a downward sloping demand curve provides the required squeeze on the profitability of "craft technology."

It is easy to see that in the new equilibrium (Q/L) equals $(Q/L)_2$, P equals $[h_1(\bar{w}, \bar{r})/\alpha]$, and craft technology is completely eliminated. If w and r change, this too, of course, would be reflected in the new equilibrium. In any case, real factor returns in terms of

---

[40] A linear homogeneous production function plus cost minimization implies a cost function linear homogeneous in factor prices.

the good in question will be higher in the new equilibrium. All
this is obvious.

What is interesting about the model is what it tells us about
the path to the new equilibrium and characteristics of the industry
along the path.

The relative importance of the craft and modern technology
will be changing as follows:[41]

$$(19) \qquad \frac{d}{dt} \log \left(\frac{Q_2}{Q_1} \right) = \lambda \left[(1 - b) \left(1 - \frac{1}{\alpha} \right) h_1(\bar{w}, \bar{r}) \right].$$

The rate of growth of Q_2 relative to Q_1 will be greater, the greater
is λ, the smaller is b (the sharing factor), and the greater the
efficiency advantage of new technology over old. If we assumed
no change in $\bar{w}$ and $\bar{r}$ and plotted Q_2/Q over time, the curve would
be S-shaped. Specifically, it would be a logistic.

$$(20) \qquad \frac{Q_2}{Q} = \frac{1}{1 + \left(\dfrac{Q_1}{Q_2} \right)_0 e^{-ct}}$$

where $c = \lambda(1 - b)(1 - 1/\alpha)h_1(\bar{w}, \bar{r})$. All these conclusions are
consistent with what we know about diffusion patterns.[42]

As the diffusion process proceeds, productivity will be rising.
If we assume that profitable firms pay either the same factor prices
or more for both factors in the same proportion, then noting that

[41]

$$\frac{d}{dt} \log \left(\frac{Q_2}{Q_1} \right) = \left(\frac{\dot{Q}_2}{Q_2} \right) - \left(\frac{\dot{Q}_1}{Q_1} \right) = \lambda \left[h_1(r_1, w_1) - \frac{h_1}{\alpha} (r_2, w_2) \right]$$

$$= \lambda \left[(1 - b)h_1(\bar{r}, \bar{w}) - (1 - b) \frac{h_1(\bar{r}, \bar{w})}{\alpha} \right]$$

$$= \lambda(1 - b) \left(1 - \frac{1}{\alpha} \right) h_1(\bar{r}, \bar{w}).$$

[42] For a survey, see Nelson, Peck, and Kalachek, *Technology, Economic
Growth, and Public Policy,* Chap. 5. Eq. 2 is derived once one notes
that

$$\frac{Q_2}{Q} = \frac{1}{1 + \dfrac{Q_1}{Q_2}} \qquad \text{and} \qquad \frac{Q_1}{Q_2} = \left(\frac{Q_1}{Q_2} \right)_0 e^{ct}.$$

$g(\cdot)$ is homogeneous of degree zero, the productivity equation has the simple form[43]

(15a) $$\frac{Q}{L} = g(\bar{w},\ \bar{r}) \left[1 + (\alpha - 1) \frac{L_2}{L} \right].$$

But under these assumptions, since Q_2/Q is a logistic, so is L_2/L.[44] Therefore, the time path of productivity will also be a (shifted upward) logistic curve with slow growth initially, then acceleration, and finally a slowing down of the rate of productivity growth as new technology becomes dominant. And under these assumptions productivity growth would be strictly due to growth of total factor productivity. With a constant $\bar{w}$ and $\bar{r}$, and with the same factors price ratios facing both groups of firms, there would be no change at all in the industry capital-labor ratio.

More realistic assumptions about the factor cost adjustment equations blur the neatness of the above result. For example, it seems reasonable to assume that, while the expanding (and profitable) firms have to pay more for labor, they may have an advantage relative to less profitable firms in gaining access to capital. On this assumption, firms using new technology would have a labor productivity differential over firms using the older technology that exceeds α, reflecting their higher capital-labor ratio induced by

43

$$\frac{Q}{L} = g(w_1,\ r_1) \frac{L_1}{L} + \alpha g(w_2,\ r_2) \frac{L_2}{L}.$$

But if $w_i/r_i = \bar{w}/\bar{r}$, then $g(w_i,\ r_i) = g(\bar{w},\ \bar{r})$. Noting that $L_1/L = 1 - (L_2/L)$, Eq. 15a follows.

44

$$\frac{L_2}{L} = \frac{1}{1 + \dfrac{L_1}{L_2}},$$

but

$$\frac{L_1}{L_2} = \frac{\left(\dfrac{Q_2}{L_2}\right) Q_1}{\left(\dfrac{Q_1}{L_1}\right) Q_2} = \alpha \left(\frac{Q_1}{Q_2}\right).$$

Thus L_2/L is the same function as Q_2/Q, except for a different constant before the exponential term.

the higher wage to interest rate ratio they face. In this case, of course, the productivity growth equation is much more complicated, nor can it any longer be assumed that L_2/L and Q_2/Q move in lock step. But the simpler result is quite suggestive.

The diffusion period would be marked by a high capital share, where the returns to capital are defined to include quasi-rents as well as interest. During the diffusion process positive quasi-rents would be made by the modern subsector (pulling its expansion) and negative quasi-rents by the craft subsector (stimulating its contraction), but the former would outweigh the latter. If we let r stand for the average interest rate, capital's share would be[45]

$$(21) \qquad S_K = \frac{rK}{PQ} + \frac{\dot{Q}/Q}{P\lambda}.$$

Notice that quasi-rents (the second term of Equation 21) will be largest when output growth is most rapid and will be negatively related to λ.

Thus far we have assumed that $\bar{r}$ and $\bar{w}$ do not change. It is interesting to augment the model with a mechanism (admittedly somewhat *ad hoc*) that would generate a change. Assume, as earlier, that capital markets are more perfect than labor markets, but now assume in addition that there is a ratchet effect in the labor market. Workers entering the modern subsector are able to force up $\bar{w}$ as well as receive wages temporarily higher than $\bar{w}$.

[45]

$$(1) \qquad S_K = \frac{PQ - w_1L_1 - w_2L_2}{PQ}$$

$$= \frac{PQ - C_1Q_1 - C_2Q_2 + r_1K_1 + r_2K_2}{PQ}$$

(using 16)

$$= \frac{rK}{PQ} + \frac{(P - C_1)Q_1/Q + (P - C_2)Q_2/Q}{P}$$

$$= \frac{rK}{PQ} + \frac{(\dot{Q}_1/Q_1)(Q_1/Q) + (\dot{Q}_2/Q_2)(Q_2/Q)}{P\lambda}$$

(from 17)

$$= \frac{rK}{PQ} + \frac{\dot{Q}/Q}{P\lambda}.$$

This could be the result of an increase in net demand for labor by the industry generally (which would occur if the product demand curve were elastic), or the formation of strong unions perhaps backed by government legislation, or both. Note that the high quasi-rents of the modern subsector, during the diffusion process, provide room for this to occur without causing losses, although, of course, the result would be a smaller growth of output and smaller decline of price over the diffusion period. Note also (from Equation 19) that such a process would actually speed up diffusion by putting more pressure on the craft subsector.[46] Thus one might assume

$$(22) \qquad \frac{d}{dt}\,\bar{w} = Z\left(S_K - \frac{rK}{PQ}\right), \qquad Z' > 0.$$

If we assume that $\bar{r}$ does not change, this mechanism will induce an increase in the capital-labor ratio. The resulting increase in output per worker would augment that due to growth of total factor productivity. But the growth in the capital-labor ratio would itself be the result of the dynamics of the diffusion process. Rising wage rates would spur it. High profits would finance it.

The above model is extremely simplified and in many ways misspecified.[47] However, it does seem to capture the spirit of a

---

[46] The phenomenon that an increase in factor costs stimulates more rapid diffusion obtains. See, for example, H. J. Habakkuk, *American and British Technology of the Nineteenth Century,* Cambridge University Press, Cambridge, 1962.

[47] First, as mentioned earlier, the assumption that new technology is neutrally better than old is very bothersome. There is considerable reason to believe that technology invented in the high-wage countries is labor saving. Perhaps this could be handled by having the shift factor be a function of factor prices; thus $\alpha(w/r)$, $\alpha' > 0$. This implies (as seems reasonable) that new technology has less of a cost-saving advantage in low-wage than high-wage countries. In addition, one would like to incorporate some kind of a learning function. Both of these modifications will be introduced later.

Second, the (implicit) assumption of independent national markets should be relaxed. One effect of some countries introducing the new technology earlier may be to exert downward pressure on price in the other countries as well. This modification, perhaps, could be handled by introducing a shift factor to the demand curve.

Third, the assumption of the same λ for expanding and declining firms or, more generally, that of a "portional" adjustment mechanism should be dropped and replaced by a more sophisticated relationship.

Fourth, for many purposes one would want to drop the assumption

diffusion point of view with respect to international productivity differences, and it certainly generates some interesting implications regarding differences between less and more developed countries.

Consider, for example, two countries that long ago had roughly equal output per worker and factor prices. One is "highly developed" in the sense that the diffusion process started a long time ago (θ is small) and is complete or nearly complete, the other "underdeveloped" in that the diffusion process started only recently (large θ) and is characterized by a small λ and a large b. Assume the product is traded internationally and world prices obtain in both countries. Further, assume that r is roughly the same in both countries because of international capital mobility. Productivity per worker would be higher in the more developed country. So would w and the capital-labor ratio. Part of the productivity and wage difference would reflect the higher capital-labor ratio, but the difference would be greater than the capital-labor ratio difference could explain. This would show up when the factor price frontier was considered. If the elasticity of substitution between capital and labor was not greater than one, the wage share would be higher in the more developed countries. An econometrician fitting a CES would ascribe the difference to a less than unitary elasticity of substitution, but a large share of it would not be due to that but to the existence of large quasi-rents in the less developed country. Only if one disaggregated would one find that a key factor explaining the productivity differentials would be the existence in the less developed countries of a large subsector of firms using older technology, firms of the type that had been largely eliminated

---

of just two competing technologies and consider a steady flow of new technology. Formally this is not hard to do. But the resulting complication of the model appears to make drawing of sharp implications very difficult.

Fifth, the model would be significantly enriched by a more explicit modeling of factor markets, in particular, analysis of the determinants of $\bar{w}$ and $\bar{r}$. One might want to relate movements in $\bar{w}$ to shifts in demand for labor relative to supply domestically and perhaps assume $\bar{r}$ is constant and equal in all countries reflecting international capital mobility. But if one were to go in this direction, one would have to be more explicit about the factor demand implications of the profit pull adjustment Eq. 17. Probably one would want to pose Eq. 17 explicitly in terms of incremental demand for factors as a function of differences between their marginal value product and their price. This, like the modification above, seriously complicates the model.

in the more developed countries. One also would find a "dual" wage structure in the less developed country.

In short, the diffusion model seems capable of quite easily accounting for certain phenomena that the neoclassical model has trouble explaining. It also generates some other specific implications of considerable interest.

Dualism in Colombian Industry

The ideas presented in the preceding section can be made more concrete, and evidence provided to support them, by an examination in detail of some of the differences between the United States and Colombia in value added per worker in manufacturing.[48] As reported earlier, in 1964 productivity in Colombian industry averaged about one-quarter that of the United States. This was roughly the same ratio as obtained in 1958, and it will be convenient to orient the discussion around 1958 data. The year 1958 provides a vantage point from which one can look forward as well as backward. Table 22 presents comparative data by industry.

These are the kinds of observations the model discussed in an earlier section of this chapter purports to explain. But Table 22, which shows great variation in productivity among firms within an industry, particularly between large and small firms, suggests that the model is inapplicable. Its "representative firm" implication is clearly violated. We want to argue that the point of view of a diffusion model is much more consistent with the data and, further, that the relatively simple "two technologies" version of this theory explains the pattern of productivity differences in Colombia surprisingly well.[49]

Colombia's recent economic history certainly reads as if it were generated by a "two technology" diffusion process. With the exception of a few industries (textile mill products and certain parts of the food processing industry), Colombia's adoption of modern technology did not really begin until after World War II. This did not mean that Colombia had no firms in other industries. In

---

[48] For a more complete analysis, see R. Nelson, *A Study of Industrialization in Colombia: Part I, Analysis.*

[49] The following presentation should be clearly recognized as an attempt to establish the reasonableness and heuristic utility of a point of view, without doing violence to the data, rather than an unbiased weighing of evidence pro and con.

1944 about 135,000 people were recorded as being employed in Colombian industry, and there were a number of firms in all two-digit industries.[50] However, it appears that in most industries virtually all firms were craft or semi-craft in their technology, producing for a local or regional market and protected by high transport costs and the absence of a modern distribution system. In the early postwar period many factors, including the improvement in transport, the import shortage experience of World War II, and the ready availability of foreign exchange due to good coffee prices, increased the perceived profitability of establishing modern industry. The resulting wave of industrialization was super-imposed upon the traditional structure of craft industry.[51]

By the late 1950s, when coffee prices broke and industrial growth slowed until it was renewed by foreign credit, most Colombian industries contained two roughly separable groups of firms. One group, generally newcomers or old firms that had transformed themselves, consisted of firms that were roughly similar to typical firms in the same industry in more developed countries. These firms were somewhat smaller, with somewhat lower value added per worker, capital per worker, and labor quality, than firms in the same industry in a developed country, but they were using roughly the same kind of technology. The other group was composed of the traditional small craft firms using significantly less modern equipment, employing quite different (and less related to formal education) labor skills, and creating far lower value added per worker. To a considerable degree these two groups produced different products. Within the so-called metal-products industry, the craft firms produced pots and pans; the more modern firms produced some parts for, and assembled, washing machines and refrigerators. But in some industries there was more direct competition. Craft firms produced shoes and furniture largely by hand or with simple power tools; modern firms produced similar products

---

[50] See the United Nations, *The Growth of World Industry: National Tables,* Vol. I, New York, 1963.

[51] For a discussion of the industrialization process in the early and mid-1950s, see the United Nations, *Analysis and Projections of Economic Development, Part III: The Economic Development of Colombia,* Geneva, 1957, and L. Currie *et al., The Basis of a Development Program for Colombia,* published for the International Bank for Reconstruction and Development, Baltimore, 1950.

TABLE 22
VALUE ADDED PER WORKER BY FIRM SIZE AND INDUSTRY, UNITED STATES AND COLOMBIA, 1958[a]
(in 1958 U.S. dollars)

Industry	Average Value Added	Firm Size (employees)					
		1-9	10-19	20-49	50-99	100-249	250+
United States							
Food	$10,321	$ 8,326	$ 7,859	$ 8,753	$ 9,979	$10,277	$11,691
Tobacco	16,733	4,833	2,886	7,038	6,286	7,404	19,338
Textiles	5,387	8,842	7,017	6,038	5,562	5,549	5,172
Clothing and footwear	5,086	8,853	6,922	5,386	4,659	4,424	4,878
Lumber	5,465	4,330	4,252	5,308	5,855	6,117	6,265
Furniture	6,759	6,788	6,449	6,477	6,627	6,521	7,144
Paper and paper products	10,276	7,979	4,479	7,793	8,704	9,588	11,237
Printing	9,169	8,100	7,798	8,329	8,883	9,362	9,962
Chemicals	17,550	12,126	12,474	13,333	14,387	16,776	19,189
Petroleum	14,056	14,108	13,561	12,454	12,033	17,408	13,773
Rubber products	9,420	8,143	7,741	8,112	8,009	8,167	10,157
Leather products	5,436	7,235	5,883	5,532	5,388	5,234	5,442
Nonmetallic minerals	9,979	8,757	8,620	8,894	8,634	10,627	10,763
Basic metals	10,646	7,866	7,495	7,726	8,697	8,877	11,185
Metal products	8,896	8,308	8,038	8,234	8,642	8,878	9,320
Machinery, excl. elec.	9,191	8,852	8,326	8,816	9,032	9,208	9,351
Electrical machinery	9,263	8,114	7,930	8,067	8,038	8,421	9,551
Transportation equipment	9,811	7,727	7,553	8,082	8,110	8,418	10,002
Other	8,320	7,500	6,777	6,735	6,581	7,189	9,432

TABLE 22 (*Continued*)

Industry	Average Value Added	Firm Size (employees)					
		1–9	10–19	20–49	50–99	100–199	200+
Colombia							
Food	$ 2,029	$ 1,019	$ 1,177	$ 2,177	$ 2,330	$ 3,526	$ 2,837
Beverages	5,187	1,308	1,519	2,053	6,019	7,124	4,826
Tobacco	7,153	416	556	986	2,971	12,243	17,575
Textiles	1,967	560	1,282	1,105	1,363	1,436	2,174
Clothing and footwear	826	600	670	720	831	960	1,414
Lumber	864	828	811	927	797	640	1,104
Furniture	890	782	684	856	975	1,028	1,511
Paper and paper products	1,958	1,230	1,223	1,993	1,611	884	3,027
Printing	1,403	869	803	1,601	1,834	1,335	1,762
Chemicals	2,983	1,863	1,562	2,818	2,667	3,364	3,855
Petroleum	6,578	3,961	3,973	2,681	—	—	7,105
Rubber products	2,185	1,047	1,475	1,256	1,403	—	2,335
Leather products	1,379	838	1,020	1,029	832	1,018	2,433
Nonmetallic minerals	1,276	578	679	857	1,235	1,141	2,117
Basic metals	1,914	1,027	2,436	2,052	1,040	2,128	1,954
Metal products	1,304	818	871	1,356	1,313	1,233	2,347
Machinery, excl. elec.	1,172	832	943	1,105	1,076	—	1,946
Electrical machinery	1,959	945	1,062	1,669	2,325	1,689	2,777
Transportation equipment	949	746	930	1,026	1,081	1,030	961
Other	1,687	1,052	1,117	1,685	2,019	1,782	1,939

NOTES:
—means "no observations reported."
[a] Exchange rate: 6.9 pesos = 1 dollar.

SOURCES:
United States——U.S. Department of Commerce, *1958 Census of Manufactures* (USA), *General Summary*, Washington, D.C., 1961.
Colombia——DANE.

using much more power equipment and a mass production organization of work. In any case, craft firms and more modern firms were included in almost every two- or three-digit industry, and it is differences across countries at the two- or three-digit level that so much recent research has sought to explain.[52]

In part the survival of a significant craft sector in Colombia can be explained by neoclassical considerations. The differences between modern and craft technology do not appear to be neutral, the former requiring much more capital and skilled labor than the latter. Thus craft technology is economically more viable in a country where unskilled and uneducated workers are cheap relative to educated workers and capital.

But a good part of the explanation seems consistent with the diffusion model rather than the neoclassical model. The late start is clear. Shortages of skilled managers and technicians clearly limited the pace of the adoption process after it started out, and at least after the mid-1950s, adoption of modern technology was limited by foreign exchange.[53] Particularly where markets were protected from foreign competition by restrictions or transport costs, there was room in domestic demand for craft firms to survive. Finally, survival was facilitated by factor market imperfections. Minimum wage legislation and labor union organization kept wages high in the modern subsector but did not extend effectively to small craft firms. As shown in Table 23, wage rates in the large firms in an industry were typically three times or more than those in small ones. Small craft firms thus had a significant labor cost advantage.[54] Partially compensating for this, however, was the apparent advantage that large firms had over small ones in access to capital. Although we have been unable to develop any systematic data to prove this, the point seems generally agreed upon by everyone familiar with Colombian industry.

[52] See C. Diaz-Alejandro, "Industrialization and Labor Productivity Differentials," *Review of Economics and Statistics,* Vol. 47, No. 2, May 1965, pp. 207–214, and E. Staley and R. Morse, *Modern Small Industry for Developing Countries,* McGraw-Hill, New York, 1965, for evidence of dualism in other less developed countries.

[53] For a more complete discussion, see R. Nelson, *A Study of Industrialization in Colombia: Part I, Analysis.*

[54] *Ibid.* The association of "large" with "modern" and "small" with "craft" will be justified later.

TABLE 23
WAGE RATES BY INDUSTRY AND FIRM SIZE
IN COLOMBIA, 1958
(in pesos)

Industry	Average	\multicolumn{6}{c}{Firm Size (employees)}					

Industry	Average	1–9	10–19	20–49	50–99	100–199	200+
Food	3,193	1,957	2,504	3,174	3,570	3,446	4,569
Beverages	5,627	2,561	3,142	4,100	5,365	5,854	6,186
Tobacco	3,791	938	1,184	1,426	2,836	5,725	7,245
Textiles	4,118	1,789	2,982	3,006	3,439	3,238	4,388
Clothing and footwear	2,433	2,000	2,129	2,225	2,513	2,679	3,289
Lumber	2,792	2,589	2,641	2,907	2,811	2,494	3,321
Furniture	3,297	3,704	2,899	3,216	3,557	3,578	4,704
Paper and paper products	4,452	2,908	3,014	3,291	4,253	2,648	6,898
Printing	4,247	2,730	3,259	3,782	5,419	4,764	5,057
Chemicals	4,710	2,906	3,174	4,696	4,629	5,096	5,391
Petroleum	12,288	2,889	4,430	7,885	—	—	13,087
Rubber products	4,993	2,707	3,114	3,867	4,039	—	5,253
Leather and leather prod.	3,436	2,128	2,461	2,983	2,964	3,653	4,615
Nonmetallic minerals	3,266	1,992	2,337	2,677	3,109	3,367	4,379
Basic metals	5,431	3,118	3,533	3,619	3,759	6,932	5,881
Metal products	3,605	2,613	2,888	3,721	4,052	3,535	4,540
Machinery, excl. elec.	3,895	3,213	3,438	3,918	4,294	—	4,571
Electrical machinery	3,994	2,947	3,628	3,827	3,828	3,599	4,871
Transportation equip.	4,500	2,791	3,310	4,356	4,505	4,541	5,414
Other	4,180	3,529	3,584	3,673	3,881	3,478	6,587

NOTE:
—means "no observations reported."
SOURCE:
DANE.

Let us consider various empirical implications of the dualism model. First, differences in value added per worker between the countries should be a function of the relative size (as measured by percent of employment) of the craft subsector in Colombia. Second, reasonably well-managed firms using modern technology should be earning a very high rate of return, even when paying wage rates significantly higher than the average in Colombia. Third, the situation in Colombia should be in flux; the modern sector should be expanding relative to the craft sector and driving it out of business in some fields.

Before we test any of these implications it is, of course, necessary to identify the craft and modern subsectors. In our discussion above

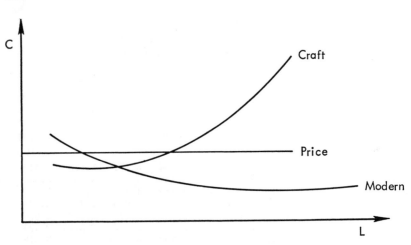

7. Unit Cost per Worker by Firm Size

we have been implicitly assuming that small firms tend to be craft
and large firms tend to be modern in Colombian industry. The
model presented earlier implies nothing of this kind. But there
are two basic reasons why one might expect this. First, economies
of scale are likely to be more important for modern technology
than for craft technology.[55] Thus the efficiency advantage of modern technology would be larger for big firms than for small. Second,
one would expect the advantages of modern technology to be
greater at a high capital-labor ratio than at low ones.[56] Given that
wage rates tend to rise and capital access tends to improve with
size, the former penalize modern firms at large firm size less than
craft firms, and the latter benefits modern more than craft firms.
Conversely, the low wage rates at small firm size benefit craft more
than modern firms.

Both of these factors would tend to lead to the distribution of
technologies by firm size that we are assuming. It can easily be
shown that these assumptions can lead to unit cost curves, as a
function of firm size, that take the shapes of those in Figure 7.
With economies of scale and access to capital less important, and
rising wage costs more detrimental to craft than to modern firms,

[55] In the model prescribed earlier, there were constant returns to scale
for both modern and craft technologies.
[56] In the model, modern technology was assumed neutrally better than
craft.

profitable operation of craft firms would tend to be limited to relatively small units. With economies of scale and access to capital more important, and high labor costs less detrimental to modern than to craft firms, profitable operation of modern firms would tend to require a certain minimal size. The result is that, at the small end of the spectrum, we would expect to find most firms to be of the craft variety and, at the large end, would expect modern firms to predominate.

This model seems to correspond quite well to the intuitions and judgments of people knowledgeable about Colombian industry. In addition, there is some empirical evidence that is consistent with the model.

When production functions are fitted to the large and small firms separately in Colombian industries, the elasticity of output with respect to capital generally tended to be significantly higher for large firms than for small.[57] It is not only that large firms operated with a higher capital-labor ratio than small firms, which they did; this one would expect simply because of the higher wage rates they faced. It is that, even at this higher capital-labor ratio, the elasticity of output with respect to capital was larger for large firms. If one assumes that within a technology the elasticity of substitution is not greater than one, this result implies that, on the average, the large firms in an industry were using a different, more capital-intensive technology than small firms.

Further, if the analysis is roughly correct, one would expect to find much greater differences in output per worker between large and small firms in Colombia than in the United States, where the craft firm subsector has been largely eliminated even in the small firm group. This is, in fact, the case. Table 22 presents the data for 1958; data for 1964 will be presented later. Notice that in the United States, with the striking exception of the tobacco products industry (where the giant firms are highly mechanized cigarette companies and the smaller firms cigar manufacturers), although value added per worker is positively related to size, value added per worker in the giant firms is seldom more than 50 percent larger than in the smaller firms. In Colombia, on the other hand,

---

[57] E. Mansfield and R. Nelson, *Production Functions for a Dual Industrial Structure: Colombian Manufacturing*, P-4150, The Rand Corporation, Santa Monica, July 1969.

TABLE 24

RATIO OF COLOMBIAN VALUE ADDED PER WORKER TO
U.S. VALUE ADDED PER WORKER, BY INDUSTRY AND
FIRM SIZE, 1958

Industry	Firm Size (employees)						
	Average	1–9	10–19	20–49	50–99	100–199[a]	200+[a]
Food[b]	.28	.12	.15	.25	.30	.52	.33
Tobacco	.43	.09	.19	.14	.47	1.65	.91
Textiles	.37	.06	.18	.18	.25	.26	.42
Clothing and footwear	.16	.07	.10	.13	.18	.22	.29
Lumber	.16	.19	.19	.18	.14	.11	.18
Furniture	.13	.12	.11	.13	.15	.16	.21
Paper and paper products	.19	.15	.27	.26	.19	.09	.27
Printing	.15	.11	.10	.19	.21	.14	.18
Chemicals	.17	.15	.13	.21	.19	.20	.20
Petroleum	.47	.28	.29	.22	—	—	.52
Rubber and rubber prod.	.23	.13	.19	.16	.18	—	.23
Leather products	.25	.12	.17	.19	.15	.20	.45
Nonmetallic minerals	.13	.07	.08	.10	.14	.11	.20
Basic metals	.18	.13	.33	.27	.12	.24	.18
Metal products	.15	.10	.11	.17	.15	.14	.25
Machinery, excl. elec.	.13	.09	.11	.13	.12	—	.21
Electrical machinery	.21	.12	.13	.21	.29	.20	.29
Transportation equipment	.10	.10	.12	.13	.13	.12	.10

NOTES:
— means "no observations reported."
[a] U.S. size groups are actually 100–249 and 250 and up.
[b] U.S. includes food and kindred products; Colombia, food and beverage industries combined
SOURCE:
Table 22.

the difference in value added per worker between large and small firms tends to be substantial.

Thus, as a first approximation at least, the association of craft with small and large with modern seems valid.[58] With this association it is possible to test three implications of the diffusion model.

To permit testing of the first implication, that Colombian productivity relative to that in the United States should be a function of the relative size of the modern subsector, Table 24 presents

[58] Richard Cooper has suggested another interpretation. The large firms in an industry tend to be able to get strong effective protection for their products, hence charge very high prices, and their high value added per worker largely reflects monopoly rents.

value added per worker in Colombia as a fraction of that in the United States by industry and by firm size within an industry. Notice how much closer the large Colombian firms were to their U.S. counterparts in terms of value added per worker than were the small Colombian firms. In industries where value added per worker in Colombia was a relatively large percentage of that in the United States, two conditions tended to hold. First, the ratio was .4 or greater for large firms (suggesting similar technology). Second, employment in these firms constituted a large share of total employment (see Table 25). Where Colombian value added per worker was small as a fraction of that in the United States, the large Colombian firms did poorly relative to U.S. firms (suggesting that many of them were not using modern technology), or employment in large firms was a small fraction of the total in the industry, or both.[59]

Regarding the second implication, the high rate of return in firms using modern technology, interviews with Colombian accountants suggest that real net rates of return on capital of 30 to 40 percent or more are typical for large firms. That this rate should be substantially higher than the average rate of return on capital in manufacturing in the developed countries is quite consistent with the difficulty (and high exchange transfer costs) of capital export.

A high rate of return in the large modern firms, together with access to credit at reasonable terms, would provide a strong inducement for the modern manufacturing sector to expand—the third implication of the dualism model. As mentioned earlier, the fall in export earnings greatly slowed Colombian manufacturing growth in the mid-1950s. By 1958, however, various foreign loans permitted a new surge of intermediate and capital goods imports and industrial growth. The pattern of post-1958 growth shown in Table 26 is revealing. Firms of over 200 employees, which in 1958 accounted for about 35 percent of employment, accounted for over 65 percent of the increase in employment achieved by the manufacturing sector as a whole between 1958 and 1964. They accounted for roughly the same percentage of the increase in value

---

[59] Again, there is the alternative interpretation of differing degrees of protection.

TABLE 25

DISTRIBUTION OF COLOMBIAN LABOR FORCE BY INDUSTRY AND FIRM SIZE, 1958 AND 1964

(percent of totals)

Industry	Firm Size (employees)											
	1-9		10-19		20-49		50-99		100-199		200+	
	1958	1964	1958	1964	1958	1964	1958	1964	1958	1964	1958	1964
Total industry	13.8	12.2	11.1	9.8	15.9	13.0	11.8	11.7	11.9	12.7	35.5	40.6
Food	23.8	23.9	14.5	13.6	19.2	15.2	16.0	11.4	10.6	12.1	15.9	23.8
Beverages	3.5	2.9	3.1	2.7	8.6	5.6	9.4	7.5	31.1	27.2	44.2	54.1
Tobacco	15.8	14.9	13.3	11.8	18.8	11.3	12.1	11.2	10.3	12.8	29.6	37.9
Textiles	2.6	2.4	2.5	2.4	5.7	6.1	4.0	4.6	6.6	5.7	78.5	78.8
Clothing and footwear	23.2	22.6	14.7	13.7	21.5	15.8	15.8	16.7	10.6	9.4	14.2	21.8
Lumber	30.1	22.7	22.9	15.3	12.9	14.0	13.2	6.6	5.8	13.4	15.2	28.0
Furniture	28.4	29.9	19.4	18.5	21.0	22.8	10.4	9.8	12.4	5.2	8.3	13.7
Paper and paper products	3.1	2.6	9.3	8.8	21.5	16.0	18.2	13.0	17.1	16.9	30.9	42.8
Printing	13.3	11.6	15.4	16.0	19.6	17.5	7.2	8.7	15.5	13.6	28.9	32.6
Chemicals	8.6	6.7	8.8	5.7	17.3	14.9	19.4	15.2	18.1	23.0	27.8	34.4
Petroleum	.5	2.7	3.3	3.3	9.2	4.6	0	5.7	0	9.4	87.0	74.3
Rubber products	1.7	1.5	5.6	2.7	5.7	8.9	2.1	4.9	0	0	85.0	82.1
Leather products	15.8	19.2	11.6	14.2	14.3	12.1	12.4	6.9	16.8	17.1	29.1	30.4
Nonmetallic minerals	14.2	13.1	13.9	10.2	16.8	13.0	8.8	11.1	13.6	10.0	32.7	42.5
Basic metals	2.4	.6	4.9	6.1	10.6	1.8	7.7	5.9	10.7	20.0	63.7	65.6
Metal products	12.2	8.5	15.0	11.6	28.3	19.3	15.1	20.6	17.9	16.3	11.6	23.7
Machinery, excl. elec.	18.5	16.5	22.1	17.5	24.7	18.9	15.8	15.8	0	6.6	18.8	24.7
Electrical machinery	10.4	5.9	11.4	9.3	21.4	12.2	21.5	15.8	8.9	16.5	26.4	40.3
Transportation equip.	15.8	12.5	12.6	13.4	15.0	11.1	9.5	13.1	6.7	10.1	40.4	39.7
Other	9.7	9.5	14.0	10.6	19.5	21.6	25.9	25.0	14.4	23.1	16.6	10.2

SOURCE:
DANE.

TABLE 26
Distribution of Colombian Labor Force
by Firm Size, 1958–1964

Year	Total	Firm Size (employees)					
		1–9	10–19	20–49	50–99	100–199	200+
1958	236,748	32,569	26,341	37,672	27,985	28,077	84,104
1959	248,540	30,938	25,863	37,741	30,183	31,301	92,514
1960	254,000	30,150	24,917	37,460	29,238	31,190	101,045
1961	264,107	30,931	25,201	39,197	31,313	31,726	105,739
1962	277,012	32,051	26,427	40,604	31,870	34,695	111,365
1963	280,520	33,252	26,792	37,321	33,794	35,638	113,723
1964	283,841	34,767	27,697	36,885	33,121	36,157	115,214

Source:
DANE.

added. These very large firms, together with those in the 100–200 employee range, accounted for about 75 percent of the growth in employment and output over the 1958–1964 period.[60]

At the same time there was a significant relative decline in employment in small firms. As employment in firms of over 200 expanded from 35 to 50 percent of the total, employment in firms of under 50 fell from 41 to 35 percent. As the percentage of value added in large firms increased from 49 to 54, that in small firms decreased from 23 to 17.[61]

Table 25 shows that these phenomena were pervasive. In most Colombian industries there was a significant increase in the percentage of employment accounted for by large firms and a decrease in small firms. The phenomena were particularly apparent in such industries as metal products, where growth of output and employment were particularly great and the percentage of employment in large firms initially was quite small.

Because the bulk of employment and output increases between

---

[60] Obviously, there are two phenomena at work here: entry of new large firms and expansion of existing large ones, and the expansion of firms that initially were middle-sized into the large firm class. The discussion above assumes that the first is the dominant phenomenon. Although we cannot prove this thesis, various pieces of evidence support it.

[61] Again, the interpretation is that the percentage did *not* decline because the small firms grew out of their initial size class.

TABLE 27
PRODUCTIVITY GROWTH BY FIRM SIZE (VALUE ADDED
PER WORKER), 1958–1964
(thousands of 1963 pesos)

	Firm Size (employees)						
Year	Total	1–9	10–19	20–49	50–99	100–199	200+
1958	26.01	11.02	12.75	19.12	24.47	36.81	35.96
1959	27.30	10.70	13.49	19.29	24.79	39.22	36.76
1960	28.60	11.57	14.51	19.75	25.83	40.19	37.67
1961	29.28	11.40	14.98	20.55	28.07	42.06	37.67
1962	30.41	12.37	15.44	20.99	25.90	43.85	39.70
1963	31.25	9.93	14.34	21.13	27.02	45.87	41.47
1964	32.83	10.05	14.80	23.54	30.31	46.97	43.29

SOURCE:
DANE.

1958 and 1964 were accounted for by the large firms, there was a substantial increase in average productivity that was independent of productivity increases in individual firms. Roughly one-fifth of the increase in value added per worker achieved over the period was the result of a shift in the composition of the work force toward the higher productivity (larger) firms and away from the small craft firms.[62] The shift was a particularly important contributor to productivity growth in the food processing industry (about 30 percent), tobacco products (25 percent), lumber and wood products (productivity would have fallen without the shift), furniture (35 percent), paper (35 percent), chemicals (most of the total), nonmetallic minerals (30 percent), and metal products (more than half).

In addition, as shown in Table 27, productivity growth in the large (greater than 100 employees) and medium-sized (50 to 100) firms tended to be significantly greater than in the small firms; indeed, productivity in the smallest firms would appear to have declined over the period. Thus the productivity gap between large

[62] The contribution of the shift to productivity growth was measured by the increase in output that would have been achieved if the 1964 distribution of employment by firm size had existed in 1958 and if the productivity of firms of different sizes as of 1958 had been maintained.

and small firms actually widened. These phenomena were pervasive, occurring in most industries.

Productivity growth in the large and medium-sized firms probably reflects three factors: a growing percentage of these firms using modern technology, the incorporation of more modern or more equipment per worker in the already modernized firms, and a growth of experience in operation by both management and labor.[63] In contrast, craft technology and productivity tended to be static.

Most of the surge of expansion of employment in manufacturing and in the large firm subsector occurred between 1958 and 1962. During this period, when employment growth in manufacturing averaged over 3 percent a year, firms of over 100 employees accounted for better than 90 percent of the total increase. Employment in firms of under 20 workers actually fell. Since 1962 there has been a significant decline in the rate of growth in manufacturing employment. In the period 1962–1964 the rate of growth of employment in manufacturing was estimated to be only about 1.5 percent a year. This was mainly the result of the drastic decline in the rate of employment growth in large firms, from about 5 percent a year to about 1.5 percent. At the same time employment in the smallest firms began to expand again. During the 1961–1966 period there would also appear to have been a significant rise in urban unemployment, suggesting that in considerable part the resurgence of employment (and self-employment) in the craft sector reflects the desperate effort of people to find any kind of work.

In the following chapter we shall examine the urban unemployment and income distribution picture in some detail. In Chapter VI we shall study the root cause of the problem—the shortage of foreign exchange.

---

[63] This learning phenomenon is ignored in the sample model presented earlier.

CHAPTER V

Urban Income Distribution in a Dual Economy

THE BASIC HYPOTHESIS

The preceding chapter presented a model of the development of the manufacturing sector in which the transition process was marked by the coexistence of a subsector consisting of modern, relatively efficient firms paying relatively high wages with a traditional subsector operating at much lower productivity and wage levels. The process of development involves the growth of the former and the decline of the latter. In addition, the productivity gap between the two subsectors, initially large, tends to widen. This reflects the exploitation of scale economies, learning, and technological progress in the modern subsector juxtaposed against a relatively static level of craft technology and efficiency. As shown in the preceding chapter, such a phenomenon is clearly characteristic of manufacturing development in Colombia.

We think that this model also suggests certain interesting hypotheses regarding the evolution of urban income distribution in the course of development. This chapter is concerned with drawing out and testing these inferences.

Given the vast accumulation of literature on the process of economic development, it is surprising that so little theoretical work has been done on the subject of income distribution. Part of the reason undoubtedly is the aggregative nature of most development models. Although these models can deal with the distribution of income by factor type (capital versus labor, for example), they can get at the equality or inequality of the income distribution only through subsidiary hypotheses about the distribution of factor ownership. In addition, these models tend to suppress what we feel to be the essential characteristics of the dualism phenomenon. As pointed out earlier, our dualism model is a relative of the models of Lewis, Ranis and Fei, and Jorgenson.[1] However, these

---

[1] A. Lewis, "Development with Unlimited Supplies of Labor," *The Manchester School*, Vol. 22, May 1954; J. Fei and G. Ranis, *Development of the Labor Surplus Economy*, Irwin, Homewood, Ill., 1964; and D. Jorgen-

models specify the dualism in terms of an agriculture-manufacturing split and repress intrasector dualism. Yet this, we want to argue, lies at the heart of the income distribution dynamics in a developing economy.

Our basic hypothesis is that the introduction of a modern sector on top of the traditional craft sector, and the widening of the productivity gap between the two, present the potential for a growing inequality of the distribution of urban income.[2] This increase in inequality is more likely to take the form of a reduction in the income share of the lower half of the distribution of income recipients than an increase in the share of the very highest income brackets. The major beneficiaries of this change are likely to be the members of (say) the eighth and ninth deciles (counting from the bottom). In short, what is commonly identified as the "middle" and "lower-middle" class will increase in relative size. This normally is thought of as the genesis of greater equality in income distribution. But if the extent of competition faced by producers in the modern subsector is limited, and if for various reasons the pace at which the modern sector can expand employment is not much larger than the growth of the working force, the introduction of a productive and progressive modern sector may split apart the urban income structure. Where the growth of the modern sector is strongly constrained, as has been the case in Colombia in the 1960s, both the wage differential and the relative size of the low-

---

son, "The Development of a Dual Economy," *Economic Journal,* Vol. 71, June 1961.

[2] This can be viewed as an extension of the hypothesis offered by Kuznets that increased inequality of income distribution over time is likely in the early stage of economic growth if the high-productivity, relatively unequal industrial sector expands relative to the low-productivity, relatively equal agricultural sector. An additional point is that in the early stages of growth the inequality of distribution of income in the urban sector is also likely to increase. Thus, where growth of the sectors of high productivity has skill or foreign exchange constraints, the shift of workers out of agriculture (perhaps spurred by an acceleration of the rate of growth of population) will not, in general, be a shift from low- to high-productivity (and income) employment, but a shift from one type of low-productivity employment to another (or to unemployment). For a statement of the original hypothesis, see S. Kuznets, "Quantitative Aspects of the Economic Growth of Nations, VII: Distribution of Income by Size," *Economic Development and Cultural Change,* Vol. 11, No. 2, Jan. 1963.

income craft sector will increase. The result is a substantial decrease in the equality of distribution of income.

This need not happen. If the modern sector faces strong competition, it may be forced to take out productivity gains in lower prices rather than higher factor incomes. If the modern sector is not in direct competition with the craft sector, the real-income benefits of high and rising productivity then will be widely spread. If the modern sector can and does grow rapidly and labor force growth is not excessive, the effect may be to lift up the entire income distribution by having a rapidly growing percentage of the work force employed at high productivity. But if, as in Colombia, there is virtually no competition within the modern sector, if the modern and craft sectors are partially competitive, if, for a variety of reasons, the growth rate of employment in the modern sector is quite slow, and if population is growing rapidly, the phenomenon we first described will come about.

The discussion thus far has been posed in terms of percentage employment in, and wage rate differentials between, the craft and the modern sectors. There is, however, a second dimension to the income distribution problem: overt urban unemployment.

A continuing high percentage of employment in stagnant low-wage craft activities cannot be separated sharply from unemployment. Where employment opportunities in the high-wage modern subsector are growing slowly relative to labor force growth, craft employment and unemployment blur into each other. As we shall discuss shortly, a large share of employment in the craft or traditional sectors is not on a contractual wage basis. Since a considerable portion is self-employment or family operation, there is scope for unemployment to take the form of partial unemployment. Nonetheless, the growth of the Colombian labor force relative to the change in the demand for labor has been sufficiently large to result in an increase in overt unemployment, and this is an important part of the income distribution picture.

In the following sections we shall consider first income distribution among the employed, then overt unemployment, and finally some important interactions between the splitting apart of the wage structure and the rate of growth of the modern sector.

The Distribution of Labor Income[3]

changes by sector

One way of partially checking the hypothesis outlined in the preceding section is to examine changes in income per worker and employment, by sector, over a period of a decade or so. To the extent that sectors differ in terms of their degree of modernity and the rankings do not change over the period in question, the argument is: first, sectors can be expected to differ significantly in growth of income per worker; second, sectors that initially have relatively high income levels can be expected to experience relatively high growth rates of incomes per worker; third, these latter sectors are not likely to experience relatively high growth rates of employment.

Data on the sectoral distribution of the labor force in Colombia are available only for the census years 1951 and 1964. National accounts data on total income by sector are available on a yearly basis. Although there are a number of difficulties with the data, two in particular seemed serious enough for us to try to correct for them. First, it is clear that the national accounts data on value added in manufacturing exclude the output of most of those employed in craft manufacturing. Table 28 is thus based on "official" figures adjusted for our own estimates of the value added in the excluded sector of craft manufacturing.[4] Second, a significant share of Colombian workers are self-employed, or work on a semi-partnership basis, particularly in small firms. Thus the wage and salary

---

[3] For a more complete discussion of the evidence on changes in income distribution in the urban sector of Colombia, see R. Slighton, *Relative Wages, Skill Shortages, and Changes in Income Distribution in Colombia*, RM-5651-RC/AID, The Rand Corporation, Santa Monica, Oct. 1968.

[4] According to the national accounts, value added in manufacturing has recently run about 15 percent less than value added in manufacturing, as estimated by the Departamento Administrativo de Estadistica (DANE). Yet the DANE data cover only about 40 percent of the labor force engaged in manufacturing as defined in the 1964 Census. Virtually all of the omitted output derives from craft manufacturing, and virtually all of value added in craft manufacturing is omitted from the national accounts. It is thus necessary to supplement the official figures with private estimates of the excluded output. Our adjustments are based on DANE data on output per worker in firms of the smallest size classes and the difference between DANE and census figures on the volume of employment in manufacturing.

TABLE 28
AVERAGE LABOR INCOME PER SALARIED EMPLOYEE BY SECTOR, 1951 AND 1964

Sector	1951			1964			Ratio of Column (6) to Column (3)
	Wages and Social Benefits (millions of current pesos)	Total Employees (thousands)	Income per Employee (thousands of current pesos)	Wages and Social Benefits (millions of current pesos)	Total Employees (thousands)	Income per Employee (thousands of current pesos)	
	(1)	(2)	(3)	(4)	(5)	(6)	(7)
Mining	67.9	34.8	1.95	526.9	47.9	11.0	5.64
Modern manufacturing[a]	365.8	169.0	2.16	3283.9	272.5	12.1	5.60
Craft manufacturing[a]	118.0	89.4	1.32	642.0	159.0	4.04	3.06
Construction	161.0	106.0	1.52	1416.1	171.5	8.26	5.43
Public utilities	14.2	9.65	1.47	279.2	12.6	22.2	15.1
Commerce	185.7	57.9	3.21	1070.0	136.5	7.84	2.44
Finance	67.8	17.3	3.91	1000.7	53.2	18.8	4.81
Transportation	193.3	94.1	2.05	1390.8	128.3	10.8	5.27
Communication	22.4	7.01	3.20	234.6	15.1	15.5	4.84
Personal services	326.6	371.8	.878	1877.0	620.3	3.03	3.45
Government services	401.0	128.7	3.12	3025.7	201.0	15.1	4.84
Not otherwise classified	n.a.	39.0	n.a.	n.a.	101.1	n.a.	
Total nonagricultural sectors	1923.7	1124.7	1.71	14,747.1	1919.0	7.68	4.49

NOTES:

n.a. means "not available."

[a] Estimates for craft manufacturing are our own. The employment figures are consistent with census estimates for all of manufacturing, but the labor income estimates are somewhat speculative.

SOURCE:

Labor income——Banco de la Republica, *Cuentas Nacionales* (mimeo).

Employment——Departamento Nacional de Estadística, unpublished data for 1951; and *XIII Censo Nacional de Población, Resumen*.

figures of Table 28 need to be augmented by imputed labor income for the self-employed. We have made estimates for this in Table 29 for three different assumptions about the ratio of average imputed labor income relative to average wage rates. Table 30 presents estimates of both paid and imputed labor income as a proportion of total value added.[5]

It is clear from Table 30 that sectors have differed markedly in terms of their growth of labor income per employee. The sectors fit roughly into two subgroups: one in which the wage rate increased roughly fivefold over the period; a second in which the increase was about threefold. For reference, the cost of living in 1964 was roughly three times what it was in 1951.

The subgroup of sectors where wage rates have been increasing rapidly roughly spans the modern portions of the economy; the low growth rate subgroup covers most of the employment in traditional activities.[6] Relatedly, and as hypothesized, all of the major sectors, except for construction, that enjoyed high rates of growth of wages in the period 1951–1964 began that period with a higher than average wage rate. Of the low growth rate sectors, all except commerce showed an average wage in 1951 that was lower than the average for the urban economy. And the high wage rate for commerce given in 1951 is probably the result of bad data.[7]

[5] The figures for imputed labor income are based on three alternative assumptions regarding the ratio between average labor income of the self-employed–employer group and wage earners: 0.8, 1.0, and 1.2. There is no direct evidence of this relationship, but there is some reason to doubt that the ratio is greater than one. The vast majority of this group (83 percent for the nonagricultural sector in 1964) are self-employed rather than employers of labor. In manufacturing, at least, value added per worker in the very small firms is less than the wages paid by larger firms. For many, self-employment represents more of an alternative to unemployment than an alternative to wage labor. Since measured unemployment increased substantially over the intercensal period, it is likely that the degree of disguised unemployment (measured in terms of declining income relatives) has been increasing. The dimensions of this possible shift are not known.

[6] Although "service" is often thought of as a "modern" sector, most of the sector in Colombia consists of domestics. Similarly, commerce in Colombia clearly is mostly traditional, although this may be changing.

[7] It is true that wages are a less reliable guide to average money income attributable to labor in commerce than almost any other sector because of the very low (about 30 percent in 1951) proportion of wage and salary employees to the total labor force. Yet the official figures show that real income per paid employee in commerce fell some 20 percent between

TABLE 29
IMPUTED LABOR INCOME BY SECTOR, 1951 AND 1964

Sector	1951				1964			
	Labor Force Other Than Paid Employees (thousands)	Total Imputed Labor Income of Workers Other Than Paid Employees (millions of current pesos)			Labor Force Other Than Paid Employees (thousands)	Total Imputed Labor Income of Workers Other Than Paid Employees (millions of current pesos)		
	(1)	(2a)	(2b)	(2c)	(3)	(4a)	(4b)	(4c)
Mining	26.4	41.2	51.5	61.7	33.3	293.0	366.3	439.6
Modern manufacturing	16.0	27.7	34.6	41.5	11.5	111.4	139.2	167.6
Craft manufacturing	186.5	197.0	246.2	295.4	213.0	688.4	860.5	1032.6
Construction	26.9	32.7	40.9	49.2	49.2	325.1	406.1	487.7
Public utilities	0.8	1.0	1.2	1.4	0.7	12.6	15.8	19.0
Commerce	127.7	327.9	409.9	491.9	245.8	1541.7	1927.1	2312.5
Finance	0.9	2.8	3.5	4.2	5.0	75.2	94.0	112.8
Transportation	28.3	46.4	58.0	69.6	47.8	413.0	516.2	619.4
Communication	0.7	1.8	2.2	2.7	0.6	7.4	9.3	11.2
Personal services	97.6	68.6	85.7	102.8	104.7	253.8	317.2	380.6
Government services	0.0	0.0	0.0	0.0	0.0	0.0	0.0	0.0
Not otherwise classified	95.9	131.2	164.0	196.8	76.5	470.0	587.5	705.0
Total nonagricultural sectors	607.7	873.3	1097.7	1317.1	788.1	4191.6	5239.2	6287.4

NOTE:

The alternative estimates (a), (b), and (c) are based on the assumptions that average imputed labor income for workers other than paid employees is equal to 80 percent, 100 percent, and 120 percent respectively of the average wage in the sector in which the worker is employed.

SOURCE:

See Table 28.

135

TABLE 30
LABOR INCOME PAID, IMPUTED LABOR INCOME, AND NONLABOR INCOME AS A PROPORTION OF VALUE ADDED, 1951 AND 1964

Sector	Paid Labor Income as Percent of Total Value Added (1)	Imputed Labor Income as Percent of Total Value Added (2a)	(2b)	(2c)	Non-Labor Income as Percent of Total Value Added (3a)	(3b)	(3c)	Paid Labor Income as Percent of Total Value Added (4)	Imputed Labor Income as Percent of Total Value Added (5a)	(5b)	(5c)	Non-Labor Income as Percent of Total Value Added (6a)	(6b)	(6c)
Mining	31.2	18.9	23.6	28.3	49.9	45.2	40.5	39.2	21.9	27.4	32.8	38.9	33.4	28.0
Modern manufacturing	28.3	2.2	2.7	3.3	69.5	69.0	68.4	38.7	1.3	1.6	1.9	60.0	59.7	59.4
Craft manufacturing	16.6	27.8	34.7	41.6	55.6	48.7	41.8	23.0	24.7	30.9	37.0	52.3	46.1	40.0
Construction	75.7	15.3	19.2	23.0	9.2	5.3	1.5	73.3	16.9	21.1	25.3	9.8	5.6	1.4
Utilities	26.5	1.9	2.2	2.6	71.6	71.3	70.9	49.3	2.2	2.7	3.3	48.5	48.0	47.4
Commerce	28.3	32.3	40.4	48.5	49.4	41.3	33.2	18.3	26.4	33.0	39.6	55.3	48.7	42.1
Finance	48.5	2.0	2.5	3.0	49.5	49.0	48.5	63.7	4.8	6.0	7.1	31.5	30.3	29.2
Transportation	36.2	8.6	10.8	13.0	55.2	53.0	50.8	46.8	13.9	17.4	20.9	39.3	35.8	32.3
Communication	53.7	4.6	5.5	6.5	41.7	40.8	39.8	55.8	1.8	2.2	2.7	42.4	42.0	41.5
Personal services	48.2	10.1	12.8	15.2	41.7	39.0	36.6	48.9	6.6	8.3	9.9	44.5	42.8	41.2
Government services	100.0	0.0	0.0	0.0	0.0	0.0	0.0	100.0	0.0	0.0	0.0	0.0	0.0	0.0
Total nonagricultural sectors	36.3	16.6	20.8	24.9	47.1	42.9	38.8	45.0	12.8	16.0	19.2	42.2	39.0	35.8

NOTE:
The alternative estimates (a), (b), and (c) are based on the assumptions that average imputed labor income per workers other than paid employees is equal to 80 percent, 100 percent, and 120 percent respectively of the average wage in the sector in which the worker is employed.
SOURCE:
See Table 28.

If the figures of Table 30 are accepted, the conclusion is inescapable that the dispersion of wage income by sector has increased. Over the 1951–1964 period workers lucky enough to be employed by the "modern" sectors experienced an annual increase of real incomes of roughly 4 to 5 percent. However, over half of the paid employees were occupied initially in sectors where the average real wage has been fairly stable.[8] The great majority of self-employed workers also were in these sectors. The percentage of total employment in these technologically stagnant sectors, if anything, increased over the period. These sectors employed 48 percent of the wage earners and paid 33 percent of all wage income in 1951; in 1964 these sectors employed 50 percent of the wage earners and paid only 24 percent of all wage income. In terms of total labor income, paid and imputed, the "traditional" sectors employed 54 percent of the labor force in 1951 and generated 45 percent of all labor income. By 1964 these sectors employed 58 percent of the labor force but generated only 34 percent of labor income.[9]

INTRASECTOR CHANGES

Implicitly we have been treating the major sectors as homogeneous. They are not. While some of the sectors are dominantly modern and others dominantly craft, many are quite mixed. The finance, communications, and public utilities sectors are almost purely modern in labor composition. The craft manufacturing and, to a lesser extent, the personal service sectors are very largely tradi-

---

1951 and 1964. This seems unlikely, particularly when it is noted that the wage per employee at the beginning of the period was nearly 90 percent higher than the average outside agriculture and was higher than every other sector but one. It seems more likely that the initial wage level was somewhat lower and the rate of growth of money wages closer to, if not higher than, the rate of increase of the cost of living.

[8] The real wage is defined here as the money wage deflated by the cost-of-living index for urban workers compiled by the Banco de la Republica.

[9] These shifts in labor income distribution are probably slightly exaggerated because of the very high figure imputed for the self-employed in the commerce sector in 1951. If average wages (and hence average imputed labor income) in commerce are assumed to have been the same as in modern manufacturing in 1951, the low growth rate sectors would have accounted for only 42 percent of all labor income, paid and imputed. Because of the relatively small number of paid employees in commerce, the proportion of total wages paid that accrued to the low growth rate subsector is changed only slightly.

tional in makeup. Other sectors, such as commerce, construction, transportation, and "modern" manufacturing, cannot be so easily classified.

Some insight can be gained by looking in more detail at "modern" manufacturing, which we examined in the preceding chapter. The theme there was duality within that sector. This was evidenced by major productivity differences between firms of different size and by major differences in wage rates. Clearly, there is a lot of craft among the modern.

During the 1958–1964 period the gap between wage rates in small and large firms increased significantly. Table 31 shows that the increase in money wages in the largest firms was more than

TABLE 31

INCREASE IN AVERAGE WAGES IN MANUFACTURING BY
INDUSTRY AND FIRM SIZE, 1958–1964

(percent)

Industry	Firms Employing Less Than 10 Workers	Firms Employing 100 Workers or More	All Firms
Food	72.8	199.8	180.4
Beverages	60.7	167.7	169.4
Tobacco	69.9	203.2	235.3
Textiles	141.7	173.2	169.1
Clothing	48.1	167.2	148.6
Wood	55.9	195.4	145.8
Furniture	57.7	178.0	116.9
Paper	115.2	196.4	200.6
Printing	63.8	159.1	149.0
Leather	129.8	138.2	140.7
Rubber	60.6	187.3	181.0
Chemicals	65.4	177.8	174.8
Oil and coal	101.1	150.4	142.7
Nonmetallic minerals	64.6	184.5	180.8
Metals	66.0	85.0	100.1
Metal products	85.8	174.5	159.6
Nonelectrical machinery	80.1	128.0	122.4
Electrical machinery	75.2	190.4	180.1
Transportation equipment	49.7	131.4	121.7
Miscellaneous industry	63.3	100.5	123.1
All manufacturing	74.7	165.7	163.2

SOURCE:
DANE, unpublished data.

TABLE 32
CHANGES IN WAGES IN MANUFACTURING BY FIRM SIZE, 1958–1964

Number of Workers per Firm	Proportion of the Labor Force in Modern Manufacturing		Average Annual Wage (current pesos)		Percentage Increase in Average Wage
	1951	1964	1951	1964	
0–9	13.8	12.2	$2,430	$ 4,246	74.7
10–19	11.1	9.8	2,984	6,344	112.6
20–49	15.9	13.0	3,704	9,137	146.7
50–99	11.8	11.7	4,253	11,335	166.5
100+	47.4	53.3	5,897	15,669	165.7
All firms	100.0	100.0	$4,643	$12,221	163.2

SOURCE:
DANE, unpublished data.

double that in the smallest—166 percent versus 75 percent. During the same period the cost-of-living index increased 94 percent. Thus the workers in the largest firms enjoyed a 37 percent increase in real income over the period. The workers in the smallest firms (clearly craft) experienced a 10 percent fall in real wages.

Table 32 shows that the major change in the wage structure was the further splitting apart of wage rates in the very smallest firms from wages in firms with more than 20 employees. Although wage rates in the middle-sized firms were substantially smaller than in the largest, the percentage differential did not increase. By and large, it appears that variations in rates of increase of wages among the different firm size groups were related to changes in labor productivity. The similarity of relative wage changes for workers in the 20–49, 50–99, and 100+ size groups reflects similar changes of value added per worker within each of the above groups.[10] Thus the anticipated internalization of productivity gains, reflecting lack of final product competition and imperfections in the labor market, was the major factor behind the splitting apart of the wage structure in manufacturing.

How the other accounting sectors of mixed type are divided

[10] In terms of constant pesos these percentage changes are 23, 24, and 22 percent respectively. For the 1–9 and 10–19 size classes, the changes in real value added per worker were −9 and −16 percent. See Table 27.

between modern and traditional components is uncertain. The construction and transportation sectors both have strong traditional subsectors that are probably proportionately more important than the traditional subsector within "modern" manufacturing as given by the official accounts. In any case, examination of intrasector differences suggests that the estimates of the preceding section regarding the percent of the work force that experienced little or no increase in real wages is probably too low.[11] A considerable portion of the workers in the sectors marked by a high growth rate of average wages probably experienced static incomes. It would appear, therefore, that the pattern of wage change over the 1951–1964 period was something like the following: an annual rate of increase of real wages (paid plus imputed) of 0 to 0.5 percent for the approximately 50 percent of the nonagricultural labor force employed in the traditional subeconomy; an annual rate of increase of real wages of about 5 percent for the 35 percent of the labor force employed in the high-wage modern subeconomy; and a 2 to 3 percent annual increase for the 15 percent or so employed in the intermediate-wage group. Although the data on income derived from agriculture are unreliable, it is generally thought that real incomes of agricultural labor have been roughly stable since the Korean War. If so, the real income per capita for nearly three-quarters of the Colombian labor force was either stagnant or increasing at a very low (no more than 0.5 percent per year) rate from 1951 to 1964. Yet the average annual increase in real output per worker during that period appears to have been about 2.1 percent.

THE SIZE DISTRIBUTION OF PERSONAL INCOME

The implication of the preceding sections is that the distribution of nonagricultural labor income is less equal now than in the mid-1950s. Labor income is a large proportion of total income, and this proportion has probably been growing. Wages and salaries

[11] If 25 percent of the employment in the so-called modern manufacturing, transportation, and construction sectors and 90 percent of the employment unspecified as to sector are assumed to be employed in the traditional mode, while 25 percent of the commerce and 7 percent of the personal services sectors are assumed employed in the modern mode, the traditional/modern (low-range/high-range) breakdown shifts from 58:42 to 63:37.

have increased greatly as a proportion of total output at factor prices since 1951. This is partly, however, the result of an increase in the proportion of wage and salary employees in the labor force relative to self-employed and other nonsalaried workers. If the incomes of the self-employed did not change relative to those of employees, the sum of labor and entrepreneurial (imputed labor) incomes for the nonagricultural sectors increased from about 57 percent to 69 percent of total value added between 1951 and 1964. In terms of (distributed) personal income, labor's share increased from 67.2 percent in 1951 to 72.6 percent in 1964.

Personal income includes income from property and entrepreneurial services as well as wages and salaries. It would be highly desirable to have separate data on the distribution of such income, but unfortunately these data are not available for Colombia. The problem of obtaining reliable information on the distribution of property and entrepreneurial income is not, of course, specific to Colombia. Income distribution data from surveys and censuses tend, in general, to miss a greater fraction of property and entrepreneurial income than wage income.[12] Although this component

[12] T. Paul Schultz, *The Personal Distribution of Income*, U.S. Congress, Joint Economic Committee, 1965, Table 13.

TABLE 33

SIZE DISTRIBUTION OF FAMILY INCOME OF
URBAN EMPLOYEES, 1953

Decile	Percentage of Total	Cumulative Percentage
1 (Low income)	3.0	3.0
2	4.2	7.2
3	5.4	12.6
4	6.0	18.6
5	7.5	26.1
6	8.3	34.4
7	9.7	44.1
8	12.2	56.3
9	15.9	72.2
10 (High income)	27.8	100.0

SOURCE:
Economia y Estadistica, No. 85, 1958, quoted in M. Taylor *et al.*, *Fiscal Survey of Colombia*, The Johns Hopkins University Press, Baltimore, 1965, p. 223.

is not much more than a quarter of total personal income, it forms a significant portion of the income of the highest income recipients. Thus income distribution surveys, in general, tend to have a downward bias to their estimates of the income share of the upper income brackets. This bias is aggravated when, as often happens, the survey was designed originally to report on labor force characteristics or consumption patterns rather than the distribution of income.

All of these problems are present in the data on the size distribution of family income for urban employees in 1953 that are given in Table 33. Although we do not know the exact sampling methodology, the fact that the survey was taken for the purpose of constructing a cost of living index, and that only "employees" were sampled, suggests strongly that the upper income brackets were underrepresented.[13] The implication is that the degree of income inequality at the top is understated. The data presented in Table 34 on a 1965 income survey for Bogota and in Table 35 on an income survey in the same year for Cali have fewer problems. Both of these studies were derived from a stratified random sample with sampling weights taken from the preliminary results of the 1964 Census.[14] Although there is probably some undercounting of property income among the highest income recipients of these 1965 samples, the degree of underestimation of incomes of the highest brackets is considerably less than for the 1953 sample.

It is thus obvious that comparisons of the 1953 and 1965 data

---

[13] This suspicion is reinforced by the finding that the average family income of workers in the top decile of this distribution is about 43 percent of that reported for the top decile of the Bogota sample of September 1965 when both figures are quoted in terms of 1964 prices. If both samples were collected on a representative basis, the implied average annual increase in the average real family income of the highest income decile would be well over 7 percent. Given the probability that nonlabor income outside agriculture has been growing at a somewhat lesser rate than the roughly 4.7 percent attributable to real personal income, it seems highly doubtful that the 1953 figures can be considered comparable to the 1965 figures. As a standard of comparison, it should be noted that the average real wage in the high growth rate sectors grew at a 4.6 percent annual rate in the period 1951–1964.

[14] For a more complete discussion of the methodology and weaknesses of the sampling procedures employed, see R. L. Slighton, *Urban Unemployment in Colombia*, RM-5393-AID, The Rand Corporation, Santa Monica, Jan. 1968, Chap. III and Appendix.

TABLE 34
Size Distribution of Personal Income in Bogota, 1965, by Individual and Family

Decile	Individual Income of Employed Workers Only[a]		Individual Income of All Members of the Labor Force		Family Income of All Members of the Labor Force		Family Income of All Families	
	Percentage of Total	Cumulative Percentage	Percentage of Total	Cumulative Percentage	Percentage of Total	Cumulative Percentage	Percentage of Total	Cumulative Percentage
1	0.8	0.8	0.0	0.0	1.2	1.2	1.1	1.1
2	1.7	2.5	0.9	0.9	2.4	3.6	2.8	3.9
3	3.0	5.5	2.0	2.9	3.3	6.9	3.3	7.2
4	4.6	10.1	3.9	6.8	4.3	11.2	4.0	11.2
5	4.7	14.8	5.3	12.1	5.7	16.9	5.1	16.3
6	6.5	21.3	6.3	18.4	6.6	23.5	6.7	23.0
7	8.0	29.3	8.2	26.6	9.3	32.8	8.3	31.3
8	11.0	40.3	10.9	37.5	11.1	43.9	12.2	43.5
9	16.3	56.6	16.5	54.0	16.2	60.1	12.6	59.7
10	43.4	100.0	46.0	100.0	39.9	100.0	40.3	100.0

Note:
[a] Comparable in conceptual terms with the distribution reported in Table 33.

Source:
CEDE, unpublished data.

must be made with extreme caution. In addition to the problem of a relatively stronger downward bias in the income share reported for the highest brackets in 1953 than for the same brackets in 1965, there is also a problem of definitional comparability. The 1953 data do not refer directly to the distribution of (family) income by family, the most relevant concept for most purposes, but to the distribution of family incomes of individual employees. Where there is more than one worker per family, there is thus some double counting of income. Fortunately, we were able to derive a distribution for Bogota in 1965 that is comparable to the 1953 data. The implications of changing the definitional basis of the size distribution of income are illustrated in Table 34.

Each of the surveys shows severe inequality in the distribution of income. According to the 1965 survey for Bogota, 40.3 percent of total personal income went to the top 10 percent of family recipients. Where the unit of observation is the individual employed person, the top 10 percent earned 43.4 percent of total personal

TABLE 35

SIZE DISTRIBUTION OF INDIVIDUAL INCOME
IN CALI, 1965[a]

Decile	Percentage of Total	Cumulative Percentage
1	0.9	0.9
2	1.3	2.2
3	2.3	4.5
4	3.0	7.5
5	4.6	12.1
6	5.2	17.3
7	6.7	24.0
8	8.5	32.5
9	12.7	45.2
10	54.8	100.0

NOTE:
[a] The sample consists of employed workers only.
SOURCE:
Centro de Investigaciones Economicas, Universidad del Valle, *Empleo y Desempleo de la Mano de Obra en la Ciudad de Cali*, Cali, 1965.

income. In Cali the top 10 percent of individual income recipients earned an even larger proportion of total personal income, amounting to almost 55 percent. Although we have no direct evidence that Bogota and Cali are representative of the entire Colombian urban sector, the data that are available from other countries suggest that the income share of Bogota's high-income families is not too different from that in other less developed countries of roughly the same stage of development. For comparison, the top 10 percent of nonfarm families in the United States received 29 percent of personal income in the early 1950s. This figure was about average for industrially developed countries. Income distribution data for the United States and a selected set of less developed countries other than Colombia are given in Table 36.[15]

[15] The United Nation's Economic Commission for Latin America has presented partial estimates of the distribution of income for eleven Latin American countries, including Colombia. Except in the case of Argentina, however, the discussion of the methodology employed in deriving these estimates is too sketchy to give an adequate impression of their reliability. The ECLA figures for the distribution of income in Colombia are given as follows: the 20 percent of the population in the lowest income brackets

The only data directly relevant to the question of the change in income distribution over time that are available for Colombia are given in Table 37.[16] In most respects these data conform to the conclusions as to the likely change in income distribution presented in an earlier section of this chapter on changes in income by sector. If the upper income decile is ignored, the distribution roughly separates itself into three parts: the first, second, and third (lowest) deciles show declining real income; the fourth, fifth, and sixth deciles show an average increase of about 1½ percent per year in real income; and the seventh, eighth, and ninth deciles show an average yearly increase in real income of nearly 4 percent. Although we suspect the decline in real incomes for the lowest deciles is exaggerated by the table, it is credible that the average income of the lowest half of the distributions remained constant, $181 in 1953 and $182 in 1965.

The problem of the noncomparability of the figures for the top deciles of the 1953 and 1965 distribution should be recognized. Any statement as to what has happened to the income share of the top 5 or 10 percent of nonagricultural income units must remain little more than a guess. If the estimates of labor income share given in the national accounts are reasonably accurate, our guess is that the share of these upper-income groups has remained roughly unchanged. Although it may have increased somewhat, certainly the increase is not as great as is suggested in Table 37.

If by "increased inequality" in the distribution of income is

---

received 5.9 percent of total income; the 30 percent of the population in the third, fourth, and fifth income deciles received 14.3 percent of total income; the 30 percent of the population in the sixth, seventh, and eighth deciles received 23.1 percent of income; the ninth decile received 13.9 percent of income; and the top 10 percent of the population received 42.8 percent of income. United Nations, Economic Commission for Latin America, "Income Distribution in Latin America," *Economic Bulletin for Latin America,* Vol. XII, No. 2, Oct. 1967.

[16] Table 37 is derived from the income data used in the preparation of Tables 33 and 34. The 1953 income figures were originally given on a monthly basis. The figures for 1953 reported here were obtained by inflating the reported decile means by the change in the urban cost-of-living index between 1953 and 1964 and converting from a monthly to a weekly basis. We have assumed that the appropriate way to make the latter conversion is to divide by four, on the grounds that this is likely to be the practice of most interviewees.

TABLE 36
SIZE DISTRIBUTION OF PERSONAL INCOME FOR SELECTED COUNTRIES: INCOME SHARES BY DECILES OF FAMILY RECIPIENTS

Percent of Families from Low to High Income	Mexico		Argentina		Puerto Rico				India		United States	
	1950 (Total)	1963 (Total)	1953 (Total)	1961 (Total)	1953 (Total)	1953 (Rural)	1953 (Urban)	1963 (Total)	1950 (Rural)	1950 (Urban)	1950-53 (Farm)	1950-53 (Non-Farm)
0-10	2.7	1.3	3.2	2.9	2.1	2.9	1.6	1.6	8.8	3.6	4.7	7.2
11-20	3.4	2.2	4.3	4.1	3.5	4.3	3.1	3.1				
21-30	3.8	2.8	5.0	4.9	4.5	12.1	9.5	4.0	10.3	4.4	10.0	12.7
31-40	4.4	3.8	5.6	5.5	5.4			5.2				
41-50	4.8	4.9	6.5	6.1	7.0	17.3	13.6	6.5	12.5	5.8	15.3	16.5
51-60	5.5	6.2	7.4	7.1	8.0			7.7				
61-70	7.0	8.0	8.3	8.1	8.9	22.9	21.8	9.4	17.1	9.2	22.5	21.2
71-80	8.6	11.3	9.8	9.8	10.9			12.1				
81-90	10.6	17.4	13.2	12.6	16.9	14.3	14.9	17.1	12.8	8.2	16.1	13.8
91-100	49.0	42.2	36.8	39.0	32.9	26.2	35.5	33.6	38.5	68.8	31.4	28.6

SOURCES:
Mexico, Argentina, and Puerto Rico——Richard Weisskoff, "Income Distribution and Economic Growth," unpublished Ph.D. dissertation, Harvard University, May 1969, Tables 5.10 and 7.6.
India and the United States——Simon Kuznets, "Quantitative Aspects of Economic Growth of Nations: VII, Distribution of Income by Size," *Economic Development and Cultural Change*, Vol. 11, No. 2, Part II, Jan. 1963, Table 14.

TABLE 37
AVERAGE REAL FAMILY INCOME BY DECILES,
1953 AND 1965[a]
(1964 pesos)

Decile	Mean Weekly Family Income of Urban Workers, 1953	Mean Weekly Family Income of Bogota Workers, 1965	Ratio of Column (3) to Column (2)
(1)	(2)	(3)	(4)
1	$105	$ 62	.59
2	146	130	.89
3	186	179	.96
4	209	234	1.12
5	260	306	1.18
6	288	356	1.24
7	334	500	1.50
8	424	600	1.42
9	549	873	1.59
10	962	2150	2.23

NOTE:
[a] The distributions being compared are the distributions for family income per worker given in Tables 39 and 40. They are *not* distributions of family income by family unit. Since this distribution involves double counting, the figure for average family income per worker will be larger than the actual mean family income. For the Bogota sample the ratio of mean family income per worker to mean family income per family is 1.23.

meant an increase in the share of the upper 5 or 10 percent of all income units, it is not clear that the recent growth experience of Colombia has resulted in increased inequality in the distribution of income. If the relevant ordinal unit is the top 25 or 50 percent of income units, the distribution of income in urban Colombia has clearly become less equal. The groups that have gained relatively the most are the skilled and semi-skilled workers in the modern portion of the urban economy who make up the seventh, eighth, and ninth income deciles. From Table 36 a similar pattern of change in income distribution is evident in Mexico and Puerto Rico.[17] The annual average rate of growth of real incomes for these groups in Colombia over the last fifteen years has been sub-

[17] In Puerto Rico, Argentina, and Mexico the income share of the top 10 percent of family recipients was relatively constant during the 1950s and 1960s. See Table 36.

stantial, perhaps as high as 4.5 percent, but their absolute level of income remains low. The mean of the seventh decile (from the bottom) of the distribution of family incomes in Bogota in 1965 was only 368 pesos per week (about $27).

Some time ago Kuznets suggested that it was likely that the early stages of development would be marked by increased inequality in the distribution of income, even though personal income is at present more equally distributed in the developed than in the less developed nations.[18] His argument was based on the implications of the gradual shift of the labor force from an agricultural sector characterized by low but relatively equally distributed income to urban sectors characterized by higher but relatively less equally distributed incomes. The distributional implications of this shift in the early stages of development would be exacerbated by the widening gap between average income originating in agriculture and that in other sectors. The data that we possess (see Table 36, for example) are consistent both with the assumptions and the conclusions of Kuznets's argument. However, the analysis and data presented in this chapter and in Chapter IV suggest that there is another factor contributing to increased inequality in the distribution of income during the early stages of development, namely, an increased dispersion of incomes in the urban sector associated with the phenomenon of dualism.

Urban Unemployment

The income distribution characteristics described in the last part of the preceding section represent the joint implications of the distribution of income among employed workers and the incidence of unemployment. A comparison of the first and third columns of Table 34, the first of which presents the distribution of income for employed workers, the third for all workers, shows that unemployment is a significant factor in depressing the income shares of the lower deciles.

Significant overt urban unemployment would appear to be a rather recent phenomenon in Colombia. Although data are scarce, the 1951 Census suggests an urban unemployment rate of no more

[18] S. Kuznets, "Economic Growth and Income Inequality," *American Economic Review*, Vol. 45, No. 1, March 1955.

than 4 to 5 percent. In contrast, by the mid-1960s urban unemployment rates may have been 10 percent or more in the major cities of Colombia.[19]

SOME CONCEPTUAL AND DATA PROBLEMS

The definition of unemployment always is a difficult problem. It is harder in Colombia than in the United States. In Colombia a completely unemployed person is rarely to be found. The existence of a large craft sector, very limited capital requirements for setting up a new operation (shoe shining, cigarette peddling), and a proclivity to extend the opportunity to participate in the small operations to needy relatives and friends mean that almost everyone can do something. Whether at significant (or even positive) marginal productivity or not is another question.

For this reason unemployment studies for the less developed countries tend to use a criterion such as employment for less than a certain number of hours per week rather than complete unemployment. In the studies we shall examine, an unemployed person is defined as an individual, fourteen years or older, working less than thirty-two hours during the sample week, who indicated a willingness to work more than thirty-two hours.[20]

To some, this criterion will seem to overstate unemployment significantly, counting many people who work a substantial week. To others, aware of the many who hang on at roughly zero productivity for more than thirty-two hours, the criterion may seem to understate unemployment.[21] Our point is that there is no correct criterion. The distinction between certain kinds of craft employment and unemployment is fundamentally blurred.

---

[19] Sample surveys gave estimated rates of overt unemployment of 8–10 percent for Bogota in 1965 and 9–16 percent in 1966. Similar surveys established rates of 10–12 percent for Medellin (1965), 12–13 percent for Cali (1965), and 16 percent for Barranquilla (1966). See Slighton, *Urban Unemployment in Colombia*.

[20] The standard work week in manufacturing is about fifty hours.

[21] It is likely that the surveys we shall examine slightly understate unemployment. The principal reason is that it is very difficult to sample the very low-income, high-unemployment areas adequately. However, it is unlikely that more representative sampling would yield substantially higher unemployment rates. For a discussion of the sampling techniques, see Slighton, *Urban Unemployment in Colombia*.

UNEMPLOYMENT RATES: TRENDS AND CHARACTERISTICS
OF THE UNEMPLOYED

As reported in the previous chapter, the period since the early 1960s has seen a significant slowdown from earlier trends in the rate of growth of employment in the modern sectors. Unfortunately, we have no data to permit comparison of unemployment trends in the 1960s with those in the 1950s. However, we do have quarterly estimates of unemployment in Bogota beginning in 1963. This series does seem to show a slow upward drift in the unemployment rate, albeit with significant cycles. Part of the variation is probably the result of seasonal factors. However, the significant (but temporary) reductions of unemployment in 1964, late 1965, and late 1966 appear to correspond to significant (but temporary) alleviations of the foreign exchange constraint. There is, unfortunately, no index of economic activity available for Bogota.

What characterizes the unemployed? For one thing, they are relatively young. They are also relatively less educated. In Bogota in 1966 the mean age of the unemployed was 25; the mean age of the employed was 33. The unemployed averaged about five years of education; the employed averaged six. The incidence of unemployment among males has generally been less than that among females.

Table 38 presents more detailed information on the effect of age and education on the incidence of unemployment. As should be expected, the inverse relationship between age and unemployment is quite strong. If we were to normalize for years of education, it is clear that the relationship would be even stronger. What might be considered surprising, however, is the apparent lack of a change in the pattern of age-specific unemployment rates given a change in the overall incidence of unemployment. Comparison of the low unemployment sample of March 1964 for Bogota with the high unemployment observations of March 1966 for Bogota and March 1965 for Cali reveals a roughly equiproportionate increase in all age-specific unemployment rates.

Although there is a tendency for the better educated to suffer relatively less unemployment, the relationship is fairly weak. There is also one important exception: those with only one year of schooling or less are generally less likely to be unemployed than those

TABLE 38

UNEMPLOYMENT RATES BY LEVEL OF EDUCATION AND AGE
(percent)

Level of Education (years)	Sample			
	Bogota March 1966	Bogota March 1965	Bogota March 1964	Cali March 1965
A. Unemployment Rates by Level of Education				
0–1	8	7	6	7
2–4	12	10	6	13
5	11	12	9	19
6–8	13	10	8	11
9–10	8	8	8	10
11	8	8	5	9
12–15	10	8	4	16
16+	2	3	4	—
B. Unemployment Rates by Age				
Age				
14–19	20	19	14	27
20–24	17	16	9	17
25–29	9	4	6	11
30–39	6	5	4	8
40+	4	5	4	8

SOURCES:
    Bogota samples——CEDE, unpublished data.
    Cali sample——Centro de Investigaciones Economicas, Universidad del Valle, *Empleo y Desempleo de la Mano de Obra en la Ciudad de Cali*, Cali, 1965.

with two to four years of primary schooling. The reversal is probably accounted for by the low level of unemployment among domestics, the least educated of the urban occupational groups.[22] There is virtually no reduction in the risk of unemployment associated with improving the level of education through the eighth year of schooling. In periods of high unemployment, the March 1966 sample for Bogota and the March 1965 sample of Cali, only university graduates enjoy a significantly lower rate of unemployment among educational groups. At such times of very slow growth even those individuals with post-secondary training of some

[22] From a study of earnings differentials associated with various levels of education in the Bogota labor market, it was also observed that the relation between years of primary school completed and earnings was insignificant among women and moderate but significantly positive among men. T. Paul Schultz, *Returns to Education in Bogota, Colombia*, RM-5645-RC/AID, The Rand Corporation, Sept. 1968.

sort do not appear to be much less susceptible to the threat of unemployment than the relatively uneducated.

There is, however, a complicating factor here in that the better educated members of the labor force tend to be somewhat younger than the average. This tendency is particularly marked for those individuals with secondary and post-secondary training. Given the strong tendency for unemployment to be inversely related to age, the apparent lack of a negative association between education and rates of unemployment partly reflects differences in the age distribution of the various education groups.

Another interesting aspect of the unemployment problem is its distribution with respect to new entrants to the labor force. The accelerating rate of growth of the labor force in the 1960s and the associated increase in unemployment would lead one to expect that new entrants to the Bogota labor force would represent a rising share of the unemployed. This, however, does not appear to be the case. The proportion of unemployed in Bogota without previous work experience has, if anything, tended to fall from 1963 to 1966.[23]

A characteristic of particular interest is unemployment of recent migrants relative to that of longer-term residents. Data on the date of migration of individuals in the sample are not available, but the proportion of the relevant group born outside Bogota can be used as a surrogate for recent migrants. Table 39 summarizes changes in the proportion of employed and unemployed born outside Bogota. There is no evidence of any recent trend toward an increase in the proportion of migrants among the unemployed. It simply is not true that it is the migrant who absorbs the ebb and flow of unemployment. It should not be inferred, however, that the native Bogotano is likely to find it more difficult to get a job than the migrant. First of all, the number of individuals born outside Bogota is only a very partial surrogate for the number of recent migrants. Second, the age distributions of Bogotanos and non-Bogotanos are quite different, the former being younger on the average than the latter. Much of Bogota's population growth is due to migration. As a result, it is common that the fathers are born outside Bogota, with the sons being natives. Since unem-

[23] See Slighton, *Urban Unemployment in Colombia.*

TABLE 39

EMPLOYED AND UNEMPLOYED BY PLACE OF BIRTH
(percent)

Sample Data	Proportion of Employed Born Outside Bogota	Proportion of Unemployed Born Outside Bogota
Dec. 1963	73	49
March 1964	71	67
June 1964	74	54
Sept. 1964	71	50
March 1965	70	68
June 1965	74	51
Sept. 1965	70	67
Dec. 1965	70	54
March 1966	72	59

SOURCE:
    CEDE, unpublished data.

ployment is strongly related to age, it would be expected that the Bogota-born segment of the population would show a higher crude rate of unemployment.

That the migrant does not seem to experience unusually high unemployment rates is still very interesting, for he labors under a disadvantage of less and probably lower-quality schooling than the average Bogota-born worker. One might infer that a potential migrant either does not move to Bogota unless he has a reasonable indication that he can get a job or returns to his original community if he is unable to secure employment reasonably quickly. Although we were unable to test this hypothesis directly in the research on migration presented in Chapter III, it is quite consistent with the findings presented there.

CAUSAL MECHANISMS

The basic conjecture examined in this chapter is that the inequality of the distribution of income will increase if growth of the modern sector is retarded after the transition from agrarianism to the dual economy is begun and if the modern sector is protected from competition. The available data for Colombia are quite consistent with this hypothesis. Although direct and complete measurement of changes of income distribution in Colombia is not possible, the indirect evidence is very strong that the inequality of the distribution of wages outside agriculture has been widening in Colombia over the past fifteen years or so.

Most of this change appears explicable in terms of a dual economy hypothesis. Wages in those sectors that are characterized by modern, changing technology have been growing rapidly relative to wages in the low-productivity sectors where technology is largely static. The effect of changes in relative wages in widening wage income inequalities has been magnified by the fact that employment in the craft subsectors appears to be growing at least as rapidly as employment in the modern subsectors. It has been further augmented by the rise of overt unemployment.

One important reason for the increase in the intersectoral wage differential is market structure. Most producers in the modern sector of the Colombian economy produce under terms of partial monopoly. By and large, the supply of labor to these producers is under union control, and wage rates are set in the context of bilateral monopoly. Monopoly and partial monopoly in selling arise from high rates of tariff protection or outright prohibition of importing items produced locally and from the small size of the local market in relation to efficient plant sizes. Although there are no reliable data on union membership in Colombia, it is comparatively rare to find a firm within the modern sector of the economy whose workers are not organized. The various unions differ radically in their nature, however, some partaking of the characteristics of company unions.

Partly because of the ability of modern firms to collect monopoly profits, the profit rate in the modern sector of the Colombian economy is relatively high. Our calculations, discussed in Chapter IV, suggest that the profit rate before taxes in modern manufacturing was at least 30 percent in 1964 and probably was closer to 40 percent. Faced with opportunities for monopoly profit, the modern sector has found it possible to accommodate to vigorous and well-organized wage bargaining and (in certain cases) to gratify the paternalistic urge to do well by its workers. The result is that the wages of many, if not most, unskilled and semi-skilled workers in the modern sector contain an important element of monopoly rent. For such workers the job is a valuable property right.[24]

The importance of monopolies in the supply of labor in influencing the wage bargain has been further amplified by the continuing shortage of imports. For many firms the effective determinant of production and employment is the availability of imported intermediate goods. In this circumstance the range of wage rates that represent feasible solutions to the bargaining process may widen.

As we stressed earlier, the rise in wages in the initially high wage sectors need not result in an income distribution problem if the majority of the labor force is employed in these sectors and is growing proportionately. But, as we showed, this has not been so, and since the early 1960s it is possible that there has been a reduction in the proportion of employment accounted for by these sectors. Up to now our discussion has treated the splitting apart of the urban wage structure and the slow growth of the modern sector as independent phenomena, but they are not. The former has contributed importantly to the latter in several ways.

First, the sharp increase in wage rates in the modern sector cannot help having influenced the capital intensity of production. Given high and rising wages, the employment growth potential of Colombia's limited investment capacity undoubtedly has been reduced.

[24] Another reason for this wage drift is the emergence of a stronger differential in the level of effective education between individuals whose cultural background is rural and those who have grown up or lived for some time in the cities. The human capital created by formal vocational training and, more important, through on-the-job training, has not been distributed equally over the population. Except for individuals with a very high level of formal education, the recent migrant finds it almost impossible to obtain employment in the most modern sector of the urban economy. To obtain access to employment in the modern economy today demands either formal education beyond the primary level (vocational or secondary training) or a substantial apprenticeship in those sectors of the economy that are technologically transitional. The urban-bred or long-term urban residents have much greater access to these opportunities. It is quite important to remember that the simple fact of employment in the most modern sector creates human capital in the individuals so employed. The on-the-job training (mostly informal) that such employees receive greatly augments their productivity relative to employees in the traditional sectors. Part of this increased productivity is simply the result of workers having grown accustomed to the demands of the "industrial system" with respect to punctuality and teamwork.

Second, the wage and price escalation in the modern sector has reduced Colombia's ability to invest and allocate investment efficiently by making it more difficult to develop export markets. The resultant further intensification of the foreign exchange shortage has encouraged a rather indiscriminate policy of import substitution. This, in turn, has fed back to enlarge the number of firms with a monopoly position, the basic factor contributing to wage-price escalation in the first place. And so the vicious cycle has proceeded.

In the following chapter we shall examine in some detail the nature of the foreign exchange constraint and how it limits Colombia's investment capability. It suffices here to note the importance of that constraint and to point out that the wage changes in the modern and traditional sectors have contributed to the continuing existence of that constraint in several respects. First, it is clear that wage pressure in the modern sector has contributed heavily to the momentum of the general inflationary sequence. The continuing price increases have eroded the relative international price effects of the spasmodic increases in the nominal exchange rate, and the peso has thus been persistently overvalued. Second, the wage drift between the modern and traditional sectors has increased the political costs of pursuing an exchange rate policy that gives an adequate incentive for the growth of new exports and the orderly substitution of existing imports. A policy of progressively increasing the exchange rate to keep pace with the rise in unit labor costs in the modern (export) subsectors will almost inevitably lead to some quickening of the rate of increase of domestic prices. The price increases will, at least in the short run, imply a reduction of real wages in the traditional subsectors where money wage rates are growing slowly. The dilemma of the policymaker is quite evident.

The question remains whether the recent changes in income distribution in Colombia reflect economic processes that are common to most countries in the initial phases of development. Our suspicion is that the Colombian experience is qualitatively typical but quantitatively extreme. In a dualistic economy there is likely to be a strong tendency toward wage drift between the modern and traditional sectors. The pressures of collective bargaining, the unequal distribution of human capital, either from increased dispersion in the distribution of the formal educational attainments of the work force or learning by doing, and the increased wage premium for labor of high quality all conspire to create a push in that direction. This wage drift is consistent with a stable distribution of income only if employment in the modern subsectors comprises a majority of the urban labor force and grows more rapidly than the total labor force. If the rate of population growth is high, the capital and skill requirements for such a rate of growth will be extremely large and difficult to attain even if the government is fortunate in its choice of economic policies and even if foreign lending is carried out on a large scale.

The Colombian situation is somewhat extreme in two respects: the capacity to import is no greater today than it was fifteen years ago, and the rate of population growth is very high. If the rate of population growth is reduced, if export (hence import) capabilities are developed, and if the quality of the labor force is upgraded such that the difficult passage from dualism dominated by traditional sectors to dualism dominated by modern sectors can be made, the pattern of increased income inequality will probably be reversed. Even in Colombia there is some evidence that income dispersion *within* the modern subsectors has decreased somewhat through time. This is characteristic of economies that have reached or are approaching economic maturity.

CHAPTER VI

Constraints on the Growth of the Modern Sector

What lies behind the slowdown in growth of the modern sector? The proximate cause surely is that international lending provided only a temporary solution to Colombia's balance-of-payments problem that resulted from the fall in coffee prices in the mid-1950s. As shown in Table 40, between 1958 and 1962 imports of intermediate goods (to operate the expanding modern sector) and capi-

TABLE 40
VALUE ADDED IN MANUFACTURING AND IMPORTS IN COLOMBIA, 1950–1966

Year	Imports (millions of current U.S. dollars, c.i.f.)					Value Added in Manufacturing (millions of 1958 pesos)
	Consumer Goods	Intermediate Goods and Raw Materials	Capital Goods	Unclassified	Total Imports	
1950	76.1	165.7	121.0	1.8	364.7	2178.5
1951	74.1	203.6	236.5	2.2	416.4	2246.8
1952	74.3	188.4	150.4	2.2	415.4	2405.8
1953	104.9	228.3	210.3	3.2	546.7	2624.6
1954	144.1	276.2	246.9	4.5	671.8	2869.6
1955	114.8	286.8	263.4	4.3	669.3	3062.8
1956	80.6	309.4	263.3	3.9	657.2	3288.1
1957	53.3	272.6	152.0	4.7	482.6	3437.8
1958	32.8	234.1	228.8	4.2	399.9	3590.2
1959	30.3	233.2	149.3	2.8	415.6	3888.8
1960	34.6	263.6	216.4	4.0	518.6	4128.2
1961	48.1	275.4	228.3	5.3	557.1	4375.8
1962	36.0	283.1	208.1	12.8	540.3	4675.9
1963	31.4	267.5	195.7	11.4	506.0	4898.6
1964	37.1	301.7	236.5	11.0	586.3	5188.2
1965	21.0	182.3	177.2	73.0	453.5	5431.5
1966	41.9	306.2	198.2	128.0	674.5	5812.0

SOURCES:
Import data, 1950–1964——John Sheahan, "Imports, Investment and Growth: Colombian Experience since 1950," Research Memorandum No. 4, Center for Development Economics, Williams College, Sept. 1966.
Import data, 1965–1966——DANE.
Value added in manufacturing——Banco de la Republica, *Cuentas Nacionales.*

tal goods (to permit its further expansion) increased rapidly. About 1961 an import ceiling was reached, precluding further rapid expansion.

The import dependency of Colombian industry is the direct consequence of the compositional characteristics discussed in Chapter IV. As of the early 1960s, some industries, usually producers of consumer goods, were almost completely modernized and had the capacity to produce enough to meet almost all of Colombia's domestic demands. In other broadly defined industries, in particular, producer goods industries, the capacity of the modern subsector was nominal or fell far short of meeting domestic demands. The former group of industries required inputs produced by the latter. Thus imports were necessary both for Colombian industry to operate at capacity and for it to expand. And the latter group of industries, although small, were also dependent on imports for operation and expansion, often to an extreme degree. Table 41 shows the import requirements of the different Colombian industries as of 1960. It was this dependency upon imports that caused such a shock to the system when exchange earnings from coffee declined and international lending took up only part of the slack.

In this chapter we shall first look behind the import dependency phenomenon, attempting to assess the factors that explain the composition of Colombian industry. Then we shall consider in some detail the nature of the import constraint in the context of a "two-gap" model. We shall attempt to elucidate why several writers recently have reached such discouraging conclusions regarding Colombia's ability to shake off her present malaise. Finally, we shall break from the conventional "two-gap" framework and suggest that at least some of Colombia's difficulties may be due to inadequate policy response to her basic problems, and that she may be far less helpless to deal with these problems than the "two-gap" analysis suggests.

INDUSTRIAL COMPARATIVE ADVANTAGE IN A
LATE DEVELOPING ECONOMY

As was shown earlier, the relative size and composition of Colombia's manufacturing sector was, and is, roughly typical for countries of comparable per capita income and size. Similarly, Colombia does not seem drastically atypical with respect to its dependence

TABLE 41
Total Import Content of Output in Manufacturing, 1960

Industry	Direct Imports of Intermediate Goods as a Proportion of Total Output	Direct and Indirect Imports of Intermediate Goods as a Proportion of Total Output
Foodstuffs	.10	.12
Beverages	.05	.09
Tobacco	.06	.07
Textiles	.11	.15
Clothing	.02	.11
Wood products	.04	.05
Furniture	.03	.07
Paper	.33	.43
Printing	.39	.41
Leather	.09	.11
Rubber	.40	.43
Chemicals	.27	.31
Petroleum	.04	.04
Nonmetallic minerals	.09	.13
Basic metals	.08	.16
Metal products	.29	.34
Machinery	.25	.29
Electrical machinery	.45	.48
Transport equipment	.31	.34
Miscellaneous	.33	.36

Source:
Derived from DANE tabulations of the distribution of imports of intermediate goods by industry and an interindustry flow table prepared by Albert Berry of the Yale University Growth Center. The interindustry matrix only reports commodity flows within manufacturing and is not an input-output table for the economy as a whole. The estimates of total import content are thus underestimated to the extent that manufacturing industries purchase intermediate goods that have a nonnegligible import content from other sectors. The estimates also ignore the import content of capital goods used up in the process of production. In notational terms the ith element of the second column is

$$\delta_{ij}|I - A|^{-1}|m_i/x_i|$$

where δ_{ij} is the Kronecker delta, A is a square matrix whose element a_{ij} is sales of the jth industry to the ith industry as a proportion of total sales of the jth industry, and m_i and x_i are direct imports of intermediate goods and output respectively of the ith industry.

on imports. The early industrialization process in Colombia, as in other countries, has resulted in a significant reduction in imported manufactured consumer goods as a fraction of total consumer purchases of manufactured products. The form of the dependence on imports has been changed, not eliminated. Although the costs of limitations on, and fluctuations in, import capacity formerly were principally in terms of the availability of certain kinds of consumer goods, the costs now are in terms of limitations on, and fluctuations in, the ability of the manufacturing sector to operate and to expand output and employment. But this too is not atypical. Delaplaine has collected data on the ratios of imports of intermediate goods and capital goods to the total domestic purchases of intermediate and capital goods. Colombia is about average for countries of similar per capita income and size.[1] Colombia's particular problems appear to be due to the unusually great falling off of traditional export earnings and inability to develop new ones. The import dependency itself appears to be a generic characteristic of countries at Colombia's state of industrialization.

CAPITAL REQUIREMENTS

Until a few years ago most economists would confidently have suggested that the likely principal factor was shortage of physical capital. The past few years, however, have not been kind to Heckscher-Ohlin's two-factor model purporting to explain international differences in industrial composition and trade, nor have they been kind to the closely related growth model discussed in Chapter IV.[2] An examination of the structure of Colombian industry appears to yield the same negative conclusions.

[1] See J. Delaplaine, "The Structure of Economic Growth in Colombia and Argentina," Development Advisory Service, Harvard University, 1966 (mimeo.), The United Nations ECLA study, *Analyses and Projections of Economic Development, Part III: The Economic Development of Colombia*, shows Colombia's imports of consumer goods as a fraction of total consumption to be less than those of any other country in South America save Argentina, Brazil, and Mexico. The same is also true for machinery and equipment and raw materials and intermediate goods, with the Colombian ratios quite comparable to those of Mexico. Although the results are hard to interpret, two other analyses also suggest that Colombia's import requirements are not atypical by world-wide standards: H. Chenery and A. M. Strout, "Foreign Assistance and Economic Development," *American Economic Review*, Vol. 56, No. 4, Sept. 1966; and H. Chenery and P. Eckstein, "Development Alternatives for Latin America" (unpublished paper).

[2] W. Leontief, "Domestic Production and Foreign Trade: The American Capital Position Re-examined," *Proceedings of the American Philosophical Society*, Sept. 1953. A discussion of subsequent literature can be found in C. Kindleberger, *Foreign Trade and the National Economy*, Yale University Press, New Haven, 1962.

Of course, the limited absolute size of Colombia's capital stock undoubtedly is an explanatory factor. As Colombia's capital stock grows, her industrial composition will diversify. However, there does not seem to be any strong tendency for the modern industries that developed in the early stages of Colombia's industrialization process to have a particularly low capital-labor ratio. The dualism model suggests that relative capital intensity of an industry in the United States may be a good indication of relative capital intensity in the modern subsector of that same industry in Colombia. Table 42 presents estimates of capital-labor ratios and capital share of value added (another measure of capital intensity) for a variety of industries in the United States. Notice that three of the large, relatively modernized Colombia industries—tobacco products, beverages, and petroleum—tended to have higher than average capital intensity. Textile mill products, Colombia's traditional ma-

TABLE 42

CAPITAL INTENSITY OF DIFFERENT U.S. INDUSTRIES

Industry	Capital-Labor Ratio (1953) Compared with Average	Capital Share of Value Added (1958) Compared with Average
Food	1.1	
Beverages	2.6	1.2
Tobacco	1.2	
Textiles	.9	.8
Clothing and footwear	.3	.8
Lumber and wood products	.7	
Furniture	.9	.8
Paper and paper products	1.4	.4
Printing and publishing	.5	.9
Leather products	.8	.8
Rubber products	1.2	1.0
Chemicals	1.6	
Petroleum and coal products	3.6	1.4
Nonmetallic minerals	1.5	1.1
Basic metals	1.2	1.0
Metal products	.7	
Machinery, excl. elec.	.7	
Electrical machinery	.8	.9
Transportation equipment	1.1	

SOURCES:
Capital-labor ratio——John W. Kendrick, *Productivity Trends in the United States*, Princeton University Press, Princeton, 1961, pp. 449, 453.
Capital share of value added——United Nations, *The Growth of World Industry: National Tables, 1938–1958*, Vol. I, New York, 1963, p. 815.

jor manufacturing export, were only slightly below average. Among Colombia's relatively efficient new industries, rubber tire processing, which has actually been generating exports, is at least of average capital intensity. Furthermore, the relatively unmodernized metal processing and machinery complex, where Colombia is largely forced to import, does not have a particularly high capital intensity in the United States.

Why was differential capital intensity of little importance in influencing the direction of early growth of modern industry in Colombia? Although the cost of capital was higher in Colombia than in more developed countries, at least during the time when Colombia stood in a relatively strong international trade position, funds could be obtained (sometimes from foreign sources) at rates not drastically higher than for investment in more developed countries. Equipment could be bought abroad at roughly world prices.[3] With capital costs roughly equalized, domestic and foreign funds will tend to be drawn into industries in which noncapital costs are a significant proportion of total costs and are low compared with costs in more developed countries (or to industries that are protected and can earn a high profit for that reason). In contrast with capital, labor is much less mobile internationally, and abundant low-wage labor certainly is the principal potential cost advantage in a less developed country. However, abundant low-wage labor translates into actual low cost only under certain conditions that are only loosely related to the labor intensity of an industry's technology.[4]

The following three conditions appear to summarize the circum-

[3] E. Mitchell, *An Econometric Study of International and Interindustrial Differences in Labor Productivity*, RM-5125-PR, The Rand Corporation, Santa Monica, Dec. 1966, finds that rates of return in different industries within a country tend to vary more than rates of return in a given industry across countries. The discussion in S. Wurfel, *Foreign Enterprise in Colombia*, University of North Carolina Press, Chapel Hill, 1965, suggests strongly that, considering the rate of inflation, the costs of money borrowed from the banks was not particularly high, if funds could be obtained at all. G. Gates, *Production Costs Here and Abroad*, The National Industrial Conference Board, 1958, reports that in many cases capital costs were not significantly higher for American subsidiaries in less developed countries than for their home operations.

[4] Of course, labor intensity raises the potential cost savings of low-wage labor. But the existence or lack of existence of the conditions appears to be more important than potential savings.

stances under which low wages result in low costs in a country in the early stages of manufacturing development. First, it must be possible to train poorly educated and inexperienced labor to tolerable levels of efficiency relatively rapidly. Second, efficient operation must be possible despite the limited size of the internal market. Third, highly competent, closely coordinated suppliers must not be needed. Industries having these characteristics naturally will tend to be the most attractive investment possibilities in the early stages. Of course, with strong protection, investment still can be profitable even when these conditions are not met.[5]

SKILL REQUIREMENTS

Although Colombian wage rates are very low compared with those in more developed countries, as is usual in the less developed countries, the work force is far less richly endowed with relevant general experience, special skills, and general and special knowledge which enable complex jobs to be learned quickly and well.[6] The explanation is to be found partly in the recency and small scale of Colombia's manufacturing development. Only a small percentage of the labor force has had work experience in modern factories, and for most workers this experience has been of short duration. In part this is the result of Colombia's underdeveloped educational system. Although a sample of the work force in manufacturing industry suggests educational attainment well above the national average, almost 70 percent of manufacturing employees had had no secondary education at all (compared with less than 20 percent in the United States). Almost 40 percent had not gone beyond the fourth grade.[7]

It recently has become clear that high education intensity, if not high physical capital intensity, provides a reasonable partial explanation of the composition of U.S. manufacturing exports. High educational requirements in an industry often are related

[5] Many of these ideas are similar to those being developed by Donald Keesing.

[6] For a general discussion, see C. A. Anderson and M. J. Bowman (eds.), *Education and Economic Development*, Aldine Publishing Co., Chicago, 1965; and F. Harbison and C. Meyers, *Education, Manpower, and Economic Growth*, McGraw-Hill, New York, 1964.

[7] Data on Colombian education are from Instituto Colombiano de Especializacion Tecnica en el Exterior (ICETEX), *Recursos y Requerimientos de Personal de Alto Nivel*, Bogota, 1965.

both directly (R&D personnel) and indirectly (requirements for a highly flexible and self-programming work force) to the technological progressivity of the industry. The evolving product cycle theory of trade in manufactures was discussed earlier.[8] Thus Colombia and other less developed countries not only have to base their manufacturing development on technology developed in advanced economies, they have to use the technology and run the associated equipment with a work force drastically less well educated.

The penalties of a largely uneducated, inexperienced work force, of course, vary from industry to industry. In any industry there are many jobs that require little skill or special knowledge. A person without much experience or education can learn to do a simple repetitive operation. But to learn to carry out a variety of tasks, and to cope with unpredictable job demands, may require education, experience, or both if a reasonable level of performance is to be quickly achieved.

The industries where Colombia had developed a reasonably large modernized sector by the late 1950s seem to be those in which most of the jobs were of the simple type. The dualism model suggests, as with capital intensity, that it is meaningful to look to advanced countries for data on relative skill requirements in the modern subsector of that industry in a developing country. As expected, big, relatively modernized Colombian industries—certain parts of the food processing complex and the textile products complex—are low skill industries in the United States by any standards. As Table 43 shows, in the United States these industries have a particularly low percentage of the work force with college degrees and a very small percentage of the work force with lengthy special training. Of the other Colombian industries that were relatively modernized—tobacco, leather goods, rubber processing (mostly tires), and petroleum refining—the first two clearly are "low skill" industries in the same sense as food processing and textiles. The U.S. data indicate that the other two are not, but it is clear that the products and activities undertaken in Colombia in these industries are different in nature from those carried out in the United

---

[8] The product cycle theory has many more elements than the technical change-skill nexus. For a good discussion, see S. Hirsch, *Evolution of Industry and International Competitiveness,* Oxford University Press, London, 1967.

TABLE 43
PERCENTAGE OF WORK FORCE IN AMERICAN INDUSTRIES
REQUIRING FORMAL EDUCATION AND TRAINING

Industry	High School but Less than College Degree	At Least College Degree	Vocational Training 2–4 Years	Vocational Training 4–10 Years
Manufacturing	22.9	4.2	18.9	5.6
Food and kindred products	18.0	2.0	18.6	1.7
Tobacco	8.5	.9	8.5	.5
Textiles	16.3	1.2	17.0	.9
Clothing and footwear	7.8	1.0	9.0	.3
Paper and paper products	15.5	2.4	13.4	3.6
Printing and publishing	42.2	9.0	21.1	28.5
Chemicals	17.8	9.4	17.4	8.8
Petroleum and coal products	21.1	11.6	20.7	10.3
Rubber products	12.6	4.0	12.6	3.5
Leather products	6.4	.9	6.2	.6
Lumber and wood products	20.3	.6	11.7	.6
Furniture	24.0	1.5	26.7	1.0
Nonmetallic minerals	16.2	3.4	16.9	2.4
Basic metals	23.4	3.3	19.6	3.7
Metal products	30.8	4.3	25.0	3.3
Machinery, excl. elec.	35.2	4.6	28.8	8.6
Electrical machinery	19.7	8.3	17.4	7.6
Transportation equipment	32.5	5.9	26.3	6.4
Professional equipment	24.7	7.5	23.8	6.6

SOURCE:
R. S. Eckaus, "Economic Criteria for Education and Training," *Review of Economics and Statistics*, Vol. 46, No. 2, May 1964, pp. 186–187.

States. The relatively high number of college graduates in the U.S. rubber and petroleum industries largely reflects scientists, engineers, and geologists, not production workers. It is interesting that many (but not all) of the industries where Colombia did not have a significant modern subsector (such as the metal processing complex) tended to be industries that in the United States had a labor force with a large percentage of college graduates in management or in production, or in which a significant fraction of the labor force had had a substantial amount of specific training, or both.

The industries where Colombia had developed a relatively large modernized sector by the late 1950s thus tended to be of the routinized, mass production type. Even for such jobs the typical Colombian new employee might require a somewhat longer training period than his better educated American counterpart to reach the same level of effectiveness. However, given low wage rates, this was not particularly costly. In most cases there was an option to compromise training somewhat, with the result that workers were less effective than a better trained worker would have been. However, this lower output or quality of work was offset by lower wages.[9] And the partially trained worker could be expected to learn to do his job better through experience.

The story was different for industries where the complicated routines are not largely built into machines or where the routines themselves are in flux. There are a few consumer goods industries that require high skills on the part of the work force. However, the most prominent examples are precision producer goods industries that require some tailoring to the special needs of the purchaser. Much machinery production is of this sort, as is production of intermediate products such as special metal castings or machined metal parts. In the United States industries producing electrical machinery equipment and supplies and professional and scientific equipment required over 6 percent of their work force to have more than four years of special training and over 7 percent to have a college degree or better. In such industries only a few complicated routines are built into the equipment. Workers often must engage in actions requiring considerable precision, and the appropriate actions may vary significantly, if subtly, depending on the product being produced at the time. In such industries the worker must be capable of doing more and more complex things and often must be able to make decisions by himself.

As many writers have pointed out, and as Leff has documented in detail in his study of the capital goods industry of Brazil, low levels of general education and shortages of academically trained high-level technicians do not preclude the development of an efficient producer goods industry.[10] Formal training in the firm can

<hr>

[9] The discussion of the tradeoffs among education, training, and learning by doing is drawn from G. Becker, *Human Capital*, National Bureau of Economic Research, Columbia University Press, New York, 1964.

[10] N. Leff, *The Brazilian Capital Goods Industry: A Case in Industrial Development*, Harvard University Press, Cambridge, 1968; and W. Baer, *Industrialization and Economic Development in Brazil*, Richard D. Irwin, Homewood, Ill., 1965. It is important to note that the industrial development of Brazil, and the development of a capital goods industry, began significantly before development in Colombia.

substitute for education and training in the schools, even if at a cost to the firm, and workers need not be trained up to levels customary in more developed countries before being put to work. Although at first costs may be high and quality low, learning by doing can offset the initial disadvantages. However, there are likely to be limits on the pace of expansion of these industries. First, the training-cost penalty is likely to be more serious than in mass-produced consumer products. Second, although low quality output may not be a serious problem for many consumer goods and may be economically efficient given the skill situation for producer goods, low quality may greatly reduce the value of the product. Johnson has given a very interesting and revealing example of what happens when unskilled labor works in a producer goods industry—for example, the making of automobile parts.[11] Low quality and variable parts simply precluded routine assembly of automobiles.

Although skill requirements are a major determinant of the way in which the structure of Colombian industry has evolved, it is not at all clear that the slowdown of the rate of growth of manu-facturing in the 1960s can be attributed to a labor skill bottleneck. The evidence is fragmentary, but the consensus among individuals who are actively involved in labor market institutions is that there are virtually no labor skills that are currently in "excess demand" in the urban labor markets of Colombia.[12] The data on changes in relative wages and unemployment among various skill classes

---

[11] L. Johnson, *Problems of Industrialization in Chile: Some Preliminary Observations,* RM-4794-AID, The Rand Corporation, Santa Monica, Dec. 1965.

[12] These "opinions and experiences" were obtained through interviews in the four major cities of Colombia: Bogota, Medellin, Barranquilla, and Cali. The sample of organizations visited included thirty-six manufacturing firms, nine universities, twenty-one government and quasi-public agencies, and four financial institutions. Although no claim is made that the sample is statistically representative of the entire labor market, considerable care was taken to secure a sample that reflected a wide variation of experience with respect to nationality of management, the kind of technology employed, size of work force, and degree of organization of the labor force. There were no small semi-craft firms in the sample, although the representatives of one organization that was interviewed, the Caja Agraria, claimed to be able to describe the characteristics of that part of the labor market that applies to such firms.

of labor are fragmentary, but they also tend to lend substance to that conclusion.[13]

SCALE REQUIREMENTS

Another factor explaining the composition of Colombian manufacturing activity is the small size of the domestic market. With the exception of such products as petroleum, the firms entering the Colombian manufacturing sector in the late 1940s and 1950s aimed for a domestic market rather than an international one. In the early stages of manufacturing sector growth, this domestic market is relatively small, particularly for producer goods.

Differences among industries in the scale of operations required for reasonably low cost production are still quite poorly understood. Different studies have seemed to yield different conclusions. However, Bain's study indicates that for many of the food processing industries small establishments can be quite efficient.[14] No other study strongly contradicts this finding. Conclusions regarding textile mill products are more mixed, but we have found no study suggesting major economies of scale beyond a level comprising about a quarter of the total Colombian market.[15] In contrast, Bain's data suggest that for some products (steel, machinery) total Colombian demand probably is smaller than the capacity of one plant of efficient size. Other studies tend to confirm scale economies in basic metals, heavy producer goods, and consumer durables.[16] Except when strong protection or other forms of encouragement or subsidy have been provided by the government (as in the Paz Del Rio iron and steel complex, and more recently in automobile assembly), it is revealing that investors have not

[13] Evidence on this point is presented in Chapter VIII.

[14] J. Bain, "Economies of Scale, Concentration, and the Conditions of Entry in Twenty Manufacturing Industries," *American Economic Review*, Vol. 44, March 1954, pp. 15–39.

[15] H. Chenery, "Patterns of Industrial Growth," *American Economic Review*, Vol. 50, No. 4, Sept. 1960, has developed regressions that seem to suggest some kind of scale effect in the textile industry. However, the reason for this is unclear.

[16] See, for example, L. Rostas, *Productivity, Prices, and Distribution in Selected British Industries*, Cambridge University Press, Cambridge, 1948; and P. S. Florence, *Investment, Location, and Size of Plant*, Cambridge University Press, Cambridge, 1950.

found it attractive to set up plants that require a very large scale market to be profitable.

SUPPLIER REQUIREMENTS

A third factor influencing Colombia's industrial composition and the pattern of dependence upon imports is differences among industries in requirements for skilled and closely coordinated suppliers. In a sense, this third factor is a special form of the first two. Both skill and scale requirements can be reduced if a firm can limit its activities to one stage of production and can look to other organizations for inputs and certain kinds of occasionally needed expertise. Both will be increased if absence of suppliers forces a firm to integrate vertically and to maintain a wide variety of technical experts.

Young, in his analysis of the economies generated by growth, commented on the rather finely worked out, and often closely coordinated, division of labor that marks certain industrial complexes in developed economies.[17] Within any nominal industry a wide variety of firms often do different things, some specializing in one kind of end-product, others in another, some producing components and parts, others assembling them. Within the automotive and heavy machinery industries, for example, there is a wide division of labor, with large firms purchasing many of their inputs, often on special order, from smaller firms. In contrast with the situation in a developed country, a new firm entering the economy during the early stages of development does not have available to it the advantages of established firms, either in products or expertise. It must either provide required specialized inputs and expertise for itself, which is expensive because of the skill and scale problems, or it must rely heavily on imports, which can also be costly.

[17] A. Young, "Increasing Returns and Economic Progress," *Economic Journal,* Vol. 38, Dec. 1928. See also Rostas, *Productivity, Prices, and Distribution in Selected British Industries;* Florence, *Investment, Location, and Size of Plant;* E. M. Hoover and R. Vernon, *Anatomy of a Metropolis,* Harvard University Press, Cambridge, 1959; and G. Stigler, "The Division of Labor Is Limited by the Size of the Market," *Journal of Political Economy,* Vol. 59, No. 3, June 1951, pp. 185–193. The whole issue of the economic consequences of the size of nations is examined in E. A. G. Robinson (ed.), *The Economic Consequences of the Size of Nations,* St. Martin's Press, New York, 1960.

Gates has shown that more often it is materials cost, rather than capital cost, that outweighs low wage rates and hence makes certain industries uneconomic (in the absence of protection or subsidy) in less developed countries.[18] Wurfel and others have commented that in many Colombian industries intermediate input costs are particularly high.[19] In part this is due to the "incomplete industrial complex" problem.

It is extraordinarily difficult to measure the degree of close coordination involved in the division of labor within an industry complex in an advanced country, even to define precisely what an industry complex or close coordination means. To some extent intracomplex sales provide a clue, although this measure misses a notion of "closely coordinated." However, it is interesting that, although the paper and printing industry, the metal products industry, and the chemicals industry in the United States are marked by large intraindustry sales,[20] intraindustry sales in Colombia were nominal. In Colombia these industries were marked by particularly high import coefficients. That many inputs need to be imported, however, does not mean that costs must be high. For certain mass-produced goods, requirements for standard inputs can be predicted in advance. In the absence of very high transport costs, the cost differential of a country importing many intermediate inputs thus need not be greatly higher than in countries with a more complete industrial complex. Even so, it is significant that, as of the late 1950s, Colombia had not yet invested heavily in industries where, in the developed countries, there is an intricate division of labor involving high skills and close coordination.

THE DYNAMICS OF GROWTH

The above discussion of comparative advantages and disadvantages in an industrializing economy is intrinsically dynamic. The very growth of the manufacturing sector tends to eliminate some of the economic disadvantages. Even in the absence of expansion and improvement of the formal education system, the skills

[18] Gates, *Production Costs Here and Abroad.*
[19] Wurfel, *Foreign Enterprise in Colombia.*
[20] M. Goldman, M. Marimont, and B. Vaccara, "The Interindustry Structure of the United States," *Survey of Current Business,* Vol. 44, No. 11, Nov. 1964, pp. 10–29.

of the work force and management tend to improve as a larger fraction gains experience. In Colombia, complementing this improvement, there has been significant expansion of vocational education and training systems. As the manufacturing sector grows, the size of the internal market for consumer goods is increased because of the relatively high incomes generated by manufacturing. The internal demand for producer goods thus is also increased. As industry begins to diversify to meet existing demands, internal capacity is more capable of meeting the specialized demands of new entrants.

In Colombia, as in other countries that have experienced the industrialization process, the result has been a slow shift in the composition of manufacturing output and employment away from the traditional first industries. As Table 44 shows, between 1958 and 1964 the chemicals and metals industries grew much more rapidly, in terms of output and employment, than did the tradi-

TABLE 44

GROWTH OF MANUFACTURING OUTPUT AND EMPLOYMENT,
COLOMBIA

Industry	Ratio of Value Added for 1964 to Value Added for 1958	Ratio of the Labor Force in 1964 to the Labor Force in 1958
Food	3.04	1.12
Beverages	3.14	1.25
Tobacco	2.29	.83
Textiles	2.56	1.12
Clothing and footwear	2.53	1.03
Lumber and wood products	2.89	1.09
Furniture	2.17	.90
Paper and paper products	6.08	1.62
Printing and publishing	3.06	1.21
Leather products	2.37	.91
Rubber products	3.64	1.37
Chemicals	3.65	1.41
Petroleum and coal products	2.72	.85
Nonmetallic minerals	3.28	1.24
Basic metals	3.43	.67
Metal products	4.93	1.87
Machinery, excl. elec.	4.92	1.53
Electrical machinery	4.83	1.91
Transportation equipment	3.36	—

SOURCE:
  DANE.

TABLE 45
INTERMEDIATE GOODS IMPORTS, COLOMBIA, 1958 AND 1964

Industry	Intermediate Goods Imports as a Fraction of Total Intermediate Goods Consumed	
	1958	1964
All industries	.26	.20
Food	.13	.10
Beverages	.26	.08
Tobacco	.20	.11
Textiles	.35	.15
Clothing and footwear	.07	.02
Lumber and furniture	.08	.05
Paper and paper products	.60	.26
Printing	.87	.48
Leather products	.19	.12
Rubber products	.77	.65
Chemicals	.60	.50
Petroleum	.03	.04
Nonmetallic minerals	.25	.13
Basic metals	.15	.19
Metal products	.64	.43
Machinery, excl. elec.	.65	.39
Electrical machinery	.80	.55
Transportation equipment	.76	.61

SOURCE:
DANE.

tional consumer goods industries. Relatedly, in the traditional industries the percentage of inputs supplied by Colombian firms rather than imports rose significantly (Table 45).

Even so, the overall ratio of intermediate goods imports to total intermediate goods consumed by the sector did not fall drastically in this period. The reason, of course, is that the import coefficients of the small but rapidly expanding industries (which were providing inputs to the more traditional sectors), although declining, were much higher than the import coefficients of the older Colombian industries. To a considerable degree the import substitution process was in the stage of import bumping, with the industries that were beginning to produce goods previously imported themselves now requiring a lot of imports.

Related to the above, but not directly shown in Table 45, between the mid-1950s and the mid-1960s the nature of Colombia's import requirements for investment (as opposed to operation) changed significantly. Over this period the ratio of the value of new capital goods imported to total investment fell somewhat as Colombia expanded her capital goods industry. But the Colombian capital goods industry itself required a significant amount of imports to operate. Thus, in effect, intermediate imports of the capital goods industries replaced direct capital goods imports without a major decline in the total import requirements for investment.

When viewed from a somewhat longer time perspective, the Colombian record in reducing import dependency is more encouraging. The estimates summarized in Table 46 show that the current ratio of imported intermediate goods to value added in manufacturing is about 40 percent less than in the early 1950s.

TABLE 46

CHANGES IN THE RATIO OF IMPORTED INTERMEDIATE
GOODS TO VALUE ADDED IN MANUFACTURING, 1951–1966[a]

Year	Imported Intermediate Goods as a Proportion of Value Added (1953 = 100)
1951	96
1952	94
1953	100
1954	106
1955	107
1956	102
1957	90
1958	77
1959	70
1960	72
1961	71
1962	69
1963	66
1964	60
1965	59
1966	58

NOTE:
[a] For purposes of this table the value of imported goods actually utilized during a given calendar year has been estimated as a weighted average of the imports of such commodities during that year and the two adjacent years. The weights are .25 for $(t - 1)$, .50 for (t), and .25 for $(t + 1)$.

SOURCE:
Value added in manufacturing——DANE, *Boletin Mensual.*

Imported intermediate goods (including fuels and construction materials)——1950–1964, John Sheahan, "Imports, Investment and Growth: Colombian Experience since 1950," Research Memorandum No. 4, Center for Development Economics, Williams College, Sept. 1966; 1965–1967, estimates prepared from unpublished material from DANE.

Two aspects of this shift deserve special comment. First, over half of the reduction in the import requirements of manufacturing took place in the period 1956–1958 when the real rate of exchange increased some 64 percent. Since quantitative restrictions on imports were also utilized widely during this period, the shadow rate of exchange rose even further. Since 1958 the real exchange rate, although quite variable, has exhibited no apparent upward trend. Second, as Colombia has expanded into the producer goods industries where scale, skill, and supplier constraints are relatively more binding, the domestic resource costs of saving foreign exchange have tended to increase. Thus, although it is reasonable to presume further reductions in import dependency, the ratio of imports to value added can be expected to fall at a declining rate, unless there is an added incentive to import substitution in the form of an increased real exchange rate.

The relationship between imports and value added is clearly a key determinant of Colombia's future growth prospects and, as such, deserves detailed analysis. In the next two sections we propose to explore the nature of the constraint on growth implied by a given import capacity and the relationship between import capacity and the structure of relative prices. Our treatment here is unabashedly theoretical. In the final sections of this chapter we shall return to Colombia, utilizing this theoretical apparatus to determine whether or not the Colombian government has in fact exacerbated the restrictive impact of a limited capacity to import by the inappropriate use of the various policy instruments at its command.

Constraints on Growth and the Room for Maneuver: An Interpretation of the Two-Gap Model

To recapitulate, the present problems of Colombian industry result largely from a structure that, first, requires a considerable volume of imports to operate at near capacity levels and, second, does not have the capability to produce large quantities of many investment goods. Two key objectives of policy are to expand the modern sector so as to increase employment and modify it so as to reduce net dependence upon imports. But to do these things requires investment, and investment requires imports. What is the room for maneuver within this vicious circle?

Vanek, in his stimulating and important study, reaches discouraging conclusions.[21] He believes that the present import constraint leaves little room for maneuver in desirable directions, that, if that constraint is not relaxed, Colombia's attempt on its own to increase investment and growth will yield very low returns. Such proposals as Currie's "Plan Colombia," which aim to increase both employment and investment through large-scale government spending programs, are not feasible when viewed in the frame of Vanek's analysis.[22] Although domestic labor certainly is available and in many sectors there is also unused productive capacity, the direct and indirect effects of increasing employment, consumption, and investment would increase import requirements beyond Colombia's present ability to pay for them. Thus, in Vanek's view, Colombia's ability to escape the impasse will be dependent largely on how much foreign aid she receives. Other studies of Colombia essentially reach the same conclusion.[23]

These discouraging conclusions have been developed within the framework of two-gap models of the constraints on development.[24] The variety of "gap" models is vast and proliferating. But, underneath the apparent diversity, all these models have a common core. This core, which contains within it the basis for the discouraging conclusions, can be developed in the following rather indirect, but illuminating, way.

Assume that an economy has available to it four basic activities: domestic production of investment goods, imports of investment goods, domestic production of consumer goods, and consumer goods imports. A unit level of an activity can be chosen as "a

[21] J. Vanek, *Estimating Foreign Resource Needs for Economic Development*, McGraw-Hill, New York, 1967.

[22] Laughlin Currie, *Accelerating Development, the Necessity and the Means*, McGraw-Hill, New York, 1966.

[23] H. Chenery and A. M. Strout, "Foreign Assistance and Economic Development," *American Economic Review*, Vol. 56, No. 4, Sept. 1966, pp. 679–733; and H. Chenery and P. Eckstein, "Development Alternatives for Latin America," unpublished paper.

[24] Chenery and Strout, "Foreign Assistance and Economic Development"; Chenery and Eckstein, "Development Alternatives for Latin America"; H. Chenery and M. Bruno, "Development Alternatives in an Open Economy: The Case for Israel," *Economic Journal*, Vol. 72, March 1962, pp. 79–103; and R. McKinnon, "Foreign Exchange Constraints in Economic Development and Efficient Aid and Allocation," *Economic Journal*, Vol. 74, June 1964, pp. 388–409.

dollar's worth." All activities require imports. The two production activities require domestic inputs as well. The activity matrix is as follows:

Activities

		I_P	I_M	C_P	C_M
Output	I	1	1	0	0
	C	0	0	1	1
Input	M	a_1	1	a_2	1
	V	b_1	0	b_2	0

The column headings are the four activities, the subscripts, P and M, standing for production and imports respectively. The first two rows are output of investment goods and consumer goods, I and C. The last two rows are use of imports, M, and domestic capacity, V (for value added).[25] A glance at Table 41 suggests an important empirical assumption for the model. It should be assumed that production of investment goods is more import-intensive and less domestic-input-intensive than production of consumer goods. Thus

$$a_1 > a_2 > 0,$$
$$b_2 > b_1 > 0.$$

Assume a given capacity to import and a given domestic production capacity. The constraints on the activities then are

$$M \geq a_1 I_P + a_2 C_P + I_M + C_M,$$

and

$$V \geq b_1 I_P + b_2 C_P.$$

We shall ignore any specialization of domestic production capacity between investment and consumer goods. Such specialization, of course, further constrains the room for maneuver. However, since the simple model already generates Vanek-like conclusions, the complication is not necessary for our purposes here.

These constraints limit the choice set for consumption and investment available to the economy to the frontier *abd* in Figure 8. If we ignored the two direct import activities, the frontier would be *abc*. But, because import capacity not used up for intermediate

---

[25] If V and M are measured in dollars, then $b_1 = 1 - a_1$ and $b_2 = 1 - a_2$.

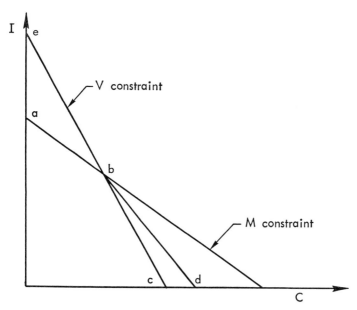

8. Investment and Consumption Subject to Import
and Capacity Constraints

goods can be directly converted, one to one, for consumer and capital goods, to the right of b the frontier is bd, not bc.[26]

If the economy is operating in the bd range, both domestic capacity and import capacity will be fully employed, imports will be used in production of consumer goods and investment goods, and, in addition, some consumer and investment goods will be directly imported. Along ab import capacity will be fully utilized, but there will be unutilized domestic capacity. The asymmetry between imports and domestic production capacity is fundamental to the two-gap model. Domestic inputs need to be complemented by imports to produce final product. Imports, in contrast, can directly provide final product (as well as complement domestic inputs).

To approach the two-gap formulation, we need, first, to introduce another constraint—a savings or minimal consumption constraint. With this additional constraint, the economy is limited to areas to the right of the savings constraint, as well as below the

[26] If V is measured in dollars, then the slope of the bd facet can be shown to be -1. The slope of the ab facet is $-a_2/a_1$.

two input constraints. Next, it is necessary to transform the investment-consumption choice set into a growth-consumption choice
set. In the standard two-gap model it is implicitly assumed that
capital is a binding constraint on domestic output. Then I can
be associated with an increase in domestic capacity, ΔV.[27]

Finally, it is necessary to transform the increment to capacity
into a percentage rate of growth and to eliminate the V constraint.[28]
This we can do by having the horizontal axis refer to C/V and
the vertical axis to the growth rate, $\Delta V/V$, which is proportional to
I/V. This is done in Figure 9. The former V constraint now becomes a constant in the problem as long as b_1 and b_2 do not change.

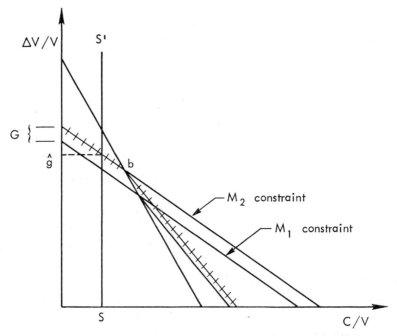

9. Rate of Growth of Output Subject to Savings and Import Constraints

The two constraints in Figure 9 that can be manipulated are the
savings constraint and the foreign exchange constraint. We now
have a "traditional" two-gap formulation.

Regarding the savings constraint, notice that the effect on the

---

[27] Specifically, $\Delta V = BI$. Obviously, depreciation is being ignored.
[28] By "eliminate" we mean, of course, eliminating it as a *variable* in
the formulation of the problem. The domestic resource constraint on production will always exist (although it may not always be binding).

growth rate of shifting SS' to the left (reducing minimal C/V) is significantly greater when the savings constraint is to the right of b than when (as depicted above) it is to the left of b. If the import coefficient for investment goods is two and one-half times that for consumer goods (this may actually understate the difference), the consumer good cost of a unit increase in investment (or a unit increase in the growth rate) is two and one-half times as great to the left of b than to the right of b.[29] Vanek is arguing that, in fact, the current position is to the left of b; thus increased savings (decreased consumption) will have limited effect on growth. And if this model does reflect reality, it would take greatly reduced consumption to gain only a little added growth; in addition, there would be rising unemployment. Although all of the imports released by cutting back consumption would be used for investment activity, the greater import intensity (lesser domestic input intensity) of investment means that the domestic resources so released would not be fully reemployed in the production of investment goods. In these circumstances employment and growth objectives are in conflict.

The relative returns to "more foreign assistance" (holding consumption constant) also vary depending on whether the economy is operating to the left or right of b. In Figure 9 notice how much more the frontier is shifted upward to the left, as compared with to the right of b, as a result of an increase in import capacity from M_1 to M_2.

In the model, as posed above, an increase in savings, like an increase in import capacity, will always permit an increase in the growth rate.[30] It is misleading to say that one or the other of these constraints is *not* binding at any time. Nevertheless, there clearly are sharp differences in the returns to more savings and returns to more imports, in terms of an enhanced growth rate, depending on whether one is to the left or right of b. In a loose sense, it

[29] We are assuming here that $a_1 = .5$, $a_2 = .2$. These are rough estimates of the direct and indirect dollar (or peso) import content per dollar (or peso) of investment and consumer goods respectively in Colombia.

[30] In some of the earlier formulations, imports used in the production of consumer goods were ignored. In this case the coefficient a_2 is zero, and the import constraint to the left of b is thus flat. Reduced consumption thus does not permit any increase in investment once consumer goods imports have been eliminated (that is, to the left of b).

can be said that, when one is to the right of b, more savings are needed, and when one is to the left of b, more import capacity is needed. This is the spirit of the two-gap distinction.

The foreign exchange "gap," which Vanek attempts to estimate, can be defined as the increase in import capacity needed to achieve a given growth target, given the savings constraint. If, in Figure 9, the growth target is $\hat{g}$, the foreign exchange gap as a function of V is proportional to the distance between M_1 and M_2. That is, if in the absence of assistance the foreign exchange constraint is M_1, an increase in foreign exchange proportional to G on the vertical axis will be just sufficient to enable the growth objective to be met, given the existing savings rate.[31] (As a bonus, the unemployment rate would be reduced as well.) Of course, the "gap" would be smaller if the savings constraint could be pushed to the left. But, given that the constraint already is to the left of b, it takes a lot of increased savings to gain only a slight reduction in the "gap."

This allegory may have considerable heuristic value as a diagnosis of the problems facing Colombia today. The system is plagued by both a low growth rate and high unemployment. As long as the import constraint is not relaxed, attempts to resolve one problem through strictly internal policies are likely to compound the other. Conversely, additional aid could be extremely productive.

It is important to note, however, that there is an extreme amount of rigidity built into the allegory. Domestic resources, which are plentiful, cannot be substituted at all for imports, which are scarce. For consideration of room for maneuver in the short run, this assumption probably is reasonably realistic.

For considering longer-run evolution of the systems, the model seems to cry out for more substitution flexibility. Indeed, the basic thrust of the past fifteen years of Colombian industrial development has been substitution—substitution of domestic production for imports. This was discussed in the preceding section. Several of the

[31] Specifically, the foreign exchange gap in dollars as a fraction of V is $(a_1/B)G$, where B is the ratio of value added to capital, a_1 is the import intensity of investment, and G is the vertical distance between the M_2 and M_1 constraints. This can be shown as follows. The required increase in the growth rate, given the savings constraint, is G. This will require an increase in I/V of G/B. The import requirements are thus $(a_1/B)G$.

two-gap models do augment the basic two-gap core by having a time trend for the import coefficients.

Yet, when the focus is on the medium and long run, rather than on the short run, and factor substitution is admitted as a possibility—indeed, is a major objective of policy—the question of incentives, costs, and factor prices, repressed in the two-gap model, naturally come to the fore. Colombia has been suffering from a recurrent shortage of imports and a surplus of certain domestic resources for a long time, to some extent since the coffee crisis of the mid-1950s, and strongly and chronically since 1961 or 1962. In such a situation the price of foreign exchange relative to the cost of domestic factors (the effective exchange rate) ought to matter. Is it not possible that Colombia compounded her problem, or at least failed to consider an important path toward alleviating it, by having a too low effective exchange rate?

THE REAL EXCHANGE RATE, EMPLOYMENT, AND GROWTH

To the extent that the government can control the real exchange rate, it can be considered an instrument of policy, a variable to be manipulated along with other instruments (such as tax, spending, and monetary policy) to achieve policy objectives. This section will explore, within the context of a highly simplified model, how the level of the real exchange rate influences the government's ability to achieve employment and growth objectives.

The concept of "*the* real exchange rate" is a convenient but misleadingly simple aphorism for a complex of things. To begin with, the real exchange rate is a ratio involving the price of foreign exchange in the numerator and the "cost" of domestic inputs in the denominator. And both the numerator and denominator are complex objects. Regarding the price of foreign exchange, there may be, and are in Colombia, multiple exchange rates depending on whether one is an importer or exporter and what one imports or exports. A system of tariffs and other import levies also influences the real "price" of foreign exchange to importers. Prohibitions on certain imports (and occasionally exports) and the complicated business involved in getting licenses also must be considered in "price." Thus the "effective" price of foreign exchange is, in general, different from the nominal price. The "cost" of domestic inputs also involves many dimensions. There are many different inputs to be considered; there are many aspects to their price. (For example, the "wages" of Colombian labor are often less than half of the total labor payments of employers.) Further, productivity and quality must be considered. Some of these dimensions of both numerator and denominator will be examined in some detail later. However, to keep the analysis and discussion manageable, we shall proceed here as if there were one real exchange rate.

It is no simple matter for the government to *control* that rate. Indeed, many Colombian policymakers, and many economists, American as well as Colombian, tend to feel a sense of helplessness about the ability to set and hold real exchange rates. They believe, among other things, that a change in the nominal exchange rate—the most natural way to try to influence the real exchange rate—leads directly to an uncontrollable pressure to increase domestic factor prices, particularly wages. As we shall discuss later, we think these fears, and others, are overly pessimistic. But suffice it to say here that varying the real exchange rate in an equation is far simpler than varying it in fact.

The level at which the real exchange rate "ought" to be set depends on the objectives of policy. Our argument in the remainder of this section is that, if the Colombians are as concerned about having more rapid growth and lower unemployment as many of their statesmen say, then the real exchange rate has been too low. Increasing it would make these objectives easier to achieve. However, a higher real exchange rate deters the achievement of other objectives. For example, if the country were more interested in higher real current consumption than in higher investment and growth, or in higher real wages of their employed rather than greater employment, then a higher real exchange rate might not be desirable. For although a higher real rate furthers the achievement of the former objectives, it reduces ability to achieve the latter.

THE BASIC MODEL[32]

Any model designed to explore the possibility of substituting domestic inputs for imports (and of increasing import capacity

---

[32] The following presentation closely follows R. Nelson, "The Effective Exchange Rate, Employment, and Growth in a Foreign Exchange Constrained Economy," *The Journal of Political Economy*, Vol. 78, No. 3, May/June 1970.

through exports) must explicitly incorporate the following characteristics of the Colombian situation. As shown earlier in this chapter, as of 1960 imports were largely intermediate goods in consumer or producer goods industries and direct purchases of capital goods, mostly machinery. Thus, if one thinks of the economy as having two sectors—one producing consumer goods, the other concerned with building new plants and equipment—the key remaining substitution possibilities were and are domestic resources—capital and labor—for imports in both, rather than further substitution of domestically produced consumer goods for imported final consumer goods.[33] And the analysis of these substitution possibilities must recognize that one of the domestic inputs, capital, itself has an import content. Similarly, in exploration of export opportunities, one must recognize that imports go into exports through both intermediate inputs and capital goods.

In order to build in these characteristics explicitly, we have been forced to make a crucial simplifying assumption—full competitive equilibrium both in the short and long run. Chapter IV argues that this is a fundamental misspecification of the development process. A second simplifying assumption is that the capital-labor ratio does not differ in consumption and investment.[34] However, with these assumptions, a quite general model can be worked out.[35]

Under these assumptions, domestic input of capital and labor can be viewed as producing domestic value added according to

$$(1) \qquad\qquad V = V(L, K).$$

Consumption and investment goods are produced from input of domestic value added and imports, with

$$(2) \qquad\qquad C = C(M, V)$$

and

$$(3) \qquad\qquad I = I(M, V).$$

[33] This is not to say that further consumer goods substitution is not possible.

[34] Examination of capital-labor ratios in producer and consumer goods industries suggests that this is not an unreasonable first approximation.

[35] For a numerical estimation of the Cobb-Douglas special case, see R. Nelson, *The Effective Exchange Rate, Employment, and Growth in a Foreign Exchange Constrained Economy*, RM-5680-AID, The Rand Corporation, Santa Monica, Nov. 1968.

To simplify the notation, the obvious subscripts on the inputs are repressed. All production functions are assumed to be linear homogeneous, with marginal products always positive within the range of relevant factor ratio variations. This last assumption is a serious restriction on the shape of isoquants[36] or on the range of factor ratios to which the model applies. In addition, it is assumed that, for any set of factor prices, the ratio of imports to value added is greater for investment than for consumption. This further constrains the shapes of the production functions.

Let w be the going money wage rate, i the short- and long-run rate of return on capital (possibly influenceable by policy), P_I the price of investment goods, and $r = P_I i$ the "rental" rate for a unit of capital.[37] Then the capital-labor ratio (in both consumption and investment activities) will be positively related to the wage-capital rental ratio.

$$(4) \qquad\qquad \frac{K}{L} = R\left(\frac{w}{r}\right), \qquad R' > 0.$$

For later convenience it is useful to note here that Equation 4 implies

$$(5) \qquad\qquad \frac{K}{V} = S\left(\frac{w}{r}\right), \qquad S' > 0.$$

Let E be the effective price of foreign exchange and P the price of domestic value added (to be specified shortly). The ratio of imports to domestic inputs in both investment and consumption will be positively related to P/E with (as one of our key assumptions) $(M/V)_I > (M/V)_c$. This implies

$$(6) \qquad\qquad \frac{M}{I} = U_I\left(\frac{P}{E}\right), \qquad U_I' > 0,$$

$$(7) \qquad\qquad \frac{M}{C} = U_c\left(\frac{P}{E}\right), \qquad U_o' > 0,$$

and also

$$(8) \qquad\qquad \frac{V}{I} = V_I\left(\frac{P}{E}\right), \qquad V_I' < 0,$$

---

[36] Ruling out, for example, less than unitary elasticity of substitution if all factor ratios are admitted.

[37] Assuming no depreciation.

and

(9) $$\frac{V}{C} = V_c\left(\frac{P}{E}\right), \qquad V'_c < 0.$$

Finally, we need the price equations

(10) $$P = P(w, r),$$
(11) $$P_I = P_I(P, E),$$

and

(12) $$P_c = P_c(P, E).$$

All partial derivatives are positive.

The prices in the equations above are hybrids. These equations obviously can be rewritten in terms of the "primitive" prices—the rate of return in capital, the wage rate, and the exchange rate. We need not, however, do this explicitly. For our purposes it is sufficient simply to note the following. First, all the product prices have to be homogeneous of degree one in w and E. The linear homogeneity of the production functions implies that Equations 10–12 are homogeneous of degree one in the variables on the right-hand side. Considering 10 and 11 simultaneously and recalling that $r = P_I i$ shows that both P_I and P must be homogeneous of degree one in w and E, given i. Then P_c must be also. Another way to see this is to recognize that a doubling of w and E will require a doubling of all product prices (including P_I) in order to keep i (the rate of return on capital) constant.

This implies that all factor proportions and input coefficients are homogeneous of degree zero in w and E. In Equations 4 and 5 a doubling of w and E (hence $r = P_I i$) will preserve the w/r ratio. In Equations 6–9 a doubling of w and E (hence P) likewise will preserve the price ratios on the right-hand side.

It now is possible to reexamine the consumption-investment choice set within a model that admits input substitution. Recall the following specification of input coefficients in the production of investment and consumer goods in the fixed-coefficient two-gap model.[38]

$$\frac{M}{I} = a_1, \qquad \frac{M}{C} = a_2, \qquad \frac{V}{I} = b_1, \qquad \text{and} \qquad \frac{V}{C} = b_2.$$

Assuming the same capital-labor ratios in both consumer and pro-

---

[38] As above, the subscripts have been repressed.

ducer goods production,

$$\frac{K}{V} = c_1, \quad \text{and} \quad \frac{L}{V} = c_2.$$

Ignoring the direct import activities, the constraints of the two-gap model can be rewritten[39]

$$M^* \geqq a_1 I + a_2 C$$

and

$$K^* \geqq c_1 b_1 I + c_1 b_2 C$$

where M^* and K^* refer to maximum availability. Assuming that the labor availability constraint never becomes binding before the capital constraint, the model is completed by the equation

$$L = \frac{c_2}{c_1} K.$$

In our new formulation the constants are turned into variables. The capital-labor ratio, c_1/c_2, is determined by Equation 4, which, given our conclusion that input ratios and coefficients are homogeneous of degree zero in w and E, can be written

(13)
$$\frac{K}{L} = \frac{c_1}{c_2}\left(\frac{W}{E}, i\right).$$

Recalling the assumptions about Equation 4, the capital-labor ratio can be seen to be positively related to w/E and negatively related to i. An increase in w (given E and i) will not leave r unchanged. However, given that $r = P_I i$ is homogeneous of degree one in w and E, the percentage change in r will be less than the percentage change in w.[40] Thus w/r must increase and K/L must rise. An increase in E will affect P_I in the same direction, hence will decrease w/r. An increase in i will also increase the rental rate on capital.

The import coefficients likewise are a function of w/E and i.

(14)
$$\frac{M}{I} = a_1\left(\frac{w}{E}, i\right).$$

(15)
$$\frac{M}{C} = a_2\left(\frac{w}{E}, i\right).$$

---

[39] The analysis will be focused on the region to the left of b in Fig. 9; hence there will not be any direct imports.

[40] Assuming both capital and labor are used in the production of investment goods.

Consideration of Equations 7 and 8 shows that import intensity varies positively with both w/E and i, since an increase in either w or i increases P, hence P/E.

The capital input coefficients are more complicated.

(16) $$\frac{K}{I} = c_1 \left(\frac{w}{E}, i\right) b_1 \left(\frac{w}{E}, i\right).$$

(17) $$\frac{K}{C} = c_1 \left(\frac{w}{E}, i\right) b_2 \left(\frac{w}{E}, i\right).$$

The first term in both equations, K/V, can be seen, from Equation 5, to be positively related to w/E and negatively related to i. An increase in w (while affecting the price of machinery) will increase w/r, through the argument presented earlier. An increase in E or i will increase r.

The second terms of the equations, V/I and V/C, also are negatively related to i (which affects the price of domestic inputs), so the total effect of a change in i upon capital intensity is unambiguous (as should be intuitively obvious). However, V/I and V/C are negatively related to w/E, for obvious reasons. Thus the effect of a rise in w/E will be to increase K/V but to reduce V/I and V/C. What happens on net depends on various elasticities of substitution. It can be shown that, for a Cobb-Douglas specification, K/I is independent of w/E, the two effects just offsetting each other, while K/C increases with w/E, the increased K/V effect outweighing the reduced V/C effect.

But, whatever the direction of response of capital intensity to w/E, it is clear that, for any given w/E and i, there is a set of linear constraints on C and I, just as in the model of the previous section. We can define both consumption and investment units as one peso or one dollar's worth at some set of basic input prices. Then, if we assume that capital goods are more import-intensive and less domestic-input-intensive than consumer goods, the M constraint and the K and L constraints will have the relative slopes shown in Figure 10. The special forms of Equations 1–3, which together with cost minimization imply the same capital-labor ratio in both consumer and capital goods production, mean that the labor and capital constraints have the same slope. The V constraint of the preceding section can be interpreted as the more binding of the K and L constraints in Figure 10.

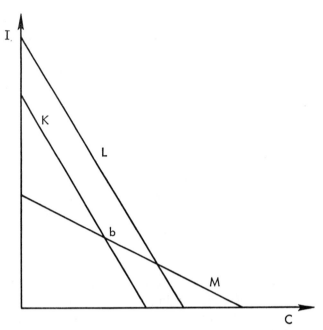

10. Investment and Consumption Subject to Capital,
Labor, and Import Constraints

With two products, three inputs, and a given set of factor prices, in general, full employment of all inputs will be impossible. Thus in Figure 10 there always will be unemployed labor.

But Figure 10 assumes a given set of factor prices. We now are able to examine the effects of factor prices on the conclusions of the two-gap model. As factor prices change, the constraints will shift. As shown above, a decrease in w/E or i will reduce the imports utilized for a given output and shift out the foreign exchange constraint. Capital coefficients can be reduced and the constraint shifted out by an increase in i. (The effect of a change in w/E is, as we have seen, ambiguous.) The labor constraint likewise can be shifted by a change in factor prices.

Under what are not unduly restrictive assumptions, there is an i, w/E combination such that, for any consumption-investment ratio, full employment of all three factors is possible. Further, if these factor prices obtain, the output of the economy, given its M, K, L endowments, is maximal along that C, I ray.

To see this, assume a given target ratio of I/C. Then, given the

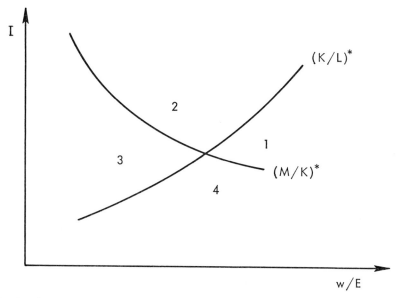

11. Capital-Labor and Import-Capital Ratios as a Function of Factor Prices

import constraint, one can plot alternative i, w/E combinations that will induce firms to use any particular K/L ratio. In particular, one can find pairs of i, w/E that will use capital and labor in the same ratio as the country's endowments. A curve for this ratio, which we shall denote $(K/L)^*$, is plotted in Figure 11. It slopes up from left to right reflecting that the capital-labor ratio is positively related to w/E and negatively related to i. Thus a higher w/E, which would increase K/L, can be offset by a higher i, which would reduce it.

If the $(K/L)^*$ curve of Figure 11 reflects the country's relative endowments of L and K, full employment of K and L will be possible only if factor prices lie somewhere along the curve. In particular, if factor prices lie to the right of the curve, in region 1 or 2, full employment of labor will be impossible. The capital-labor ratio that firms are motivated to use will be higher than the country's endowments. Capital will become a constraint before labor. Thus having factor prices in regions 1 or 2 implies that the K constraint lies inside the L constraint in Figure 10. A similar argument shows that, if factor prices are in region 3 or 4, the L constraint lies inside the K constraint. The condition for the

K and L constraints to coincide is that factor prices lie along the $(K/L)^*$ curve.

Similarly, ignoring the L constraint, one can plot alternative pairs of w/E and i that will induce any given M/K ratio. There is some ambiguity with respect to the slope of the curve. In the Cobb-Douglas case, since M/K is positively related to both w/E and i, the curve slopes down from left to right. A higher w/E, which would increase M/K, must be offset by a lower i, which would reduce M/K. The curve associated with the country's availabilities of these inputs has been drawn sloping down in Figure 11 and denoted $(M/K)^*$. But, in general, nothing can be said (or is necessary to say for our purposes) about this slope.

Only if factor prices lie somewhere along the $(M/K)^*$ curve will full employment of both K and M be possible. If factor prices lie above the curve, in region 1 or 4, firms will be induced to use an import-capital ratio larger than the country's endowment. Thus the import constraint will not permit the capital stock to be fully employed. (Region 1, then, contains factor prices that cause unemployment of both capital and labor.) Conversely, in regions 3 and 2, at full employment of the capital stock, the excess import constraint lies inside the capital constraint. If prices are in regions 2 and 3, the capital constraint lies inside the import constraint. If factor prices lie along the curve, the two constraints intersect at the ray.

In Figure 11 the $(K/L)^*$ and $(M/K)^*$ curves intersect once and only once. Their intersection, of course, defines the set of factor prices at which full employment of all factors can be attained. Given our assumption that all factors have positive marginal productivity for all relevant factor ratios, this set of factor prices yields maximal output along the C, I ray as well as full employment. Of course, factor prices that will induce business firms to use factors in the ratios reflecting availability is a necessary, but not sufficient, condition for general full employment and maximal output along the given ray. In addition, the overall level of demand (given C, I proportions) must be "right" so that not only the ratios of factors demanded but total quantities equal the country's endowments. But, given "right" factor prices, this is a "macro" question. Assuming that government fiscal and monetary policy can adjust the overall level of demand to equal capacity, the remaining condition is that of good fiscal-monetary policy.

There are some difficult questions regarding the conditions under which the curves will intersect and under which they will intersect only once. The assumption that marginal products are positive within the range of relevant factor proportion variation appears sufficient to ensure intersection.[41] This implies, for example, that the nation's capital-labor ratio is not so low that the marginal productivity of labor at "full employment" is zero (as will happen at very low K/L if the elasticity of substitution is less than one). It also implies that imports are not so scarce that domestic inputs have zero marginal productivity in capital goods production (as could happen at high V/M ratios if the elasticity of substitution is less than one). Conditions for the intersection to be unique, if there is one, are less clear to us.

Thus far we have ignored the possibility that export earnings, and hence import capacity, may also be sensitive to factor prices. Assume that, given domestic capacity,

$$(18) \qquad\qquad M = B + Z\left(\frac{E}{p_c}\right)$$

where B can be interpreted as net foreign borrowing. The form of $Z(E/p_c)$ assumes that only consumer goods are exported and that the foreign exchange proceeds from exports are positively related to the exchange rate and negatively related to their price in local currency.[42] There is no reason, of course, why the exchange rate for exports has to be the same as the exchange rate for imports. There may be multiple nominal rates; in addition, the structure of tariffs and subsidies may cause these rates to diverge. If they are proportional to each other, these discrepancies can be incorporated in the Z of Equation 18. If this is assumed, then it easily is seen that the introduction to the equation of a term sensitive

[41] The "within the range of relevant factor proportions" caveat is important. We shall elaborate later.

[42] In addition, with exports admitted into the system as a function of relative prices, the C in the constraint inequalities no longer is "domestic" consumption. To obtain domestic consumption requires the subtraction of exports.

to the exchange rate specifying the import supply constraint will pivot the $(M/K)^*$ curve clockwise.

Imports will be greater at a low W/E (hence a low (P_c/E)) and less at a high (W/E) than if import capacity were insensitive to the exchange rate.[43]

THE POLICY OPTIONS RECONSIDERED

The introduction of factor substitution possibilities suggests that domestic policy may be far less helpless in influencing employment and growth possibilities than the simple two-gap model would lead us to believe.

With factor substitution possibilities, employment can be increased without reducing investment; indeed, it is possible to increase employment, investment, and consumption at the same time. With a given capital stock, an increase in employment (a higher labor-capital ratio) shifts the $(K/L)^*$ curve of Figure 11 to the left because, as Equation 13 shows, to achieve a higher L/K requires a lower w/E for any i. The simplest case to analyze geometrically is one of no change in the C, I ratio and hence no shift of the $(M/K)^*$ curve. The new equilibrium, with greater employment, more consumption and investment, the same capital stock, and the same level of imports (or imports constrained by Equation 18), requires, then, a lower w/E.[44] (If the $(M/K)^*$ curve slopes down from left to right, a higher i also will be required.)

The discussion above hints at the possibility of getting something for nothing. This is both true and untrue. It is true in the sense that the option is open to get more consumption and more investment. The Keynesian situation obtains. It is untrue in that real wages must fall for those employed. For working through what happens to the price of consumption goods shows that an increase in E will increase P_c. (A decrease in W will cause a less than proportional fall in P_c.) Thus there is a tension between higher employment and lower real wages for those employed. This is a

---

[43] We are assuming that the import supply curve is not "backward bending" within the range of exchange rates considered here. With the possibility of multiple rates, of course, there is no reason why the import rate cannot be increased, holding the export rate constant, if export demand is believed inelastic.

[44] In either case the $(M/K)^*$ curve does not shift.

traditional tension, and a politically real one in such countries as Colombia.

Given a level of employment, the costs of shifting the mix of output toward more investment and less consumption are clearly real. But in this model this shift is at least possible without the added costs of increasing unemployment. In this model, as in the fixed coefficient model, investment is more import-intensive, less domestic-resource-intensive, than consumption. Thus an increase in investment relative to consumption will require a reduction in the import intensity of both. This will require a decline in the price of domestic inputs relative to imports. In terms of Figure 11, an increase in the investment-consumption ratio shifts downward the $(M/K)^*$ curve.[45] The $(K/L)^*$ curve does not change, reflecting the assumed equality of the capital-labor ratio in consumption and investment. (Note the symmetry to the analysis in the preceding paragraph.) Full employment of all factors in the post-shift situation thus requires a decline in w/E and a decline in i.[46]

It is possible to obtain these same conclusions from analysis focused on the demand and supply of foreign exchange. In Figure 12 the supply of foreign exchange is positively related to (E/W) given our assumption concerning the form of Equation 18.[47] The demand for imports for any given C, I ratio is a decreasing function of E/W, reflecting the possibility of substituting domestic products for imports. Given our assumptions, it is clear that either an increase in employment associated with an increase in both C and I or an increase in I relative to C shifts the demand curve to the right and hence must lead to an increase in (E/W). Put another way, these changes are possible given an increase in (E/W).[48]

The ability to change the real exchange rate gives a wide variety of options in a situation where initially there is unemployed labor. It is clear that a given increase in employment can be used totally to increase investment, or totally to increase consumption, or any of

[45] It is required that M/V decrease in both activities; this requires a fall in P/E. To achieve this requires a fall in W/E, or i, or both.

[46] That both W/E and i must fall is required in order to preserve the K/L ratio.

[47] Net of imports used to produce exports.

[48] As we have drawn Fig. 12, an equilibrium exchange rate "exists." Vanek has argued that there may not be an equilibrium exchange rate

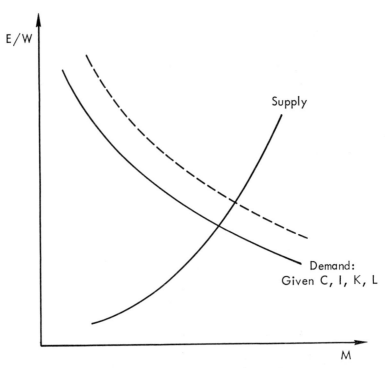

12. Demand for and Supply of Foreign Exchange as a
Function of the Real Exchange Rate

a wide variety of combinations in between. The case of a proportional increase in C and I is not unique. As shown in Figure 13,
the frontier of possible increases in C and I from a given increase
in employment must be concave (just as the C, I frontier, in general,
must be concave).[49] A greater than proportional increase in invest-

___

for a very high investment rate. His argument rests, first, on the case
that, beyond a point, world demand for Colombian exports may be inelastic,
the supply curve thus bending backward. If it is possible to separate
the export rate from the import rate, policy can make the supply curve,
at most, perfectly inelastic. The second argument is that, beyond a point,
the possibility of substitution of domestic production for imports stops,
and thus the demand for imports is bounded from below as E/W rises.
Further, the minimal import level rises as the investment rate rises. We
think this quite likely is correct, and an equilibrium exchange rate may
not exist for a very high investment rate. But we do not think Colombia
now is at this rate or anywhere near it.

[49] This is the well-known implication of linear homogeneous production
functions, with one of the goods (investment) using a different factor mix
(a higher M/V) than the other. The formal proof will not be given here.

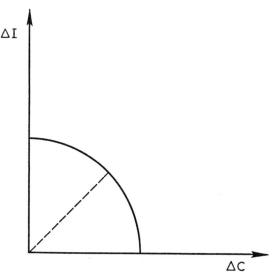

13. Investment-Consumption Production Frontier

ment will require a greater decline in W/E than the proportional increase case; a greater than proportional increase in C will require less decline in W/E. This makes good economic sense. The increase in employment relative to the capital stock calls for a decline in W/E. The increase in employment relative to the capital stock calls for a decline in W/E relative to i, but any point along this new $(K/L)^*$ schedule will sustain the new, higher labor-capital ratio. Since investment is more import-intensive than consumption, a high investment-consumption ratio requires a higher exchange rate relative to W and i than does a high consumption-investment ratio.

Just as with the two-gap formulation, it is possible to translate the C, I choice set of the neoclassical model into a growth rate – consumption rate diagram. The "inside" activity analysis frontier of Figure 14 (abd) is drawn assuming that factor prices generate full employment of all factors at point b and they are fixed at that level. The "outside" neoclassical frontier (fbg) is drawn assuming factor prices adjust so as to generate full employment of all resources along the ray. In particular, W/E is lower at the high investment (growth rate) end of the curve than at the high consumption end.

In Figure 14, if the target growth rate exceeds $\hat{g}$, there will

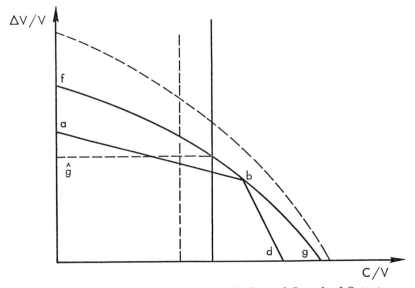

14. Comparison of the Constraints on the Rate of Growth of Output
with Fixed and Flexible Factor Prices

be a foreign exchange "gap." But if we are to the right of the savings constraint, say, at point *b,* increases in savings can do more to close the gap than is implied by the fixed coefficient model, assuming factor costs can be varied. Instead of the two-gap "kink," there are smooth diminishing returns to both increased savings and increased aid alone and complementarity between them. The diminishing returns to increased savings (reduced consumption) simply reflect the diminishing returns to domestic inputs, holding imports constant. Diminishing returns to aid reflect the same phenomenon the other way. The feature that aid yields greater returns in terms of growth at a high savings rate than at a low savings rate is retained in this model, reflecting the greater import intensity of investment. But an increase in aid increases the marginal productivity, in terms of growth, of increased domestic savings.

Thus substitution possibilities mean that domestic policy can do more to increase employment, can have greater impact alone on growth, and is more important as a complement to foreign aid in influencing the growth rate than the fixed coefficient two-gap model implies. However, achievement of these potentialities depends on the instruments of policy that a government can use.

In particular, the government must first have some ability to influence the C, I level and mix; and, second, it should be able to influence the effective exchange rate and the equilibrium rate of return on capital. As discussed earlier, this is not a trivial problem.

DYNAMICS OF PRODUCTIVITY GROWTH, WAGE INCREASES, AND THE EXCHANGE RATE

The analysis thus far has been essentially static. But with a positive investment rate the capital stock will be growing. In Colombia capital growth has averaged five or six percent a year over the past decade. Total factor productivity has been advancing at roughly 2 or 3 percent a year.[50] And, of course, the labor force has been growing. As these developments proceed, the set of factor prices consistent with different employment and growth rates changes. It is clear that under conditions of growing labor efficiency and expanding capital, rising money and real wages are perfectly consistent with constant or expanding employment and a constant exchange rate. However, if the rate of wage inflation is too great, either the rate of growth of employment and output of the system or the exchange rate must erode.

To understand the nature of the dynamic relationships, it is useful to make two additional assumptions and to indicate an implied "invariance" property of the model. The first assumption is that productivity growth is "labor augmenting." (A special case is that the production function is Cobb-Douglas and technical change is neutral.) Since labor's share is about .4, this means that the 2 or 3 percent annual growth of total factor productivity is equivalent to a 5 to 7 percent annual increase in "effective" labor. The second assumption is that, for a given ratio of Colombian prices to the exchange rate, exports will grow at the same rate as domestic GNP. Let the system be in equilibrium, in the sense of intersection of the two curves in Figure 11, for a given level of labor effectiveness, the money wage rate, and the exchange rate.[51] Then the same equilibrium will obtain if the money wage

---

[50] See Chapter VIII for details and calculations.

[51] By "equilibrium" here we do not mean to imply that there is full employment of all factors, but simply that the employment levels are consistent with factor prices.

rate and labor effectiveness change in the same proportion, so long as the $(K/L)*$ curve is interpreted as pertaining to the ratio of capital to effective labor. Thus the equilibrium set of prices, interpreted as above, will be invariant to equal proportional changes in capital and effective labor.

The labor augmenting assumption implies that one efficient laborer is exactly equivalent to two inefficient laborers each having half his "effectiveness" and charging half his wages. Therefore, $(W/A)/E$ can be substituted for W/E along the horizontal axis of Figure 11, the $(K/L)*$ curve consequently being respecified as $(K/LA)*$, where A is an index of labor effectiveness. The export potential assumption implies that a given increase in both K and LA will increase M in the same proportion. Hence the $(K/M)*$ curve is invariant to equal proportional changes in capital and effective labor.[52]

All this implies that effective labor input will grow at exactly the same rate as the capital stock if W grows at the same rate as A, holding E constant or, more generally, if W/A and E increase in the same proportion. (Thus increases in the exchange rate exactly offset wage rate increases proceeding faster than productivity growth.) Using the Colombian "numbers," balanced growth equilibrium, in the sense above, is consistent with a rate of increase in money wages that is about 5 to 7 percent faster than the rate of increase in exchange rate. With a 5 to 7 percent annual increase in the capital stock, balanced growth of capital and effective labor would imply no employment growth at all. With A and K changing over time, the "equilibrium" in Figure 11 can be associated with this "balanced growth" configuration. Shifts in the curves will be associated with deviations from "balanced growth." For a given investment rate, a faster growth of employment (in this case positive employment growth) can be associated either with a shifting to the left of the $(K/LA)*$ curve (a rising labor-capital ratio and hence a fall in $(W/A)/E$) or a rate of increase in money wages that is less than the sum of the rates of productivity growth and exchange rate erosion. Faster capital growth, implying a higher ratio of investment to consumption, is associated with a downward shift in the $(K/M)*$ curve and thus also with a smaller rate of growth of the money wage rate relative to the exchange rate.

[52] The $(K/LA)*$ curve is invariant to these changes by definition.

There is thus a multidimensional tradeoff among the growth rate of money wages, changes in the exchange rate, growth of real wages, growth of employment, and growth of the capital stock. If the rate of growth of labor efficiency is about the same as the rate of growth of the capital stock,[53] a rapid acceleration in the rate of growth of employment will require that $(W/A)/E$ fall. This requires that wage pressure be contained, or the exchange rate steadily increased, or both.

AN INTERPRETATION OF COLOMBIA'S ECONOMIC DIFFICULTIES

The model sketched in the preceding sections provides an interesting interpretation of the economic difficulties Colombia has been experiencing over the past decade. In particular, the model suggests that, given the initial trauma of the fall in coffee prices, a considerable portion of Colombia's subsequent problems may be the result of, or at least were made unnecessarily severe by, an inadequate foreign exchange policy.

Before we argue this point in detail, we must drop the simplifying assumption that there is only one price of foreign exchange. Colombia has until recently operated with a multiplicity of nominal exchange rates. At various times there have been separate rates for proceeds of coffee exports, proceeds of exports other than coffee, capital transactions, capital imports by petroleum companies, and various categories of imports. The "nominal" rates have been only part of the "effective" price of foreign exchange. Tariffs, generalized exchange taxes, taxes on the repatriation of foreign exchange earned from coffee exports, an implicit tax on imports levied in the form of a requirement to maintain deposits at the central bank in advance of actual payment for imports, and various sorts of tax rebates have formed an important part of the actual peso cost or proceeds of transactions involving foreign exchange. Further, in attempting to control the excess demand for foreign exchange, the Colombian authorities have relied heavily on quantitative restrictions of various sorts as well as manipulation of price incentives. The structure of nominal exchange rates since 1951 is given in Table 47. The concurrent structure of "effective

---

[53] There is no implication of causality here.

TABLE 47
Nominal Exchange Rates, 1951–1968
(Colombian pesos per U.S. dollar at end of period)

Year	Quarter	Principal Selling Rate (before tax)	Principal Buying Rate (before tax)	Buying Rate for Proceeds of Manufac- tured Exports (before tax)	Free Rate or Capital Rate
1951	1	2.51	2.50	2.50	2.50
	2	2.51	2.50	2.50	2.50
	3	2.51	2.50	2.50	2.50
	4	2.51	2.50	2.50	2.50
1952	1	2.51	2.50	2.50	2.50
	2	2.51	2.50	2.50	2.50
	3	2.51	2.50	2.50	2.50
	4	2.51	2.50	2.50	2.50
1953	1	2.51	2.50	2.50	2.50
	2	2.51	2.50	2.50	2.50
	3	2.51	2.50	2.50	2.50
	4	2.51	2.50	2.50	2.50
1954	1	2.51	2.50	2.50	2.50
	2	2.51	2.50	2.50	2.50
	3	2.51	2.50	2.50	2.50
	4	2.51	2.50	2.50	2.50
1955	1	2.51	2.50	2.50	2.50
	2	2.51	2.50	4.01	4.01
	3	2.51	2.50	3.87	3.87
	4	2.51	2.50	4.16	4.16
1956	1	2.51	2.50	4.38	4.38
	2	2.51	2.50	4.66	4.66
	3	2.51	2.50	4.51	4.51
	4	2.51	2.50	6.86	6.86
1957	1	2.51	2.50	6.42	6.42
	2	5.96	5.96	5.96	5.96
	3	5.94	5.94	5.94	5.94
	4	6.22	6.22	6.22	6.22
1958	1	6.11	6.10	6.10	7.24
	2	6.81	6.10	6.10	7.84
	3	6.43	6.10	6.10	7.74
	4	6.40	6.10	6.10	8.23
1959	1	6.40	6.10	8.03	8.03
	2	6.40	6.10	7.98	7.98
	3	6.40	6.10	6.75	6.75
	4	6.40	6.10	7.01	7.01

TABLE 47 (*Continued*)

Year	Quarter	Principal Selling Rate (before tax)	Principal Buying Rate (before tax)	Buying Rate for Proceeds of Manufactured Exports (before tax)	Free Rate or Capital Rate
1960	1	6.64	6.10	6.75	6.75
	2	6.70	6.50	6.82	6.82
	3	6.70	6.50	7.00	7.00
	4	6.70	6.50	7.23	7.23
1961	1	6.70	6.50	8.00	8.00
	2	6.70	6.50	8.36	8.36
	3	6.70	6.50	8.71	8.71
	4	6.70	6.50	8.82	8.82
1962	1	6.70	6.50	8.85	8.85
	2	6.70	6.50	8.74	8.74
	3	6.70	6.50	8.90	8.90
	4	9.00	9.00	11.09	11.09
1963	1	9.00	9.00	9.99	9.99
	2	9.00	9.00	9.99	9.99
	3	9.00	9.00	9.99	9.99
	4	9.00	9.00	9.99	9.99
1964	1	9.00	9.00	10.04	10.04
	2	9.00	9.00	9.99	9.99
	3	9.00	9.00	9.98	9.98
	4	9.00	9.00	12.82	12.82
1965	1	9.00	9.00	14.02	14.02
	2	9.00	9.00	19.82	19.82
	3	9.00/13.50	13.50	13.50	18.20
	4	9.00/13.50	13.50	13.50	18.29
1966	1	9.00/13.50	13.50	13.50	17.87
	2	9.00/13.50	13.50	13.50	16.14
	3	9.00/13.50	13.50	13.50	16.35
	4	9.00/13.50	13.50	13.50	16.30
1967	1	13.54	13.51	13.51	16.30
	2	14.54	14.48	14.48	16.30
	3	15.36	15.30	15.30	16.30
	4	15.82	15.76	15.76	16.30
1968	1	16.04	15.98	15.98	16.30
	2	16.32	16.25	16.25	16.32
	3	16.61	16.54	16.54	16.61
	4	16.95	16.88	16.88	16.95

SOURCE:
International Monetary Fund, *International Financial Statistics.*

TABLE 48
Effective Exchange Rates, 1951–1967
(Colombian pesos per U.S. dollar)

Year	Quarter	Selling Rate to Importers (average for period)	Buying Rate for Coffee Exporters (end of period only)	Buying Rate for Exporters of Manufactured Goods (average for period)
1951	1	2.90	2.09	2.50
	2	2.90	2.09	2.50
	3	2.90	2.09	2.50
	4	2.90	2.19	2.50
1952	1	3.16	2.21	2.50
	2	3.16	2.24	2.50
	3	3.16	2.26	2.50
	4	3.16	2.29	2.50
1953	1	3.11	2.31	2.50
	2	3.11	2.34	2.50
	3	3.11	2.36	2.50
	4	3.11	2.38	2.50
1954	1	3.10	2.38	2.50
	2	3.10	2.38	2.50
	3	3.10	2.38	2.50
	4	3.10	2.38	2.50
1955	1	3.08	2.50	2.50
	2	3.08	2.50	3.00
	3	3.08	2.67	3.94
	4	3.08	2.50	4.01
1956	1	3.04	2.68	4.27
	2	3.04	2.86	4.52
	3	3.04	2.93	4.59
	4	3.04	3.18	6.42
1957	1	3.13	3.15	6.42
	2	3.20	4.11	6.19
	3	5.88	4.10	4.20
	4	6.29	4.28	4.80
1958	1	6.92	4.72	5.92
	2	8.37	5.00	5.98
	3	8.29	5.02	5.98
	4	8.05	4.84	5.98
1959	1	8.54	4.81	8.03
	2	8.28	4.74	7.82
	3	7.73	5.11	7.36
	4	7.73	5.03	7.09

TABLE 48 (*Continued*)

Year	Quarter	Selling Rate to Importers (average for period)	Buying Rate for Coffee Exporters (end of period only)	Buying Rate for Exporters of Manufactured Goods (average for period)
1960	1	8.12	5.10	6.65
	2	8.36	5.43	6.66
	3	8.42	5.44	6.79
	4	8.42	5.38	6.99
1961	1	8.34	5.80	7.50
	2	8.34	5.76	9.18
	3	8.34	5.76	9.61
	4	8.34	5.72	9.81
1962	1	8.37	6.30	9.78
	2	8.37	6.35	9.77
	3	8.37	6.41	9.74
	4	8.97	6.96	11.31
1963	1	11.01	7.05	11.30
	2	11.01	7.01	11.19
	3	11.01	7.02	11.19
	4	11.01	7.01	11.19
1964	1	11.03	7.30	11.19
	2	11.03	7.30	11.18
	3	11.03	7.30	11.18
	4	11.03	7.30	13.15
1965	1	11.67	7.67	15.53
	2	11.67	7.67	16.59
	3	11.96	8.50	16.40
	4	14.88	8.50	15.12
1966	1	16.82	8.94	15.12
	2	17.08	8.94	15.12
	3	17.53	9.35	15.12
	4	17.91	9.94	15.12
1967	1	17.02	10.00	15.95
	2	17.38	10.99	15.95
	3	18.04	11.67	17.04
	4	18.76	12.13	17.33

SOURCE:
    Derived from Table 47 and information provided by the Departamento Administrativo de Planeación of the Colombian government.

rates" (nominal rates adjusted for tariffs, tax differentials, import deposit requirements, and subsidies) is given in Table 48.[54]

The multiplicity of exchange rates has been further compounded by the enormous degree of dispersion within Colombia's tariff structure. For example, the range of tariffs on automotive vehicles is from 2 to 450 percent, for clothing from 5 to 150 percent, for basic iron and steel products 10 to 100 percent. The average tariff on goods actually imported was about 22 percent in 1967, but, given the degree of rate dispersion, this figure is virtually meaningless as an index of the degree of protection built into the tariff structure.

The numerical examples given above refer to the height and dispersion of nominal tariffs. From the point of view of effect on resource flow, however, a more relevant variable is the effective rate rather than the nominal rate. By "effective" rate we mean the percentage increase in factor payments (including profits) that is "made possible" by the tariff structure.[55] Where tariffs on inputs

[54] The estimates of the effective exchange rate paid exporters of manufactured goods take account of the estimated value of tax rebates or dated tax certificates and the costs of export taxes, if any. It does not include an adjustment for import rebates under Plan Vallejo. The coffee rate is that reported by the International Monetary Fund. It includes adjustments for export taxes, taxes on exchange certificate turnover, and differences between the surrender (*reintegro*) price per unit exported and the New York price. The effective rate on imports includes exchange certificate taxes, the so-called remittance taxes, consular fees, and estimates of the average tariff rate and the average opportunity cost of funds frozen in import deposits. The figures given as the selling rate to importers are based on the average cost of tariffs and import deposits for all nonexempt imports.

[55] In algebraic terms, the effective tariff rate is $(V - W)/W$, where W is value added at world prices and V is value added, or the sum of factor payments including profits, at domestic prices, the assumed difference between world and domestic prices being the tariff. This reduces to $(t_f - at_i)/1 - a$, where t_f is the average tariff on final product, t_i is the average tariff on intermediate goods (weighted by the share of each intermediate good in the pre-tariff cost of production of the final product in question), and a is the pre-tariff ratio of the value of all intermediate goods to the value of final product. The object of this reformulation of the concept of protection is to provide an ordinal index of the likelihood that the tariff structure will induce a net inflow of resources into a given sector.

There are, in fact, a number of conceptual difficulties with this definition. In particular, the justification for expressing protection in terms of pre- and post-tariff value added depends upon the assumption that all resources other than intermediate products are not in infinitely elastic supply. With

are less than the tariffs on outputs, the effective rate exceeds the nominal rate.

In general, Colombian tariffs on final products are greater than the rates on intermediate goods, and the effective rate of tariff protection is thus in excess of the nominal rate. As can be seen from Table 49, in 1966 the average tariff rate on intermediate goods was less than that on final product on all but three of the twenty two-digit manufacturing industries.[56] In well over half the cases the difference between rates on input and output was substantial. In addition, there appears to have been a strong tendency for those industries with the highest rates of nominal protection on output to enjoy the highest ratios of output tariffs to input tariffs.[57] The implication of this finding is that the dispersion of effective tariff rates is even greater than the dispersion of nominal rates.

With this degree of tariff dispersion, it is clear that there is a good deal of "water" in the rate structure. In these cases the effect of tariffs is essentially indistinguishable from outright prohibition of imports, another policy instrument used by the Colombian gov-

---

respect to Colombia, a strong case can be made for the assumption that most classes of labor are in something like infinitely elastic supply to producers in the modern sector. In this case labor should be treated as an intermediate good with zero tariff, and the rate of effective protection is the proportionate increase in factor payments other than wages made possible by the tariff. In this case the levels of effective protection will be much higher than those given by the definition first proposed. For a discussion of these problems, see W. M. Corden, "The Structure of a Tariff System and the Effective Protective Rate," *Journal of Political Economy,* Vol. 74, No. 3, June 1966, pp. 221–237.

[56] The "tariffs" reported in Table 49 embody both the nominal tariff and an implicit tariff of goods whose importation into Colombia was forbidden at the time the data on nominal tariffs were collected. The allowance made for implicit tariffs is excessive. Since import prohibition is more common among final products than intermediate goods, there is something of an upward bias in these estimates of the difference between tariff rates on those two classes of goods. As near as we can judge, however, the general tendency for rates on final products to be higher than rates on inputs holds even in the absence of an estimate of "implicit" tariffs.

[57] The Spearman rank correlation coefficient between the height of the tariff on final product and the ratio of tariff rate on final product to tariff rate on inputs according to the data of Table 49 is .80. The evidence of association between these variables is significant at the 99 percent confidence level. Note that this relationship holds even though the absolute value of input and output tariff appears to be somewhat correlated.

TABLE 49

AVERAGE TARIFFS ON OUTPUTS AND INPUTS BY INDUSTRY
IN 1966[a]

(1964 commodity weights)

Industry	Average Rate on Final Products	Average Rate on Intermediate Products
Foodstuffs	206%	173%
Beverages	195	160
Tobacco	301	192
Textiles	170	137
Clothing	500	177
Wood products	227	186
Furniture	400	177
Paper	200	135
Printing	236	64
Leather	123	191
Rubber	196	56
Chemicals	94	105
Petroleum	107	103
Basic metals	44	43
Nonmetallic minerals	127	140
Metal products	177	50
Machinery	187	91
Electrical machinery	150	142
Transportation equipment	260	75
Miscellaneous industry	239	177

NOTE:

[a] The measured tariff in these calculations combines both the nominal tariff and an estimated "implicit" tariff on goods whose importation is prohibited. In the latter case, the Argaez-Plazas assumption was that the ratio of Colombian prices to world or import prices was $2(1 + t)$ instead of $(1 + t)$, t being the tariff rate. The "implicit" tariff on prohibited goods is thus $[2(1 + t) - 1]$ or $(1 + 2t)$ instead of the actual tariff t. Although it does seem useful to make some allowance for the price effect of import prohibition, the assumption actually used in these calculations allows for much more of a price effect than appears reasonable. This shows up particularly in the figures for the furniture and clothing industries, the importation of a large proportion of the output of those two industries being on the prohibited list. Unfortunately, we did not have the information needed to recalculate the "implicit" tariff for less extreme assumptions.

SOURCE:

G. Argaez and C. Plazas, "Estudio Preliminar Sobre la Eficiencia de la Industria en Colombia," Departamento Administrativo de Planeacion, unpublished manuscript.

ernment to control the excess demand for foreign exchange. Current import policy places a commodity into one of three groups: a "free" or automatic license list where protection is provided only by the tariff and the nominal exchange rate; the prior license list, the volume of licensing being adjusted by the trade authorities in accordance with the current and expected net foreign exchange reserve position of the country; and the prohibited list.

In the short run, the excess demand for foreign exchange has been controlled by the more or less coordinated implementation of a variety of policy instruments. In periods of substantial pressure on exchange reserves, excess demand has been damped by shifts of commodities to the prohibited or prior license list, a slowdown in the rate of approval of import licenses, an increase in import deposit requirements (an implicit import tax), adjustment of the differential between the effective rates on imports and exports, direct controls on capital export, restrictions on credit creation by the banking system, and, in periods of great stress, an increase in the nominal exchange rate or rates (devaluation). It is not clear, however, whether there has been a conscious long-run exchange rate policy.

To understand this uncertainty, it is necessary to consider briefly the recent history of wages and prices in Colombia. Since 1957 the rate of increase in money wage rates has averaged well above 10 percent a year, significantly in excess of productivity growth. This has proved incompatible with stable prices. Indeed, between 1957 and 1966 the index of domestic prices of goods other than foodstuffs increased some 276 percent. As shown in Table 50, the year-to-year variation in the rate of wage and price inflation was quite variable. The price level increased more than 25 percent in 1963 and about 18 percent in 1965. However, in 1960 and 1961 prices increased only 3 percent and 5 percent respectively. In 1967 and 1968 the rate of inflation was about 7 percent. This increased to 10 percent in 1969.

As a result of this high and variable rate of inflation, the pattern of change of the structure of nominal (or effective) exchange rates is rather different from the pattern of change of the structure of "real" exchange rates as given in Table 51. For example, the substantial increase in the nominal rate of exchange on imports between 1963 and 1964 (Tables 47 and 48) was accompanied by a rate of price increase sufficiently high to imply (Table 51) that the real import rate actually fell (there was an effective exchange revaluation). More important, the real import rate in 1967 was actually less than in 1958. There is a similar absence of an upward trend in the exchange rate applicable to manufacturing exports.

TABLE 50
RATES OF INCREASE OF WAGES AND PRICES, 1958–1967

Year	Quarter	Percentage Increase of Salaries	Percentage Increase of Wages	Percentage Increase in the Cost of Living (workers)	Percentage Increase in Wholesale Prices Other than Foodstuffs
1958		13.9	8.6	7.9	16.4
	1	3.5	2.9	1.9	4.8
	2	4.6	1.9	4.4	5.4
	3	3.7	.9	.8	4.2
	4	1.4	2.7	.5	1.1
1959		8.9	11.4	7.7	6.9
	1	2.3	.9	3.1	1.0
	2	2.6	3.5	3.2	2.9
	3	1.3	3.4	.1	2.6
	4	2.5	3.3	1.2	.3
1960		8.6	11.1ᵃ	7.5	3.1
	1	2.7	.8	1.4	.5
	2	1.9	3.1	2.0	1.3
	3	2.4	5.0ᵃ	.9	.5
	4	1.3	2.0	3.2	.7
1961		9.4	12.0	5.5	5.0
	1	2.0	1.3	2.7	2.6
	2	2.4	3.3	3.7	.8
	3	2.9	3.8	−2.3	.7
	4	1.8	3.1	1.3	.8
1962		12.6ᵃ	17.8ᵃ	6.1	7.4
	1	2.7	2.4	1.4	1.0
	2	3.3ᵃ	5.1ᵃ	1.3	1.7
	3	2.7	5.4	1.5	1.3
	4	3.2	4.2	1.7	3.2
1963		24.1	37.8	35.4	25.5
	1	12.7	24.9	16.7	17.1
	2	4.6	4.3	8.1	3.3
	3	1.8	2.4	2.0	2.2
	4	3.3	3.3	5.3	1.6
1964		11.2	11.3	8.5	6.7
	1	3.4	3.2	4.3	2.4
	2	4.1	2.2	7.9	1.2
	3	1.2	2.1	−3.7	1.9
	4	2.1	3.2	.1	1.1
1965		14.4	12.8	14.3	18.2
	1	3.1	1.7	1.6	2.2
	2	5.2	2.8	4.8	3.1
	3	2.1	3.0	.8	6.8
	4	3.2	4.6	6.5	5.0
1966		12.7	11.6	12.7	13.7
	1	4.1	3.1	5.1	4.8
	2	4.7	3.7	4.3	2.9
	3	1.6	1.4	.4	3.3
	4	1.7	2.8	2.3	1.1
1967ᵇ		7.5	5.5	5.0	3.7
	1	2.8	2.5	2.0	1.6
	2	4.6	2.9	2.9	2.0

NOTES:

ᵃ Adjusted for change in sample.

ᵇ Six-month figures only.

SOURCES:

Departamento Administrativo de Estadistica, *Boletin Mensual*, Bogota, 1958–1967.
Banco de la Republica, *Revista del Banco de la Republica*, Bogota, 1958–1967.

TABLE 51
Average Real Effective Exchange Rates for
Imports and Minor Exports

Year	Quarter	Index of Wholesale Prices (1958 = 100)	Index of Real Effective Import Rate[a] (1958 = 100)	Index of Cost of Production[b] (1958 = 100)	Index of Real Effective Minor Export Rate[c] (1958 = 100)
1958	1	92	95	92	108
	2	96	110	96	104
	3	101	103	101	99
	4	103	99	103	97
1959	1	104	105	104	129
	2	106	99	106	124
	3	110	90	110	113
	4	110	90	110	109
1960	1	110	94	110	100
	2	112	96	112	99
	3	113	95	113	100
	4	114	94	114	101
1961	1	116	91	116	106
	2	117	90	117	128
	3	118	90	118	133
	4	119	89	119	135
1962	1	120	89	120	133
	2	122	88	122	130
	3	124	86	124	127
	4	126	91	126	145
1963	1	143	98	143	125
	2	154	91	154	116
	3	157	89	157	114
	4	160	88	160	112
1964	1	163	86	163	110
	2	166	85	166	108
	3	169	84	169	106
	4	171	82	171	123
1965	1	174	86	174	143
	2	179	83	179	149
	3	188	81	188	140
	4	199	95	199	121
1966	1	210	102	210	115
	2	217	101	217	111
	3	224	100	224	107
	4	230	99	230	105
1967	1	233	93	233	103
	2	238	93	238	107
	3	243	95	243	112
	4	245	98	245	109

Notes to Table 51 on page 210.

NOTES TO TABLE 51:

ᵃ The average effective exchange rate is defined as the nominal rate adjusted for exchange certificate taxes, consular fees, the so-called remittance taxes, and estimates of the average tariff rate and the opportunity cost of funds frozen in deposit requirements. The real effective rate is the effective rate deflated by the Colombian wholesale price index (excluding foodstuffs). The latter adjustment ignores the effects of changes in the foreign export price of Colombian imports, but since IMF data do not give evidence of a trend in c.i.f. import prices for Colombia, this complication can be ignored for most purposes.

ᵇ This index is an index of the cost of manufactured exports. It is a composite of separate indexes of the cost of labor (average hourly wage of workers in manufacturing as reported to DANE), the cost of imported intermediate goods (the effective exchange rate on imports), and the cost of domestically produced intermediate goods (the wholesale price index excluding foodstuffs). The respective weights are 13.5 percent, 13.5 percent, and 73 percent and were developed by A. Urdinola and R. Mallon in *Policies to Promote Colombian Exports of Manufactures*, Economic Development Report No. 75, Development Advisory Service, Harvard University, 1967.

ᶜ The effective rate on minor exports is defined as the nominal rate adjusted for export taxes and tax rebates. The real effective rate is the effective rate deflated by the cost of production in manufacturing.

SOURCES:

Price data were taken from the *Revista del Banco de la Republica*. Data on nominal exchange rates are those given by the International Monetary Fund, *International Financial Statistics*. The adjustments from nominal to effective exchange rates are based on information collected by the Departamento Administrativo de Planeacion of the Government of Colombia.

Thus, whether adopted consciously or not, the Colombian government has appeared to follow (at least until very recently) a long-run exchange policy characterized not only by a high degree of rate dispersion, with rates on imports higher than on exports, but also by a tendency to maintain the average of the *real* exchange rate structure at the level established during the stabilization program of 1957–1958.[58] This policy, conscious or unconscious, has had a number of pernicious effects. Because of extreme rate dispersion, there has been a strong bias in favor of import substitution relative to export development (other than coffee). This bias has become progressively more costly as Colombia has moved beyond the early and easy phase of import substitution and into industries where capital, skill, scale, and supplier requirements are more onerous. The inference that the exchange differential between import substitution and export development has induced an important misallocation of resources requires, of course, the assumption that Colombian exports are sensitive to the real rate of exchange on exports. Our own estimates suggest that this is, in fact, the case.

[58] It should be noted that the "exchange stabilization" of 1957–1958 was as much the result of severe quantitative restrictions as of changes in the nominal (or real) exchange rate.

For the period 1960–1967 the short-run elasticity of response of agricultural exports other than coffee (valued in terms of foreign currency) with respect to the real exchange rate appears to be about 1.0. The short-run elasticity of response of nonagricultural exports can be estimated as about 0.8.[59] By that we mean that a 10 percent increase in the real exchange rate for minor exports has recently been associated with a 10 percent increase in the dollar volume of minor agricultural exports and an 8 percent increase in the dollar volume of nonagricultural exports (other than fuel oil) within a period of no more than three months from the date of the rate change. In the period 1953–1959 supply response to devaluation was typically spread over a longer period, since the

[59] These estimates were obtained from the regression equation

$$\log Y_t = a + b_1 \log X_{1_t} + b_2 \log X_{2_t} + b_3 W_{1_t} + b_4 W_{2_t} + b_5 W_{1_t} + u_t$$

where Y is the volume of exports, X_1 is the real effective exchange rate, X_2 is the volume of total world exports, and W_1, W_2, and W_3 are dummy variables introduced to capture quarterly variation over the first three quarters of the calendar year. The data are quarterly observations, t being the appropriate time subscript. This regression model is the most successful of those developed by John Sheahan in *The Response of Colombian Exports to Variations in Effective Exchange Rates*, Research Memorandum No. 11, Center for Development Economics, Williams College (mimeo). The elasticity estimates obtained by A. Urdinola and R. Mallon, *Policies to Promote Colombian Exports of Manufactures*, Economic Development Report No. 75, Development Advisory Service, Harvard University, 1967, have the virtue of being based on a better measure of effective exchange rates than that used by Sheahan, but their data are yearly observations. Sheahan has shown conclusively the necessity of using quarterly data.

The regression equations that we have obtained on 1960–1967 quarterly data (with standard errors of regression coefficients indicated in parentheses) are as follows:

(a) Y = agricultural exports other than coffee,
$\log Y_t = -5.04 + 1.06 \ \log X_{1_t} + .871 \log X_{2_t}$
$(.46)\phantom{\log X_{1_t} + }(.31)$

$ + .30W_{1_t} + .46W_{2_t} + .26W_{3_t}$
$(.16)(.16)(.16)$
$R^2 = .45, F\text{-value} = 4.07;$

(b) Y = nonagricultural exports other than petroleum and fuel oil,
$\log Y_t = -13.28 + .77 \log X_{1_t} + 2.79 \log X_{2_t}$
$(.28)\phantom{\log X_{1_t}}(.19)$

$ + .03W_{1_t} + .46W_{2_t} + .26W_{3_t}$
$(.10)(.10)(.10)$
$R^2 = .90, F\text{-value} = 44.12;$

rate of erosion of the real exchange rate through domestic price increases was less rapid. For that period the elasticity of response of all minor exports (measured over a period of not more than *six* months) following a change in the real exchange rate was in the order of 1.6.

Another cost of extreme tariff dispersion and quantitative restrictions has been the establishment or strengthening of monopolies. This has further served to foster the splitting apart of the wage structure and the rapid upward drift of wages in the modern sectors of the economy.

Another set of deleterious effects (the focus of the model of the preceding sections) is attributable to the chronic overvaluation of the peso. First, given the hesitancy of the government to maintain a wide differential between the effective rates on imports and minor exports, the relatively low average real exchange rate has retarded the development of new export industries. Second, the overvalued (too low) exchange rate (together with low tariffs on items that Colombia has no immediate intention to produce) has encouraged a degree of capital and import intensity of production that is inappropriate to her resource endowment.[60]

(c) Y = all minor exports (including fuel oil),

$$\log Y_t = -6.14 + \underset{(.27)}{.72} \ \log X_{1t} + \underset{(.17)}{1.57} \log X_{2t}$$

$$+ \underset{(.09)}{.12 W_{1t}} + \underset{(.09)}{.20 W_{2t}} + \underset{(.09)}{.17 W_{3t}}$$

$$R^2 = .79, F\text{-value} = 18.40.$$

Note that the elasticity of response of all minor exports (the elasticity corresponding to Sheahan's estimates) is less than that for either agricultural minor exports or nonagricultural exports other then petroleum and fuel oil. The difference is explained by the inclusion of fuel oil exports in the data for all minor exports. Given the special exchange circumstances surrounding the export of petroleum products by foreign firms, it is not surprising that fuel oil exports should prove to be unrelated to variations in the effective exchange rate for minor exports.

[60] The point here is not (necessarily) that Colombia should produce more sugar and bananas, but simply that import substitution should proceed with close attention to the realities of comparative advantage as they are foreseeable in the reasonable future. We are quick to admit the difficulty of specifying this reality. We are also quick to admit the relevance of the infant industry argument in many circumstances. The point here is that we feel that many of the implicit judgments by Colombian policymakers about the future course of changes in comparative advantages have been faulty.

The unsatisfactory rate of growth of income and employment in the 1960s thus appears to be in large part the result of an inappropriate long-run foreign exchange policy. In particular, "the exchange rate" has chronically been too low. The fall in coffee prices in the mid-1950s meant that a large increase in the real exchange rate was required if Colombia were to continue her previous employment and growth experience. The increase in the real exchange rate accomplished during the 1957–1958 stabilization period was clearly insufficient to serve as a long-run rate target consistent with Colombia's growth aspirations.[61]

The fall of coffee prices in the mid-1950s can be interpreted as a shift to the left in the supply of foreign exchange schedule facing Colombia (Figure 12), or a shift down in the $(M/K)^*$ curve (Figure 11). Maintenance of full employment equilibrium required either an allocation of resources *away* from investment and toward consumption (which would conserve on foreign exchange) or an increase in (E/W), both of which would increase foreign exchange earnings and tend to push down the import intensity of both investment and consumption.

The 1961 development plan called for an increase in the investment rate. The implication that this required an increase in the effective exchange rate appears not to have been recognized. The result is that the system has operated in region 4 of Figure 11—excess demand for foreign exchange, excess supply of domestic inputs. The investment rate has in fact fallen, but not sufficiently to avoid the development of significant domestic slack.[62] As will be discussed in the following chapter, from time to time devaluation has been undertaken. But almost always the target has been (implicitly) to restore the effective exchange rate of 1958, not to achieve a higher rate. As a result, even after devaluations there still have been the two-gap symptoms, and a belief has developed that they are a necessary fact of life. The possibility that the long-run real exchange rate target has been set too low does not appear to have received much serious consideration.

A complicating issue is that the rate of increase of money wages

[61] This is not to say that Colombia ought to have devalued by a greater proportion in 1957–1958. The point is simply that the rate established at that time was not an adequate benchmark or target for long-run development policy.

[62] The decline has not been deliberate, of course.

in the modern sectors of the economy has persistently exceeded the rate of growth of productivity and gives every sign of continuing to do so. The causal mechanism behind the Colombian inflation is highly complex, and we have no intention here of attempting to establish the relative importance of monetary and "structural" factors in producing price changes. Suffice it to say that, for various reasons, the rate of increase of domestic costs is likely to be significantly higher than the rate of increase of international prices. The real exchange rate implied by a given devaluation in the nominal rate of exchange will thus tend to erode through time and, at times, at a spectacular rate. This fact of economic life is completely inconsistent with the view that devaluation is a once-and-for-all policy instrument. Yet, until recently, that is precisely how changes in the exchange rate were portrayed in the context of Colombian politics.

We suspect that the tendency to view "the" exchange rate as a fixed instrument of policy is in large part the reason why the Colombian exchange rate has been chronically overvalued. If so, the key question is whether a different approach to foreign exchange policy is politically possible. To answer this, we must first answer the question, "Why did the Colombian government adopt the foreign exchange policy described in this section?" That is the subject of Chapter VII.

The Political Determinants of Colombian Foreign Exchange Policy

The fall in the price of coffee in 1957–1958 was a major setback to Colombia in her efforts to achieve a rapid pace of economic development. In the face of this severe and permanent change in the terms of trade, Colombia would have had difficulty maintaining into the 1960s the rate of economic growth characteristic of the 1950s even with the wisest and most farseeing of foreign exchange policies. In fact, however, the Colombian policy response was not farseeing. The foreign exchange policy that has emerged, consciously or unconsciously, in the aftermath of the coffee crisis is in part the extension over time of techniques developed to cope with short-run exchange crisis and in part the reflection of that autarchic strategy of growth associated with Raul Prebisch and the ECLA school of the 1950s.[1] This policy, which we shall call the "disequilibrium system," has been characterized by strong reliance on administrative allocation of resources in the form of quantitative trade restrictions, trade licensing, and pricing by administrative decision. The evidence of Chapters IV, V, and VI is that this policy response has been inadequate. Perhaps the most dramatic evidence of its inadequacy is that, in a country characterized by substantial excess capacity in many sectors, the government has found it necessary from time to time to control the excess demand for foreign exchange by means of general restrictions on aggregate demand.

The problem to be explored in this chapter is why, in the face of this record of failure, Colombian foreign exchange policy has developed its present characteristics. Our basic argument is that the failure of Colombian exchange policy to cope satisfactorily with the severe foreign exchange shortage is more the result of political constraints on policymaking than informational or ideological constraints. The government's perception of the importance

---

[1] A strategy that Prebisch has since in large part rejected. See R. Prebisch, *Towards a New Trade Policy for Development,* United Nations, Geneva, 1964.

of the foreign exchange problem has indeed been blunted by an ideology of growth that is widely shared within the ranks of the modernizing elite, but its choice of foreign exchange policy has primarily been determined by a calculus of the relative political costs of policy alternatives.[2]

By *political* constraint we mean either (1) limitations on the government's freedom to make policy, imposed by the need of the political leadership to retain the support of broad groups within the electorate, or (2) the inability of the government to maintain both policy initiative and independence vis-à-vis more narrowly defined economic interest groups. Both types of political constraint are relevant in Colombia. The restraint on freedom of policy choice imposed by the competition for dominance within the existing party structure between modernizing and traditional elites is obvious in a political environment such as Colombia's, where the nonelite elements of the party hierarchies are increasingly oriented toward populistic objectives. The constraints imposed by interest group actions are equally important but more subtle in their exercise. The constraint imposed by the use or threat of use of overt pressure on the Congress or the presidency by economic interest groups is both visible and important. That the careers of many members of the bureaucratic elite involve movement back and forth between the government and institutions committed to furthering the objectives of the entrepreneurial elite may represent a further constraint on governmental actions, but one more difficult to appraise.

By *ideological* or *informational* constraint we mean the inability of the policymaker to perceive the full range of options, or the complete set of consequences of a particular decision, because of certain assumptions or preconceptions about the nature of the growth process that he is unwilling or unable to reexamine. In Colombia the most important of these preconceptions is that administrative pricing decisions can be used to compensate for most of the inadequacies of an imperfectly competitive market system.

[2] It is by no means obvious that this should have been the case. For example, in his *Economic Policy-Making and Development in Brazil, 1947–1964*, Wiley, New York, 1968, Nathaniel Leff has argued that the Brazilian failure to deal adequately with its foreign exchange constraint can be explained primarily in terms of the ideology of growth held by the political elite. In discussions with other students of Brazilian politics, we understand that this thesis is debatable.

A second preconception, now held less strongly than in the past, is that excess demand for foreign exchange can be dealt with satisfactorily in the long run without securing a dramatic increase in the supply of exports.

There are two main themes that emerge from our analysis. The first is that the preference for the "disequilibrium" system that is typical of policymaking in most of the less developed nations is in large part rooted in the characteristics of what we commonly call democracy. A government whose leaders are conditioned primarily by such incentives as power, "visibility," or prestige that are intrinsic to the political system, whose major objective is to retain the support of the electorate, has a strong tendency to adopt comprehensive exchange controls, maintain an exchange rate that undervalues foreign currency, and accord producers of import substitutes a high degree of protection from foreign competition. In a pluralistic democracy the disequilibrium system is likely to be abandoned only if the government's leadership rejects it on ideological grounds, and such a policy reversal is unlikely to be permanent unless an overwhelming majority of the political leadership of the nation shares that commitment.

The second conclusion of this chapter is that the objectives of the program-oriented political elite in Colombia in large part lead to a preference for some type of disequilibrium system of foreign exchange policy. This, in turn, reinforces the preferences of those leaders who lack program commitments. The tendency to administrative allocation of foreign exchange and extreme dispersion of tariff rates is thus the result of a long series of bargains between a bureaucratic elite intellectually committed to the notion of providing a detailed prescription for allowable economic change and an economic elite convinced that the advantages of markets protected from competition outweigh the likely costs of finely detailed government intervention.

There is no need to presume that this reinforcement derives only from those ideologies that stress the advantages of autarchic development. A simple commitment to the belief that efficient and equitable growth requires a substantial degree of administrative allocation of resources will tend to strengthen the preference for each of the elements of the disequilibrium system, with the exception of the bias against provision of increased incentives to export.

The first section of this chapter will recapitulate briefly the recent political history of Colombia and discuss the objectives and place in society of the major political power groups. The second section attempts to portray the structure of incentives and constraints that underlies the economic policymaking of the central government. The final section is devoted to the determinants of foreign exchange policy.

POLITICAL POWER GROUPS IN COLOMBIA

The recent political history of Colombia is a complex record of two separate but related arenas of competition. The first, and probably still the most important, is the competition for the traditional rewards of politics—money, jobs, status, power—among leaders who attempt to manipulate the loyalties of the Colombian population to the Liberal or the Conservative parties. The second is the competition between those leaders primarily conditioned to this traditional style of politics and others who have also been motivated to transform Colombian political and social institutions to conform to modern economic reality and to hasten the development of that reality.

HISTORICAL AND INSTITUTIONAL BACKGROUND

The competition for the traditional rewards of politics has taken place both within and between the major political parties. The competition between "traditionalists" and "modernists" has for the most part taken place within the confines of the separate parties, although the emergence in the 1960s of the Alianza Nacional Popular (ANAPO) as an alternative to the two historic parties threatens an extension of this competition to the interparty level.[3]

The competition between the "traditionalists" and the "modernists" is a relatively recent phenomenon. It is customary to date it from the advent of the first administration (1936–1940) of the Liberal President Alfonso Lopez Pumarejo. The competition for the traditional rewards of politics is the legacy of the political style developed in the nineteenth century. The traditional style of

---

[3] The ANAPO is the first electorally significant Colombian political movement in this century to operate outside the label of either the Liberal or Conservative parties. It was founded by ex-President (1953–1957) Gustavo Rojas Pinilla.

Colombian politics invokes an emotional, moralistic, and tenacious attachment to hereditary loyalties. At its highest level it threatens physical survival. Twice within the twentieth century this threat has been sufficient to promote civil war. The first of these conflicts was the War of the Thousand Days from 1899 to 1902. The second was the so-called *Violencia* of 1948–1953.[4] The memory and the consequences of this last episode of violence, the last great eruption of traditionalist competition, continue to influence the structure of Colombian politics.

The pivotal importance of *la Violencia* to subsequent political developments results in large part from the consequences of the actions taken to bring the conflict to an end. The assumption of political power by the military in 1953 was initially accepted by many political leaders as the only possible means of ending the armed conflict between partisans of the Liberal and Conservative parties. However, the independent political ambitions evidenced by General Gustavo Rojas Pinilla, subsequent to his accession to the Presidency, convinced the leadership of both parties that a continuation of the Rojas regime threatened the very existence of the traditional party system of government. The eventual opposition to Rojas of virtually all elements of the political and economic leadership of the country led to a further military intervention in 1957 and the resumption of constitutional government in 1958.

This reestablishment of political power in the hands of the historic political parties was preceded by an agreement between the Liberals and Conservatives in the so-called Pact of Sitges to restrict the level of "traditionalist" political competition. This restriction was accomplished by a series of agreements over executive and legislative parity that constitute the National Front system of government,[5] the current constitutional basis for government in Colombia.

There are elements that are new in the National Front politics

---

[4] A series of skirmishes, terrorist attacks, and mass political murders that is estimated to have taken between 100,000 and 200,000 Colombian lives, roughly 1 percent of the population.

[5] The National Front system calls for alternation of the Presidency (every four years) between candidates of the Liberal and Conservative parties and equal representation for each party within the national and departmental (state) legislatures and municipal councils. It also calls for parity in executive appointments. The terms of the system are currently being revised.

of the 1960s and 1970s, but much is rooted in the past.[6] A high degree of party identification by individual lower and lower-middle income class voters remains. In rural areas, in particular, this identification still is quasi-religious in intensity. In these areas the traditional pattern of bloc voting still obtains, the bulk of a given community voting for the candidate endorsed by the local political "chief" (*cacique*) who, in turn, has endorsed the candidate sponsored by the regional political leader (*caudillo*) with whom he has formed a semi-permanent alliance.

In urban Colombia the political structure is more complex. Many voters in lower and lower-middle income areas still can be expected to follow the endorsement of neighborhood leaders who have formed alliances with the municipal structure of one of the major party factions. However, the urban party leadership is less able now than in the past to achieve electoral success with an appeal rooted in little more than the historic mystique of the party label. As a result, the strategy whereby the urban professionals attempt to maintain the electoral loyalty of their clientele is changing. More attention is given to economic events (not economic policy issues), and political argument is increasingly cast in the populist mold. Political campaigns are organized to exploit the public's sensitivity to the issue of inflation and the widespread belief that inflation is causally related to the increased pressure on the real-income levels of the lower and lower-middle income classes of recent years. The notion that the economic plight of these classes is related to the slow rate of growth in the modern sector is not well rooted in the electorate.

Another characteristic of current-day Colombian politics that derives from the past is that a primary motivation for virtually all participants in political life continues to be found in the rewards intrinsic to the political system itself—jobs, money, power, prestige, and "visibility."[7] In particular, the opportunity to achieve visibility

---

[6] In the following discussion of party characteristics and structure, we are enormously indebted to the ideas and writings of Richard Maullin of The Rand Corporation. For published material, see James Payne, *Patterns of Conflict in Colombia*, Yale University Press, New Haven, 1968, Chaps. 9 and 10; and Robert H. Dix, *Colombia: The Political Dimensions of Change*, Yale University Press, New Haven, 1967, Chaps. 8 and 9.

[7] The theme developed by James Payne in his highly stimulating *Patterns of Conflict in Colombia* is that political conflict in Colombia is essentially

is a compelling incentive. Although there is something of a hereditary element in the determination of position within a party hierarchy, advancement within that hierarchy is essentially a function of the demonstrated ability to deliver votes. As such, politics represents one of the important avenues for upward mobility in Colombia.

It is important to stress, however, that the dominance in Colombian politics of considerations intrinsic to the political system itself is gradually abating. This development is perhaps the chief "new" element in the politics of the National Front period. A "new breed" of politician is emerging—leaders who are *also* committed to the modernization of existing institutions and who have distinct notions about the policies needed to effect such changes. The motivation of most members of the political class is thus becoming a complex amalgam of "modernist" and "traditionalist" objectives colored by a common quest for patronage, leverage, and status.

Another "new" element in the politics of the current period is the reduced level of competition between the two historic parties. Much of this is the result of the constitutional constraints on maximum political loss or gain that is implied by the National Front arrangements. A further restraint is the fear of breaking down the tenuous arrangements that curb the intense interparty rivalry, a competition so severe in the recent past as to have produced a situation of near anarchy in many rural areas of the country. The memory of *la Violencia* is the dominant influence on many of the older generation of political leaders. Finally, there is the fear common to the upper hierarchies of both the Liberal and Conservative parties of the emergence of an authoritarian populist alternative to the historic polyclass parties.

This reduction in the level of interparty competition has been purchased at a cost, however, for the degree of competition within the parties has correspondingly increased. This increased factionalism has greatly complicated the political spectrum. It is not suffi-

nothing more than a competition for position (and the traditional rewards of position). That is, all political leaders can be described as being pure traditionalists. This is an oversimplification of the Colombian political reality. Much of the recent political conflict in Colombia is explicable only in terms of competition between "modernist" and "traditionalist" objectives. This competition is more than a conflict between individuals. It is also evident in the successive actions of individual political leaders.

cient any longer to identify a person or a group as Liberal or
Conservative. The Liberal party has been divided into an "official"
faction and the Movimiento Revolucionario Liberal (MRL), until
1968 a faction in opposition.[8] The Conservative party in recent
decades has been divided into "official" (Ospinista) and Lauro-
Alzatista factions, both of which have from time to time found
it strategic to refrain from participating in the National Front government. A further splintering of the Conservative party occurred
in 1969 as a result of Belisario Betancur's decision to contest the
presidential election outside the National Front framework.[9] Within
these major factions there are important subfactions. Further
complicating this alignment is the ANAPO of ex-President Rojas,
for all intents and purposes an independent party, but for constitutional (legal) reasons identified as an opposition group of Liberals
and (chiefly) Conservatives.

These phenomena—high party identification, the importance of
"intrinsic" objectives, the fear of populism, restricted interparty
competition, and heightened party factionalism—are responsible
for what we feel to be the most important behavioral characteristics
of the two historic parties: the relative lack of control by top leadership over the subordinate leadership within a party, and the
tendency of the Liberal and Conservative parties to offer essentially
the same policy solutions to the various problems facing the
country.

The relative lack of control of the party apparatus by the party's

[8] Party factionalism is essentially a matter of competition for the traditional rewards of politics, rather than a struggle between "modernists" and
"traditionalists," although there is perhaps a growing tendency for the
modernists to identify with the "official" party factions supporting the National Front coalition. A faction will go into opposition if it feels that
its participation in the National Front coalition is not sufficiently advan-
tageous in terms of patronage and other prerequisites of power. The absorp-
tion of the MRL into the "official" Liberal party in 1968 efter eight years
of opposition was the result of a recalculation of the relative advantages
of cooperation and opposition to the National Front, not a reassessment
of differences in ideology or policy perception.

[9] Belisario Betancur began his political career as a protégé of former
Conservative President Laureano Gómez. Subsequently he joined the forces
of the political enemies of Gómez. His rhetoric leans heavily toward
promises to defend the national patrimony from exploitation by foreign and
domestic big business and to shift the distribution of income in favor of
labor.

top leadership has two important consequences. First, the top political leadership is strongly sensitive to the judgments formed by subordinate elements of the hierarchy in making its own appraisal of the costs and benefits attendant upon a given policy change. The leadership is further dependent on the party structure because there are no public opinion polling organizations that can provide information on the tenor of public feeling on policy issues. In the absence of more precise techniques, many political leaders have come to rely upon the network of party workers for estimates of public sentiment. The emergence of an authoritarian-populist alternative (ANAPO) to the traditional party factions has further increased the sensitivity of the top leadership to the judgments of the lower party apparatus. As a result, there are a number of problem areas in which even the more extrinsically motivated top leaders do not feel able to maintain a substantial measure of policy freedom vis-à-vis the party rank and file. As we shall see, one of these areas is exchange rate policy. A more direct consequence of the relative lack of control of the party apparatus by the top leadership is the congenital difficulty of securing legislative support for the policies advocated by the executive.

The phenomenon of negligible programmatic or policy differences between the Liberal and Conservative parties derives from the constraints on interparty competition and the essential irrelevance of program objectives to the motivation of much, if not most, of the membership of the party apparatus. This tendency to sameness of policy obtains in spite of substantial differences in the constituency and ideological heritage of the two parties. The Liberals tend to be the majority party in the cities. The Conservatives are dominant in most rural areas.[10] The Liberal party has grown up with a Manchestrian, republican doctrine that in some cases has had positivistic or Marxian embellishments. The Conservative ideology has historically stressed the value of maintaining the hierarchical principle of personal relations and has been influenced by Hispanic traditions of state control of economic activity. Yet, except for the issue of church-state relationships, it is not now possible to identify marked differences between the two parties on matters of economic policy. Neither the evidence

[10] For example, see Payne, *Patterns of Conflict in Colombia*, p. 235.

of public statements of party leaders nor questionnaire surveys of the attitudes of these leaders is inconsistent with the hypothesis that the parties are polyclass institutions whose objectives are not related in any close way to the composition of the party's electorate.[11]

With this background we are ready to consider the current structure of political power in Colombia. For our purposes we think this structure is best defined in terms of the interactions among and between five distinct groups: (1) an element within the traditional parties committed to both the modernization of existing institutions and the traditional rewards of politics; (2) those elements within the traditional party hierarchies that are committed to the maximization of the rewards accruing to successful participants in party activities but are either indifferent or opposed to the modernization of existing institutions; (3) groups outside the traditional two-party structure, most of whom are uncommitted ideologically but are oriented to the exploitation of popular discontent, but some of whom are committed to a revolutionary socioeconomic transformation of society that is to be initiated by violence; (4) economic interest groups; and (5) the government bureaucracy.

THE MODERN ELITE

The modern political elite of Colombia is a heterogeneous group of politicians and administrator-technicians (*tecnicos*) operating within the traditional political parties. Those who are best classified as professional politicians are generally at or near the top of their party faction's hierarchy. Included in this group are both ex-President (1966–1970) Carlos Lleras Restrepo and the current President Misael Pastrana Borrero. The *tecnicos* are those of the educated elite, often with specialized training or experience, who have sought out and established a personal relationship with various influential members of the party hierarchy.

A good many of the upper hierarchy of each of the traditional party factions are in general agreement concerning the "modern" objectives, but the purest expression of the modern ideology by professional politicians is probably to be found in the writings and speeches of the *La Ceja* group within the Liberal party. There are numerous links between the modern elite and elements within

[11] *Ibid.*, Chap. 4.

the business sector and the liberal professions that are concerned with socioeconomic modernization. The Sociedad Economica de los Amigos del Pais (Liberal) and the Centro de Estudios Colombianos (Conservative) are particularly important in this connection as public forums and private clearinghouses for modern policy.

Although there are obvious problems with identifying a given set of objectives as *the* program of the modernists, most of this group shares a commitment to the following set of beliefs: economic development is essential not only as a means of raising the material standard of living but as a prerequisite to the modernization of a society whose organization is still dominated by the hierarchical principle that roles are assigned on the basis of class rather than ability; the public sector must be the "leading sector" in the development process, the critical policy instrument being a large public investment budget devoted to the provision of an economic infrastructure and the elimination of bottlenecks not attacked by the private sector; the characteristics of the market mechanism in Colombia are such that detailed public control over relative prices and the direct allocation of scarce resources such as foreign exchange are necessary to secure a socially acceptable distribution of the economic gains of development; and modernist policy objectives must be institutionalized within the public sector through creation of a bureaucracy that is substantially independent of the party structure.

It is important to stress that the focus of the modernizing group is on socioeconomic "efficiency," rather than on the redistribution of wealth. This is not to say that changes in the distribution of income are not sought as an objective or gain from modernization, but that the means for achieving such changes are seen to be changes in the distribution of the capacity of individuals to contribute to total productivity, and not direct transfers or publicly imposed changes in the distribution of wealth.[12] To the extent that there is a political ideology common to the modern elite, it is a

---

[12] This appears the essential concept, for example, in the theory of the *Economia de Abundancia* as enunciated by President Carlos Lleras Restrepo. See his essay "La economía de la abundancia fuente a la escasez," in A. Lleras C. *et al., Los Caminos del Cambio,* Ediciones Tercer Mundo, Bogota, 1966.

corporativist concept of society as an organic whole. Although the paternalism inherent in the group's perception of its own role in the development process provides a strong link with the traditional style of politics in Colombia, the relatively widespread acceptance of the objective of weakening the hierarchical basis of social organization indicates a fundamental change in the political process. The basis for this change is partly a matter of idealism, but the primary motivation is a pragmatic perception of the likelihood that the socioeconomic stresses accompanying industrialization will prove incompatible with traditional political institutions, unless the latter acquire greater executive capability and adapt to changing circumstances.

THE TRADITIONAL ELITE

The pragmatic aspect of the motivation of most of the modern elite makes the distinction between a modern and a traditional political elite difficult to draw in practice. Relatively few leaders influential in the factional hierarchies are strongly committed to the ideology of modernization. The great bulk of the professional political class in Colombia, as in other countries, is primarily oriented to maximizing the traditional rewards to participants in the political process. These rewards are primarily material and accrue chiefly in the form of jobs, which carry an important element of social status. In recent years the menu of rewards has become more complex—access to government credit, government contracts, access to foreign exchange, and favorable tax or tariff treatment—but for most professional politicians the dominant incentive is still jobs.

Although the objectives of this traditional political class are unrelated to matters of economic policy, there are several policy issues in which the interests of the modernists and traditionalists are directly opposed. One such issue is the matter of increasing the executive capacity of the government through professionalization of the bureaucracy. Another is the principle to be employed in allocating public investment funds. On questions of fundamental reform of economic policy, the traditional group is perhaps best characterized as being resistant to change in existing policy but sensitive to strong swells of what passes for public opinion and to the threats to political stability embodied in fiscal or exchange crises. This group can be expected to respond pragmatically to the policymaking leadership of the modernists in certain circumstances. For example, the powerful demonstration effect of the Cuban revolution and land reform provided the pragmatic incentive for the cooperation between the modernists and certain elements of the traditional elite that was essential to the passage of Law 135 (the land reform law) of 1961.[13] Similarly, the near economic paralysis and unprecedented inflation of early 1963 prompted a traditional-dominated Congress to permit widespread administrative reforms urged by modern elements, including the establishment of effective governmental control over the Central Bank (*Banco de la Republica*).

Both the strength and nature of the traditional group is evident in the intensity and form of Congressional opposition to the constitutional reforms initiated by President Lleras Restrepo in 1968. Only the threat of resignation (of a popular chief executive) and an exceedingly intricate series of negotiations among the leadership of the Liberal party and the dominant faction of the Conservative party were sufficient to secure a transfer of budgetary initiative from the legislature to the executive, and this was achieved only at the cost of abandonment of a proposal to reduce the size of an unwieldly Congress.[14]

The continuing dependence of the modernists on the electoral apparatus assembled by the traditionalists was further evident in the events of the elections of 1966. Although the presidential candidacy of Carlos Lleras Restrepo had been endorsed by the national directorate of the *oficialista* (National Front supporting) factions of the two traditional parties, Lleras chose to entrust the direction of his campaign to a bipartisan committee composed of modernists. In the course of the electoral campaign, however, it became apparent that the Congressional strength of dissident factions of the Liberal and Conservative parties together with the opposition party organized by Rojas Pinilla (ANAPO) was likely to create a legislative-executive stalemate. As a result, Lleras was forced to abandon his policy of reliance on the modernists and seek the help of those traditional elements of the Liberal and Con-

[13] Albert O. Hirschman, *Journeys Toward Progress,* Anchor Books, New York, 1965, p. 193.
[14] *El Espectador* (Bogota), 19 Nov. 1968.

servative parties who were supporting the National Front.[15] The near defeat of Pastrana, the National Front candidate for the presidency in 1970, is likely to strengthen further the power of traditionalist elements within the major parties.

GROUPS OUTSIDE THE TRADITIONAL PARTY SYSTEM

The only electorally significant political group operating without the endorsement of major figures in the two historic parties is the ANAPO. In the presidential election of 1970 it very nearly achieved a plurality for its founder and leader, Gustavo Rojas Pinilla, and it has enjoyed important electoral successes at the local level, particularly in some of the large cities. As an organization, however, it is critically dependent on the personal image of ex-President Rojas. It represents a conglomerate of interests, some ideological, others purely opportunistic. The ideological content of ANAPO defies description in terms of a simple left-right classification, embracing as it does neo-Peronists, admirers of the Falange, various arch-Catholic conservatives, and former supporters of the MRL; but the image created by Rojas is one of appeal to the working class masses and hostility to an "oligarchy" whose mechanism of control is the traditional political parties.

There is a great deal of doubt that the ANAPO will survive its leader, and it is not at all certain that any other leader or group will be able to manipulate the Rojista formula with a similar degree of success. Nevertheless, ANAPO's success has certain implications for the future structure of politics in Colombia. In particular, the electoral appeal of a populist alternative to the gradualist, efficiency-oriented program of the modern elite has been demonstrated, and leaders within the traditional parties may become further emboldened to offer populist solutions to the country's problems. To some extent the ability of the modernists to play an important role at the apex of the traditional party hierarchies has depended on the absence of an effectively competitive strategy of government that the traditional elements could invoke. The redistributive-populist package of ideas currently associated with

[15] For a more extended discussion of this episode, see Richard L. Maullin, *The Colombia-IMF Disagreement of November–December 1966: An Interpretation of Its Place in Colombian Politics,* RM-5314-RC, The Rand Corporation, Santa Monica, June 1967.

ANAPO may provide such a strategy, and the modern elite may find itself increasingly embattled in its efforts to retain the support of the traditional party mechanism. This appears to be the most likely challenge to the existing structure of political power in Colombia. There is today no significant threat from those groups whose opposition to the current leadership of the traditional parties is based on the appeal to violent revolution.[16]

ECONOMIC INTEREST GROUPS

Although the recent resurgence of political factionalism rooted in the appeal of a simplistic form of populism is potentially of great significance to the future structure of Colombian politics, probably the most important political change in Colombia during the period of the National Front has been the gradual supplementing of the traditional style of interparty political and ideological warfare by a politics of pressure groups. The industry associations, labor unions, and entrepreneurial organizations have grown in importance in the progress of policymaking. There are two major factors in the emergence of this relationship between the economic interest groups and the government. The first is the ineffectiveness of the traditional party organizations as aggregators of the wide variety of economic interest group claims. The second is that the administrative capability and technical expertise required to implement the development strategy of the political elite can often be supplied only by the organizations formed to further special group interests.

The nature of the relationship between the economic and political leadership of Colombia is complex. There is a strong tendency to view the modern elements of the political parties and the management of the technologically modern sectors of the economy as being part of a homogeneous national elite.[17] In some respects

---

[16] The most important of these organizations are the Fuerza Armada Revolucionaria Colombiana (FARC) and the Ejercito de Liberacion Nacional (ELN). The former organization controls some territory in remote rural areas and possesses a surprising capacity for self-defense, but there is some doubt whether its ambitions extend to the control of the national government. The latter group has more orthodox revolutionary goals, but its ambitions appear to exceed its means by a very wide margin.

[17] See, for example, Dix, *Colombia: The Political Dimensions of Change,* pp. 389–417. For a contrasting view, see James L. Payne, "The Oligarchy

this view is warranted. There is a growing tendency for both groups to share in the part of the ideology that stresses the value of achieving a society less dominated by the principle of hierarchy. Both groups stress the importance of the state in the development process and share a common aversion to populism. Yet there are also some significant differences in the outlook of the two groups. The unity of the political leadership with respect to social class is generally exaggerated. The distaste for the message of populism on the part of many members of the modern elite is founded on a judgment that such programs are economically inefficient, rather than on a rejection of their implications for the distribution of income. And the consensus on the role of government in the development process quickly disappears when questions of the usefulness of particular instruments of economic control arise. Thus there is a real need to revise the notion that Colombia is dominated by an oligarchy that controls both political and economic power in a single embrace. The economic and political leadership represent groups that are surprisingly independent in membership and motivation.

The primary distinction between the nature of the objectives of the modern elite and the special interest groups is that the latter see themselves as petitioners for redress of government decisions rather than as bargainers over policy in the formulation stage. This is particularly so for such organizations as ANDI (the National Association of Industrialists) and FENALCO (the National Federation of Merchants) whose membership base encompasses diverse interests. Groups such as the Cottongrower's Association and the Cattleman's Association whose concerns are more narrowly defined, chiefly with government policy with respect to sector prices and the sectoral allocation of credit, are more likely to take a direct part in the initial stages of policy formulation. Although the primary focus of most of these special interest groups is reactive, while the government bureaucracy directed by the political

---

Muddle," *World Politics,* Vol. XX, No. 3, April 1968, pp. 439–453. For a discussion of recruitment patterns for the political leadership, see Payne, *Patterns of Conflict in Colombia,* pp. 36–45. Data on the origins of business leaders have not been developed in any detail, but a discussion of some relevance is to be found in Aaron Lipman, *El Empresario Bogotano,* Ediciones Tercer Mundo, Bogota, 1966, Chap. 5.

elite retains the responsibility for the initial formulation of policy, it does not follow in the least that these organizations are not ultimately of critical significance in determining just what policy will be carried out. The ideological commitment of the modern elite impels the government to adopt a strategy of detailed prescription for allowable economic change, but the limited technical and decisionmaking capacity of the government bureaucracy implies that the details of that prescription will be strongly influenced by those groups that best understand its effects, namely, the relevant interest group organizations. There need be no implication here of either corruption or political favoritism. That the interest groups are normally the sole source of supply of the data needed for policymaking is, in general, sufficient to guarantee some degree of influence over the government's economic decisions.

The organizations founded by various entrepreneurial groups have an unquestioned interest and ability in protecting their clientele from potentially adverse decisions. It is more difficult to argue that these organizations are strongly motivated to act so as to preserve the vested interests of entrepreneurs as a class. In a certain sense, of course, these organizations are conservative in terms of the usual left-right spectrum. Nevertheless, much of the current entrepreneurial class in Colombia is strongly influenced by a conception of society as an organic whole; and the wealthier element, at least, is more or less strongly committed to the notion that the ownership of property implies a social responsibility.

In this respect there has been a substantial change over time in the objectives of the organizations established by the propertied class. The predecessor to ANDI, the National Economic Association of Employers (APEN), was organized specifically to combat the economic policies advocated in the 1930s by President Lopez Pumarejo (in particular, to prevent the growth of labor organizations). In contrast, ANDI, although an organization of the industrial elite or superelite, tends to the view that the most efficient means of protecting the interests of the economic elite is rapid economic growth itself. This focus on "efficiency" and increasing the rate of economic growth sets a certain bond between the economic elite and the modern political elite—a relatively new political development in Colombia.

It is easy to exaggerate the extent to which the economic elite

is willing to subordinate its historically narrow focus on class interests for a somewhat broader conception of national interest. For
all its expressed concern for truly national objectives, ANDI remains an organization dedicated to the furtherance of the interests
of big business. The small manufacturers of Colombia have accordingly deemed it necessary to establish their own organization, the
Association of Small Industrialists (ACOPI).

The above discussion has been primarily concerned with the
characteristics of the special interest organizations established by
the entrepreneurial class. The role played by the national confederations of labor unions, the most important of which are the
Colombian Labor Federation (CTC) and the Colombian Workers
Union (UTC), is sufficiently different to warrant separate
consideration.

One important source of difference in the nature of the political
influence wielded by labor and entrepreneurial groups is the hierarchical difference between the entrepreneurial and working classes
and the character of much of the dominant political caste. Much
of the effectiveness of the pressures exerted by the entrepreneurial
organizations derives from the ability of the leadership of such
groups to take advantage of personal, family, and client relationships with members of the modernizing political elite. There are
fewer ties of this sort for union leadership to exploit. Furthermore,
the union movement is not as free of political party ties as are
the entrepreneurial organizations. The CTC has had historically
close ties with the Liberal party and at various times has been
virtually a creature of that party. The UTC was founded by the
Jesuits to counter the communist influence in the CTC and had
definite ties with the Conservative party in the 1950s. It is not
now identified with a particular party faction, but it has sponsored
its own slates of candidates under traditional party labels.

The major constraint on the potential power of a class-oriented
movement energized by labor groups is probably the inherent organizational weakness of the national labor federations. The individual unions that make up these confederations have been
reluctant to allocate either responsibility or funds to the national
organizations. This split reflects a dilemma that has continued to
plague the union movement in Colombia—the inconsistency of
the objectives of maximizing the economic gains of existing union

membership and representing a working class that is mainly employed in technologically traditional environments where union organizations are not practicable. Only on certain issues such as inflation, where the interests of the unionized (modern sector) and nonunionized (traditional sector) labor force appear to be identical, is there an obvious opportunity for union leadership to represent "class" interests. In many respects the membership of the stronger labor unions represents an industrial "aristocracy," and the local leadership of the union movement is unwilling to sacrifice the relatively secure economic advantages that can be obtained by elevating the unionized work force to the status of a noncompeting group for the uncertainties of a strategy of class-oriented objectives.

For these reasons the influence of labor organizations on policy decisions is muted and complex. On matters such as reform of the labor code that are of immediate relevance to all union leadership, the consultative status of labor organizations has been institutionalized either by law or by custom. In these areas the role of the labor confederations is analogous to the role of the entrepreneurial groups in such questions as the sectoral allocation of credit. The unions have also succeeded in obtaining direct influence over the administration of labor law by securing the appointment of congenial individuals to the judicial apparatus responsible for labor law. Yet certain individuals within the labor movement also have nascent ambitions to use their organizational positions to achieve broader political objectives. This possibility that the labor organizations might be used as a vehicle for the vigorous exploitation of a populist political program, in combination with the uncertain structure of power within the labor federations, makes the potential influence of the union organizations over economic policy very difficult to evaluate.

THE BUREAUCRACY

A professional technical caste within the government whose outlook is identified with the special interests of the various bureaucratic units that house it is not yet an important force to be reckoned with in the process of policy formation in Colombia. At the moment the executive competence of the ministries and independent government agencies is highly dependent on the initia-

tive of a few top-level *tecnicos* who are associated with members
of the professional political elite.

This state of affairs is slowly changing, however, for one of
the major canons of the modernist ideology is the necessity of
creating an administrative bureaucracy that possesses both a strong
analytic and implementing capability and substantial policymaking
autonomy. Because of the tradition of substantial ministerial independence vis-à-vis the presidency and the difficulty of revitalizing
organizations whose functions, structure, and pay scale are a matter
of legislative approval, this movement to strengthen the capacity
of the executive branch has chiefly taken the form of delegating
policy responsibility to newly established independent executive
agencies. The agency responsible for implementing the existing
land reform legislation (INCORA) is the best example of this
form of organization. The Planning Department (Planeacion) is
another. In each case the line of authority flows directly to the
office of the presidency. In the main, the staffs of these organizations are both technically capable and possessed of program
commitments.

In the particular area of foreign exchange and trade policy,
the role played by the *tecnico* group is somewhat complex. A large
number of bureaucratic units are involved in the formulation of
foreign exchange policy—the Planning Department, the Ministry
of Finance, the Central Bank, the Superintendency of Foreign
Trade, and the Ministry of Development. Yet although the responsibility for policy is bureaucratically diffuse, in practice most
policy inputs come directly from the President or the Monetary
Council (Junta Monetaria).[18] The dominant nonpolitical influence
on the Monetary Council has come from the two *tecnicos* designated as participating but nonvoting members, individuals who
are allied with, or are protégés of, important political leaders.

This state of affairs is more or less typical of the present policymaking role of the high-level technical expert in Colombia. The

[18] Established by Law 21 of 1963 to consist of the Minister of Finance,
the Minister of Development, the Minister of Agriculture, the Head of
the Planning Department, the Manager of the Bank of the Republic, and
two "permanent" technical experts, the last named having a voice but no
vote in the deliberations of the group. For a discussion of the functions
of the Junta Monetaria, see Oscar Alviar, *Instrumentos de Direccion
Monetaria en Colombia*, Ediciones Tercer Mundo, Bogota, 1967.

influence of the program-oriented *tecnico* is exercised through personal relationships established with upper-level members of the professional political caste, rather than through formal bureaucratic relationships. In most cases the organizational routines of the government bureaucracies do not impinge on the decisions of the government leadership in any important way, and their outputs are only marginally significant in shaping policy discussion.

THE INCENTIVE AND CONSTRAINT STRUCTURE OF ECONOMIC POLICYMAKING IN A DEMOCRACY

The previous description of the characteristics of the major political groups in Colombia suggests that, in many respects, the behavior of the Colombian government may conform to that implied by the model of rational political behavior posited by Anthony Downs's economic theory of democracy.[19] That is, political leaders act so as to maximize the probability of attaining (or retaining) office, subject to the constraint that selection is through a process of free elections; and voters act so as to maximize their utility income (including that part accruing from government action), subject to the constraint that information and its utilization are costly. In terms of policy formation, the key proposition implied by this model is that government policies are thought of simply as a means of holding or attaining office.

If stated in a reasonably strong form, the general (and obvious) proposition that governments formulate policies with an eye for maximizing electoral rewards has a number of implications with respect to the likely outcome of the economic policymaking process. Three of these implications appear to us to be of particular importance. First, there is a high degree of inertia with respect to reconsideration of a policy whose effects on the distribution of real income are both blurred and diffuse. Second, there will be a strong tendency for policy to be made in a piecemeal fashion and implemented by special purpose policy instruments. The policymaking system will be relatively sensitive to the desires for policy change of special interest groups as long as perception of

[19] Anthony Downs, *An Economic Theory of Democracy*, Harper, New York, 1957. For a similar opinion, see Payne, *Patterns of Conflict in Colombia*, p. 254. Eduardo Santa, *Sociologia Politica de Colombia*, Editorial Iqueima, Bogota, 1955, offers an analysis of Colombian politics that is also in many ways characteristic of the general model posited by Downs.

the effects of such policy change on income distribution is likely
to be confined to a small portion of the electorate. Third, if a
policy instrument is widely believed to have significant effects on
the distribution of income, it will be utilized in a manner that
is believed to redistribute income from the "rich" to the "poor."

The remainder of this section will examine these three characteristics of policymaking in a democracy in the particular context
of Colombian political institutions.

POLICYMAKING INERTIA

The economic policymaking system in a democracy such as that
of Colombia is prone to inertia when confronted by policies whose
ramifications regarding income distribution are possibly extensive
and not well understood. A policy will not be reexamined unless
a party (or party faction) believes that it is likely to be to its
advantage, having balanced out potential supporters and opponents
to such a reexamination of policy. The policymaking system will
thus resist the attempts of a program-oriented political innovator
to force a thoroughgoing reappraisal of a major policy instrument
unless he can demonstrate that there has been, or will be, a substantial change of sentiment within the electorate or unless he can
engineer such a reappraisal through a complex strategy of log-
rolling and shifting alliances.[20] Given the crudity of the system
whereby political chieftains in the less developed countries obtain
information concerning the sense of the electorate, and given the
essential difficulty of explaining or "propagandizing" to such an
electorate any but the most simplistic of conceptions of the economic effects of broad economic policies, so-called reform mongering by charisma is likely to be successful only under fairly special
circumstances. "Reform mongering" by "sheer politicking" is constrained by the limited authority possessed by the factional lineup
within the major parties[21] and by the tendency to "opposition for

[20] For a classic description of the techniques of so-called reform-mongering, see Albert O. Hirschman, *Journeys Toward Progress*, Chap. 5.

[21] The phenomenon of limited authority of leadership is not confined
to the party hierarchies. Traditionally, responsibility for policymaking initiative within the central government has been delegated to the executive
cabinet. This is very much a function of the personality of the President
and the extent to which he has program commitments, however. Guillermo
Leon Valencia (1962–1966) and, to a lesser extent, Alberto Lleras Camargo

opposition's sake" implied by the importance of the "visibility" incentive to participants in political life.[22]

The fear of the consequences of unconstrained interparty competition (a fear fed by the memory of *la Violencia*) may also serve to increase policymaking inertia in Colombia. This influence cuts two ways, however. The opposition to a given policy change may use the threat of withdrawal from the National Front coalition to stymie the proponents of that change. On the other hand, the government may induce factions that have no interest in securing a policy change to accept that change by equating policy support with a vote of confidence in the National Front system. If there is no conflicting wave of public sentiment, and if the issue poses no threat to the long-term electoral balance between the major parties, a president who is willing to play the game of brinkmanship may be able to force an agreement over policy change simply on the grounds that the alternative to agreement is a breakdown of the guarantees of equal (or similar) access to political resources that make up the National Front system and a threat to civil order. For the Liberal Carlos Lleras Restrepo the National Front served to some extent as such a lever. For the Conservative Guillermo Valencia the National Front arrangements served as a restraint. The differences reflect both the greater factional instability of the Conservative party and the difference in the political personalities of the two leaders, in particular, the much stronger program commitments of Lleras.

The limited authority and capability of the technical bureaucracy is a further important source of policymaking inertia. The absence of a bureaucracy whose primary mission is the evaluation of the total effects of foreign exchange policy—in particular, an organization whose output would supplement and provide a counterweight to the advice of those technical advisors whose primary responsi-

---

(1958–1962), tended to view the office of the presidency in this traditional way. Under Carlos Lleras Restrepo, policymaking initiative was largely centralized in the hands of the President. The makeup of his executive cabinet (fewer party "chiefs" and more *tecnicos*) reflected this change.

[22] For an articulation of the argument that "reform-mongering by sheer politicking" is strongly constrained by the characteristics of the political structures of the less developed countries, see Charles W. Anderson, "Reform-mongering and the Uses of Political Power," *Inter-American Economic Affairs,* Vol. 19, No. 2, Autumn 1965.

bility is controlling the general level of prices—is partly responsible for the unwillingness or inability of the Colombian government to approach the foreign exchange problem in an innovative or comprehensive manner. In the main, the government has been relatively passive in accepting the terms of reference or general policy guidelines put forth by the international lending consortium headed by the International Monetary Fund. That is not to say that the Colombian government has not vigorously opposed the Fund's policy proposals at various times, but there has been a strong tendency for the government's *tecnicos* to formulate policy changes only in response to proposals initiated from outside and to avoid policy formulations whose orthodoxy (as defined by the IMF) they feel to be suspect.[23]

The policymaking system in Colombia and other such countries is saved from complete inertia with regard to broad-gauge policy because of (1) the program (policy) commitments of those party leaders who "wear a modernist as well as a traditionalist hat," (2) "traditionalist" recognition that complete inertia with respect to policymaking (the natural consequence of hyperfactionalism) threatens the continued existence of traditional political institutions, and (3) the operation of constraints or pressures external to the policymaking system. This last effect appears to be the key element in provoking recent major policy changes in Colombia.

An example of such an external constraint is the limit on a country's external debt that is established by the policies of foreign commercial banks and the international lending authorities. The most likely reason for a reconsideration of foreign exchange policy is bumping against the limits of international borrowing capacity.

---

[23] The policy changes following Lleras's rejection of the consortium's policy proposals in the fall of 1966 (which we discuss at a later point in this chapter) represent a reversal of this tendency only in part, for although the certificate system ultimately adopted was primarily the creation of *tecnicos* in the Monetary Council and the Planning Department, the President himself was the prime mover of this change. At the time of the refusal to maintain a devalued fixed exchange rate, no contingency plan existed. The notion of a flexible certificate rate had not yet been generated by the technical bureaucracy as an alternative preferable to the existing fixed rate system. It was devised as a crash response to the President's demand for a policy short of outright devaluation that could conceivably be acceptable to the international lending consortium and could provide the framework for a policy of exchange austerity if that acceptance were not forthcoming.

This happened in Colombia in 1957–1958, 1962, 1964–1965, and 1966–1967. Yet, where reexamination of policy is forced by external pressures, any policy change will be postponed as long as possible.

In a policymaking environment of the sort we have described for Colombia, there will be a strong tendency to tie policy changes that the leadership feels to be required, but electorally threatening, to policy changes forced by external pressures. Policies that entail a certain gross political cost—tax increases or implementation of new taxes, restrictions on the rate of increase of credit, and increases in the price of foreign exchange—will thus tend to be bunched. The democratic policymaking environment also encourages the utilization of policies whose benefits are quickly apparent but whose costs are likely to accrue with some time lag, such as the financing of government expenditure through the forced saving financed by inflation. Given the Colombian political structure, there is thus good reason to expect abrupt fluctuations in the level of economic activity.[24]

In the recent political history of Colombia there are two conspicuous examples of the tendency of the "modernists" to use external pressures for policy change to induce acceptance of major policy departures. The first of these is the set of tax and administrative reforms proposed (and partly put through) by Finance Minister Sanz de Santamaria as part of his devaluation package in the fall of 1962. The second is the thoroughgoing reformulation of foreign exchange policy carried out by President Carlos Lleras Restrepo in early 1967.

It should be stressed, however, that it is difficult to use such incidents to support the hypothesis that international lending authorities have substantial "leverage" in inducing a country to

[24] Given the importance of the import constraint and the historic tendency for the real exchange rate to erode during the period following an abrupt devaluation, it does not appear an exaggeration to say that the major determinant of the amplitude of Colombian business fluctuations is the limit on commercial arrears established by the foreign banking community in conjunction with the lending decisions of the International Monetary Fund and the Agency for International Development. The interval between turning points of crises is (in the absence of an abrupt shift in the price of coffee) primarily a function of the government's monetary policy, which is, in turn, primarily a function of the electoral strength of the current National Front coalition.

make policy changes that it would not undertake in the absence of external pressures. Sanz de Santamaria's reforms of 1962–1963 were clearly in the spirit of the policy changes sought by Colombia's international creditors, but they were not adopted on that account. They were adopted because the top leadership of the National Front coalition was convinced (on programmatic grounds) that such changes were desirable and because the concurrent monetary-exchange crisis provided an opportunity for this top leadership to effect these changes without provoking the violent, opportunistic opposition of dissident factions that would have been likely under ordinary circumstances.

The reform of foreign exchange policy promulgated by Lleras Restrepo in 1967 was in fact radically different from the change urged by the International Monetary Fund. Although the existence of international liquidity pressures in late 1966 clearly required that some change be made in existing exchange policy, the thoroughgoing reform actually adopted—replacement of a fixed rate system by a quasi-floating rate system and suspension of the privilege of unrestricted capital export at the "free" rate—was not the change that the policymaking system had come to accept as the required response to liquidity crisis. In this case the external "constraint" was invoked in a new and inventive fashion. The (potentially unpopular) exchange reform was explained, not as a change required to maintain solvency, but as a change required to maintain policy sovereignty.[25]

THE TENDENCY TO USE SPECIAL PURPOSE POLICY
INSTRUMENTS

The tendency to use special purpose policy instruments stems both from the inherent responsiveness of a democratic policymaking system to the wishes of special interest groups and from the desire in such a system to have administrative control over the allocation of costs and benefits from policy decisions. The responsiveness of a democratic policymaking system to the needs of special interest groups derives from the basic proposition that, in such a system, a policy will be adopted if a minority strongly favors it and the majority is either unopposed or apathetic. The key ex-

[25] Maullin, *The Colombia-IMF Disagreement of November-December 1966: An Interpretation of Its Place in Colombian Politics.*

planation of this responsiveness thus lies in the fact that, in many cases, only the special interest group affected by a given policy change is likely to be aware of (or concerned about) the actual effect of that policy change on the distribution of income. An example of such a policy change is the establishment of a "supertariff" to force the substitution of domestic production for imports where the good in question is not an input into the domestic production of other goods. In a political environment such as Colombia's, where the vast majority of the electorate is only dimly aware of both the range and effects of the government's policy instruments, the only effective opposition to special interest group demands is likely to come either from the technical bureaucracy of the government or from special interest groups with conflicting demands.

The incentive to fragmented policy response derives from the basic proposition that, where a change in policy is required (perhaps because of the operation of a constraint external to the political system), a policy instrument that gives the implementing government discretionary control over the allocation of the costs and benefits associated with that change in policy is likely to result in a greater increase (or lesser decrease) in electoral support than one that does not. For example, a government will prefer to cope with an exchange crisis provoked by a sudden and massive reduction in the supply of foreign exchange by administrative controls, rather than by rationing scarce exchange through the price mechanism (allowing a sudden and large increase in the price of foreign exchange). Or, to take a similar example, a government that anticipates an extreme inflation (provoked, let us say, by the monetary excesses of the previous administration) will prefer to employ a mixed strategy involving both indirect monetary-fiscal instruments and direct controls on prices of goods important to the cost of living, rather than rely exclusively on indirect policy instruments.

There are a number of strong reasons for these preferences. One is, of course, that the government wants to obtain the power to reward its friends and punish its enemies. The critical factor, however, is the government's need to convince the public that its policies are either neutral with respect to the distribution of income or are resulting in a more equal distribution. The income-distributional effects of changes in indirect policies may be particularly sensitive to market imperfections and variations in group bargaining strength.[26] Under such circumstances the public is quick both to perceive such distributional changes as actually occur and to imagine changes that are, in fact, not occurring. The changes are conceived of as "profiteering" and hence as an unjust increase in the inequality of income distribution. In these circumstances the government will feel obligated to supplement indirect policy instruments with direct controls designed to forestall the changes in the distribution of income that the public may anticipate (or to convince the public that a strong effort is being made to forestall such changes).

We have already alluded to still another important reason why the Colombian government tends to use a strategy of fragmented policy instruments. Political leaders conditioned by "traditionalist" objectives, political leaders conditioned by the additional programmatic commitment toward increasing the rate of economic development, and the *tecnicos* of the bureaucracy each tend to the ideological commitment that equity and efficiency considerations are best served through a system of complex administrative controls. For the "modernists" this commitment results from a belief that the market structure is too imperfect to permit extensive reliance on indirect controls. For the "traditionalists" this commitment is simply a modern-day reflection of the Colombian (more properly, Hispanic) tradition of formulating policies in terms of complex structures of administrative controls. These beliefs are, in turn, congenial with the preferences of most of the special interest organizations. The more fragmented the policy, the easier it is to marshall the political muscle required to shape particular parts of it to individual preferences, and the more dependent the executors of that policy are on the information and expertise that is unique to those who are the object of that policy.

THE INCOME DISTRIBUTION OBJECTIVE

A democratic policymaking system opts for policies that are widely believed to shift income from the "rich" to the "poor" (and

---

[26] We do not wish to argue that such changes in income distribution as may occur in periods of extreme disequilibrium (or, more properly, periods of extreme change in the degree of disequilibrium) are permanent. A rapid rate of inflation is quite possibly consistent with a stable distribution of income. We suspect that there are changes in income distribution associated with sudden changes in the rate of inflation, however.

hence improve the income position of the majority). This is an obvious implication of the basic postulates that political leaders and voters are "rational" and elections are "free." This is not to say, however, that democracy will increase the equality of income distribution. The disproportionate sensitivity of the system to special interest groups counters the effects of the basic egalitarian objective.

Where the distributional effect is readily apparent, the policies of the Colombian government are strictly in accord with this general egalitarian preference of democracy. The income tax is highly progressive (and an increasingly vigorous and efficient effort is being mounted to collect it), excise taxes tend to be substantially higher for "luxury" consumption goods than for items of general consumption, and direct controls are administered with greater vigor over prices of items important to the general cost of living than over those of intermediate goods.[27] Further, even where the effects of a policy on the distribution of income are not easily determined, the government's policy preferences are sensitive to the redistributionist objective if a large segment of the public holds a strong belief about the distributional consequences of that policy.

The mechanism described above is one of the chief reasons why the Colombian government does not rely heavily on changes in the nominal exchange rate in its effort to cope with the chronic problem of excess demand for foreign exchange. In the public mind, devaluation is associated with inflation, which, in turn, is associated with an increase in the inequality of the distribution of income.[28] The validity of these associations is highly question-

[27] The Taylor Report's estimate of the incidence of taxes levied by the national government suggests that the distribution of income after federal taxes is somewhat more equal than the distribution before taxes. Local government taxes are regressive, however. See Milton Taylor et al., *Fiscal Survey of Colombia,* The Johns Hopkins University Press, Baltimore, 1965, p. 227.

[28] It is somewhat paradoxical that the distributional objective deters devaluation and not inflation, even though the opposition to devaluation stems from its association with inflation. The explanation for this difference lies in the fact that the inflation (or, more properly, the public recognition of the inflation) that results from a monetary decision develops with a time lag. The inflation may even develop only in a subsequent administration. This, in fact, did happen in Colombia in the period 1961–1963. The monetary excesses of the last two years of the Lleras Camargo administration did not yield a rapid rate of increase of prices until the first year of the Valencia administration. The public reaction to devaluation is immediate,

able,[29] but, to a democratic government such as Colombia's, reality is what is believed by the public, not what is believed by the *tecnico*.

The Foreign Exchange Policy Preferences of a Democracy

Knowledge of the style of decisionmaking described in the previous section is critical to an understanding of why the governments of the less developed countries have, in general, been reluctant to adopt policies that would lead to a more open economy, with the exchange rate rather than quantitative restrictions playing the dominant role in equilibrating the supply and demand for foreign exchange.[30] A disequilibrium exchange system and a protectionist trade policy are integral to the maintenance of public support of the governing coalition. Such a policy is politically "legitimate."

The implication of this argument is that the foreign exchange policy preferences the Colombian government has revealed in the past are likely to hold in the future unless there is a fundamental change in political institutions. The same would be true for any other democratic government facing the same syndrome of problems. We can codify these preferences as follows: a system of differentiated effective exchange rates is preferred to a unified effective exchange rate; a low exchange rate is preferred to a high exchange rate; and, in periods of strong exchange disequilibrium, rationing of foreign exchange through exchange controls is preferred to rationing through a price system.

DIFFERENTIATED EFFECTIVE EXCHANGE RATES

The primary instrument for obtaining a complex system of differentiated effective exchange rates is a system of variable tariffs. The preference for a variable as opposed to a fixed tariff is virtually

---

however, and the reaction is inevitably directed toward the implementing government.

[29] We shall discuss the relationship between devaluation and the rate of increase in prices in Chapter VIII.

[30] The Colombian policy response is in no sense unique. For a general discussion of trade and exchange policy drawing from the experience of Brazil, Chile, Colombia, Pakistan, and Turkey, see Charles P. Kindleberger, *Liberal Policies vs. Controls in the Foreign Trade of Developing Countries,* Agency for International Development, Office of Program Coordination, 1966 (mimeo, n.d.).

implicit in the tariff concept. What is peculiar to Colombia is the wide differential between the tariff rates on goods produced in Colombia and the rates on goods not produced domestically but imported as inputs into the process of production—the extreme degree of tariff dispersion.

The preference for tariff dispersion, and hence a differentiated effective exchange rate structure, derives from the Colombian government's sensitivity to the demands of producers wanting to enhance (or establish) the profitability of their activities through tariff protection. This protection is sought in two ways. A high tariff rate is sought for goods produced, a low rate for items used as inputs. Given the relatively simple structure of manufacturing in Colombia (the proportion of outputs of most manufacturing industries used as inputs by other sectors of manufacturing is relatively small), the award of a high degree of effective tariff protection has not often until recently invoked the threat of a political loss symmetric to the political gain so far as the special interests of producer groups are concerned. Given the general apathy of the public toward the economic effects of tariff policy, the calculus of political gains and losses inherent in a tariff decision has been confined to the balance of preferences of the producer groups.

It would be a gross exaggeration, however, to imply that the policymaking system in Colombia passively implements the tariff petitions of producers as long as they are unopposed by other producers. A technical bureaucracy is interposed between the producer groups and the professional politicians in the tariff-making process, and these *tecnicos* are motivated by a far more complex set of incentives than that of simply maximizing the electoral support of the governing coalition. The extent to which this group has been able to shape the tariff structure in accord with allocative efficiency criteria is, however, not entirely clear. For example, the tariff reform of 1963 was ostensibly dominated by criteria formulated by a *tecnico* group. In fact, these criteria formed a loose agenda for bargaining, rather than a basis for restructuring the tariff so as to achieve a more efficient allocation of resources, and in certain important respects the degree of tariff dispersion was greater after the reform than before.[31]

[31] The three criteria announced as guiding the tariff reform of 1963 were that the tariff should vary according to the "social utility" of the good

Although the bargaining strength of the *tecnicos* of the government tariff authority now appears to be sharply constrained, the balance of bargaining power is gradually shifting in their favor. Part of the explanation for the increased influence of the *tecnico* group is that the grant of protection through super-tariffs is increasingly an action that creates losses to other producer groups. As import substitution expands into the realm of intermediate goods, the political calculus becomes difficult, and program criteria such as allocative efficiency are likely to be more relevant. Extreme protection in the form of import prohibition has become much more difficult to obtain, and super-tariffs for new industries are now likely to be awarded for a limited period of time only.

Even so, in the foreseeable future this enhanced role of the technical bureaucracy is more likely to reduce the "water" in the tariff structure than deny more protection for import-substituting entrepreneurs, owing to the political strength of the incentive to economize on foreign exchange. Although there is now a considerably more sophisticated understanding of the likely impact of import substitution on total import demand than there was ten years ago, the goal of import substitution still retains a basic appeal to many *tecnicos* and most political leaders in the modernist camp. In an economy whose development prospects are sharply constrained by limited access to foreign exchange, the advantages of reducing the need to import a given commodity are readily apparent. The opportunity costs of increased misallocation of resources are not. Calculations of net foreign exchange savings resulting from given investments have become more realistic, but the

---

in question or the good to which it is an input in the process of production, the degree of fabrication, and the producer's need for protection. In practice, the "end use" and "degree of fabrication" criteria appear to have had little relevance to the determination of rates *on goods actually produced in Colombia*. Although comparison of the pre- and post-reform tariff structure is made difficult by the complex mixture of specific and *ad valorem* rates applicable to the pre-reform period, the evidence suggests that the increase in rates on final products was greater than the increase in rates on intermediate products for a majority of two-digit industries. Further, those industries whose effective tariffs increased more than their nominal tariffs tended to be the most dependent on the import of intermediate goods. See the data assembled by G. Argaez and C. Plazas, "Estudio Preliminar Sobre la Eficiencia de la Industria en Colombia," Departamento Administrativo de Planeacion, Bogota, 1966 (unpublished).

habit of comparing the domestic resource costs of alternative means of reducing the excess demand for foreign exchange with some efficiency benchmark is not ingrained. Under these circumstances a very high degree of tariff dispersion will be tolerated if such a policy appears to yield a net direct saving of foreign exchange.[32]

The lines of conflict are thus drawn between the innovating entrepreneur and the *tecnicos* dominated by the goal of import substitution, on one hand, and the import-substitute-using entrepreneur and the efficiency-oriented *tecnicos,* on the other. The recent recommendation by the Institute for Industrial Development that the growth of the metallurgical industry be stimulated by increased dispersion between the tariffs on items that are (or are capable of being) locally produced and items that are inputs into the metalworking process suggests that the bargaining power of those who stress the need of the government to be receptive to the protectionist needs of new industries is still dominant. In the short run this suggests a continuation of the trend toward increased tariff dispersion.

A differentiated exchange rate structure may also be obtained through a system of multiple nominal exchange rates. At present Colombia does not maintain such a system, except for coffee. In the past she has often resorted to this device. A variety of motives have been involved, in each case readily explicable in terms of the incentive structure of policymaking discussed in the previous section. A low rate of "official" transactions has been maintained to reduce the peso cost to the government of repayment of official foreign debts. A low rate was paid on the foreign exchange imports of petroleum companies in lieu of a requirement (that could not be negotiated) to repatriate the foreign exchange proceeds of petroleum exports. A multiple rate system was maintained for commodity imports in order to keep down the rate of increase of

[32] In this connection it should be stressed that the tariff structure resulting from a process of progressive import substitution is likely to approach that of a uniform (high) tariff only in mature economies. In an economy just beginning to modernize, the extension of protection involves both increases in tariffs on goods produced and reductions in tariffs on goods imported as inputs. The pattern in which the tariff structure will evolve is thus one of ever-increasing fineness of detail with a wide differential between protected and unprotected goods. In the initial stages of development it is quite possible that the ratio of "protected" to "unprotected" goods will decrease.

domestic prices of certain basic commodities. A low rate was paid
on repatriated coffee earnings in order to discourage further investments into the coffee sector and finance the purchase of excess
coffee production.[33]

OVERVALUATION OF DOMESTIC CURRENCY

The second of the generalized foreign exchange policy preferences of a democracy desiring more rapid economic growth—a
preference for low nominal exchange rates—needs more careful
specification. Involved here is a preference for an average nominal
rate of exchange that is less than the rate that would eliminate
excess demand for foreign exchange given the country's growth
targets and given the pattern of taxes and subsidies that defines
the relationship between the nominal and effective exchange rates.[34]
Where there is a further tendency for the domestic rate of inflation
to be substantially in excess of the rate of change of prices of
goods in international trade, this statement should be augmented
to include a preference for a lower rate of increase in the price
of foreign exchange than is required to maintain the existing level
of excess demand for foreign exchange given the real growth target.

The identification of the exchange rate with national prestige
is a phenomenon found in virtually every country. Devaluation
is never a popular act with the electoral majority, although it may
be in the interests of certain minority groups. Yet although this
preference appears to be fairly general, the strength with which

[33] The recent decision to abandon this multiple rate system reflects the
increasing administrative sophistication of the government. In each of the
cases mentioned above, it was realized that the same effects could be
achieved through a system of taxes and subsidies that would have the
further advantage of greater administrative flexibility. A similar structure
of *effective* exchange rates was maintained, but with a different set of
policy instruments. The government's decision to unify the nominal rates
applicable to capital and commodity transactions is not easily explained,
however. Part of the reason is that capital export is currently subject to
very strict administrative controls. We have already discussed the generalized
preference for administrative allocation as opposed to market allocation
in periods of extreme disequilibrium. It is not clear why no substantial
exchange tax is levied on capital export.

[34] For certain growth targets there may in fact be no equilibrium (effective) rate of exchange. In such circumstances the preference for "low"
rates should be defined as a preference for a rate lower than the rate
that would minimize excess demand for foreign exchange.

it is held in Colombia is in large part the result of factors that are particular to that country. We shall discuss the origin of the preference for an overvalued peso under the following headings: the encouragement of import substitution through tariff dispersion; the dominance of coffee among Colombia's exports; redistributionist objectives; and bureaucratic influences.

Tariff policy. The role of tariff policy in contributing to the preference for an overvalued peso is implicit in our earlier discussion. Producers who desire a high effective rate of exchange in order to protect their domestic monopolies from foreign competition are generally able to do so through tariff manipulation. The protection embodied in a high nominal exchange rate is not necessary, and the increase in costs implied by a high nominal rate is not wanted. As long as a large proportion of inputs into manufacturing is imported and the rate structure is highly dispersed, Colombian industry can obtain a high degree of protection from a relatively low average tariff. This being the case, the manufacturing sector is induced to lend its support almost unanimously to a policy of establishing an average effective rate of exchange, inclusive of tariffs, that substantially overvalues the peso.

Coffee policy. It is clear why the possibility of extreme tariff dispersion reduces the interest of import-substituting manufacturers in a high average effective exchange rate. One would expect, however, strong pressures for a higher exchange rate structure to come from exporters or would-be exporters to serve as a political counterweight. In Colombia such pressure is minimal. The reason is the legacy and the politics of coffee, traditionally Colombia's nearly sole export and still her dominant source of foreign exchange.

For well over a decade, because of the expansion of production in other countries and because of the price and income-elasticity characteristics of world coffee demand, the volume of coffee produced in Colombia has been well in excess of what can profitably be marketed. Given Colombia's adherence to the International Coffee Agreement and the voluntary limitations on export volume that such membership entails, this problem of surplus production is likely to persist in the forseeable future.

Colombia has tried to meet the problem of surplus coffee production through the following institutional arrangements. First, a domestic coffee support price has been established in order to maintain real incomes in the coffee sector at some reasonable level of parity with incomes in the rest of the economy. Second, a complex set of taxes falling on the various transactions deriving from the sale and export of coffee production has been established, the most important of which is a differential between the effective rate of exchange on proceeds from coffee export and the main rate.[35] In general, the revenue derived from this set of implicit and explicit taxes on the coffee sector has been sufficient to finance the coffee surplus. At various times, however, the financing burden has been shifted in part to the rest of the economy.[36]

[35] This "complex set" of taxes is indeed complex. The first element is a tax in kind levied on the private exporters of coffee to equalize the relative profitability of export by private firms and export by the quasi-public National Federation of Coffeegrowers (FEDECAFE). The latter organization needs this equalization because of its responsibilities for export promotion, research and development, and the encouragement of crop diversification in the coffee-growing areas.

The real source of finance of the coffee surplus derives from the taxes (explicit and implicit) on the repatriation of foreign exchange earnings from the export of coffee. The "tax" results both from the maintenance of an exchange differential between the buying rate applicable to repatriated coffee earnings and the selling rates applicable to imports or capital export and from the difference between the *reintegro* price of coffee and the actual selling price. The *reintegro* price determines how many dollars a coffee exporter must surrender at the rate of exchange applicable to coffee. If it is less than the actual price, the exporter may exchange the remaining dollars at the rate of exchange applicable to capital imports, and the actual exchange differential on coffee is less than the nominal differential. The "tax" deriving from the differential between the coffee rate and the main rate is by far the more important of the two. At various times this differential has been established by a nominal exchange rate applicable to coffee proceeds that was separate from the nominal rate on imports. Currently it is established as a percentage of the certificate rate of exchange. For a discussion of coffee tax policy, see Richard M. Bird, "Coffee Tax Policy in Colombia," *Inter-American Economic Affairs*, Vol. 22, No. 1, Summer 1968, pp. 75–86.

[36] Although the surplus is purchased by the semi-official National Federation of Coffeegrowers (FEDECAFE), the ultimate financial responsibility rests with the government. At times when the differential between the coffee rate and the main rate has been very low—and the exchange "profits" accruing to the government have been correspondingly low—FEDECAFE has resorted to borrowing from the central bank in order to finance its purchase of the surplus. In recent years agreements with the international consortium of public lenders has provided a strict limit to this sort of operation. Where necessary, FEDECAFE continues to borrow from foreign commercial banks, however.

This institutional structure has induced the coffee sector to focus on the instrumentalities that establish the differential between the effective rate of exchange on coffee and the nominal rate, rather than on the nominal exchange rate itself. Just as with the import-substituting manufacturers, the possibility of differential exchange rates has resulted in a reduction of the pressure to maintain a higher average rate of exchange. The critical factor here is that the ratio between the effective rate on coffee and the main exchange rate is a policy variable, rather than a fixed element of the exchange structure. In this circumstance the coffee sector will be more inclined to use its political influence to change the domestic support price and the exchange rate differential—policies specific to the coffee sector itself—than to lobby for a higher exchange rate structure, a strategy that would put it in direct conflict with other special interest groups.[37] In the past this tendency to view the coffee rate and the import (main) rate as separate policy instruments actually has been sufficiently strong so that, on occasion, the coffee sector has been motivated to oppose devaluation packages offered by the government.[38]

In these circumstances the political leaders and *tecnicos* of the Colombian government have been caught in a web of conflicting objectives. On one hand, the political leadership wants to avoid the substantial loss of electoral support that would result from any abrupt drop in producer income. The coffee producers are a large, well-organized, and articulate bloc of voters. On the other hand, the government *tecnicos* and the program-oriented political leaders would like to reduce the coffee surplus. The high taxes

[37] The relationship between the domestic support price of coffee and the coffee rate of exchange is close but not one-to-one. The profitability of coffee export at a given rate of exchange can be maintained in the face of an increase in the domestic support price (and fixed world prices) by an adjustment of the *reintegro* price. This sort of adjustment is "fine tuning," however, and a large increase in the support price will ultimately call for a proportional increase in the coffee rate if export profitability is to be maintained.

[38] Such was the case with the devaluation proposals of Finance Minister Sanz de Santamaria in the fall of 1962. Since the government's proposal did not call for an increase in the coffee rate, the coffee sector threw its weight to the opposition. This posture continued until the government agreed to a simultaneous (although smaller) increase in the rate on coffee dollars.

on the coffee sector that are integral to supporting the surplus are a continuing source of political friction, and the recurrent possibility that a sudden drop in international coffee prices would make the cost of financing the surplus (at a politically acceptable domestic support price) too large to be borne by the coffee sector alone threatens the government with the spectre of having to choose among further expansion of the money supply, higher taxation, or the cutback of other government expenditures.

To the extent that the government pushes the objective of supporting real incomes in the coffee sector in the face of falling international coffee prices, it is creating some upward pressure on the general structure of nominal exchange rates. Because of the nature of this objective and because the differential between the coffee rate and the main rate is not fixed, this mechanism is exceedingly unlikely to result in an upward pressure on the structure of *real* rates, however. To the extent that the government pushes the objective of reducing the coffee surplus—and this objective appears to be increasingly important to the program-oriented leadership—it is actually creating a downward pressure on the real rate structure.[39]

It may be objected that the arguments we are raising here are inconsistent. In the first case we have posited that the coffee sector treats the effective exchange rate on coffee transactions as a policy instrument that is distinctly separate from the main import rate. In the second case we have suggested that political leaders interested in reducing the burden of the coffee support program assume that there is an intimate relationship between the coffee rate and the main rate of exchange. Our reply is that the arguments are indeed asymmetric, but not inconsistent.

The coffee interests are well aware that the support price of coffee is closely dependent on the main rate of exchange. They are also aware of the strength of the political opposition to increases in the main rate and the potential danger to coffee sector

---

[39] If the government were able to increase the differential between the coffee rate and the main rate of exchange, this need not be the case. Such a change is politically very difficult, however. In election years it is essentially impossible. In most circumstances the only feasible way to secure a domestic support price of coffee that is sufficiently low to contribute to the resolution of the problem of excess production is to keep the main rate of exchange on imports low.

interests if that opposition were inclined to formulate its advocacy of low exchange rates in terms of a low rate structure, rather than a low import rate. In order to maintain coffee sector incomes at a high level of parity, the coffee sector has thus sought to separate the bargain over the coffee rate (and support price) from the discussion of the main import rate and thereby isolate those political leaders most concerned with the problem of surplus production from their potential backers in the manufacturing and commercial sectors. In periods of falling international coffee prices, those leaders and *tecnicos* for whom reduction of the coffee surplus is an important objective have tried to counter this strategy by tying the coffee and import rates together. This strategy is most likely to create a political coalition effective in restraining the coffee sector's pressure for a higher support price (and a higher coffee rate) when the differential between the coffee and import rates has narrowed to the point that government net revenue from exchange profits has declined substantially and when the finance of the coffee surplus requires funds derived from outside the coffee industry.[40]

Objectives with respect to income distribution. Although the nature of the objectives of special interest groups is of undoubted importance in determining the preference of the Colombian political system for low exchange rates, probably the most important cause of this bias is the widespread belief by much of the electorate that devaluation implies inflation, which, in turn, is believed to shift income from the "poor" to the "rich." Indeed, these beliefs have achieved such wide currency as to become a slogan used

[40] Although the complex of forces deriving from the government's coffee policy appears to enhance the government's preference for low exchange rates, particularly a low import rate, it also creates something of an upper limit to the extent to which the peso can be overvalued (a lower limit to the exchange rate). If a very low import rate is maintained in the face of a continued increase in domestic prices relative to world prices, the need to maintain a domestic price of coffee that is in reasonable parity to the general level of prices will result in the gradual erosion of the differential between the import and coffee rates of exchange. As the differential narrows, there is both a squeeze on the volume of government revenue and a gradual shift of the burden of the support program from the coffee sector to the rest of the economy. As this process continues, groups lobbying for maintenance of the existing import rate gradually perceive an increased threat to the economy's fiscal and monetary stability and eventually come to acquiesce in or support a higher rate structure.

by those political groups attempting to develop populist electoral support. Although the act of devaluation is politically unpopular in virtually any circumstance in all countries, the extent to which the devaluation issue has penetrated the consciousness of the politically active population in Colombia is extraordinary. As one Colombian close to (Liberal) President Lleras Restrepo recently put it, "Politically, devaluation goes hand in hand with extreme unction." This perception is not unique to the Liberal party. In the spring of 1965 the Conservative President Guillermo Leon refused to accede to very strong pressures for devaluation raised by the country's foreign creditors and many Colombian financial and business leaders on the grounds that such an act would cause a "revolution."

The extreme unpopularity of devaluation in recent years can probably be traced to the Colombian experience with the devaluation of December 1962. In the year following that devaluation (an increase in the main selling rate of about 35 percent), the national cost-of-living index increased some 43 percent (two-thirds of this increase falling in the first six months of 1963). Although wages and salaries also climbed sharply, the net effect of this inflation was to reduce the real incomes of most urban workers and to exacerbate the growing inequality of the distribution of income.[41] Although the main basis for this inflation can be found in the tremendous liquidity overhang at the time of the devaluation and in the very large increase in the minimum wage that was voted as virtually a companion piece to the act of devaluation itself, the root cause of the inflationary spiral in the eyes of the voting public was the devaluation.

The fact that the rate of price change following the devaluation of September 1965 was relatively modest did little to dispel this image. Most politically active Colombians continue to see devalua-

---

[41] The official statistics for salaried workers show a 24 percent rate of increase of income for 1963. The corresponding rate for workers paid on an hourly basis is 38 percent. Both statistics refer only to workers employed in what we have called the "modern" sector of the urban economy. Although the data are scanty, our evidence suggests that, except for domestic workers, those people employed in the traditional sectors of the economy received a lesser increase in money incomes than those in the modern sectors.

tion as a primary cause of inflation and see inflation as a vehicle for the redistribution of income from the poor to the rich.

It was with this perception of public opinion that Carlos Lleras Restrepo faced the monetary crisis of late 1966. The opposition to the National Front had enjoyed considerable success in the elections of 1964 and 1966 with the tactic of accusing the government of favoring the devaluation route, and Rojas Pinilla, the leader of the ANAPO, had endlessly accused Lleras of preparing for another devaluation. In these circumstances Lleras felt that the orthodox devaluation package called for by the International Monetary Fund was not only a less efficient (in terms of its effect on growth) response to the crisis than the set of detailed administrative controls implied in his "economy of abundance" strategy but also a dangerous threat to the delicate balance of political power. In particular, Lleras was concerned that an orthodox "spasm" devaluation would destroy his already fragile popular support and make impossible the amendments to the constitutional system that he felt were essential if the nation were to make an orderly transition from the temporary arrangements of the National Front system to more permanent political arrangements. His consequent rejection of the IMF proposals, accompanied by imposition of a system of complete exchange controls, has thus to be thought of less as an indication of a pure preference for the "disequilibrium" system of foreign exchange policy than as an indication of his perception of the importance of enhanced access to foreign exchange relative to enhanced public support of the office of the presidency.

Given this objective, Lleras's refusal to accept the IMF proposal was a major success. The appeal to nationalism inherent in his portrayal of the crisis as an attempt by the Fund to force a policy that was insulting to the administrative capability of the Colombian government enhanced his personal prestige enormously and, more important, placed the opposition in the delicate position of either having to accede to whatever alternatives to orthodox devaluation the government might devise or running the risk of being accused of a lack of patriotism.[42] In the period immediately following the confrontation with the IMF, Lleras made use of the new-found

---

[42] For a good discussion of the political forces operating during this crisis, see Maullin, *The Colombia-IMF Disagreement of November–December 1966: An Interpretation of Its Place in Colombian Politics.*

prestige of his office in a manner virtually as imaginative as his actions during the crisis itself. The rate applicable to capital trans-actions was raised to the level of the preexisting free market rate, and, after a brief period of indecision, a quasi-flexible rate system, the so-called certificate market, was established for commodity transactions.[43] Although the opposition, particularly ANAPO, tried to identify these actions as "devaluation," the government suc-ceeded in avoiding such onus by simultaneously maintaining the fiction that the certificate rate was a "free" rate susceptible only to the free play of "supply and demand" and restricting the effective demand for exchange certificates sufficiently to ensure that the ini-tial rate of increase of the certificate rate (the main exchange rate) would not be too rapid.

Although the certificate system established a mechanism that, in theory at least, should relieve the government of some of the community pressure to maintain low exchange rates, the Lleras administration was fairly cautious in permitting the certificate rate to increase. During the first full year of operation of the certificate system, the rate increased some 18 percent.[44] Since the unification of the certificate and capital rates in June 1968, however, the rate of increase has slowed considerably. In calendar 1968 the certifi-cate rate increased only 7 percent. The rate of increase in 1969 was less than 6 percent.[45] This slowdown apparently reflected Lleras's judgment on what sort of rate of change was publicly

[43] In essence the certificate system is a controlled auction. Exporters are required to trade foreign earnings for dated exchange certificates, which they then sell for domestic currency. Importers are required to purchase foreign exchange with these certificates. The fact that the dated certificates can be exchanged at par for only a very limited period, and the additional requirement that would-be purchasers of foreign exchange must also have an exchange license and (in most cases) an import license, enable the government (through the Monetary Council) to maintain close control over the price of exchange certificates. The certificate system is essentially the same as the exchange system maintained in Colombia in the period 1957–1958. It was proposed by *tecnicos* within the Monetary Council and the Planning Office in response to the President's request for an alternative exchange system to that previously proposed by the IMF and rejected by the President.

[44] The increase of the domestic wholesale price index over this period was 6.4 percent.

[45] The increase of the domestic wholesale price index was 5.5 percent in 1968 and about 10.0 percent in 1969.

acceptable. The relatively rapid increase of the exchange rate during 1967 could be explained to the community simply as the result of "natural market forces" bringing the certificate rate up to the level of the rate in the free market that prevailed prior to the November 1966 crisis. Once this level had been achieved, a considerably more cautious policy was felt necessary. Thus, even though a system has been adopted that removes most of the political drama from devaluation, gradual rate changes being substituted for the "spasm" devaluations implicit in the "fixed" rate system, the government's perception of the potential political costs involved in exchange rate increases appears to have changed but little. The worst aspect of the fixed rate system—large cyclical variation in the real exchange rate—has been obviated, but there is little evidence at present that the government has a conscious policy of permitting the real certificate rate to increase through time so that administrative allocation of foreign exchange can ultimately be largely replaced by market allocation.

The influence of the bureaucracy. The net effect of the technical bureaucracy's influence over tariff policy is probably to restrain the policymaking system from giving full vent to the preferences of the professional politicians. It is not at all clear, however, that the bureaucracy has played an effective role in weakening the preference of the political system for an overvalued peso, even though many of the government *tecnicos* are well aware of the problems that such a policy preference entails and would prefer to see a more rapid rate of devaluation. The reason for this lack of influence is the central role played by the *tecnicos* of the Monetary Council (Junta Monetaria) in the foreign exchange policymaking process and the priority that they have given to the goal of controlling inflation relative to the goal of increasing the growth of output and employment.

This dominance of the price control criterion over the broader development criterion in the policy analysis of the *tecnicos* attached to the Monetary Council reflects the conditions of the Council's creation, the hyperinflation of 1963. As initially conceived, the Council was to provide a means of establishing government control over the supply of money, a function previously exercised in large part by the quasi-private Central Bank (Banco de la Republica).

The problems associated with the primary mission of the Council, the creation and implementation of instruments of monetary control, have tended to dominate the thinking of the Council's technical staff to the point that foreign exchange policy has been viewed primarily as an aspect of monetary policy.[46]

The consequences of this parochial bias have been important. In technical discussions of the consequences of devaluation, the primary emphasis has been placed on the immediate fiscal-monetary consequences of changes in the exchange rate, rather than on the effect on the maximum feasible real rate of growth. The comparative calculus of the inflationary effects of increases in the costs of imported intermediate and capital goods and the relatively deflationary effects of increased government tariff revenue, along with an increased volume of money frozen in the form of advanced import deposits (*depositos previos*), has dominated the concerns of decisionmakers. Little, if any, attention has been given to the question of the price responsiveness of exports, other than coffee, or to the elasticity of substitution between domestic products and imports.[47] As a result, monetary instruments have to a large extent replaced the exchange rate as a means of controlling the excess demand for foreign exchange.[48] And there have been distressingly

[46] There are two separate phenomena at work here. The first is the tendency of policy advisory groups to present a very limited set of policy alternatives for final decision by the political leadership. Where the alternatives offered for final decision are the output of a single bureaucratic unit, the set of alternatives will be limited not only in number but in the extent to which they differ in substance. The second phenomenon is the tendency of a policymaking bureaucracy to seek out the political leadership's ultimate policy objectives if the policy problem faced by that bureaucracy is complex and has not been parcelled out to a number of separate organizations. In Colombia and in any other democratic country where the political leadership is not programmatically motivated, the highest political priority will be given to the goal of maintaining a stable distribution of income, or insuring against public perception of changes in that distribution. In circumstances where a single group or institution has an advisorial monopoly over both monetary and exchange policy, the technical output of that institution will reflect that preference, and there is a lessened chance that the *tecnico* group will induce the political leadership to modify the disequilibrium system of foreign exchange policy.

[47] The Planning Department has attempted to study such questions, but its bureaucratic output has not (at least until very recently) been as important in influencing the decisions of the Monetary Council as the output of the Council's technical staff.

[48] This is less true now than before the adoption of the certificate system.

few well-placed *tecnicos* to point out the inadequacies of a policy of controlling the demand for foreign exchange by depressing aggregate demand in an economy where excess capacity is the rule rather than the exception.

EXCHANGE CONTROL AND IMPORT LICENSING

A government that maintains an overvalued exchange rate is necessarily going to have to maintain some degree of administrative control over the allocation of foreign exchange. It is not necessary, however, that it *prefer* to do so. Exchange control and import licensing may well be perceived as a gross cost entailed in achieving the net advantages implied by a less-than-equilibrium exchange rate. But this does not appear to be the way they are viewed in Colombia. The majority of Colombian political leaders and *tecnicos* see exchange control and import licensing as policy instruments that are exceedingly useful means of achieving their objectives.

There are several reasons for this attitude. Probably the most important is the belief by most of the modern elite that the changes in the structure of production that would most likely result from market allocation of foreign exchange would be far from optimal from the point of view of maximizing the country's long-term growth potential. This belief, in turn, rests on a number of subsidiary considerations: the desire to prevent the import (or perhaps production) of "luxury goods"; the desire to prevent capital flight; the recognition that most local producers in the modern sector produce under terms of partial or total monopoly; the conception that the establishment of certain industries will entail substantial external economies (the bottleneck industry hypothesis); and a faith that the techniques of detailed sector planning can be used to reduce the incidence of excess capacity. In the absence of detailed public control over the distribution of credit, administrative allocation of foreign exchange is seen as the only policy instrument to alleviate each of these deficiencies.

The preference for administrative control over foreign exchange is not confined to those political leaders imbued with a faith in economic planning. These controls allow both traditional and modernist politicians to perform useful services for their petitioners and thereby construct a network of patron-client relationships that is useful, if not essential, to advancement within a factional hierarchy. The apparent rarity of overt pecuniary corruption in the import license system further increases the scope for the exercise of personal political influence. This ability of individuals with good political connections to obtain reconsideration of, and perhaps redress from, unfavorable licensing decisions by the foreign trade authority provides a safety valve that is probably essential to the smooth functioning of an import control mechanism as complex as that maintained in Colombia. This is probably the most important reason that the politically powerful economic interest organizations have not mounted a concerted campaign to restrict the scope of administrative control over imports, even though there appears to be substantial dissatisfaction with the foreign exchange system among businessmen taken as a group.[49]

The system of direct exchange and import controls cannot be characterized as a "popular" policy.[50] But it is a system that is widely accepted. It will continue to be accepted as long as the administrative bureaucracy retains its reputation of being generally free from pecuniary corruption and the community continues to view foreign exchange as a "national resource" that must be used in the best interests of the nation as a whole. Yet although the principle of administrative allocation of foreign exchange is widely accepted, the exercise of tight import controls (a very limited list of goods not subject to prior license and a relatively low volume of foreign exchange allocated to the private sector) over an extended period of time is politically costly. A government that is determined to placate the general public by maintaining a fixed or nearly fixed exchange rate (thus alleviating fears of inflation) will eventually find itself forced to maintain import controls of such rigidity that substantial portions of the modern business sector will actively press for a more liberal allocation policy and even come to advocate devaluation (if there is good reason to believe that a change in the exchange rate would allow an increase in the volume of exchange offered to the public).

[49] For evidence of business (chiefly small business) attitudes, see A. Lipman, *El Empresario Bogotano*, Ediciones Tercer Mundo, Bogota, 1966, Chap. 7.

[50] This is particularly true of import licensing. That part of the exchange control system that limits profit repatriation by foreign-owned firms is, as might be expected, extremely popular.

This alternation in the relative intensity of the business sector's demand for larger exchange allocations for imports and the general public's demand for a stable price of foreign exchange is the key to the government's foreign exchange policy behavior and the essential determinant of the exchange reserve cycle. As net exchange reserves increase in the period following resolution of an exchange crisis (devaluation), the business sector's pressure for larger exchange allocations (which may or may not take the form of a pressure to reduce the number of items requiring prior license) also increases. Ultimately these pressures become sufficiently insistent that the government leadership faces the choice of accommodating the business sector's demands or facing the tactical opposition of a significant portion of the preexisting National Front coalition.[51] An eventual relaxation of import controls is thus virtually mandatory, and if, as has been the case in the past, the liberalization of import policy is both abrupt and considerable, the resulting increase in pressure on exchange reserves is very likely to induce a destabilizing shift in exchange rate expectations. At this point the balance of influence over policy is likely to shift from the spokesmen for business sector interests to those who choose to advocate the interests of that part of the public actively concerned with the redistributive effects of inflation. Tight exchange and import controls will be reimposed, and the existing exchange rate will be maintained until such time as something approaching consensus on the untenability of that rate can be secured. The replacement of a policy of fixed exchange rates by the exchange certificate (quasi-flexible rate) system should permit a considerable dampening of the exchange reserve cycle, but as long as the "real" exchange rate remains at anything like current levels, conflicting political demands for increased exchange allocations and stable foreign exchange prices will persist.

[51] The campaign waged against the continuation of the relatively austere monetary and exchange policies of Finance Minister Agudelo Villa in 1961 by economic interest groups and the factional press is a classic example of this mechanism. For a description of these maneuvers, see the prologue written by Edgar Gutierrez Castro to Hernando Agudelo Villa, *Cuatro Etapas de la Inflacion en Colombia,* Ediciones Tercer Mundo, Bogota, 1967, pp. 31–45.

CHAPTER VIII

Future Development Policy

We now have traced the roots of Colombia's economic difficulties. We have considered the population explosion, the fall in the death rate that triggered it, and the factors that may begin to dampen it by reducing the number of children parents want to have. We have examined the flow of people to the cities, pushed by rapid population growth and pulled by a belief that life would be better in urban communities. The Colombian manufacturing sector, the principal factor in the dynamics of urban economic growth, has been analyzed in considerable detail. We have suggested that the manufacturing sector can be understood only if its fundamental dualism is recognized. The process of growth can be interpreted as the grafting onto, and then the gradual replacement of, a low productivity craft sector by a much higher productivity sector using modern technology, the rate of replacement of the traditional technology sector increasing as the initial scale disadvantages of the infant modern sector are partially overcome by growth, as labor and management learn to operate the new technology, and as suppliers become more efficient.

We have studied the consequences of the slowdown in manufacturing development that occurred in the early 1960s. With employment in the modern sector expanding slowly, yet with steady upward pressure of wage rates in the modern sector, we have watched the wage structure split apart. The limited fruits of slow growth have been taken out largely in the development of a small middle class with rising incomes, with a large part, perhaps a majority, of the growing urban population continuing to subsist at real-wage levels that appear to have changed but little since the early 1950s. We also have studied the rise of overt urban unemployment, noting, however, that the lines are blurred between craft employment and unemployment and that, because of the possibility of craft employment and through influences on migration rates, overt unemployment is to a degree at least self-regulating.

The causes of the slowdown have been traced to the import dependency of the evolving modern sector, the fall in coffee prices in the mid-1950s, and the failure of policy to find a way to increase Colombia's access to foreign exchange. Dependency on imports for many capital and intermediate goods was traced to the skill, scale, and network of suppliers that are required for efficient production—factors that Colombia can hope to improve only slowly. We examined in detail how stagnant or slowly growing foreign exchange earnings can constrain the growth of output and employment and how the requirement to maintain continuous focus on balance-of-payments problems can, on one hand, strip room for maneuver from fiscal and monetary policy and, on the other, cause the appearance of the symptoms of recession.

Finally, we have studied the policymaking process regarding foreign trade and exchange and attempted to see why it has failed to cope with the problems. We have studied political organization, the groups involved directly and indirectly in the policymaking process, and the evolution of the policies themselves. Our conclusions were that the more traditional theories explaining inadequate policies did not adequately depict the situation. The failure to take the actions needed to permit a more rapid rate of growth is indeed partly the result of the actions of powerful groups seeking to enhance their special interests, but these interests have been pursued within the context of a pluralistic democracy. The policies adopted are politically legitimate. They will continue to be politically legitimate until politically significant groups who are disadvantaged by the current disequilibrium system propose and argue forcibly for an alternative policy.

In this concluding chapter we attempt to draw from our analysis of the development process certain broad implications with regard to sensible development policy. As before, while the Colombian situation will provide our specific context, we think the analysis is broadly applicable, and our discussion will be presented broadly. We shall examine, in turn, three major policy areas: first, population growth; second, policies toward education and transfer of technology; third, foreign exchange policy. We shall then return to the policymaking process to examine the possibilities of political innovation.

POPULATION POLICY

There appears to be an evolving consensus that a more effective population policy is an imperative if underdeveloped countries, faced like Colombia with high fertility and rapid population growth, are to make substantial headway toward resolution of their development problems.

Of course, it clearly is naive to believe that population growth represents a simple subtraction from income growth in determining the growth of personal welfare. In the first place, per capita national income certainly is only a very partial index of welfare. The wide range of general problems with this index are well known and need not be discussed here. More generally, in the context of this discussion it must be stressed, and recognized, that children and people cannot be considered simply as claimants on a national income "pie." Parents and society assign value to children that transcends their future productive potential. Viewed simply as an economic investment, at reasonable rates of discount, children are a very bad investment indeed, but this is scarcely an argument for everyone to stop having children.

In the second place, the growth of output and income and the growth of population are not independent of one another. They would not be independent even if labor had zero marginal productivity. They certainly are not independent when labor itself contributes to production. Rather, the relationships are much more complex, involving the effects of population growth on the growth of the labor force and factors other than labor and on the marginal productivity of the different factors. Economic growth in developing countries is not sufficiently understood today to permit estimates with any precision of the effects of population growth on output and output per capita. However, some of the relationships are beginning to come into clearer focus.

Population growth retards the growth of physical capital per capita, if not necessarily the aggregate capital stock. In low income countries, rapid population growth sustained by high birth rates is likely to depress average private rates of saving. Since high fertility levels are achieved by bearing children for a longer time, rather than by a drastic shortening of the intervals between births, a much larger proportion of births in high fertility populations are to parents over age 30. A consequence of this pattern of high fertility and child spacing is a shorter period after rearing children when parents have the opportunity to save from current earnings without depressing their own consumption. High fertility and high dependency rates are likely to be associated, therefore, with low household savings.

The public sector's opportunities to save and invest its resources in tangible productive assets are also eroded by population growth, for public expenditures on social infrastructure are closely tied to population growth, urbanization, and the youthfulness of the population. On an *a priori* basis there is thus good reason to infer that high fertility in conjunction with low incomes depresses the fraction of domestic product saved and invested in directly productive physical capital. The empirical evidence, though limited, confirms these conclusions. For example, Leff has found a significant negative relationship between the proportion of the population below 15 years of age and per capita national savings.[1]

Moreover, even if per capita savings rates were not lower but the same, growth of population would tend to retard growth of capital per head. For a given capital-population ratio, the faster the rate of growth of population, the higher must be per capita savings to sustain a given growth of capital per head. Thus the effects of rapid population growth appear doubly pernicious.

It is likely that, in a regime of rapid population growth, a smaller fraction of the population reaches the progressively higher rungs on the educational ladder, and improvements in health proceed less rapidly. Data are not available to confirm this supposition. But high fertility probably retards the rate of improvement in human resources or "capital" for exactly the same reasons that it retards growth of physical capital per worker. Although rapid population growth ultimately implies rapid growth of the labor force (in spite of low participation rates of married women), it implies a labor force with a high fraction of untrained and inexperienced (and relatively unproductive) workers.

The total effects of rapid population growth on growth of aggregate income or output are ambiguous. The likely effect on growth of per capita income is not. Rapid population growth reduces the rate of formation of both physical and human capital per worker while increasing the supply of inexperienced and unskilled workers.

[1] Nathaniel Leff, "Population Growth and Savings Potential," preliminary report to the Office of Program Coordination, AID, Washington, D.C., Nov. 1967.

The consequence is a strong tendency to perpetuate economic dualism.

These factors are of unquestionable importance in shaping Colombia's development prospects. The natural rate of increase in population is, and has been of late, relatively high by international standards. A reduction in the birth rate, even if achieved very quickly, would not alter the fact that Colombia will see a rapid increase in the labor force for the next decade or two simply from the growing up of people already born. The large flow of people from the country to the city is also likely to persist for many years even if the birth rate were quickly reduced. Nevertheless, there is good reason to believe that population policy, if vigorously pursued, could make its effects felt in the near future. A reduction in the birth rate might permit an increase in national savings and investment, thus making it easier to deal with the near-term surge of the labor force at the same time that it slows down the growth of the labor force fifteen years hence. By taking some of the strain away from Colombia's sorely taxed educational resources, a decline in the birth rate could make it easier to ensure that the next generation of Colombian workers will be better qualified for jobs in modern industry. By reducing the growth rate of labor relative to capital, a decline in the birth rate would enable a larger share of the new work force to be absorbed by the modern sector.

FACTORS INFLUENCING THE BIRTH RATE

We believe the model presented and tested in Chapter II provides a useful way to look at population policy. To recapitulate, the model assumed that, within limits, families exerted relatively effective control over the number of children they had. The concept of a family size goal was central in the model we hypothesized, and we found confirming evidence that certain factors of the environment were strongly associated with the number of children families were having. In particular, availability of primary schooling for children seems to exert a significant negative impact on the desired number of children, for a variety of complex reasons. Obstacles to child labor and employment opportunities for women likewise seem to lower the family size goal.

Given the family size goal, the child mortality rate can be expected, and was found, to influence the birth rate by determining the number of births needed to achieve the goal. Downward shifts in the death rate can be expected to be followed, with a lag, by downward shifts in the birth rate.

Finally, access to and costs of birth control can be expected to influence the birth rate. First, the costs and inconvenience of birth control itself probably influence the family size target. Second, in a period of transition, like that now taking place in Colombia, where the child death rate has fallen significantly from traditional levels, one can expect birth control information and access to influence the speed at which the birth rate is brought down to the desired level. Some limited evidence about this process was provided in Chapter II. More will be presented shortly.

POLICY OPPORTUNITIES

On the basis of the preceding analysis, it appears sensible to view a population policy as involving two basic elements: distribution of birth control information and devices, and influencing family size goals.

Until recently it often was argued that only a small proportion of the population in developing countries understood the feasibility of limiting births, or wanted to. The analyses of Chapter II, which show significant variation in birth rates associated with factors that could be expected to influence the desired birth rate, cast strong doubts on the assertion that few parents limit births.

Other studies have indicated that, although parents almost always do exert a degree of birth control, in many cases the size of the family wanted is substantially smaller than that being achieved.[2] These studies have found that many individuals have an interest in, and curiosity about, new methods for controlling births, but that few have actual knowledge of these methods. It seems fair to conclude that existing channels for distribution have not reached the majority of parents demanding modern methods of family planning. For the individual with limited regional mobility and little, if any, formal education, the costs of locating, evaluating, and effectively adopting a new method of birth control are large and have heretofore effectively barred access to these

[2] B. Berelson, "KAP Studies on Fertility," in *Family Planning and Population Programs,* University of Chicago Press, Chicago, 1966.

innovations. It is typical, therefore, to find contraceptive users more frequent among the better educated, higher social and economic classes in the developing countries. Scant evidence is found, in the absence of a public family planning program, that this innovation spreads rapidly through the society.

Historical evidence casts doubt on the likelihood of rapid diffusion of contraceptive knowledge and use through private channels of communication and commerce. It is well established that, by the end of the seventeenth century, birth control had taken root among the upper classes of European society, but nowhere did fertility decline on a wide scale, except in France, before the mid-nineteenth century. Although the attractions of having a large number of children may have diminished more rapidly among upper than among lower classes, it is nevertheless generally believed that practice of contraception among lower classes was retarded more by the inaccessibility of information than by lack of motivation.[3] Although it is reasonable that public support for the diffusion of family planning and contraception should hasten the process of its acceptance, it remains to be shown precisely how effective large-scale public programs can be in accelerating the rate of diffusion and thereby narrowing the differences in the rate of contraceptive use between high and low socioeconomic classes.

With most family planning programs in their initial stages, there are few data with which to answer this question. Two repeated surveys that have been collected for areas in Korea and Taiwan are relevant here. These studies show that contraceptive use in all classes tends to increase with the start of a national family planning program, this increase being most noticeable among the lower classes.[4] The ratio of the rate of contraceptive use among high to low economic classes was equal to four before the program in the two Korean communities was initiated (Table 52). In Koyang, where the more intensive program was mounted, the ratio fell to 1.07 in two years; in Kimpo it fell to 1.25. The farmer-non-farmer ratio declined from about two to less than one in Koyang;

[3] J. Sutter, "The Action of Birth Limitations on Genetic Composition of Populations," in *Fertility and Family Planning: A World View,* University of Michigan Press, Ann Arbor, 1969.
[4] It is actually quite striking that the highest IUD acceptance rates first recorded in Korea were among farming communities of low literacy.

TABLE 52
RATIO OF CONTRACEPTIVE USERS IN VARIOUS CLASSES
BEFORE AND AFTER A PUBLIC FAMILY PLANNING
PROGRAM IN TWO KOREAN COMMUNITIES

User Ratio	Koyang (intensive program)		Kimpo (only national program)	
	Before	After	Before	After
High to low economic status	4.40	1.07	4.17	1.25
Nonfarmer to farmer	2.00	.95	1.70	1.44
Wife's education—primary school plus to none	5.25	1.82	4.14	2.40
For All Women				
Percent using some form of contraceptive	8	38	12	17
Percent using more reliable form of contraceptive[a]	2	29	4	11

NOTE:
[a] Condom, sterilization, and IUD.
SOURCE:
Sook Bang, "The Koyang Study: Results of Two Action Programs," *Studies in Family Planning*, No. 11, April 1966, Table 7, p. 8.

in Kimpo the fall was somewhat less. A wife with more than a primary education was some four to five times more likely to be using some form of contraception before the program than her counterpart with no education. After the program this ratio was reduced to about two. In each case the reduction in the ratio was greater in the community where the more intensive public family planning program was undertaken.

The Taichung data summarized in Table 53 confirm the same consequences of the public family planning program as those traced in the two Korean towns.[5] The frequency of contraceptive use be-

[5] For our purposes the Taiwan data are not exactly comparable to those for Korea, but, because they are based on larger samples and include greater detail, they deserve attention. The pre-program study refers to contraceptive use, while the latter survey reports only those who accepted contraceptives in the program, omitting persons who continue to use their own means and thus are not "acceptors." It would therefore appear that the ratio of contraceptive users after the program was launched in 1965 would actually fall somewhere between the initial ratio of users and the final ratio of acceptors (both given in Table 53). As in the Korean case, in every instance the more intensive program brought the ratio of acceptors among social and economic classes closer to unity.

fore the program was launched in 1962 was about three to four times greater among high school graduates than among those with less than a primary education (education of either husband or wife). After exposure to the program in 1965, those accepting contraception in the program were only 1.1 to 1.5 times more frequent in the higher education group than in the lower. When families were divided into high and low income classes, the ratio of contraceptive use fell from 2.3 to 1.1 in the regularly covered regions of Taichung. Just as the ratio of contraceptive use among disparate economic and social classes diminished with the intensity of the public family planning program, the ratio of contraceptive use among couples with five or more children to

TABLE 53

RATIO OF WOMEN AGE 20 TO 39 EVER USING
CONTRACEPTION PRIOR TO A PUBLIC FAMILY PLANNING
PROGRAM, AND RATIO ACCEPTING A METHOD OF
CONTRACEPTION IN PROGRAM IN TAICHUNG, TAIWAN, BY
DEMOGRAPHIC AND ECONOMIC CHARACTERISTICS

Contraceptive User Ratio	Ever Used Means of Family Limitation Before Program, 1962	Acceptance Rate in Program by July 31, 1965	
		Regular Program	Intensive Program
Wife's education—senior high school graduate versus less than primary	3.27	1.28	1.13
Husband's education—senior high school graduate versus less than primary	3.56	1.50	1.24
Husband's occupation—white collar-professional versus farmer	3.71	1.35	1.08
Household income—NT $2,500 or more versus less than NT $1,000	2.30	1.07	n.a.
Number of living children—five or more versus none	7.00	7.66	10.00

SOURCE:
Ronald Freedman and John Y. Takeshita, *Family Planning in Taiwan: An Experiment in Social Change*, Princeton University Press, Princeton, 1969, and unpublished tables circulated with the manuscript.

couples with no children increased from 7.0 to an acceptor ratio of 10.0 in the regions subjected to the more intensive program.[6]

The evidence is that these programs have not only accelerated the diffusion of contraceptive knowledge and practices and equalized the frequency of contraceptive use among diverse social and economic classes, they have done so within the remarkably short span of two years. The ability of these public programs to penetrate all segments of society regardless of their innovative advantages is a powerful argument for direct public action in this field, rather than indirect public subsidy to private commercial channels of information and distribution. In all probability, the latter policy would maintain class differentials in access to, and use of, modern contraception.

Given that many families are having more children than they want, programs to increase access to modern birth control methods can have a rapid and powerful impact. There is good reason to believe that this condition also obtains in Colombia. Published survey findings are available only for Bogota in 1964, but other fragmentary evidence suggests the situation is more acute today in less metropolitan areas of Colombia.[7] About two-thirds of the

---

[6] Freedman and Takeshita confirm this pattern by other statistical methods that show that social and economic characteristics of the respondents are more helpful in predicting contraceptive use before the program than in predicting acceptors from the sampled population after the program has been in operation. A multivariate linear relationship is assumed to exist between a variety of economic, social, and demographic features of the respondent and her use of some form of contraception before the family planning program and her acceptance of some form of contraception in the program. Freedman and Takeshita found that the wife's education, husband's occupational status, and household income with six other socioeconomic variables helped to explain 18 percent of the variance in contraceptive use before the program among the women age 30 to 39. But these same variables accounted for only 1 percent of the variance in acceptance in the program. On the other hand, the demographic variables, such as the number of living sons and daughters and the number of children alive and wanted, explained 13 percent of the variance in program acceptance. The authors conclude, "Clearly, the social variables are much more important in relation to prior use of contraception than for acceptances in the program." Takeshita and Freedman, *Family Planning in Taiwan: An Experiment in Social Change,* Princeton University Press, Princeton, 1969, p. 179.

[7] Alfredo Aguirre, "Colombia: The Family in Candelaria," *Studies in Family Planning,* No. 11, April 1965.

married women interviewed in Bogota reported they wanted no more children. In the United States the proportion is one-half; in Taiwan it is only 45 percent.[8] There was a general receptivity among all classes for the adoption of birth control, and a majority regarded the lack of money as an acceptable reason for preventing additional births. The completed family size in Bogota implied that parents were having on the average 4.8 children while the expressed "ideal" number of children was 3.6. Consistent with the evidence from Taiwan and Korea, contraceptive use was more frequent among the upper classes. As seen in Table 54, better educated women were more likely to have used some form of contraception. They were also more likely to have used a modern, reliable

TABLE 54

IDEAL AND ACTUAL FAMILY SIZES AND CONTRACEPTIVE
USE BY WIFE'S EDUCATION, BOGOTA, 1964

Wife's Educational Attainment	"Ideal" Number of Children All Minors[a]	Actual Number of Live Births All Unions[b]	Actual Number of Live Births After 15 Years or More than One Union[c]	Percent of Catholic Women Having Ever Used Contraceptives[d]
No Schooling	4.5	5.3	6.5	14.6
Some primary	4.3	3.9	5.5	28.2
Primary graduate	3.8	3.8	4.7	39.7
Some secondary	4.0	3.6	4.1	59.5
Secondary graduate	4.1	3.6	—	74.0
University	3.9	1.8	—	70.0
All women	4.2	3.9	4.8[e]	39.4

NOTES:

[a] Estimated from Rafael Prieto Duran and Roberto Cuca Tolosa, *Analisis de la encuesta de fecundidad en Bogota*, Monografia 19, CEDE, Bogota, 1966, Table 151.

[b] *Ibid.*, Table 11.

[c] *Ibid.*, Table 455.

[d] Carmen A. Miro, "Some Misconceptions Disproved," in Bernard Berelson (ed.), *Family Planning and Population Programs*, University of Chicago Press, Chicago, 1966, Table 13, p. 629.

[e] Bernard Berelson, "KAP Studies on Fertility," *ibid.*, Table 2, p. 658.

method. Although the better educated wife sought fewer births, she nevertheless managed better in achieving her "ideal" than the

[8] Berelson, "KAP Studies on Fertility," in *Family Planning and Population Programs*, Fig. 2, p. 659.

less educated.[9] Most of the unwanted births in Bogota are apparently to families where the mother has had less than a primary education, and it is toward this group that a publicly supported planning program must be aimed if equal access to modern methods of birth control is to be assured for all parents and if birth rates are to fall substantially.

But there is no reason why population policy must stop with birth control. The studies described earlier indicate that it is possible to influence the birth rate by influencing the number of children people want to have. This can be done directly by various tax and subsidy schemes. There does exist an economic argument for a transfer tax, for, in addition to the costs of children that are borne by the family directly, the society as a whole bears costs in the form of education, health, and welfare services that children consume. Although the average taxpayer is also a parent, without user fees the individual parent's tax is unrelated (or perhaps negatively related) to his children's use of these government-supplied services. An efficiency argument may be made for transferring these social costs to the parent.

A policy of directly charging parents for their children's consumption of public services would discourage the purchase of such services by the poor, however. This is inconsistent with the social objective of fostering, rather than discouraging, the use of health and educational services by the lower income classes. Moreover, until knowledge of modern methods of birth control are virtually universal, it seems ill-advised to place severe penalties on those who are least able to alter their circumstances. Thus, although it may be argued on efficiency grounds that parents should absorb the costs of public services their children will consume, a birth tax generates inequitable side effects, particularly if modern birth control has not percolated through all strata of society. A transfer payment to parents for avoiding children may be a preferable mechanism for rationalizing this aspect of public-private population policy without significantly altering the existing redistributional function of the tax-expenditure system.[10] However, such a proposal

[9] Rafael Prieto Duran and Roberto Cuca Tolosa, *Analisis de la encuesta de fecundidad en Bogota,* Monografia No. 19, Centro de Estudios Sobre Desarrollo Economico (CEDE), Bogota, 1966, Table 355A.
[10] One difference between the tax and transfer schemes would be that

is today highly unrealistic politically. It is possible, in many ways more attractive, and much more feasible to try to influence desired family size by means other than direct payments. In particular, policy might be focused on various aspects of the parent's environment in order to provide an incentive for a reduction in fertility.

The regression results of Chapter II suggest that one promising route to the reduction of family size goals is expanding school facilities for young children. Another is facilitating greater labor force participation by women through labor legislation and industrial policy. Finally, it seems quite likely that public health programs that improve the chances for child survival will lead relatively quickly to a more than compensating decline in fertility if they are complemented by a strong birth control program. Although the well-known facts of high infant and child mortality in low income countries would appear, at first glance, to deter rapid population growth, the analysis of Chapter II suggests just the reverse may be closer to the truth.

These factors tending to reduce average family size—greater economic opportunities for women, more schooling for children, and lower infant and child mortality—are already coming into play. Since child spacing is a subtle form of family planning that is uncommon in less developed countries, most persons seeking birth control methods already have the number of living children they want. Consequently, the demand for birth control and the subsequent decline in birth rates should lag ten to fifteen years behind the decline in child death rates and be most noticeable among women 30 years or older. Because of the reduction in child mortality that has already occurred in Colombia, one might expect that a large number of the women reaching the age of 30 to 35 in the 1960s would desire the means to avoid additional births.

---

parents who had already decided to avoid having additional children would nevertheless receive a transfer payment as an economic rent. Some detail in graduating the size of transfer payments according to the likelihood that parents of a certain age, parity, and open birth interval would have additional offspring could substantially reduce the size of these rents, however. Another difference between the tax and transfer systems would be that the tax system would generate additional government revenues while the transfer system would be costless for the government (if rents were eliminated and if the discount rate used to compute the size of the transfer payment were equal to the cost of current government borrowing).

The evidence from Bogota supports this conjecture. After the birth rate has once begun to decline, there will be a potentially fertile group of women controlling their fertility through reliable means of birth control, and fluctuations in child mortality may then become more closely associated with (replacement) fluctuations in birth rates. Where means of reliable contraception remain difficult to secure, abortion and dissolution of marital unions may become more frequent than is already evidenced in Colombia.

If this reasoning is sound, some reduction in fertility in such countries as Colombia is likely in the 1970s, and family planning programs may facilitate this process by providing parents with humane and safe methods of preventing unwanted births. But, to achieve a much lower level of population increase, many more parents must find the objective of a smaller number of living children more attractive than they do now. If society places a high priority on slowing population growth, it must be willing to expand those health, education, labor, and welfare programs that will promote selected changes in the social environment and induce more parents to scale down their family size goals. Such changes in attitudes may tend to follow more or less automatically in the wake of urbanization and a general industrialization effort, but this is no reason not to accelerate the process. Government programs and policies could make specific contributions by strengthening the incentives and improving the opportunities for women to find employment outside the home, in fostering more universal school attendance, and by allocating more resources to health and welfare programs aimed at ending the regime of high infant and child mortality.

Policy Toward Education and Technology

A principal benefit of slowing the pace of population growth would be to relieve some of the pressure on Colombia's sorely taxed educational and technological resources. In this section we consider ways in which these resources may more effectively foster rapid structural transformation.

THE ROLE OF EDUCATION IN THE MODERNIZATION PROCESS

Knowledge about the role of education in the economic development process is both strong and weak at the same time. It is strong in that there are a number of significant empirical relationships that seem to hold. It is weak in that, although these relationships correspond to common sense, very little in the way of formal theoretical work has been done that really explains them.[11]

The relationships between level of per capita GNP and various measures of educational attainment on the part of the population are both striking and well known.[12] It is clear, however, that causality runs from high incomes to ability to support a high level of education, as well as from high educational attainment to high output per worker. Thus these data alone tell little about the productivity of education as an investment in economic growth. Even so, it is probably significant that several of the most rapidly developing countries in terms of per capita output—Japan, Taiwan, Israel, South Korea—have education levels above the average for countries with comparable per capita income. Not only is there some tendency for a certain national level of (or distribution of) education to be associated with a given level of productivity, but educating the work force above that level pulls up productivity.

Despite the well-known strength of the empirical relationship between education and productivity, rigorous understanding of just how education contributes to effectiveness on a job, or to the range of jobs a worker can handle with at least minimal effectiveness, is very weak. Formal analysis of the effect of the supply of people with various educational backgrounds tends to vacillate between assuming fixed educational requirements for a job and assuming that a better educated worker is a perfect (but more productive) substitute for a lesser educated worker. More recent work, positing diminishing marginal productivity to the number of people with skills, is an important formal step forward but does not really come to grips with the mechanism relating education to productivity.[13]

[11] See the excellent review and original analysis of the theoretical and empirical literature by Zvi Griliches, "Notes on the Role of Education in Production Functions and Growth Accounting," Report 6839, Center for Mathematical Studies in Business and Economics, University of Chicago, Sept. 1968.

[12] See, for example, the data presented by F. Harbison and C. Myers in *Education, Manpower and Economic Growth*, McGraw-Hill, New York, 1964.

[13] E. Mitchell, *An Econometric Study of International and Interindustrial Differences in Labor Productivity*, RM-5125-PR, The Rand Corporation, Santa Monica, Dec. 1966.

Our analysis in Chapter VI, we think, provides some clues. We argued that in modern industry the training programs for a variety of jobs have been designed so that they can build on a base provided by the formal educational system. The more the new worker brings to his job, the less the time and expense involved in training him up to a given level of proficiency. The resulting implication is that education is a substitute for experience, as well as employer-provided training, for a given level of worker proficiency in a job. Or, given a cost constraint, educational attainments of the work force act as a limit on pace of expansion of employment in an activity, the limit being greater or lesser depending on the fraction of jobs that require special skills and the amount of combined education and experience needed to achieve minimum acceptable skill levels.

Several studies enrich and reinforce this point of view. In advanced countries one finds a strong relationship between the pace at which technology is changing in an industry and the education levels (particularly the percent of highly educated people) in the work force.[14] Where jobs do not change, the costs to an employer of training a relatively poorly educated worker or letting him gain experience on the job need be incurred only once. Where technology, hence the nature of jobs, changes often, trainability for a variety of jobs becomes pivotal, and the advantages of a strong education base on the part of a worker can be very important.

In contrast, the ability to learn rapidly to cope efficiently with a wide variety of circumstances, any one of which may require some considerable skill or understanding, has limited payoff when the world is relatively static. Perhaps this explains why, although certain high skills are needed in craft technology, these tend to be taught on the job, and the demand for people with high formal education is limited. It points, also, to the reason why education, at all levels, may be especially important in economies beginning to modernize rapidly. Craft experience has little relevance to making sensible choices regarding whether or not to adopt modern technology and what kind to adopt, or how to run the operation once started, or what to do when a machine breaks down. In a country just beginning to modernize, relevant experience is scarce.

[14] D. Keesing, "Impact of Research and Development on U.S. Trade," *Journal of Political Economy*, Vol. 75, No. 1, Feb. 1967, pp. 38–48.

In a very real sense, the less developed countries are in the peculiar position of being forced to substitute education for experience if they are to expand their modern sector rapidly and efficiently.

In most development models the manufacturing sector is faced with an elastic supply of labor.[15] However, the model does not distinguish between kinds of labor. The performance of a country's educational system may be a key factor in determining the elasticity of supply of effective labor. If the supply of relatively well educated people at all levels is limited, rapid expansion of employment may rapidly lead to high costs. With a better educated work force, the lower levels of average experience associated with rapid expansion of employment may carry less penalty. A modernizing economy that opts for the hothouse environment of protection may be able to live with high costs. The Colombian experience, however, suggests that, if rapid growth of output and employment is the objective and the balance of payments is an important constraint, this is not a viable long-run strategy. For an economy that opts for openness and an export market, educational policy may be the key to making that strategy work.

DIRECTIONS FOR EDUCATIONAL POLICY

In this section we want to make three points about the directions of educational policy in Colombia. First, there is strong evidence of high social productivity of education (and strong private incentives to acquire it) at the lower and middle levels of the educational ladder. The conjectures discussed in the preceding section about the growing importance of education are borne out by rate-of-return data. Second, improving the quality of education appears to be becoming an increasingly important consideration. Third, there are some mysteries and important problems with regard to the productivity of higher education.

Table 55 presents our estimates of rates of return to education of different levels in Colombia, together with rate-of-return data on other countries taken from published studies. Note first that the rate of return at the lower and (particularly) middle levels is high, and that this seems to be consonant with data from other countries. Second, it can be seen that the estimated rate of return

---

[15] Consider, for example, the "classic" model of Arthur Lewis and the subsequent systems posited by Ranis and Fei or Jorgensen.

TABLE 55
INTERNATIONAL COMPARISONS OF RATES OF RETURN TO EDUCATION

Country Year Type of Rate	Colombia[a] 1965 Private	Colombia[a] 1965 Social	Mexico[b] 1963 Private	Chile[c] 1959 Social	Venezuela[d] 1957 Social Urban	Puerto Rico[e] 1959 Private Urban	Philip- pines[f] 1966 Private	India[g] 1960–61 Private	U.S.A.[h] 1959 Private North-White
Approximate educational levels									
1. Primary over none	18	15	45	24	82	28	9	17	22
2. Middle over primary		27	17	29	17	14	29	14	16
3. Matriculation over middle	34		15	17	23	15	12	12	16
4. University over matriculation	5	3	40	12				10	10

NOTES:

[a] Bogota men——T. Paul Schultz, *Returns to Education in Bogota, Colombia*, RM-5645-RC/AID, The Rand Corporation, Sept. 1968, Table 7 and p. 36.

[b] Men——M. Carnoy, "Rates of Return to Schooling in Latin America," *Journal of Human Resources*, Vol. II, No. 3, Summer 1967, Table 7, p. 368.

[c] Men and Women——A. Harberger and M. Selowsky, "Key Factors in Economic Growth in Chile," paper at Cornell University Conference, "Next Decade in Latin American Development," April 1966 (mimeo).

[d] Urban males presumably——C. Shoup, *The Fiscal System of Venezuela*, The Johns Hopkins University Press, Baltimore, 1959.

[e] Men——H. R. Carby-Samuels, "Income and Returns to Education in Puerto Rico," University of Chicago, Aug. 30, 1965 (mimeo), Table XII, p. 22.

[f] Men——J. Williamson and D. DeVoretz, "Education as an Asset in the Philippine Economy," Institute of Economic Development and Research, School of Economics, University of the Philippines, Discussion paper 67–15, Nov. 6, 1967, Table 5.3.1. p. 39.

[g] Men——A. M. Nalla Gounden, "Investment in Education in India," *Journal of Human Resources*, Vol. II, No. 3, Summer 1967, Table 2, p. 352.

[h] Men——G. Hanoch, "An Economic Analysis of Earnings and Schooling," *Journal of Human Resources*, Vol. II, No. 3, Summer 1967, Table 3, p. 322.

to higher education in Colombia is extremely low, and that in other countries (with the exception of Mexico and Venezuela) such rates of return also are relatively low.

In order to interpret these data and to be able to look into the future, we undertook an extensive interview study of Colombian employers and have examined time-series data on wage rates for different occupational classes.[16] Perhaps the most important conclusion we have drawn from our interviews is that the mid-1960s was a period of flux. When Colombia began its post-World War II surge of industrialization, there was a definite general skill shortage problem. Foreign firms establishing plants in Colombia often felt it necessary to import virtually all skilled manpower, even down to the level of bulldozer operator. This is no longer true. In the opinion of most observers of the Colombian labor market, there are virtually no labor skills that are currently in "excess demand."[17]

TABLE 56
CHANGES IN WAGE RATES BY OCCUPATION,
BOGOTA, JULY 1964 – MAY 1967

Occupation	Percentage Increase in Hiring Salaries
Unskilled labor	38
Semiskilled machine operators	36
Skilled mechanics	29
Messengers	23
Semiskilled office workers	24
Secretaries	22
Skilled clerical workers	22
Professional accountants	25
Engineers	26

NOTE:
The increase in the working class cost-of-living index in Bogota over this period was 37 percent. The cost-of-living index for the middle class increased 39 percent.
SOURCE:
Unpublished data collected by Industrial Relations Consultants, Bogota.

[16] See note 12, Chap. VI.

[17] See R. Slighton, *Relative Wages, Skill Shortages, and Changes in Income Distribution in Colombia*, RM-5651-RC/AID, The Rand Corporation, Santa Monica, Oct. 1968.

Data on wage relatives also tend to confirm the argument that there is no general skill shortage in Colombia. Table 56 shows that since 1964 the wage rate of professionals has declined relative to that of skilled labor, and that of skilled labor has declined relative to that of semi-skilled and unskilled labor. It is not fully apparent when the wage structure began to change. There are no good data prior to 1964, only opinions.

It is extremely difficult to interpret these data, either the relative compression of wage differentials by level of skill and profession or the interview assertions that Colombia does not at present suffer from many skill shortages. There clearly are several factors at work, and it is important that one try to separate them. First, since the early 1950s there has been a significant increase in the percentage of new entrants to the Colombian labor force who have progressed higher up the educational ladder. Table 57 shows the sharp across-the-board rise in the percentage of people in school from 1951 to 1964. University enrollments have increased fourfold since 1951, and the proportion of this enrollment in engineering, natural science, and agriculture has doubled. There has been an equally dramatic increase in vocational school enrollments and graduates. Enrollment in public vocational schools increased from 19,400 in 1951 to 38,000 in 1957 to 71,000 in 1963. The

TABLE 57

STUDENTS PER HUNDRED POPULATION BY AGE, SEX, AND REGION, COLOMBIA, 1951 AND 1964

Age in Years	Total Population				Cabeceras or Urban Population				Other Regions or Rural Population			
	Male		Female		Male		Female		Male		Female	
	1951	1964	1951	1964	1951	1964	1951	1964	1951	1964	1951	1964
5–9	17.3	25.6	17.6	26.3	27.5	36.9	27.6	36.9	12.0	15.1	12.0	15.7
10–14	39.7	58.2	38.0	56.1	59.6	76.2	55.6	70.7	28.8	40.7	26.1	39.1
15–19	13.7	26.6	9.5	22.0	26.6	43.2	16.1	31.5	6.2	9.5	3.9	7.5
20–24	2.8	5.9	.9	2.3	6.2	10.6	1.6	3.6	.6	1.0	.2	.5
25–29	.6	1.0	.3	.4	1.3	1.8	.5	.6	.1	.2	.1	.1

SOURCES:

Censo de Poblacion de Colombia 1951 Resumen, Table 11, p. 37, and Table 39, p. 188. *XIII Censo Nacional de Poblacion (Julio 15 de 1964) Resumen General*, Table 7, pp. 33ff., and Table 41, pp. 143ff.

national apprentice program (SENA), which began in 1958, now graduates over 40,000 students each year.[18]

This rapid change in the conditions of labor supply was the direct result of government recognition of the overt skill shortage problem of the 1950s and the assumption that the rapid growth of industry in that period would continue. Since the early 1960s, however, Colombia has exhibited recession-like symptoms. Although employment in modern manufacturing increased about 18 percent between 1958 and 1962, it increased only 3 percent between 1962 and 1966. As a result, the growth of demand for skilled labor has lagged greatly behind the growth of supply. Wage relatives have changed, and unemployment rates among the better educated have increased.[19] It would be extremely desirable to be able to determine whether the current situation of redundant skills is a phenomenon of recession or an indication of a changing secular balance between supply and demand. We cannot, in fact, make that discrimination, although we suspect the former interpretation is more likely to be the true one.

Although the clarity of the long-run educational policy implications of the interview evidence is thus badly obscured by a temporary phenomenon, there are some clues worth considering. First, the rate of return on primary and secondary education of existing quality is still relatively high, but it is increasingly likely that a premium will be placed on improved quality. Second, although the average rate of return on investment in higher education of the present quality and distribution of fields appears to be low, there is likely to be a high rate of return on high quality advanced education in certain fields.

Even with recession there still seems to be strong demand for persons capable of moving into high-level managerial jobs. At the present time only a small proportion of the Colombian urban economy is managed by professionals, but the proportion is growing.[20] The chief bottleneck today to the expansion of "profession-

[18] SENA, Division of Human Resources, Bogota, 1967 (mimeo).

[19] Unemployment among SENA graduates appears to be particularly serious. For example, 28 percent of the graduates of the SENA vocational training program in Barranquilla were unemployed in 1965.

[20] We are not sure that it is possible to give an adequate definition of "professionalism" or "professional management." The essence of what we are trying to identify with such words is the habit of constant reexamination

alism" in business management is probably the limited capacity of the educational system to train management specialists.[21] This is one important skill class that is not currently in "excess supply." In the past the demand for such individuals has been small, and it is more this fact than any inherent inertia on the part of Colombian educational institutions that explains the current thinness of supply. The rapidly increasing demand for management specialists can probably be ascribed to a number of factors. One is the higher level of educational attainments of the younger generation of "owner-managers." Another is that many Colombian businessmen have served their managerial apprenticeships in foreign firms.

Relatedly, there also appears to be considerable demand for high quality technical people. The demand for engineering graduates from schools such as the Universidad de los Andes or the Universidad Industrial de Santander is currently quite brisk, and the real wages paid such graduates appear to have grown at a rate that is similar to the average for all industrial workers in recent years. The fortunes of the technical graduates of lesser qualification do not appear to have been so favorable. The need now is to secure a better fit between the patterns of enrollment and demand (fewer automobile mechanics) and to upgrade course quality.

Yet if increased stress is going to be put on quality of education, the educational system is going to be putting out people who have options outside the country. If there are lags in the evolution of demand, Colombia's investment in education may be reaped by other countries. Colombia is already experiencing a significant

---

of the profitmaking possibilities of the firm. Typically, this will involve the acquisition of sufficient technical expertise to permit reevaluation of production processes in light of changes in technological opportunities, a nonpassive attitude toward product and market development, and a strong concern for the possibilities of increasing administrative efficiency through specialization.

[21] The undergraduate faculty of business at the Universidad del Valle may dispute this assertion on the grounds that it has had some difficulty in placing all of its graduates. We suspect that this difficulty will disappear quickly once the facts that this faculty is in existence and that it is an operation of high quality are more widely publicized outside Cali. In both Bogota and Medellin the demand for management specialists does not appear to be satisfied.

brain drain. Therefore, it is imperative that educational policy be complemented by measures aimed at increasing the effective demand for highly trained people. One appealing route would be to invest in activities directly involved in the technological transfer process, such as industrial R&D and technical consulting and information services. The rate of return to these activities might be very high. We say "might" because, despite Strassman's recent pathbreaking work, the subject is still very poorly understood.[22]

THE NATURE OF THE POLICY PROBLEM

Industrial R&D in a less developed economy. For agricultural research the case can be made that soil types, temperature and rainfall conditions, the insect and pest populations, and other characteristics of the environment tend to be unique to the country or area, and hence technology that works well in developed economies may be ill-adapted to less developed ones. There is strong evidence in support of this argument, for in many cases U.S. seeds and techniques have not worked out well in a less developed country. In addition, there are examples of very high payoffs to indigenous agricultural research and development, such as the Rockefeller corn and rice varieties and barley technology for Colombia.

This sort of argument does not apply readily to industrial R&D. Technology developed in advanced countries, although not necessarily optimal, nonetheless can generally be used to considerable economic advantage in the less developed countries. Late developing countries are, in a very real sense, blessed by the legacies of the advances in technology achieved through efforts of the developed countries.

There is a counterargument, however, suggesting that certain kinds of industrial R&D may yield a high rate of return in the less developed countries. In this connection, two conceptually distinct kinds of industrial R&D appear particularly relevant to Colombia.

One is what might be called "special circumstance" or "adap-

---

[22] W. Paul Strassman, *Technological Change and Economic Development,* Cornell University Press, Ithaca, 1968. Also see E. Staley and D. Fulton, *Scientific Research and Progress in Newly Developing Countries,* Stanford Research Institute, Menlo Park, 1961.

tive" R&D aimed at the different factor supply situations of a less developed country.[23] The arguments here are much like those regarding agricultural R&D discussed above, although less powerful. The development literature has noted for some time that process and product invention and design in developed countries have been pulled in the direction of satisfying the product demands and cost constraints of a high-income, high-wage, capital-and-skill-plentiful, large-scale economy. That the technologies and the programs and equipment in which they are embodied are in most cases economically efficient relative to traditional technology, even in the vastly different environment of the less developed economies, is testimony to the magnitude of the advances achieved. Nevertheless, the argument remains that research, development, and design aimed at doing even better under the demand patterns, resource endowments, and scale constraints of the less developed countries could result in a more economic technology.

Another set of arguments for an industry-related R&D effort by a developing country derives from the need to anticipate the future technological manpower requirements of a rapidly changing industrial structure. In the early stages of the industrial modernization process, a large fraction of high-level education of scientists and engineers will have to take place in universities abroad. As the economy develops, and as the number of foreign-trained technical experts grows, it will become increasingly possible, and economic, to carry out a growing fraction of a high-level education in the home country. But both the direct returns to industrial development and the ability of the country to increase its high-level teaching capability progressively will depend in good part on the ability of the country to hold its trained people and to keep them up to date. In turn, this may depend on the existence of what several people concerned with this problem have called "centers of research excellence."

The short-run payoffs of such an R&D program must be viewed as indirect, in terms of educating and holding people, rather than direct, in terms of the development or adaptations of new tech-

---

[23] For a good discussion, see Strassman, *Technological Change and Economic Development.* Also see R. Eckhaus, "Notes on Invention and Innovation in Less Developed Countries," *American Economic Review,* Vol. LVI, No. 2, May 1966.

nology. In the long run such direct payoffs will emerge, and they will become increasingly important as the economy moves into the technically progressive fields. In designing such research centers, the critical consideration is orienting research capabilities in the direction of those kinds of industries the country is likely to develop in the reasonably near future. Thus the Mexican programs in the fields of physical and organic chemistry appear to compare favorably with the Indian decision to put resources into the nuclear energy field.

Together these arguments, one for adaptive R&D to permit better exploitation of comparative advantage, the other relating to the complementarity of a research program of excellence and the education function and the holding of scientists and engineers in a country, provide a qualitative justification for industrial R&D as at least a minor portion of a developing country's investment budget. Unfortunately, there have been few studies, to our knowledge, that permit assessment of the actual returns to industrial R&D in developing countries.[24] In most countries it is clear that very little is done. In countries where some industrial R&D is carried on (principally in public facilities), there seems to have been little in the way of systematic appraisal of the actual returns. Most of the laudatory comments regarding industrial R&D in a less developed country really amount to statements that such and such an institution has been established and still survives.

Consulting and information services. The appropriate kind and magnitude of investment in technical consulting and information services also involve a set of difficult and unexplored questions. The questions are quite different, however. The argument that industrial R&D should play a limited role in a developing economy's investment budget is the other side of the argument that the rate of return is very high from adopting existing technology. This might appear to imply a high rate of return to activities aimed specifically at speeding and facilitating the adoption and learning process.

Unfortunately, there is very little in the way of usable information regarding how an industrial extension service should be set up, or exactly what it should do, if it is to have a substantial

---

[24] Again, Strassman, *Technological Change and Economic Development,* has provided what little knowledge we have.

impact. The limited U.S. experience has not been analyzed in any depth. There is a voluminous literature about productivity centers established under the European Recovery Program that presents arguments for their establishment and roughly describes their activities, but it provides no information at all to enable assessment of their impact. Perhaps largely as a result of habits of thought developed in the European Recovery Program, productivity centers have been springing up in many less developed economies for some years now. Again, there is literature describing their rationale and what they tend to do. For example, a survey of several productivity centers in Asia describes their activity in terms of symposia and conferences, training courses, studies, visits by home groups abroad and consultations at home with foreign experts, and special consultation services.[25] This appears to be a typical menu of activities. It is all probably quite splendid, but no one appears to have studied the effects of these activities very carefully or systematically.

THE CURRENT SITUATION IN COLOMBIA

Colombia's stock of scientific and engineering manpower appears to be about average for Latin American countries of comparable per capita income.[26] Brazil, with roughly comparable per capita income, has about three times as many engineers as Colombia and is roughly three times the size. Argentina has a significantly higher fraction of engineers to population, but also a much higher capita income. However, in recent years Colombia's output of new engineering graduates has been relatively high by Latin American standards. In 1961 Colombia graduated 575 engineers, significantly more per capita than Mexico or Brazil. By

[25] C. Wolf, R. Gangadhavan, and K. C. Han, *Industrial Productivity and Economic Growth,* Asian Productivity Organization, Tokyo, Dec. 1964. See also Strassman, *Technological Change and Economic Development.*

[26] There were roughly 7,000–8,000 engineers and physical scientists in Colombia in the mid-1960s. Unfortunately, the principal source of information on industrial employment of highly educated persons does not differentiate between administrators with and those without scientific or engineering training. Hence the recorded employment of scientists and engineers in Colombian industry is very low. For these data see the Instituto Colombiano de Especializacion Tecnica en el Exterior (ICETEX), *Recursos y Requerimientos de Personal de Alto Nivel,* Bogota, 1965.

the mid-1960s yearly output had risen to around 700. The output of natural scientists is appreciably smaller.[27]

Very few of these technically trained individuals are employed in what might reasonably be called research and development. In a nearly exhaustive study of the largest Colombian firms, Hadley reported that only five could be considered as pursuring R&D activities.[28] The pattern of dependence on foreign sources for new technology is also present for technical consulting and information. The Institute of Technological Research (IIT) is an important domestic source of technical information, but it has less than fifty professional scientists and engineers on its staff. In the main, Colombian firms appear to rely on technical assistance relationships with some foreign firm, either a firm maintaining equity interest, an equipment or materials supplier, or a technical consulting firm. It thus appears that foreign technicians play a major role in the investment, plant layout, and design decisions of Colombian firms.[29]

Given this tradition of dependence upon foreign sources for technical services, and given the slowdown in the 1960s in the rate of growth of manufacturing, Colombia has had serious trouble in preventing the emigration of its newly trained scientists and engineers. Between 1960 and 1965 Colombia was surpassed only by Argentina, among Latin American countries, in the number of professional and technical workers migrating to the United States.[30] In 1964 alone 70 engineers migrated to the United States, and many more to Venezuela. The drain of engineers was significantly less from Brazil and Mexico, both of which have many more engineers and graduate more each year. Interview evidence suggests that some of the "emigrés" consider that working in the United States is "graduate training" and ultimately return to Colombia. But, given the low salaries of engineers and scientists in Colombia relative to those in the United States or even Venezuela, the brain-drain problem has to be considered serious.

[27] Pan-American Health Organization, *Migration of Health Personnel, Scientists and Engineers from Latin America,* WHO, Washington, D.C., 1966.

[28] G. Hadley, *Some Characteristics of Colombian Industry,* Universidad de los Andes, Bogota, 1965.

[29] Strassman, *Technological Change and Economic Development,* reports a similar situation in Mexico and Puerto Rico.

[30] Pan-American Health Organization, *Migration of Health Personnel.*

POSSIBLE POLICY DIRECTIONS

In these circumstances it is necessary to look at education and the technical consulting and development services discussed above as part of a single package. A significant increase in adaptive R&D and improvement in the technical consulting machinery both require an increase in the quantity and average quality of the engineers and scientists coming out of the educational system. But the Colombian economy must also find a way to provide these people with employment opportunities that are sufficiently attractive to deter their emigration.

It appears to us that it is possible to design such a complementary package of policies. Indeed, a complementary package is implicit in the diagnosis. The private rate of return on higher education simply is not high in Colombia, nor does it seem to be in other countries of comparable development levels where data have been analyzed. While it seems that the return to higher education in engineering is above average, the brain drain in Colombia, and in other countries, testifies that the private marginal productivity of an engineer is higher in the more developed than in the less developed countries. If one believes that private returns to scientists and engineers in industry reflect long-run social marginal productivity reasonably accurately, there is little case for increasing government investment in high-level scientific and engineering education. If one believes that the long-run social returns to a growing pool of high-level technical talent is far above short-run private returns, and that private perception of these returns is distorted by a lack of "professionalism" in management, then one has a case for investment in education. But as long as the earnings of technically trained people in Colombia are significantly below their opportunities abroad, one also has a case that education is not enough.

There are several reasons for being hopeful that the demand for relatively high-level technical personnel will increase. First, the major thrust of the policies to be suggested will be to increase competitive pressure on Colombian firms and force them to pay more attention to questions of productive efficiency and product quality. Second, an easing of the import restraint will permit a significantly higher level of investment in capital equipment. Even so, the extent of market disequilibrium is such that government establishment and support of institutions engaged in industrial R&D and technical information services is probably needed. It is important that Colombian firms have access to high-level technical expertise, without being committed at the start to hiring such people full time. Even apart from the learning aspect, in a country where the number of scientists and engineers is limited and most firms are small, a strong case can be made that a considerable portion of technical expertise should be in a common pool, rather than scattered in separate firms and generally not fully employed at high-level work.

The argument that firms need to learn to use such personnel strengthens the case and suggests as well two facets of policy that might not otherwise be obvious. First, some strong mechanism for inducing utilization of the service may need to be developed. One such mechanism is to have some kind of technical audit and, if recommended, a technical consulting arrangement as a prerequisite for credit under government-run credit programs. Colombian firms are far more likely to approach a public agency for credit than for technical assistance, and they are far more likely to take advice when better performance is a requisite for that credit than when a public agency tries to push advice on them. Second, a major function of a technical assistance service is to give private firms experience with the returns to the employment of high-level technical people and thereby induce an increase in the demand for such services. The possibility that the technical service itself would become a major supplier of technicians to the private sector thus should not be viewed as a problem. Indeed, the flow of personnel from the technical service to industry is virtually a prerequisite to the success of the program.

The advantage of having such an institution linked closely with Colombia's engineering schools would appear considerable. In the first place, it could serve as the research and consulting outlet for faculty, making faculty positions more attractive and attracting Colombia's top talent to the research and consulting organization. Relatedly, contact with such an institution might serve to better acquaint academicians and advanced students, many of them trained in the United States, with the real problems and opportunities of Colombian industry. The institution would also serve as a natural source of first employment, if no more attractive offer beckoned, for new graduates.

TOWARD A MORE OPEN ECONOMY WITH A MORE REALISTIC EFFECTIVE EXCHANGE RATE

In Colombia, as in many other less developed countries, foreign exchange availability is the key constraint on future progress. Relaxing the constraint is not a sufficient condition for more satisfactory growth. But it certainly is necessary. Policies to deal with this problem by promiscuous encouragement of import substitution, and quantitative restriction of imports to effect this and to regulate demand for foreign exchange, have reached a dead end. In this section we shall present arguments for a policy of letting the effective exchange rate play a progressively larger role in equilibrating supply and demand for foreign exchange and in guiding import substitution and export development and, relatedly, for progressively opening up the economy to external competition. This prescription is scarcely novel, but that does not make it any easier to implement. Neither does it make it any less necessary. Without such a change we do not see how a country with Colombia's present resource endowments and size can hope to improve its economic performance significantly.

THE IMPERATIVE OF A MORE REALISTIC AND FLEXIBLE EXCHANGE RATE

Colombia's exchange policy has resulted in an average real rate of exchange that is too low to be consistent with rapid growth of output and employment in the modern sector. Colombian policymakers periodically, if not chronically, have thus been forced to restrict aggregate demand to keep the balance of payments from getting out of hand. As a result, the Colombian economy has exhibited symptoms of recession—slow growth of employment in the modern sector, increases in overt unemployment, and a rise in covert unemployment in the form of resurgence of low-productivity, low-wage craft firms. These symptoms call out for expansive policy. But expansionary fiscal and monetary policy is not possible, given the balance-of-payments bind.

That the balance-of-payments constraint is crucial, has not, we think, been adequately recognized.[31] Although many economists have called attention to the problem, it has been easy for policy-makers to maintain the view that the degree of disequilibrium in the foreign exchange market is not severe. Indeed, one of the most important consequences of the short-run, plaster-patch policies that the Colombian government has adopted has been to dull perception of the basic problem. Heavy reliance on quantitative import restrictions permits policymakers to develop and maintain the illusion that long-run supply and demand for foreign exchange are more nearly in balance than is actually the case. Tight fiscal and monetary policy, which restricts total demand, compounds the illusion. Policymakers, observing that when controls are relaxed import surges are temporary and output increases are limited, can argue that, given the constraints on demand, foreign exchange availability is not a serious restraint on expansion. They are right, except that the principal reason that demand is limited is the expectation that the disequilibrium system (and the fiscal-monetary policy associated with it) will continue to be imposed.

There are two broad policy problems here. One is somehow lifting the average real exchange rate structure up to a level more consistent with rapid growth. The other is keeping it there in the face of domestic inflation. If both requirements are to be fulfilled, Colombia will probably be forced to maintain a policy of flexible exchange rates.[32]

[31] Vanek obviously is an exception.

[32] It is extremely important that this recommended devaluation be accomplished gradually, rather than through a series of large once-and-for-all changes in the exchange rate. A good discussion of the economic costs of the latter (conventional) approach is given in H. Dunkerley, *Exchange Rate Systems and Development in Conditions of Continuing Inflation,* Report No. 37, Development Advisory Service, Harvard University, 1966. The political costs are probably even more important. An abrupt devaluation receives far wider publicity and is far more likely to provoke a climate of opinion that leaders of dissident or competitive political factions can exploit than a creeping devaluation. The fact of devaluation is less deeply imbedded in the public mind if the change is gradual and less clearly identified as being the result of actions by the government. The issue here is not one of money illusion, but rather the extent to which the public is inclined to focus upon devaluation as a simplified explanation of the wide variety of economic ills facing society, many or most of which may have only the most tenuous connection with the fact of devaluation itself.

There is another important reason why the gradualist approach is necessary. In an economy such as Colombia's, where administered pricing is

One might be tempted to propose more effective wage and price control as a substitute for a flexible exchange rate. In principle, at least, a large share of the commodities manufactured in Colombia are now subject to price control. The government also has considerable legal authority to influence wage bargains. Yet, in fact, the government's efforts at price and wage control have been more in the nature of forays than a systematic policy. This should not be surprising. The problems of administering a detailed price control system have seriously strained the government apparatus even of countries as well endowed with administrative resources as the United States. This is not to say that public regulation of public utility rates and of the prices charged by a few key monopolized industries is either impossible or undesirable. But a comprehensive and efficient price control system covering large congeries of products is beyond Colombia's administrative reach.

It is thus reasonably certain that Colombia will have to abandon the objective of a fixed nominal exchange rate. Internal prices cannot be expected to be stable. As discussed in Chapter VI, even if employment is assumed fixed, an annual increase of wages of 5 to 7 percent (the rate of growth of labor efficiency) is probably the maximum consistent with stable prices. The average trend over the past decade greatly exceeds this, although there has been some diminution of wage pressure in the past several years. Opening up the economy to external competition—a theme we shall discuss shortly—may somewhat damp inflation, but more rapid employment growth is very likely to speed it up.

In this connection we must note the argument that progressive devaluation would be largely self-defeating in that it would feed back to fuel further wage and price increases and ultimately estab-

---

common and government price controls are ubiquitous (although often evaded), an abrupt devaluation will provide the justification for simultaneous price increases or demands for increases in price ceilings by virtually every sector of the economy. Since these price increases include allowances for both anticipated increases in costs and past cost increases that have not yet been reflected in price decisions, the rate of inflation immediately following a large devaluation may be much more rapid than would have been necessary simply to cover increases in the costs of direct and indirect imports. This bunching of price increases leads to an exaggerated perception of the relationship between devaluation and inflation and thus further intensifies the public hostility to devaluation as a means of stimulating growth.

lish a wage-price spiral. Yet, for such a mechanism to be important, there must be a strong relationship between money incomes of domestic factors of production and the exchange rate. It is not sufficient simply to establish that devaluation will lead to price increases because of the increased cost of imports. For Colombian manufacturing as a whole, the ratio of direct imports of intermediate goods to the value of output was about 14 percent in 1960. The average direct plus indirect import content was about 21 percent.[33] Thus, if the money incomes of domestic factors— wages and profit rates— were independent of the exchange rate, a 5 to 10 percent yearly devaluation would add no more than 1 or 2 percent to the rate of increase in the price of manufactures and a somewhat smaller amount to the cost of living. This seems well within the bounds of political acceptability.

It is, in fact, quite difficult to establish a relationship between the price of domestic factors and the rate of exchange using Colombian data. If the experience of the hyperinflation of early 1963 is ignored, regression analysis shows no significant relationship between the rate of increase of the money wage rate and the rate of change of the exchange rate.[34] The regression of changes in wholesale prices on changes in the exchange rate and changes in wages yields results that are consistent with the hypothesis that changes in domestic factor prices are not related to changes in the exchange rate.[35] Analysis of the relationship between price

[33] See Table 41.

[34] The hypothesis that wages are related to the exchange rate was tested by estimating the parameters of the equation

$$(W_t - W_{t-1})/W_{t-1} = \alpha + \beta(E_t - E_{t-1})/E_{t-1} + u_t$$

for semi-annual data from 1958 through 1967, the data for the first six months of 1963 being omitted. W is the average value of the DANE index of hourly wages in manufacturing for the period in question; E is the average effective rate of exchange on commodity imports. The null hypothesis that β was zero could not be rejected, the standard error of the regression coefficient being more than twice as large as the coefficient itself. Even less significant results were obtained when a lagged relationship was assumed.

[35] The relationship between the price level and the exchange rate was examined by estimating the parameters of the equation

$$(P_t - P_{t-1})/P_{t-1} = \alpha + \beta(E_t - E_{t-1})/E_{t-1} + u_t$$

for semi-annual data from the period 1958–1967, P being the average

changes by two-digit industry and the import content of output
also suggests that the relationship between the price level and the
exchange rate is what would be expected if the exchange rate and
domestic factor prices were unrelated.[36] We must conclude, there-

---

level of the wholesale price index reported by the Banco de la Republica
for the six-month period in question, and E being the average effective exchange rate on commodity imports for the period. If the price index that
excludes foodstuffs is used, and if the data for the first six months of 1963
are excluded, the estimated parameters (the standard error of the regression
coefficient indicated within the parentheses) are

$$(P_t - P_{t-1})/P_{t-1} = .0345 + \underset{(.04)}{.23}(E_t - E_{t-1})/E_{t-1}, \qquad R^2 = .68.$$

The average proportion of total import content of production in manufacturing over the period was in the order of .20. If P is defined as the
wholesale price index including foodstuffs, the estimated parameters are

$$(P_t - P_{t-1})/P_{t-1} = .0347 + \underset{(.07)}{.19}(E_t - E_{t-1})/E_{t-1}, \qquad R^2 = .32.$$

If the data covering the hyperinflation of early 1963 are included, P
being the wholesale price index excluding foodstuffs, the estimated parameters are

$$(P_t - P_{t-1})/P_{t-1} = .0352 + \underset{(.07)}{.32}(E_t - E_{t-1})/E_{t-1}, \qquad R^2 = .57.$$

The fact that the regression coefficient relating prices to the exchange
rate is higher for this period than appears warranted given our pricing
hypothesis is the result of a correlation between devaluation and certain
excluded variables. If the parameters of the model

$$(P_t - P_{t-1})/P_{t-1} = \alpha + \beta_1(E_t - E_{t-1})/E_{t-1} + \beta_2(W_t - W_{t-1})/W_{t-1} + u_t$$

are estimated, W being the DANE index of hourly wages in manufacturing,
the exchange rate coefficient is reduced to the value calculated for the
1958–1967 period when the data for early 1963 were excluded. The actual
estimate is

$$(P_t - P_{t-1})/P_{t-1} = .082 + \underset{(.05)}{.23}(E_t - E_{t-1})/E_{t-1} + \underset{(.09)}{.46}(W_t - W_{t-1})/W_{t-1},$$

$$R^2 = .84.$$

[36] The simplest interindustry pricing model consistent with the hypothesis that the relationship between devaluation and price change is limited
to the shifting forward of total import cost is given by the equation

$$\Delta P_i/P_i = \Delta P^*/P^*[1 - (m_i/x_i)] + \Delta E/E(m_i/x_i) + u_i$$

where P_i is the price of the product of the ith industry, P^* is the common
price index of domestic factors and intermediate goods for all industries, E
is the exchange rate, and (m_i/x_i) is the ratio of total import content of

fore, that the concern over the inflationary consequences of devaluation probably has been greatly exaggerated.

Finally, we wish to stress that the advantages of a higher, more
flexible exchange rate are not confined to the increased supply
of foreign exchange and the improvements in resource allocation
that would accrue to such a policy. An additional benefit would
be the freeing of fiscal and monetary policy. If fiscal-monetary
policy is forced to have a key role in restraining excess demand
for foreign exchange, these instruments are not available for spur-
ring the growth of output and employment. This is the ultimate
cost of an overvalued peso—a depressed level of aggregate demand
that cannot be alleviated through conventional fiscal-monetary pol-

---

production to total production of the ith industry. This model assumes no
productivity change. If productivity change is uncorrelated with import
content (which appears to be the case in Colombia), this pricing hypothesis
can be tested by estimating the parameters of the equation

$$(\Delta P_i/P_i)/(\Delta P^*/P^*) = \alpha + \beta(m_i/x_i) + u_i^*.$$

If the hypothesis holds, the estimate of β should approximate the prespecified value $[(\Delta E/E)/(\Delta P^*/P^*) - 1]$. Where P^* is the index of the cost
of manufacturing calculated for the earlier discussion of the real effective
exchange rate for exporters of manufactured goods, E is the effective rate
of exchange on commodity imports, and P_i is the wholesale price index
for the ith industry as given by the Banco de la Republica (data being
available for all two-digit industries other than printing), the estimates are

$$(\Delta P_i/P_i)/(\Delta P^*/P^*) = .623 + 1.1(m_i/x_i)$$
$$(.42)$$

for the period 1953–1958, and

$$(\Delta P_i/P_i)/(\Delta P^*/P^*) = 1.133 - .59(m_i/x_i)$$
$$(.38)$$

for the period 1958–1964. The standard errors of the regression coefficients are given in parentheses. For the earlier period the regression
estimate of 1.1 should be compared with the actual value of $[(\Delta E/E)/(\Delta P^*/P^*) - 1]$ of .5. Since the nominal and shadow rates of exchange
diverged substantially during this period, the finding that the estimated
coefficient is somewhat larger than the figure implied by the pricing model
is not surprising. This is precisely what one would expect if the users of
imported intermediate goods valued these goods at their scarcity price instead
of their nominal price. For the later period the value of the term $[(\Delta E/E)/(\Delta P^*/P^*) - 1]$ is $-.46$. This compares with the regression estimate of
$-.59$. Since the nominal and shadow prices of foreign exchange appear
to have moved in a more or less parallel fashion over the 1958–1964
period, the consistency of the two figures is what one would expect if the
pricing model were appropriate.

icies. The Colombian government has made it very clear to the international agencies that it intends to retain complete control over foreign exchange policy decisions even if these decisions should result in a lessened flow of international lending. The point that the Colombian government must understand, however, is that a poor choice with respect to foreign exchange policy will ultimately destroy their freedom of choice with respect to fiscal-monetary instruments.

OPENING THE ECONOMY

The second major policy reform that is needed relates to the "structure," rather than the level, of the real exchange rate. The benefits to Colombia would appear great if somehow policy could, first, provide greater balance between the incentives for exporting and import substitution, second, greatly reduce the maximum allowable rate of effective tariff protection[37] and, third, dismantle some of the structure of quantitative controls. While this broad

[37] The critical first step in tariff reform is the reduction of rate dispersion within individual tariff chapters or sections. In practice, the policy guideline established for the average rate of protection for various broad classes of goods (for example, the tenfold classification used in the tariff revision of 1964) is less important as a determinant of the ultimate tariff structure than the guideline on the range of permissible rates within each class. The more complex the criteria for exemptions from the target rate and the wider the permissible deviation from that rate, the more likely it is that the tariff system will degenerate into a line-by-line review tariff with the structure of individual tariffs more reflective of the relative bargaining strengths of domestic producers than a strategy of compensating for certain deficiencies of the price system.

The tendency for administration of the exemption process to blur beyond all recognition the broad allocative criteria established by upper-level decisionmakers suggests that a successful tariff reform can be achieved only if the range of possible rate deviation is small and if the criteria for exemption are limited in number and more or less automatic in their application. It is highly important that the administrators of the tariff system be able to plead an incapability of dealing "flexibly" with the problems of individual producers. Without this protection they will be extremely vulnerable to bargaining pressure. There is also the question of whether the tariff bureaucracy has access to the kind of information needed to administer a complex set of criteria of exceptions. One possible basis of reform that appears administratively feasible is to permit all producers who are currently enjoying higher rates of protection than the common rate established for the relevant tariff section or chapter to obtain a tariff differential that is initially equal to their current price (up to some agreed maximum) but declines through time according to a prespecified schedule. A similar

prescription is "old hat," some of our arguments for it are rather different from the traditional ones. It is to these "new" arguments that we now turn.

Our views are heavily colored by the belief that manufacturing development is essentially a process of structural and technological transformation of the sort discussed in Chapter IV. There we showed that differences in inputs (particularly capital and education) fall short of explaining why such countries as Colombia are so poor. These differences in inputs are also incapable of fully explaining growth over time.[38] Only one-third or so of the increase in productivity in Colombia is explicable in terms of the growth in capital per worker.[39]

---

privilege could be offered new industries. Both a maximum initial tariff differential and a time schedule for the reduction and eventual elimination of this protection should be specified. The quest for administrative simplicity suggests that maximum protection be stated in terms of nominal rather than effective rates, although it would be desirable if the tariff authority were to retain the right to adjust this maximum downward in cases where the apparent difference between nominal and effective rates is very large.

[38] It has been known for some time that a "difference-in-inputs" model has only partial explanatory power regarding growth of productivity over time in developed countries. Bruton's recent study extends this conclusion to less developed countries, including Colombia. See Henry Bruton, "Productivity Growth in Latin America," *American Economic Review,* Vol. LVII, No. 5, Dec. 1967.

[39] Assuming a Cobb-Douglas relationship,

$$\frac{\Delta\left(\frac{Q}{L}\right)}{\left(\frac{Q}{L}\right)} = \frac{\Delta A}{A} + \alpha\frac{\Delta\left(\frac{K}{L}\right)}{\left(\frac{K}{L}\right)}$$

where $\Delta A/A$ refers to productivity growth not explained by growth of the capital-labor ratio and α is capital's "share" of value added.

But

$$\frac{\Delta\left(\frac{K}{L}\right)}{\left(\frac{K}{L}\right)} = \frac{\Delta K}{K} - \frac{\Delta L}{L},$$

and

$$\frac{\Delta K}{K} = \frac{I}{Q}\frac{Q}{K} - \delta$$

where I/Q is the ratio of gross investment to value added (assumed .14),

When one looks at manufacturing development as a structural transformation, rather than as a neoclassical process of factor accumulation, total factor productivity differences across nations and the growth of total factor productivity in the development process are not mysterious at all. The structural transformation model suggests that there are at least three major subprocesses involved. First, there is an innovation in an unconventional sense: the decision (by someone who can directly or indirectly organize economic activity and has access to resources) to invest in modern, rather than in traditional, technology. Second, there are learning phenomena internal to the innovating firm: improvements resulting from accumulated experience on the part of management and the work force in operating with new technologies. Third, there are accommodation and adjustment phenomena outside the firm: induced innovation and learning by suppliers and consumers, and policy responses by government to facilitate the evolution of an environment where efficient operation of modern technology is possible and encouraged.[40]

This difference in viewpoint between the transformation model of development and the neoclassical model is of far more than academic interest. In several important respects the models pose the policy problem in a different light.

First, in comparison with the neoclassical view that puts almost total weight upon the investment rate and the allocation of investment as the key variables on which policy should operate, the structural transformation view assigns considerable weight to increasing somehow the pace and effectiveness of innovation and learning. The effectiveness of investment appears to be powerfully related to the extent to which new investment flows into promising

---

Q/K is the output-capital ratio (assumed .5), and δ the depreciation rate (assumed .02). Thus $\Delta K/K = .05$. Assuming $\Delta L/L = .03$, and $\alpha = .6$, growth of capital per worker can explain a growth of productivity of roughly .012 a year. The observed rate of growth of value added per worker in Colombian manufacturing during the period 1958–1964 was .035 (3.5 percent).

[40] Baranson has provided an extremely interesting case study of how the policy environment can cripple the capability of a firm using modern technology to develop efficiently. See J. Baranson, "Technical Adjustment to a Developing Economy: A Study in the Transfer of Technology by an International Corporation," unpublished Ph.D. dissertation, Indiana University, 1966.

nontraditional industries and to the speed with which these new enterprises learn to operate efficiently. Countries apparently differ significantly in the extent to which their environment is conducive to selective and effective innovation and learning. An important objective policy, then, must be to create an environment conducive to innovation. It is, of course, possible that rapid growth of total factor productivity is a natural concomitant of a high investment rate, but Bruton's study suggests this is not so. His data also show that neither growth of output nor growth of employment is closely linked to the growth of capital.[41]

Second, the structural transformation model implies that it is very difficult to predict the evolution of comparative advantage, for the cutting edge of expansion both is, and should be, firms with coefficients significantly different from the industry average. Within the group of modern expanding firms one would expect, and hope for, changes in input coefficients over time in response to growth of output, experience, improvement in supply conditions, and other factors. One would expect an uneven pace of innovation and learning among industries, with significant changes in relative product attractiveness (including both price and quality) as well as input coefficients. If the system of incentives is permissive, variation on growth rates may transcend variation permitted by domestic demand functions (which in themselves may have considerable sensitivity to price and quality) by the development of export markets.

In the context of an analysis attempting to shed some empiricall light on the balanced versus unbalanced growth controversy, Swamy has examined the relative "balance" of expansion in high-growth versus low-growth countries.[42] His findings are that the faster the growth rate, the greater is the discrepancy from a pattern of industry growth predicted from either strict proportional growth or growth related to income elasticities of demand. Swamy's study suggests a macroeconomic analogue to the apparent differences in environments for innovation and learning mentioned earlier. The difference in environments appears strongly related to

[41] H. Bruton, "Productivity Growth in Latin America."

[42] D. Swamy, "Statistical Evidence of Balanced and Unbalanced Growth," *Review of Economics and Statistics,* Vol. XLIX, No. 3, Aug. 1967, pp. 288–303.

the ability to tolerate, or, better, make profitable, rapid opportunistic growth of an unbalanced kind. Sensible policy must be designed with an eye to permitting and encouraging opportunistic growth.

Ability to predict in detail the promising export industries is thus sorely limited. Neither with respect to variety nor with respect to variation over time within any category could Colombia's minor export performance over the past six years have been predicted. In the Adelman-Sparrow model,[43] Colombia's export potential industries were limited, on the basis of performance in the 1950s, to coffee, petroleum, and bananas. Thus the model simply missed the whole point.

Similarly, there are enormous problems involved in sensibly implementing a policy that involves industry-by-industry or firm-by-firm evaluation of requests for "infant" industry protection. The firms to be encouraged almost certainly will have, and will be expected to have, input coefficients and costs significantly different from those of existing firms. Further, costs and input coefficients are expected to change over time with growing scale and experience. Both of these considerations make the kinds of predictions needed for effective implementation of the policy extremely difficult and uncertain.

We believe that these considerations provide powerful arguments for greater reliance on the effective exchange rate structure to allocate imports and stimulate exports and for use of the opportunity and pressure of international competition as a key instrument of public control. We think these arguments are a significant addition to, sometimes a substitution for, the neoclassical ones.

The neoclassical argument in favor of an open economy has been couched in terms of the advantages to be derived from exploitation of comparative advantage. Partly because of the inability of economists to designate areas of comparative advantage and disadvantage, and partly because of the belief that, for almost any factor prices and in almost any industry, efficiently operated modern technology is more productive than craft production, it seemed sensible to many countries during the 1950s to encourage manufacturing development by providing a protected domestic

---

[43] Irma Adelman and Frederick T. Sparrow, "Dynamic Linear Development Planning" (mimeo, n.d.).

market for all comers. As the experience of Colombia and other countries that have gone this route now shows clearly, "efficiently operated" is a key qualification. There is now increasing awareness of the relationship between efficiency and scale of production and of the need to develop export markets if the problem of excess capacity is to be dealt with.[44] But reliance on a more discriminate, but protection-based, policy of import substitution and export promotion also faces severe problems in the absence of competition. The problem of "selection," discussed earlier, is extremely hard. And once protection has been granted (and is viewed as being in the public interest), incentives for the "infant" to grow up are very difficult to apply with any vigor.

More generally, a closed economy presents very serious problems of public control of industry in a small country. Those countries that have gone the protectionist route with little emphasis on exports have found themselves increasingly faced with a dilemma. On one hand, they have eroded the ability of the price system to generate incentives and pressures that will spur efficiency and regulate product and factor prices so that the prices of factors in different uses are similar and relative prices are roughly consonant with relative marginal costs. On the other hand, they have gained a much keener awareness of how difficult and costly it is to attempt to use a sensible, detailed regulatory policy from the center. In the past there has been a strongly optimistic tradition within the Colombian government concerning the difficulties of administrative allocation, so much so that necessity has become a virtue in the eyes of many. This tradition is by no means dead, but an increasing number of the younger planners and administrators understand the empty, *pro forma* nature of many of the direct control procedures. It would therefore seem that, even if there were no facts of life with respect to comparative advantage to consider, awareness of the problems of public control of industry in a small, protected economy would call for the use of imports or the possibility of imports as a control device.

[44] The changes in attitudes among the *tecnicos* within (or potentially within) the government reflects many of the considerations that prompted Prebisch to revise his ideas about development policy. See R. Prebisch, *Towards a Dynamic Development Policy for Latin America*, United Nations, Geneva, 1964, for a provocative and influential discussion of the role of import substitution.

The Policy Process

The preceding sections have presented a limited, but far-reaching set of policy reforms. In presenting them, we run the risk of being twice damned. The package is in no meaningful sense optimal. On the other hand, the package may not be politically feasible or, from the point of view of revealed political preference, even desirable. At best this reform package may be considered naive; at worst it may be considered ideological imperialism. We think the question of political feasibility is the more serious complaint. The question of optimality bothers us considerably less.

POLICYMAKING IS NOT AN OPTIMIZATION PROCESS

It is clear that, in principle, any policy problem can be posed in terms of three components: the objectives and some kind of a weighting scheme that together define a welfare function; a set of instruments at the control of the government that can be used in varying ways; and the set of constraints and relations that determine the outcome of any policy choice in terms of the value taken on by the various objectives. The problem of policy choice, then, can be viewed as picking the set and levels of instruments that maximize the welfare or objective function subject to the constraints.[45]

But we do not think it fruitful to view global policymaking in this way. The variety of different objectives and different points of view regarding their relative desirability, the vastness of the number of instruments that can be used in different ways, and the complexity of the constraints on economic development and lack of solid quantitative knowledge regarding them combine, we think, to rule out the useful posing of overall economic policy as an optimization problem.

One fundamental problem is the very meaning of a "social preference function."[46] But beyond that, in a situation of "social" choice, compounded by great complexity and uncertainty, the distinction among ends, means, and "the way the system operates"

[45] For a good summary discussion of policy optimization models, see B. Hickman (ed.), *Quantitative Planning of Economic Policy,* The Brookings Institution, Washington, D.C., 1965, Chap. 1.

[46] See K. J. Arrow, *Social Choice and Individual Values,* Wiley, New York, 1951.

invariably breaks down in a political environment. For example, is price stability an end in itself (related, say, to income distribution), or is it desired because it is believed conducive to growth and balance-of-payments equilibrium? Is government regulation or spending to be viewed solely as a possible instrument for the achievement of an objective or as something that colors the whole tone of the economic system, something to be desired or disliked in itself? Disagreement about policy may stem from disagreement about either values or analysis. Agreement on policy may be possible even when people disagree on values or analysis. Under these circumstances the results of alternative policies are in large part debated rather than calculated, and policies invented rather than selected. Differences in interest tend to be logrolled to achieve a coalition capable of agreeing to some choice, rather than objectively balanced in some utility function.

It is for such reasons that Braybrooke and Lindblom have pointed out that global policy is not dealt with globally.[47] The policy arena simply has to be divided, often in an *ad hoc* and expeditious way, into a set of subareas with the attention of the higher-level policymaking apparatus sometimes focused on one small subset of these, sometimes on another. Policy is considered at a high level only when "problems" caused by existing policy become a matter of open dispute, or when another problem on the agenda calls for reconsideration of that policy. A premium is placed on getting rid of the requirement to focus on a particular area when others may be compelling attention. The resolution of the problem at the higher level, if it can be achieved at all, usually amounts to the chartering of an institution with a prescribed set of instruments under its control and a rough set of decision rules as criteria for dealing with the problem. Once the institution is chartered, responsibility for carrying out the policy is delegated, and detailed overview of the institution from a high level may be quite nominal.

Once policymaking is viewed in this way, three kinds of constraints not typically considered by the optimization model are seen to be of pivotal importance. The first is a resource constraint. The limited amount of resources available for policy implementa-

[47] D. Braybrooke and C. Lindblom, *A Strategy for Decision: Policy Evaluation as a Social Process,* The Free Press, Glencoe, Ill., 1963.

tion at any given time constrains the range of policies that can be effectively administered. The second is the constraint on the number of issues that the top political leadership can consider effectively within any given time period. The "issues" constraint limits the degree of high-level control over the separate institutions that make policy on an operational basis. Finally, there is the subtle constraint implied by the phenomenon that institutions and policies once created are difficult to abandon. Further, their existence seriously constrains the room for maneuver in dealing with new problems.[48]

Each of these constraints is important to a normative evaluation of economic policy in Colombia, but the "resources" constraint is particularly significant. Given the government's difficulty of augmenting its limited administrative resources, policies can be applied selectively and sensibly in only a few areas at any one time unless there is strong incentive to comply voluntarily. A quasi-equilibrium system with the effective exchange rate approximating a free market rate needs little administration and monitoring to be effective. A system of import licensing and quantitative exchange controls will inevitably result in distortions. Policies aimed at detailed control will not, in general, have stated objectives that are different from a more macroeconomic policy. But the effects will be different from those intended. Much evasion must be expected. Most important, the administrative decision rules adopted will have to be crude. The import licensing criteria are a case in point. Simple and stable decision rules are likely to be close to optimal only when contingencies can be predicted in advance. The essence of the development process is that they cannot be predicted.[49]

Normative policy judgments must also be made with full awareness that policy choice today will affect what is feasible tomorrow.

[48] A. Hirschman, *The Strategy of Economic Development,* Yale University Press, New Haven, 1958; and W. Stolper, *Planning Without Facts,* Harvard University Press, Cambridge, 1961. Both stress the importance of these kinds of constraints.

[49] This is not to argue that it is foolish to attempt any form of microeconomic control, only that microeconomic control is effective in very limited areas. Trying to exert it in too many areas at once is diabolically well designed to scotch the development process rather than further it. We think the policies discussed earlier represent a judicious balance between what is necessary to cope with the problems and what is administratively feasible.

In the first place, existing policies and institutions mold the way that problems are perceived. The legacy of treating the foreign exchange problem as one of crisis management has obscured the basic nature of the problem. With tight restrictions on demand, it is hard to see how large the foreign exchange gap really is. With policies focused on import substitution through quantitative protection, it is hard to see that there may be major export options. It is recognized that prices are not competitive. But, with the exchange rate played down as an instrument, the possibility that this conclusion can be changed by changing the exchange rate tends to be overlooked.

In the second place, policies tend to develop a vested interest. If a policy continues over any considerable period of time, people and groups will have learned to accommodate themselves to it in the sense of finding ways to live with it, or take advantage of it, as best they can. The vesting effect on that segment of the public that has learned to accommodate to a policy complements the vested interest of the administrators who staff the institutions charged with policy implementation. As a result, the institutionalized policies may become quite insulated from the control of the elected officials at the center, and an effective coalition against change may form in a particular policy area.

The nature of the high-level political machinery that proposes, adopts, modifies, and destroys policies and policy institutions is of pivotal importance. It is significant that Japan, Mexico, Taiwan, and Israel, all countries that have had relatively successful development experience, have been able to achieve a considerable degree of continuity in politics. And, in the first three cases, conscious policies were invoked and enforced over time to erode powerful existing interest groups and to build a vested interest in the new departures. These countries were able to engage in successful long-term economic planning, but not in the neoclassical policy model sense. Rather, the planning involved the ability to specify certain problem areas and policies regarding them that happened to be pivotal and fruitful in generating development and to push on with these policies steadily despite what, for a time, was strong opposition. We suspect that these high-level judgments were rarely, if ever, the result of any careful optimization analysis. Rather, they represented ability, or luck, in getting a coalition of sufficient power to persevere with the policies agreed upon, even though the short-term results may not have been impressive.

Trying to pose Colombia's economic policy problem as an optimization problem may actually make it more difficult for effective policy to evolve. As Lindblom and Wildavsky have stressed, agreement on policy often is achieved because of, not in spite of, the fact that the issues are not fully clear.[50] Groups with very different objectives can come together on policy precisely because the conflict of objectives is never permitted to come fully into the open and because they differ in their comprehension of the problem and in their belief about what the policy actually means.

POLICYMAKING AND POLITICS: THE
POSSIBILITY OF INNOVATION

The critical question is thus not whether the policy changes that we have recommended are optimal, but whether they are politically feasible. Existing Colombian development policies reflect certain fundamental characteristics of the Colombian political process that will not be changed easily. We also feel vulnerable to the charge of ideological imperialism, for it is hardly clear what ground the outsider has for making normative judgments regarding the net impact of policies that mostly affect Colombians.

With respect to the Colombian policymaking process, two things are quite evident. First, the process by which policies are made and men governed has a value that transcends the specific policies that system produces. Colombians have a great (and, given their history, a legitimate) fear of disturbing the stability of the political system for the sake of securing a particular policy change. In concerning ourselves with the problem of achieving a greater rate of economic growth, it is quite possible to forget that the most critical of the problems facing Colombia is that of maintaining a political mechanism that is capable of resolving factional conflicts without resort to violence. The "National Front" solution to this problem has worked fairly well, but it was not conceived of as a permanent arrangement. A new set of decisions regarding the permissible area of competition between the political parties will

[50] C. E. Lindblom, "The Science of Muddling Through," *Public Administration Review*, 1959, and *Intelligence of Democracy*, The Free Press, Glencoe, Ill., 1965; A. Wildavsky, "The Political Economy of Efficiency," *Public Interest*, No. 8, Summer 1967, pp. 30–48.

thus have to be made, and this consideration, together with related constitutional issues concerning the distribution of power between the executive and legislative branches of government, will dominate the political thinking of Colombian leaders in the immediate future. If a proposed economic reform is deemed likely to engender sufficient opposition to the government in power to be an important threat to that government's chance of securing such constitutional reforms, it will not be implemented.[51]

The second clear characteristic of the Colombian policymaking process is that, by and large, the policies that have been selected have not engendered strong opposition. Colombian economic policy is politically legitimate. Most Colombians do not seem to be upset by the protection given to special interest groups, for special treatment has been traditional in the Colombian political culture. There are few groups lobbying for a more balanced support of exports and import substitution. Those individuals who have already secured property rights in jobs in the modern sector see no reason to change the policies that have created those rights. Those who have not been fortunate enough to secure such employment perceive their misfortune in terms of inflation and the traditional gulf between rich and poor, rather than in terms of the slow rate of growth of the modern sector. In part the existing policy is not under serious challenge simply because the consequences of a change in policy are uncertain and electorates are averse to taking risks. We suggest, however, that the most important reason why it is not seriously challenged is because the groups in society that are likely to gain from reform of the disequilibrium system do not perceive those gains, while the groups that benefit from current policy are well aware of the potential losses entailed in a major modification of foreign exchange policy.

[51] In saying this, we do not mean to imply that economic reform and devaluation are mutually exclusive objectives. A considerable degree of continuity in politics is itself a prerequisite to the successful implementation of any development strategy, and the essential issue of constitutional reform in Colombia is obtaining the necessary degree of consensus as to the mechanism regulating political succession. Yet though complementary in the long run, in the short run constitutional reform and economic policy reform are competitive. The alignment of forces resisting change in these areas is different, and two separate coalitions, each with its own set of costs in terms of political concessions, must be assembled if both reforms are to be achieved.

To point out that current policy is legitimate, that it reflects the balance of policy preferences of the electorate, is not to say that it cannot be changed, however. In fact, a conspicuous example of the potential instability of policy preferences is to be found in the recent history of Colombian foreign exchange policy. Although the quasi-flexible (certificate) rate system that the Lleras government adopted is now apparently quite acceptable to most political groups, many of these groups showed a strong preference for a fixed-rate system only a few years ago.

This preference for a system of fixed exchange rates derived largely from a distaste for uncertainty, fears by exporters and importers of a wide divergence between actual and expected peso prices and fears by the administrators of the exchange system (chiefly the bureaucracy of the central bank) about their ability to control rate fluctuations. An additional source of prejudice against rate flexibility was the deep-rooted suspicion that such a policy would lead to destabilizing speculation.

These preferences have been weakened, and probably reversed, because the government, in judiciously leaking information concerning its future rate target and in maintaining a rate that is stable in the short run, has satisfied the business community's conception of acceptable rate uncertainty. This confidence, together with the more stable flows of demand for imports and exports that are implied by a more stable real exchange rate, has apparently induced the business sector to accept the quasi-flexible certificate system. A policy that was initially established by administrative decree, and whose legitimacy derived only from its association with the right of self-determination of economic policy, has been further legitimized by a shift in policy preferences. This is the consequence of political innovation.

In certain circumstances, then, it is thinkable that political innovation can result in a significant departure from the policies of the past. Such changes are possible if either the policy perceptions (hence preferences) of groups important to the policymaking process change or the balance of policymaking influence between groups of different perceptions shifts. In fact, we think there is some reason to believe that both perceptions and the political balance between groups of different perceptions will be less stable in the future than in the past.

The first reason for believing that policy preferences in Colombia are likely to be increasingly unstable is that it is becoming more difficult to protect, or somehow subsidize, the interests of a particular producer group without simultaneously hurting the interests of another producer group. The days in which the costs of special treatment of special interest groups are borne almost exclusively by consumers are rapidly drawing to a close. As the structure of the economy grows more complex, the old harmony of the policy of import substitution becomes dissonant.

A second reason for believing in the increased instability of the revealed preferences of the Colombian policymaking system is the changing importance of the technical bureaucracy and the changes that are taking place in its ideology of growth. Although there is some question about the degree of influence over the policy-making process currently exercised by the *tecnico* group, *tecnico* influence is undoubtedly increasing. Perhaps more important, the policy perceptions of this group are changing. Although the old commitment to administrative allocation of resources remains, there is now considerably less faith in autarchic or semi-autarchic strategies of growth.[52] Most of the *tecnicos* and business spokesmen who have urged special tariffs and favorable tax treatment for "basic industries" are now urging tariff rebates, subsidized credit, and favorable exchange treatment for exporters; and to the extent there is still an asymmetry in the relative valuation of augmented exports and import substitutions, it derives from a sophisticated, if somewhat exaggerated, perception of possible differences in the secondary benefits (for example, backward linkages) inherent in export growth and import substitution.[53]

---

[52] Although the ideology of growth that has been intellectually dominant in Colombia has stressed the centrality of import substitution, it has not embraced the position of extreme autarchy—in particular, the exportable surplus theory of trade—that has been current in some other countries. The exportable surplus theory implies that a country should only attempt to export the "surplus" that is "left over" after the domestic market has been "adequately" supplied. If the theory is strictly construed, a good will not be exported if its domestic price is rising. For a discussion of the impact of this ideology on Brazilian trade policy, see Nathaniel Leff, *Economic Policy-Making and Development in Brazil. 1947–1964*, Wiley, New York, 1968, pp. 81–83.

[53] As the *tecnico* groups gain further experience with the range of the domestic resource costs of saving foreign exchange involved in import substi-

A third reason for believing that policy change is more likely to be feasible in the future than it has in the past is the growth in importance of a low-income urban electorate for whom the traditional loyalties and hatreds are increasingly irrelevant and whose (electoral) sensitivity is increasing. The results of the election of 1970 illustrate dramatically the electoral significance of this group. We confess, however, that the precise policy changes likely to result from this shift in electoral balance are almost impossible to predict. The pressures resulting from the increased complexity of the economy and the increased policy role of the technical bureaucracy are almost certain to create an environment conducive to the adoption of the sorts of policies we have proposed in this chapter. The pressures resulting from the growth in importance of a low-income urban electorate may well make such policy changes even more difficult to accomplish than they are now.

What appears most likely is that the emergence of a large low-income electorate will result in an increase in the electoral productivity of an appeal to authoritarian populism, a view that loosely joins the notions that society is dichotomized into the "people" and the "oligarchy," that the industrialization process is yielding disproportionately small benefits to the "people," and that this process is undermining the "traditional" values of society. The ideological content of this electoral strategy is thus highly complex. Populism is neither "liberal" nor "conservative." But if it develops outside the mold of the traditional political parties—in particular, if it develops in the authoritarian mold of ANAPO or a similar, successor organization—it is certain to be antagonistic to the sorts of policy changes that we have proposed.

Fundamental to this antagonism is the priority that policies resulting from the pressure of authoritarian populism are likely to

---

tution projects of the "showcase" variety, this ideological asymmetry will become even less pronounced. There is already evidence that the upper-level *tecnicos* in the government are keenly aware of both the critical importance of augmenting the supply of foreign exchange and the need to establish an upper limit to the domestic resource cost of reducing foreign exchange needs through import substitution. This tendency of the *tecnico* group to think in terms of "shadow" rates of exchange is also beginning to extend to the field of tariff policy. Within the *tecnico* elite, at least, discussion of tariff rates is increasingly being conducted in terms of effective, rather than nominal, rates of protection.

give to the objective of redistribution of income relative to the objective of growth. The main thrust of authoritarian-populist policy would be to try to force an increase in the share of income accruing to labor. Given the difficulty of enforcing wage regulations in the traditional or craft sector, this would probably redound most to the benefit of labor in the modern sector. The wage drift between the modern and traditional sectors would tend to accelerate. The emergence of authoritarian populism would also probably result in the resurrection of certain of the mythic elements in policymaking that the government's technical bureaucracy has attempted in recent years to eradicate. In particular, some version of the autarchic strategy of growth is likely to be dusted off and resubmitted as a solution to the Colombian economic malaise.

If, as seems more likely, much of the pressure created by the increased appeal of the populist message is channeled within the framework of one or more of the traditional parties, the consequences for policy change are more ambiguous. It is by no means certain that a political innovator cannot ultimately use these pressures to supplement his electoral base within the traditional polyclass parties and exploit that base to carry out policy changes whose benefits are too diffuse to be electorally attractive today. It is precisely this diffuseness that makes policies of the sort we have advocated so difficult to advocate. The distribution of benefits is less well perceived than the distribution of costs. It is possible that the latent appeal of populism can provide a remedy for that weakness by permitting a more effective invocation of the interests of the "people" in opposition to the interests of special groups. If, as is possible only in a polyclass party, a political innovator can build a political base on an appeal to populism that is not so shrill as to proscribe effective cooperation with the preexisting elites, the growth-oriented policies we have recommended can be adopted.

We certainly do not want to predict whether or not this will happen. We do believe, however, that the policies now being used are not viable over the long run. Population will grow and migrate to the cities looking for work. A technical bureaucracy with an ideological interest in "efficiency" will continue to evolve, and the conflicts of interest latent in the present system will become increasingly apparent. New wine cannot be contained by old bottles.

INDEX

ACOPI (Association of Small Industrialists), 232

Adelman, Irma, 301

age: and migration rates, 54, 67, 72 (tables of, 50, 69, 70, 71); students per hundred by, 281; and unemployment, 149, 150, 151–152

Agency for International Development (AID), 90, 239n

agricultural activity: and birth rates, 39; and migration rates, 55

agricultural exports, 211

agricultural research, 284

agricultural wages, 57n, 57–58n; compared with other sectors, 78, 147; and family size, 19; and migration, 62, 67; stability of, 139

Agudelo Villa, Finance Minister, 261n

ANAPO (Alianza Nacional Popular), 218, 222, 223, 228, 256, 311

ANDI (National Association of Industrialists), 230, 231–232

Arrow, Kenneth J., et al., 92–100 passim

Bain, J., 168

balance of payments problems, 91, 157, 263, 291

Banco de la Republica, 227, 234, 257

banks, foreign and commercial, and debt limits, 238

Betancur, Belisario, 222

birth control, 29–30, 275; access to modern methods, 267–268, 271, 273; and birth tax, 273; costs, 13, 42, 267; and educational level, 269, 272; and health programs, 274–275; history of, 268; in Korea, 268–269; lag in demand for, 274; receptivity to, 272; in Taiwan, 28, 37, 42, 43, 270–271

birth rate, 3–4, 9; and age of parents, 29, 35, 37; and childhood mortality, 15–16, 23, 25, 30, 31, 274–275; data, 17–18, 24; determinants, 9; and education, 37, 265–266; and environment, 20, 42; and labor force, 266; and migration, 72; and opportunity income, 11; Puerto Rico, 24, 25, 26, 27–28; rural-urban differences, 45n; Taiwan, 24, 28, 29, 30, 35–39. See also family size goal

birth tax, 273

births, spacing of, 28–29, 43, 264, 274

Bogota: birth control use, 272, 273; educational returns data, 61; family income, 146; family size goals, 271–272; growth, 47; manufacturing work force, 101; migration to, 48, 54, 55, 152; personal income distribution, 142–143, 147; unemployment, 147–152; wage rates, 288

brain drain, 102, 283, 288–289

Braybrooke, D., 304

Bruton, H., 300

bureaucracy, 233–235; on devaluation, 257; foreign exchange policy, 234–235, 237, 260; independent of parties, as modernist goal, 234; policy formulation, 230–231, 234–235, 242, 310–312; professionalism of, 226; tariffs, 245–246, 257. See also tecnicos

Cali: individual income, 143; migration to, 54; population growth, 47; unemployment rates by age and education, 149, 150

capacity constraints in two-gap model, 176–177

capital: access to, 118, 120–121, 123; constraint, 186–190; cost of, 162; exports, 123, 207; imports, 199; input coefficients, 187, 188; per capita, and population growth, 264; and quasi-rents, 111; rate of

Selected Rand Books

Averch, Harvey, John E. Koehler, and Frank H. Denton, *The Matrix of Policy in the Philippines,* Princeton University Press, Princeton, 1971.

Becker, Abraham S., *Soviet National Income 1958–1964,* University of California Press, Berkeley and Los Angeles, 1969.

Bergson, Abram, *The Real National Income of Soviet Russia Since 1928,* Harvard University Press, Cambridge, Massachusetts, 1961.

Bergson, Abram and Hans Heymann, Jr., *Soviet National Income and Product, 1940–48,* Columbia University Press, New York, 1954.

Chapman, Janet G., *Real Wages in Soviet Russia Since 1928,* Harvard University Press, Cambridge, Massachusetts, 1963.

Cooper, Charles and Sidney Alexander (eds.), *Economic Development and Population Growth in the Middle East,* American Elsevier, New York, 1971.

Downs, Anthony, *Inside Bureaucracy,* Little, Brown, Boston, 1967.

Goldhamer, Herbert and Andrew W. Marshall, *Psychosis and Civilization,* The Free Press, Glencoe, 1953.

Gurtov, Melvin, *Southeast Asia Tomorrow: Problems and Prospects for U.S. Policy,* Johns Hopkins University Press, Baltimore, 1970.

Halpern, Manfred, *The Politics of Social Change in the Middle East and North Africa,* Princeton University Press, Princeton, 1963.*

Harman, Alvin J., *The International Computer Industry: Innovation and Comparative Advantage,* Harvard University Press, Cambridge, Massachusetts, 1971.

Hirshleifer, Jack, James C. DeHaven, and Jerome W. Milliman, *Water Supply: Economics, Technology, and Policy,* University of Chicago Press, Chicago, 1960.

Hitch, Charles J. and Roland N. McKean, *The Economics of Defense in the Nuclear Age,* Harvard University Press, Cambridge, Massachusetts, 1960*

Hoeffding, Oleg, *Soviet National Income and Product in 1928,* Columbia University Press, New York, 1954.

Johnson, John J. (ed.), *The Role of the Military in Underdeveloped Countries,* Princeton University Press, Princeton, 1962.*

Johnson, William A., *The Steel Industry of India,* Harvard University Press, Cambridge, Massachusetts, 1966.

Johnstone, William C., *Burma's Foreign Policy: A Study in Neutralism,* Harvard University Press, Cambridge, Massachusetts, 1963.

Kershaw, Joseph A. and Roland N. McKean, *Teacher Shortages and Salary Schedules,* McGraw-Hill, New York, 1962.*

Leites, Nathan and Charles Wolf, Jr., *Rebellion and Authority,* Markham, Chicago, 1970.

Liu, Ta-Chung and Kung-Chia Yeh, *The Economy of the Chinese Mainland: National Income and Economic Development, 1933–1959,* Princeton University Press, Princeton, 1965.

* Also available in paperback.

Lubell, Harold, *Middle East Oil Crises and Western Europe's Energy Supplies,* Johns Hopkins University Press, Baltimore, 1963.

Marschak, Thomas, Thomas K. Glennan, Jr., and Robert Summers, *Strategy for R&D,* Springer-Verlag, New York, 1967.

McKean, Roland N., *Efficiency in Government Through Systems Analysis: with Emphasis on Water Resource Development,* Wiley, New York, 1958.

Moorsteen, Richard, *Prices and Production of Machinery in the Soviet Union, 1928–1958,* Harvard University Press, Cambridge, Massachusetts, 1962.

Nelson, Richard R., Merton J. Peck, and Edward D. Kalachek, *Technology, Economic Growth and Public Policy,* Brookings, Washington, D.C., 1967.

Pascal, Anthony, *Thinking About Cities: New Perspectives on Urban Problems,* Dickenson, Belmont, California, 1970.

Pincus, John A., *Economic Aid and International Cost Sharing,* Johns Hopkins University Press, Baltimore, 1965.

Rosen, George, *Democracy and Economic Change in India,* University of California Press, Berkeley and Los Angeles, 1966.

Scalapino, Robert A., *The Japanese Communist Movement, 1920–1966,* University of California Press, Berkeley and Los Angeles, 1967.

Stepan, Alfred, *The Military in Politics: Changing Patterns in Brazil,* Princeton University Press, Princeton, 1971.

Trager, Frank N. (ed.), *Marxism in Southeast Asia: A Study of Four Countries,* Stanford University Press, Stanford, 1959.

Wolf, Charles, Jr., *Foreign Aid: Theory and Practice in Southern Asia,* Princeton University Press, Princeton, 1960.